THE UNITED STATES
OF AMERICA

THE UNITED STATES
OF AMERICA

A CONCISE HISTORY

By

H. C. ALLEN

FREDERICK A. PRAEGER, *Publishers*

NEW YORK · WASHINGTON

BOOKS THAT MATTER

Published in the United States of America in 1965
by Frederick A. Praeger, Inc., Publishers
111 Fourth Avenue, New York 3, N.Y.

Second printing, 1965

All rights reserved

© H. C. Allen 1964

Library of Congress Catalog Card Number: 65–12440

Printed in the United States of America

TO
DENIS BROGAN
AND
RONALD McCALLUM

Preface

THIS VOLUME differs in form from most of the others which have preceded it in the series. Partly this is because I have deliberately chosen to discuss the history and politics of the United States almost entirely in historical rather than half in historical and half in analytical terms. I have done this because I believe that most Europeans, and especially most Britons, tend to see the American system of government (largely owing to the existence of the written constitution of the United States and to the relative shortness of American history), in a two-dimensional – even somewhat shallow – way, with no proper perception of its depth. Yet the American achievement can only be fully understood in terms of the growth and development of the United States over three and a half centuries.

Partly also the volume is different because the United States is a larger and more powerful country than any previously included in the series, which makes the task of describing its history and institutions within such a compass as this a truly formidable one. It was said many years ago that it had ceased to be possible for a single historian to write the history of the United States from primary sources. I have come to the conclusion that it is very nearly as impossible nowadays for one author (at any rate one as ill-equipped as I am for the exercise by training, background and capacity) to tell the story of the United States from the vast numbers of secondary works which pour from the presses in ever-increasing numbers. To all the many historians, unnamed as well as named in the text, on whose studies I have necessarily drawn, I acknowledge my profound debt.

It is customary on these occasions, sometimes with a vaguely formal – if not perfunctory – air, to give thanks to those of one's colleagues on whom one has inflicted the preliminary reading of one's text. In this case my tribute is real, sincere and heart-felt. There are doubtless still many errors of fact and interpretation (to say nothing of omission) in the book: for these I am entirely responsible. Had it not been for the painstaking and illuminating comments of my friends, these errors would be far more numerous.

I should like to express my gratitude to Herbert Nicholas for his welcome advice on the last two chapters. I should like to thank R. Calhoon and K. Hinman for their assistance in the preparation of Appendix II. And I should like most warmly to acknowledge the invaluable help of those tutelary saints who patiently read and helpfully criticised the whole manuscript – Charlotte Erickson, Dick Pear, Jack Pole, Jim Potter and Dick Reinitz.

Thanks are due to the copyright owners Stephen Vincent Benét and Rosemary Carr Benét for permission to use the lines I quote from *John Brown's Body*.

I should also like to thank Sheelagh Taylor and Nazneen Razwi for their uncomplaining, cheerful and indispensable work at the typewriter.

Little Chalfont   H. C. ALLEN
May 1964

Contents

Maps

Chapter 1

Setting and Settlement

THE United States of America occupies the great central portion of the North American continent. It is flanked on the north by Canada and on the south by Mexico, and, like them, it stretches from the Atlantic to the Pacific oceans.

These two extensive bodies of water isolate the Americas from the large Eurasian land-mass, with its African and Australasian projections; and, though Americans have always tended to think of their geographical situation primarily in terms of the separation of the Western Hemisphere from the old world, the United States is also effectively isolated from South America. It is thus somewhat over 1,600 miles from New Orleans to Panama, and the islands of the Caribbean are no more than stepping-stones from north to south, while neither railroad nor trunk-highway yet runs vertically through the narrow Central-American isthmus. Similarly, though air routes now cross the Polar regions, the Arctic wastes insulate the United States and Canada to the north. Thus North America, which has been for more than a century dominated, physically, economically and politically, by the United States, is in effect in an island position: this fact has profoundly influenced its development.

North America is closest to Eurasia in just those forbidding areas of northern cold. To the east it is fairly close, through the island links of Greenland and Iceland: to the west it is closest of all through the eccentric American peninsular state of Alaska, across the mere 23 miles of the Bering Strait. In the warmer climate of the south, the narrowest gap between the new and the old worlds is South and not North American, that between the western tip of Africa and the eastern tip of Brazil, though this distance is not far short of the approximately 2,000 miles from Newfoundland direct to Ireland. The other eccentric American state, Hawaii, which lies in mid-Pacific, is just over 2,400 miles from the western seaboard of the United States and much farther from any other mainland. From San Francisco straight to Yokohama is some 4,500 miles, and it is just over 3,000 from New York to Liverpool. The geographical insularity of the United States is thus, broadly speaking, remarkably complete.

It was, moreover, by these three routes – the North-Western, the North Atlantic and the South Atlantic – that America was, at different epochs, discovered and populated, and it is a measure of the importance of sheer distance in America's history that, despite all the difficulties of the frozen north, it was in the North-West, which is closest to Eurasia, that men seem first to have entered the continent. Though the evidence is scanty, it has consistently directed attention to this area. It has also indicated that man's arrival was relatively recent, for there are no known early anthropoid remains in America. It is likely that savages of Mongolian origin crossed the Bering Strait between 25,000 and 10,000 years ago and were the ancestors of the American Indian.

The next adventurers to discover America never constituted more than a trickle, and this very soon dried up and disappeared without leaving any permanent mark. Though the evidence is tenuous, it seems probable that around the tenth and eleventh centuries Norsemen, skilled in seamanship, crossed to North America by stages through Iceland and Greenland, thus pointing the way, even if for the moment abortively, for the final and conclusive conquest and settlement of the continent from the east. The third, and ultimate, European migration, which achieved this some five centuries later, made it certain that North America, including the United States, would develop as part of a Western and basically European civilisation which had its origins around the Mediterranean and was to centre in due course upon the Atlantic basin.

This decisive occupation of the Americas began, however, far to the south. Between about 30 degrees north and 30 degrees south the predominant Trade Winds blow from east to west; north of that the Westerlies prevail. Though the Vikings, with their greater reliance on oars, were able to beat from island to island against these westerly winds, there was a natural and necessary impulse for the more skilled seamen of the fifteenth and sixteenth centuries to take advantage at first of the favourable Trade Winds. Thus the initial major discoveries and settlements of this era were around the warm Caribbean. This gave an advantage to the southern nations of Europe, for though the winds frustrated the tendency which some observers have noted for American emigrants to follow parallels of latitude (Madrid is on much the same latitude as New York and Lisbon as Philadelphia), seamen from the Mediterranean region were obviously better situated to catch these winds which lay to their south.

There were, however, other reasons, at least equally important, why it was in fact especially Portugal and Spain which first explored and exploited the New World. The main European motive, apart from the search for knowledge, for the geographical discoveries which began around the period of the Renaissance was economic, the desire to find better maritime trade routes to the East. This commerce had in the past been mainly in the hands of Mediterranean merchants, such as those of Genoa and Venice, but the inhabitants of the Iberian Peninsula, facing, as it were, both the inland sea and the open oceans, were best situated to adapt the rudimentary seafaring techniques of the Mediterranean to the far more difficult problems of world-wide navigation. Thus the Portuguese caravel came to supplant the less sea-worthy Genoese carrack, and by the end of the fifteenth century Portugal had opened up the route to the Indian Ocean by the Cape of Good Hope. At just this time Spain became a formidable, and in the end successful, rival, largely as a result of the attainment of her national unity and the expulsion of the Moors from this, their last, foothold in Europe. It was thus under Spanish auspices that, beginning in 1492, the Genoese seaman, Christopher Columbus, in the course of persistent efforts to sail westwards round the world to the East, discovered (though never realising it) the continents of North and South America.

The ascendancy of Spain (which partly produced, and partly resulted from, her imperial conquest of most of South, Central and southern North America) was not long to remain unchallenged. From the fifteenth century onwards England, France and the Low Countries had sought to take part in the new discoveries and commercial ventures. In 1497, for instance, another Genoese, John Cabot, who had become a naturalised Venetian, laid the foundation of Britain's claim to North America by leading an expedition sponsored by Henry VII to Newfoundland. By the end of the sixteenth century, these more northern nations, and especially England and Holland, were to surpass the Spaniards and Portuguese in maritime skills, perhaps because they had to learn all their seamanship on the open seas and were not partly restrained by a Mediterranean inheritance. They, too, expanded their Oriental commerce, they searched – with less success but equal avidity – for gold and silver, they developed more fully such enterprises as the fisheries and the fur trade. Ultimately, in the course of the seventeenth and eighteenth centuries, they were to undermine and openly despoil the huge empire which Spain had built up, and they were also to participate, even more fully than Spain or Portugal, in the creation of great overseas colonies of settlement.

This enormous and unprecedented historical movement which historians have called the Expansion of Europe thus had two almost concurrent phases or aspects, a great commercial expansion and a vast migration of peoples; and it was essentially in the end a movement deriving from and affecting Europe as a whole. From it resulted not only the fact that the entire earth had, within four centuries, come in a very real sense to constitute for the first time a single world, but also the fact of that European domination of the globe (in Australia and Africa no less than Asia and America), which has been one of the most remarkable phenomena in modern history. This unique ascendancy of Europe was made possible fundamentally by its revolutionary technological developments both for peace and war. It was these new skills which gave Europeans the power to conquer, or overwhelmingly to influence, the rest of mankind. The United States was to be not only in many respects the most important result of this process, but also, because she was the greatest of the colonies of settlement, a dominant – for a period the exclusively dominant – nation of that Western world of which Europe came to form but a part.

The eventual power of the United States was based upon the great extent, variety and richness of the territory that she had come to occupy during her two and a half centuries of settlement and expansion, which was virtually complete by 1867 when she acquired Alaska. The main body of the continental United States is just under 3,000 miles from east to west, at its widest part near the Canadian border, and it is somewhat over 1,500 miles from New Orleans north to the 49 parallel, along which much of that border runs. It has an area of more than 3 million square miles, which is over two-thirds the size of Europe including European Russia. The great width of the country and the compressive effect of the Great Lakes and the Gulf of Mexico (scarcely more than 750 miles apart and forming at once natural boundaries and splendid natural routes of travel and communication) have combined with the fact that the great European settlements were all on the eastern seaboard to give a predominant east-west trend to American development; the persistent movement of people from east to west has indeed been of signal importance in the history of the United States.

The physiographical structure of this vast area has, with the variety of its climate, produced marked regional differences. The main physical features of the United States are three; the great area constituted by the Atlantic coastal plain and the rich open lands of the Mississippi valley, the great Cordillera mountain region of the west, and the uplands of the Appalachian region in the east. The chief constituents of the Cordilleras, apart from the long, low Coasta

Range, are the bones formed by the Cascades and the Sierra Nevada, and the great mass of the Rocky Mountains, which fill in this western third of the United States; these ranges attain in places heights of more than 14,000 feet. The Appalachians, which divide the eastern coastal plain from the prairies of the middle west, only rise to 6,000 feet. The coastal plain is narrow in the north, but broadens to a width of 250 miles or more in the south where it merges into the great heartland of the Mississippi valley, which is in places 1,500 miles from north to south and more than 1,000 miles across and is for its size perhaps the most fertile area of land in the world: it is the core of America's strength. Other areas add to the variety; the well-watered valleys of the north Pacific coast; the Great Valley of California, which is, with irrigation, wonderfully productive; the Great American Desert, which occupies the south-western area of the Cordillera plateau; and the sub-tropical peninsula of Florida, spared the cold of the continental winter by the seas which lie around it.

Temperature and rainfall also accentuate this variety. One can enjoy winter sports in high summer in the Cordilleras and warm sea bathing in midwinter in Florida. The mean annual temperature of the United States is 52 degrees fahrenheit and the annual average temperature-range between 40 degrees and 70 degrees approximately, but these overall figures conceal sharp differences. Summer temperatures of 90 degrees are common in most parts of the United States and in winter 10 degrees and more of frost are frequent; North Dakota can be almost literally arctic, the south-east and south-west sub-tropical. Similarly, an annual average rainfall of some 26 inches (compared with 40 inches in Britain) covers variations from as low as 5 inches in Utah to as high as 60 inches in the vicinity of the Gulf of Mexico. One of the main formative facts in the development of the United States has been that, as the people moved westward across the great tract which stretches from the Appalachians to the Rockies, they found it progressively more arid and more difficult to cultivate or exploit.

This variation of climate and terrain is reflected in a correspondingly wide variety of vegetation. There are six main natural areas or types of growth; the coniferous forests of the north-east, the Great Lakes and the north-west; the broad-leaved forest and meadow of the Appalachians and the eastern Mississippi Valley; the warm evergreen forests of the south; the temperate grasslands of the prairies; the sparse semi-desert of the south-west; and the true cactus-desert of the extreme south-west. There has therefore been an equal, or even greater, variety of agricultural produce. Grain and timber, to cite a few examples, come from the north-west; citrus fruits exclusively from the south-west and Florida; cotton, rice and sugar from the South; corn (American-style) and winter wheat predominantly from the central area of the middle-west and the Atlantic seaboard; spring wheat from the northern middle-west; dairy products from the Great Lakes and the north-east; livestock and wool from the mountain states in the west. The United States can produce almost every type of agricultural commodity she needs, with the exception of certain tropical products such as coffee and tea, bananas and pineapples. She has developed some synthetics, such as rubber, to the point where it can be used for almost all purposes for which natural rubber (which she does not produce) has been employed.

The United States has been similarly well endowed by nature with mineral resources. There have been within her present borders abundant, or relatively abundant, supplies of gold, silver, copper, zinc, lead, iron and bauxite, and of coal, oil and natural gas. There have not been many important minerals which she has not produced in considerable quantities, and for which she has thus been heavily dependent on imports; chrome and tin are examples of these negligible deficiencies. Many of her resouces, however, she has used at a prodigious rate, such as iron, for which she is now becoming increasingly reliant on the outside world. The same is true of other resources than minerals, such as timber, though here serious efforts at rebuilding reserves have been made in this century. But it seems probable that the coming of synthetics and plastics, as well as atomic energy, may make this enormous consumption-rate less of a problem.

The true wealth of America's resources, however, can only be fully gauged on a comparative basis. To take but a few examples: between 1848 and 1898 the United States led the world in the production of gold; in the late 1920's she produced 70 per cent of the world's oil and 50 per cent of its copper; at the same period she was growing 54 per cent of the cotton of mankind and 62 per cent of its corn; in 1939 tobacco was only her sixth crop in value, but it was the largest tobacco crop in the world, and she produced more oats and barley than any other nation; in the same year she led in the production of hogs, was second in cattle and third in sheep; and, as befits an industry which has been important from the beginning of America's history, from the oceans round her shores, as well as her inland waters, she still harvests more fish and sea-food than any other nation except Japan.

In one final respect has the physiography of the United States been vitally important to her development. She is a country, a sub-continent, of great rivers, especially on the Atlantic seaboard where her history began. Not only did the waterway of the St. Lawrence and the Great Lakès (matched by the sea route of the Gulf of Mexico) make penetration into the middle-west by water possible, but they both in effect linked up with the world's greatest navigable river system, the Mississippi-Missouri, with its long eastern tributaries such as the Ohio. On a smaller scale numerous and bountiful rivers flowed from the Appalachians into the Atlantic. Thus river transport was possible from the first coastal settlements up to the 'fall line' at the foot of the mountains (where the rapids and water-falls begin), and, after relatively easy portages, down its westward flowing arms to the Mississippi itself; from New Orleans in the south one could return to the east coast by sea. This formed in the early years a magnificent water route from east to west, and was one of the keys to American development. And just at the moment when, west of the Mississippi, the rivers were hampering westward movement because they were sparser and less navigable and, above all, flowed in the wrong direction, the steam boat (and in the end the railroad) appeared, as by a miracle, to solve the problem and make further expansion possible. Thus the lack of navigable waterways in the west was of little consequence, while its rushing torrents were waiting to make the United States the biggest producer of hydro-electric power in the world.

This great good fortune in communications was of vital significance in American history, for the gravest problem of the United States has always been that of maintaining the unity of her extensive territories. The wide variety of her regions, or 'sections' as they are called, was of the greatest economic value to her. When the United States, which then contained no territory west of the Mississippi, came into existence in 1783 it constituted the largest free-trade area in the world, and as Adam Smith was pointing out at the time division of labour and consequent industrial growth depended on the extent of the free market. But America was only able to derive full economic benefit from her size and resources because national unity was maintained; in the era before the railroad, the automobile and the aircraft, this was only made possible by her waterways. They were the bonds that held the federal union together, economically, socially, and politically.

Yet the geographical sections, each encompassing a number of states, developed, and retained, real and important, if often changing and not very clearly defined, differences. In colonial times New England, the middle colonies, and the South had distinct economic

and social structures; in the era of Jacksonian Democracy the states
west of the Appalachians had a certain unity; the Civil War came
near to disrupting the Union and to making a new nation of the
Deep and the Upper South, and the South has – as a counterpart to
the North – retained (despite or because of disastrous defeat in the
Civil War) a separate identity until very recent times; by the end of
the nineteenth century the middle-west, lying between the Appalachians and the Rockies, had in many respects become the dominant
section in American life; in the twentieth century the mountain
states, the Pacific north-west, and above all California have acquired
sectional characteristics and significance. The sections and their
differences are hard to delimit and describe with precision, but are
none the less actual, and highly influential. American life cannot be
understood without an understanding of them.

In many respects the section most complex and difficult to understand but at the same time the most important has been one which
no longer exists, the frontier – if indeed it can properly be classified
as a section. From the earliest settlements until the end of the nineteenth century, as the American people pushed unceasingly out-
wards along the natural and man-made routes of communication –
a movement 3,000 miles westward on a front of 1,000 miles, more or
less – their skirmish line of scouts and pioneers and hunters was
continuously probing a wilderness, sporadically roamed or sparsely
settled by tribes of Indian savages. Behind this line of exploration
and exploitation came that of settlement, thin at first and then
thicker. The ever-changing zone occupied by these advance-guards
of civilisation is the American frontier, vastly different in character
and effects from the precise and rigid frontier lines to which Europe
had become accustomed.

The westward movement, voracious in its consumption of land
and of nature's animal, vegetable and mineral wealth, was remorseless in the way it drove before it, elbowed aside, and came near,
as it sometimes seemed, to exterminating the native Indians,
who numbered perhaps three-quarters of a million in the present
territory of the United States in the seventeenth century. Until very
nearly the time that the frontier was declared closed by the Census
Bureau in 1890, when the Indians had ceased to be a menace, they
were decimated by – in addition to their own tribal conflicts and
customs – the wars, whisky, diseases and political ruthlessness of
the white man. In the early days they made some small contribution
to the skills and way of life of the newcomers – the techniques of the
hunter, for example, and the gift of native American crops, such as
corn and potatoes – but it would be a mistake to romanticise a way

of life barbaric, cruel and bloodthirsty, even if white unscrupulousness cannot be condoned. When the Indian was utterly crushed, the conscience of civilisation awoke; from the time of the Dawes Act of 1887 (approximately at the time of the last Indian wars) the Indians have increasingly come to be, especially during the New Deal era, well-cared-for wards of the American government. Today there are probably substantially more Indians in the United States than there were when the first settlers came. They either live, poorly for the most part, in reservations, as near to their traditional life as modern conditions (including the tourist avid for the products of their splendid arts and crafts) allow, or become fully absorbed into American life as normal citizens. No critic can be taken seriously who doubts the benefit mankind enjoys from the fact that the United States is occupied, not by the scattered and primitive red man, but by nearly 200 million inhabitants enjoying the highest standard of living in the world.

The Indian problem, however, though it was an important aspect of the frontier, was not the essence of it; this lay in the continuous existence of abundant and fertile 'free' land, which he was not really capable of cultivating at all. This fundamentally made possible the expansion of the population of the United States at a rate not far from the famous norm enunciated by Malthus, doubling itself every twenty-five years. According to the much criticised, but basically justified, views of Frederick Jackson Turner, one of the greatest of American historians, the moving frontier had profound effects upon American development. This was the case whether it was the frontier of the hunter, of the miner seeking precious metals, of the pastoralist with his sheep or cattle, of the plantation owner with his slaves, or of the pioneer farmer, who remained much the most important of these figures prior to the industrialisation of the post-Civil War period. The frontier can, in general terms, fairly be held to have been a great agency of Americanisation, which promoted the sense of nationality. It was also a great promoter of democracy, of social equality, of political freedom; it bred self-reliance and individualism and liberty. It helped to give to American society its optimism and its special energy, as well as its vital strain of radicalism. Throughout the first three centuries of American history, the frontier, wherever it had reached, tended to be a section with ideas and interests which ran counter to the more conservative ones of the longer established areas behind it. The west, for example, was an 'under-developed', a debtor area, perennially favouring cheap land, inflationary money policies and government aid for improvement of communications. Usually opposed to it were the eastern sections, which, though themselves often having an adverse balance of payments with Europe, frequently tended to believe in a stable currency, controlled westward development and conservative government finance. Not only was this division between east and ever-changing west a continually re-emerging theme in American history, but the frontier process preserved a high degree of flexibility and mobility in the life of the United States and its people.

In a sense this division between east and west was a muted version of the graver divergence between the new and the old world which appeared as soon as the first settlements were made and which steadily widened thereafter until it reached its apogee in the era of the American Revolution. It was in large degree a natural consequence of augmenting distance, decreasing intercourse and widely differing environments. But just as, in the event, the unity of the United States was preserved, so, despite political independence, America always remained an integral and increasingly essential part of Western civilisation; the American people, indeed, were by mid-twentieth century to become ever more aware of the fact. As Walter Prescott Webb pointed out in *The Great Frontier* the United States as a whole, along with other areas of overseas settlement, has been in effect the 'frontier' of Europe and has had some effects of a similar kind upon European development. The mass movement of European peoples, more than 40 millions of them in the course of American history, across the ocean to the United States, a migration perhaps unprecedented in human history, has been comparable to the westward movement in America itself. As Tocqueville wrote, 'This gradual and continuous progress of the European race towards the Rocky Mountains has the solemnity of a providential event. It is like a deluge of men, rising unabatedly, and driven daily onward by the hand of God.' There has in a very real sense been a community of the North Atlantic basin which perhaps reached the height of its power in the years after the Second World War. Now, with the rise of modern Russia and the new China, linked (though the strength of the link may be increasingly doubtful) by their common Marxist ideology, the West, essentially reliant upon a sea power centring in the North Atlantic, is challenged by the Communist bloc, rooted in the vast expanse of the Eurasian land mass.

The bonds which tie America to Europe have been, of course, strongest between Britain and the United States. The mother country left an indelible mark upon America, in its tongue, in its racial composition, in its law, in its political institutions, and in its social habits and ideas. Nor did the intimate connection cease with the Declaration of Independence. The English-speaking element

continued for a considerable period to be the most important in
American immigration; with the rise of democracy their political
lives grew once more closer akin; for many years in the nineteenth
century their economic relations remained so close and extensive
that they constituted what has been properly called an Atlantic
economy; their social intercourse waxed rather than waned with the
passage of the years; and in and after the Second World War they
were in the closest political alliance. But though there has been a
special Anglo-American relationship, America also bears the marks
of the influence of all Europe and shares in the whole European
heritage. She is today the dominating member of the Western community of nations.

   The debt of the United States to Europe as a whole, and not only
to Britain, is clearly shown by the wide variety of the early settlements in what is now the territory of the United States. Widely
ranging and scattered journeys of exploration went on throughout
the sixteenth century. A Florentine, Giovanni Verazzano, sailed
along the eastern seaboard on behalf of France in 1524, searching
for a route to India, but Portuguese and French (and in due course
English) sailors had been fishing on the Newfoundland Banks since
very soon after Cabot's voyage twenty-seven years before. Jacques
Cartier penetrated down the St. Lawrence as far as Quebec in 1535,
but his attempt to found a colony there in 1541 failed disastrously.
The English took up seriously the search for a northwest passage
with the voyage of Martin Frobisher which began in 1576, the year
before Drake's circumnavigation of the globe. The efforts of Sir
Humphrey Gilbert and Sir Walter Ralegh to plant colonies in Newfoundland in 1583 and on Roanoke Island in North Carolina in
1587 both ended in total failure. Meanwhile, far to the south, Spain
had both explored, and made a settlement in, the territories border-
ing upon her already flourishing empire. In 1513 Ponce de Leon
visited Florida, and in 1539 De Soto began there, and ended on the
Mississippi, a great four-year journey; in 1540–2 Coronado explored
the arid lands to the north-west of Mexico. In 1565 Pedro Menendez
de Avilés founded at St. Augustine, on the east coast of Florida, the
first permanent European settlement in the present United States.
   It was not till forty-two years later that a second foundation followed, that of the English at Jamestown, Virginia; then, in the
following year, the Frenchman, Champlain, set up a base in Acadia
(Nova Scotia) and founded Quebec; and in 1609 the Spaniards
established themselves at Santa Fé in New Mexico. Others soon
entered the field. In 1609 Henry Hudson, an English agent of the

Dutch East India Company, explored the river named after him, and during the following years Holland set up fur-trading posts in the present State of New York. In 1626 the Dutch 'purchased' Manhattan island from the Indians – for goods worth $24. In 1638 a group of Swedes established themselves on the Delaware River, whence they were expelled by the Dutch in 1655. Within a very few years it is recorded that in New Amsterdam no less than eighteen languages were being spoken, which is conclusive evidence of the early international character of American immigration.

But English settlement became the most intense. The Spaniards developed their hold on their vast territories in Florida and the south-west, but it was military and pastoral in character, and therefore sparse and precarious compared with their empire in Latin America. The French consolidated their base on the St. Lawrence in Canada, and from it ranged farther than anyone else into the still unknown and mysterious North American continent; by 1682, for example, the Sieur de la Salle had descended the entire length of the Mississippi from the Great Lakes and planted the flag of St. Louis at New Orleans. Holding a few strategic posts by military force, they cultivated the friendship of the Indians and built up through them the great fur trade which was long to be the economic mainspring of Canadian life. But their base, both physically and in terms of population, was in the long run to prove too narrow to sustain so vast an area of activity. At the beginning of the eighteenth century, France, encircling the British coastal belt of colonies, might have seemed to hold all the cards, but by the Seven Years War in 1756 it was to be clear that the great increase in the strength, population and resources of these colonies, built up behind the protective barrier of the Appalachians and constantly augmented by immigration from and trade with the mother country and the old world, had made it more likely that the destiny of the sub-continent lay in their hands.

It would be wrong, however, as far as the seventeenth century is concerned, to give any impression of certainty or solidity in the American colonies in the first fifty years of their existence. They still had the appearance of pitifully small bodies of settlers clinging to the outermost edge of a harsh and alien wilderness. Colonisation is as much, and sometimes more, the result of 'push' than of 'pull'; of pressures to leave the mother country rather than attractions in the new land. What led Englishmen to leave their homes for ever, facing the known hazards of a long and arduous voyage and the largely unknown perils of a new life, whether arising from the savage natives or the strange conditions of America?

The main elements of 'push' were social and economic on the one hand and political and religious on the other. England was experiencing economic difficulties and seemed to contemporaries to be over-populated; one of the only means of making one's way in the old world, or even of living at all, sometimes seemed to be to leave it. The country, too, was in the throes of religious intolerance and political strife; the desire to live according to one's own beliefs in one's own way was a vital motive for emigration. The 'pull' was more simply and predominantly economic and social. It is true that the spirit of adventure of the Elizabethan era still played a part, that missionary zeal to convert the heathen was also a factor and that Puritan desire to found God's 'city on the hill' in the New World was a significant influence, but in all likelihood none of these compared in importance with the desire to make a living and if possible to get rich. Gold beckoned them at first, as it had the Spaniards, but when this hope faded, it was succeeded by the more solid, if slower, expectation of prosperity through agriculture and trade. In part colonies came to subsist of themselves, by farming and fishing; in part to live by trade, in cereals or great staple crops such as tobacco, or in natural products such as fish and fur and timber. All these, the main motives for colonisation, can be seen at work in the British foundations, during what American historians call the colonial period.

Chapter 2

The Colonial Period

For thirteen years, Virginia, which had developed from the Jamestown settlement of 1607, remained the only English colony. Founded by a trading company formed for the purpose, it was a classic example of the economic motive for colonisation: it hoped for gold, but survived by agriculture and trade. Its grip on life was precarious for its first few years and it was held together only by the tough assumption of leadership (in a manner already unmistakably characteristic of the democratising effects of the American frontier) by a Captain John Smith; between 1612 and 1614 the settlers began to cultivate tobacco, a crop which they could sell easily at home, where the smoking habit had caught on in recent times. Their difficulties were far from over yet, and the colony had to be taken over by the Crown in 1624, but they had pointed one way to the future before the second colony was founded, at Plymouth, Massachusetts, in 1620. The inhabitants of Virginia numbered more than 1,000 by this date, they were exporting more than 30,000 pounds of tobacco a year, and they had elected their first representative assembly, later to be known as the House of Burgesses.

The New England settlement, made by a group who came to be known as the Pilgrim Fathers, was an equally classic example of another motive for colonisation, the religious. A number of the settlers were Separatists, or Congregationalists, who had fled from England to Holland more than ten years before, in order to be able to worship in their own fashion. They had been allowed by James I to obtain a patent from the Virginia Company to settle in northern Virginia; actually they settled just outside its boundaries, but got subsequent permission from the New England Company to remain where they were. Although the expedition was financed by English merchants in return for seven years labour by its members, the colony was fundamentally one in which its founders sought a new life for religious reasons. The strength of their faith showed itself in the fortitude with which they faced the prospect, and the reality, of this hard and rigorous existence, for which many of them were ill-fitted by their experience; the strain of idealism (albeit of a stern character) and of independence and political self-reliance which they brought with them, showed itself in the compact for their government which they drew up on board the famous *Mayflower* on 11 November 1620. Because they never succeeded in securing a charter it became the original constitution of the colony. It declared 'We . . . Do . . . solemnly and mutually in the Presence of God and one another, covenant and combine ourselves together into a civil Body Politick, for our better Ordering and Preservation . . .' Though never in such dire straits as the founders of Jamestown, the inhabitants of Plymouth numbered only 300 after ten years, and in the next year, under the newly incorporated Massachusetts Bay Company, nearby Boston was founded.

Boston was the largest, most carefully prepared, and best equipped of the colonial settlements yet made by Britain, and it soon absorbed the earlier Plymouth colony. The charter of the new Company gave effective and permanent control to a small minority of the 'godly' settlers, and did not require their officials to meet together in the mother country. Representative institutions were shortly established, with a governor and deputy governor, a council, and a legislature known as the General Court; all these were elected by the 'freemen', originally shareholders in the company. Though the number of voters was soon enlarged, church membership, which was limited, remained a prerequisite for the franchise, and Congregationalist orthodoxy was sternly enforced. Neither the concept of toleration nor the separation of Church and State were yet recognised in Massachusetts, any more than they had been in Virginia, although there (even though the Anglican church predominated) a greater practical tolerance tended to prevail. But the Puritans of New England had none the less left the mother country to escape the control of the Anglican church, even if they were not prepared to extend toleration to others. There thus arose in America, from the earliest days of colonisation, a fundamental fact for the history of tolerance in the United States and the world – that there was almost as wide a diversity of religious beliefs as there were settlements. Toleration was always to be essential for America because uniformity was impossible, indeed inconceivable.

Already in 1634, under a charter granted to Lord Baltimore, Maryland, named after the French Catholic wife of Charles I, had been settled as a refuge for English Catholics. Like Virginia, it thrived through tobacco, but as a 'proprietary' colony it was slower to gain representative government from its Roman Catholic rulers. But the growth of the always substantial Protestant element in the

ordinary population, swelled by Puritan emigration from episcopalian Virginia, led to the passage in 1649 by the Maryland assembly
of the famous Toleration Act, which provided that any believer in
the divinity of Jesus Christ should be allowed to worship un-
molested, although it strictly forbade denial of the Trinity. In New
England in 1636, Roger Williams was expelled from Massachusetts,
in effect for demanding religious toleration, and settled in what was
to be known as Providence, capital of the later colony of Rhode
Island. Here for the first time – and for a long period it stood alone –
was a community in which, for reasons of principle, all religious
sects enjoyed freedom of worship.

During the middle years of the century Puritan settlements spread
widely in New England for economic, and not merely religious,
reasons. In 1639 settlers in the Connecticut Valley drew up the
Fundamental Orders of Connecticut, patterned on the system of
Massachusetts and seeming somewhat more liberal. Settlers to the
north in what were later to be New Hampshire, Vermont and Maine
inaugurated another constantly repeated American tendency; they
entered lands of other proprietors, and even other countries, such as
the French here and the Dutch to the south. In the nature of things,
however, it was virtually impossible to prevent, or later to control,
them. The manner in which these New England settlements were
reabsorbed into Massachusetts before finally becoming independent
of the Bay Colony illustrated what was to be in the future a characteristic American method of annexing neighbouring territories by
infiltration.

In the fertile lands of the South, stretching away from the Tidewater area of the Chesapeake, such collisions of jurisdiction (which
might have been more serious because the scale of expansion was so
much swifter than in the poorer and harsher area of New England)
did not occur because of the vast unclaimed spaces to the west and
south. The character of development, too, was very different in the
two sections. In New England, during the seventeenth century,
expansion was more orderly, more carefully planned, more closely
controlled; whole new townships were established, in Massachusetts
for example, under the authority of the General Court, with land set
aside for church and school and village green. More than three-
quarters of the hardy population were subsistence farmers, and the
nature of the soil and climate kept economic inequalities in the
countryside to a minimum. Already indeed the remainder of the
New Englanders had turned their attention from this harsh agriculture to pursuits which brought some of them considerable wealth,
such as fishing, lumbering, shipbuilding, local manufactures, and

trade with the West Indies, especially in molasses which they turned into rum and re-exported. In the warm rich soil of Virginia and Maryland, by contrast, there was an increasing tendency towards land speculation and the growth of large land holdings, the latter especially in the more settled coastal region. The importation of Negroes to augment the supply of labour, as emigration from England dwindled after the Restoration of Charles II in 1660 (which marked in the mother country the coming of more settled times and the disappearance of the idea of over-population), led to the permanent establishment of slavery. By the end of the century there were probably more than 10,000 slaves in Virginia, and tobacco was increasingly grown on large plantations run with slave labour, especially as the exhaustion of the soil necessitated rapid expansion into new lands. It made possible greater wealth than subsistence farming, but like so many great staple crops it put its producers very much at the mercy of an unpredictable and uncontrollable international market, which can be seen in the serious decline in tobacco prices in the late 1660s.

Politically, as well as economically, there was, even setting aside the Negro question, probably by this time less equality in Virginia than in New England. There were also, well as the aristocratic political system functioned in Virginia, more signs of political variety and flexibility in the North; in 1643, for example, 'The Confederation of the United Colonies of New England' was formed and, though it proved abortive, it was the first of the efforts of the colonies in America to work together institutionally. Though it was, in the exceptional circumstances of the Civil War in Britain, set up partly to co-operate in dealings with foreign powers, its main object was to combine against the Indians, who were still formidable enemies to expansion. In Virginia the failure of the government to give protection from the Indian menace was the occasion, in 1675, of the first American frontier rebellion against the established authorities, led by one Nathaniel Bacon. It derived its strength, and its success until the death of Bacon nearly a year later, from the economic grievances of the small farmers and their resentment at their lack of say in their own government. But although the Indians were long to hinder the advance of the frontier and often to terrorise its bold but scattered pioneers, they had already ceased to be a fundamental menace to the white man, with his superior weapons and economic techniques, for by 1688 there were about 200,000 settlers in the mainland colonies.

This extraordinary growth since 1607 owed most to the great opportunities of the new land and to the hardiness and energy of the first Americans, but something also to the neglect which their affairs enjoyed during the political turmoil, in the remote mother country, which lasted until the Restoration. After that date there was a new burst of colonial enterprise from Britain. In 1670 a small group of proprietors, who had been granted a charter by the King in 1663, founded Charleston; their effort, under the 'Fundamental Constitutions of Carolina', drawn up (ironically in some ways, in view of the later American opinion of him as a great democrat) by John Locke, to establish an elaborate system of social and political hierarchy, failed to take root in the actual soil of the New World, but it may possibly have helped to give to South Carolina the aristocratic tone it long maintained. When in the first decade of the new century rice, cultivated by slave gangs, became its staple crop, the economic basis for oligarchy had been found. The much less fertile North Carolina, which became a separate colony in 1691, remained dependent on farming and the supply of naval stores to Britain, and, being peopled largely by dissatisfied migrants from Virginia, acquired a totally different, radical, complexion.

In 1664, in the Anglo-Dutch war, New Netherland was acquired by England, and the King's brother, James, Duke of York, received a very large grant of land in the area, which included the Dutch settlements and was now called New York. The new régime, although more liberal than the old, was perhaps the least democratic in the colonies, but the Duke, himself a Catholic, did grant religious toleration. Almost at once, he made a separate gift of what was later to become New Jersey to two of his loyal followers; as a result of a number of Quakers gaining control of West New Jersey, it, like Rhode Island, became a haven for the persecuted.

So, too, on a much larger scale, did Pennsylvania, which was founded by one of the greatest of Quakers, William Penn, in the area between Virginia and New York granted to him by Charles II in 1681. In accordance with Quaker ideals Penn organised what was perhaps the most liberal constitution in the world, with a legislature elected on a very broad franchise. But it was still the aristocratic world of seventeenth-century Europe, and the constitution left a great deal of power in the hands of the governor and a small council of land-owners. Opposition to Penn's administration was persistent, especially after he favoured the cause of James II in 1688, and in 1701 he issued a Charter of Privileges; this was even more liberal and remained the constitution of the colony until 1776. Meanwhile Pennsylvania, with its capital Philadelphia carefully planned before the first settlers arrived, burgeoned as no other colony had done. In less than a decade it had developed a flourishing trade with the

West Indies in meat, flour and wheat, and had more than 12,000 inhabitants, including the first great wave of German immigrants to America. In 1704 the tiny colony of Delaware became separate from Pennsylvania, but the latter soon became the wealthiest of all the colonies.

Only one further colony was to be founded before the American Revolution, Georgia in 1733. Its leading figure, James Oglethorpe, planned not merely religious toleration but a settlement which should be a refuge for debtors, still liable in England to a hopeless imprisonment until their debts were repaid. The government favoured its establishment as a military outpost between South Carolina and the Spanish colony of Florida. Georgia began with a stern prohibition of slavery and remained weak – a monument almost to the economic ineffectiveness of excessively paternalistic philanthropy – but in due time gained its prosperity as a characteristically Southern plantation and slave-owning society. Thus by the end of the Colonial Period there was a virtually continuous line of settlement from New Hampshire, in the vicinity of French territory to the north, to Georgia, whose borders ran with Florida in the south; and in the west the line was already by this date well into and beyond the foothills of the great protective barrier constituted by the Appalachians. In not much more than a century and a half the position of the British colonies had become one of great natural strength. In 1750 they probably had a population of about a million and a half; some 700,000, including 300,000 Negro slaves, in the South; somewhat under half a million in New England; and approximately 400,000 in the Middle Colonies. (The latter sections contained an increasing proportion of non-British settlers, which began to augment the growing differences between the colonists and the people of the mother country.) There were by contrast only 65,000 white men in New France at this time to sustain the much more ambitious territorial claims of the French government.

It was with France that the main British conflict in America, as elsewhere, was fought in the century before the American Revolution. Britain's seventeenth-century rivals had already given ground before her; Holland she had defeated in war, of which New York was among the spoils, and Spain had steadily declined in power until she was formidable only when in alliance with France. The American colonists were necessarily in some degree involved in the great cycle of Anglo-French wars, but the names by which they called the first three of them show how much they recognised that they were primarily of European origin and significance – King

William's War (1689–97), Queen Anne's War (1701–13) and King George's War (1744–8). In all three, the colonial campaigns were subordinate and largely ineffective; the colonies were not themselves seriously threatened, and the only permanent acquisition was Nova Scotia in the treaty of 1713.

But the Seven Years War (1756–63) marked the culmination of an increase in the importance of America which had in fact been going on for some time, and its colonial name, the French and Indian War, illustrated not only this but also the far greater involvement of the colonists themselves. Hostilities with the French had indeed broken out in America long before the war began in Europe, and the colonies had even, at a meeting in Albany in 1754, considered, only to reject, a plan for inter-colonial union drawn up by Benjamin Franklin with the object of facilitating co-operation in the conduct of the fighting. William Pitt, later Earl of Chatham, was the first English leader to make British overseas possessions his main objective, to think in terms of the Empire rather than of Europe. Of the brilliant victories of Britain under his leadership he declared, 'America was conquered in Germany'. In fact General Wolfe's capture of Quebec was of crucial importance, but Pitt's phrase got the priorities right; America was the grand object of the war. Though the peace, at Paris in 1763, was made by lesser men, Britain won the whole of Canada and all the interior east of the Mississippi from France, and East and West Florida from Spain. France retained only two small islands in the St. Lawrence and fishing rights off Newfoundland, and had to cede New Orleans and all her claims west of the Mississippi to her ally, Spain. With Britain at the highest peak of power she had ever yet reached, the American colonies were henceforth released almost entirely from any serious foreign threat to their liberty. In a sense their only real political contact with the outside world was now with the mother country, and their new-felt freedom of action was to put increasing strain on their relationship with her.

Formally, that relationship was an independent and distinctive one in the case of each of the thirteen existing colonies. (New Hampshire, Massachusetts, Rhode Island, Connecticut, New York, New Jersey, Pennsylvania, Maryland, Delaware, Virginia, North Carolina, South Carolina and Georgia.) Originally the colonies had been broadly of three types, the chartered company, the proprietary colony, and the royal colony, but there had been, after the Restoration of 1660 and even more after the establishment of Parliamentary supremacy in 1688, efforts by the British government to simplify the system and make it more uniform; after 1696 these were directed by the Board of Trade and Plantations which was set up in that year. The efforts met with limited success. The attempt, for example, begun in 1684, to enforce a union of colonies (to be called the 'Territory and Dominion of New England' but including also New York and New Jersey) collapsed after the Revolution of 1688, to the joy of the member colonies, who not only hated the abolition of their assemblies, the attempt to enforce Anglican worship, and the dictatorial governor, Sir John Andros, but were also quite unprepared to accept any long-term measures of co-operation. There was, however, a tendency for the Crown to take over individual colonies if the occasion arose, and by 1763 all except five were Crown colonies; Connecticut and Rhode Island were still incorporated under their own charters, and Pennsylvania, Delaware and Maryland remained under their proprietors.

All the colonial governments, however, whether directly under the Crown or not, had the same basic problem of reconciling the particular interests of their colonists with the general interests of the mother country, now ruled by Parliament. There was a strong tendency for this situation to find expression through similar institutions. The executive – in the royal colonies a governor – represented the central authorities in Britain, and had considerable powers, such as appointing some officials, summoning and dissolving the colonial assembly, and vetoing certain types of legislation passed by it, usually in accordance with instructions received from the Privy Council and seldom revealed to the colonists. The assembly was elected by the colonists, on a franchise which was restricted but much less narrow and corrupt than that on which the British House of Commons was elected, and acquired considerable powers both of legislation and taxation. In some colonies the conflict between the imperial and the local interests centred around the voting of the salaries of certain officers, especially the governor, and in some the existence of a council, usually nominated by the executive, gave great colour to the colonial belief that their system was a close replica of government at home through King, Lords and Commons. The more the disputes came to focus upon the voting of money – upon taxation – the more the colonists came to think of themselves as successors of Pym and Hampden, fighting in different circumstances the same battle for self-government against royal tyranny.

In fact, since 1688 at least, the authority of the imperial government was exercised by Parliament, which was even more blind to the fact that it was not representative of the colonies than to the fact that it did not in any full sense represent the people of Great Britain themselves. Nevertheless it had in reality directly legislated for the colonies to an increasing degree since the seventeenth century. The great growth in the prosperity of the colonies and in the mother country's sense of what that might mean to her own wealth coincided with the establishment of Parliamentary control. All the colonial powers in Europe shared the competitive nationalist view, commonly called Mercantilist, that colonies existed primarily for the benefit of the parent country and that colonial economic development should be stringently controlled in order to ensure that it continued to enrich the homeland. This system of control in the First British Empire took shape in a series of enactments, generally known as the Navigation Acts, the first of which were passed during the Commonwealth in 1650 and 1651 and specifically aimed against Dutch competition. There were other important Navigation Acts in 1663, 1673, and 1696, so that, except for relatively minor alterations and extensions, the system was in full operation early in the eighteenth century.

It had five main features. The first was the protection of British (including colonial) shipping, both for commercial and naval reasons, by giving a monopoly of the colonial carrying trade to British built and manned ships. The second was the restriction of the export of certain 'enumerated' commodities, such as tobacco, and indigo, and later rice, and later still furs, to England alone, though they could be re-exported thence; this was to encourage their growth in the colonies and at the same time to make sure that the commerce in them passed through Britain, where the merchants could make a profit on them and the government could tax them. The third was an effort to give a monopoly of the imports of the colonies to the British merchant and manufacturer by a very high tariff on all goods except those imported through England, which enabled the government in Westminster to tax all goods imported into England for re-export to the colonies and which encouraged the purchase by the colonies of goods manufactured in Britain. The fourth was the prohibition in the colonies of trades and industries, such as that in woollen products in 1699 and iron rolling and slitting in 1750, which might compete with those of the mother country. The fifth was the restriction of the export of specie to the colonies, and the prohibition of the minting of coin or the issuing of paper money there; this exacerbated the already grievous colonial shortage of currency, which is, as was to seem clear from later American history, a persistent, apparently inevitable, problem in any frontier, debtor, society.

Yet the Navigation Acts were very probably more liberal than those of any other colonial power, and often benefited the colonies almost as much as Britain. The shipping monopoly, for example, led to a flourishing shipbuilding industry and shipping trade in the northern colonies. Some of the enumerated commodities, which came principally from the South, such as tobacco, were given an absolute monopoly of the home market; others, such as sugar, were highly protected against foreign competition; and export bounties were paid on yet others, such as naval stores. Furthermore, a number of important colonial products, like grain from the middle colonies, were not enumerated at all. The protection of British manufactures, too, was less onerous than it seems; thus customs duties were in some cases refunded when articles from abroad were re-exported from Britain to the colonies, while Britain's industrial supremacy was such that her goods were for the most part the cheapest in the world. Finally, the currency shortage was in part a result of the adverse trade balance of the colonies, which was itself an indication of the extent of highly beneficial British investment in the colonies.

The most important alleviation, however, of the Mercantile system was the ineffectiveness of its operation. It would be going much too far to say that it was more honoured in the breach than the observance, but it was always difficult to apply the regulations rigorously in so vast an area so distant from the seat of the imperial government. This tendency was heightened during the first half of the century when a British government, like that of Walpole, could, in its search for political stability and economic development, almost make a policy of passivity, especially towards the colonies. During these years of what Burke in a famous phrase called 'salutary neglect', the 'trade of America', as he also put it, 'increased far beyond the speculations of the most sanguine imaginations'. The total trade (exports plus imports) of the American mainland colonies with England rose from around £500,000 a year at the beginning of the century to something approaching £3 million on the eve of the Revolution. Population multiplied similarly and in the twenty-five years after 1750 increased, by approximately a million, to 2,500,000. (Its structure, as a result, was remarkably youthful.) Considerable elements in this population had come to live by trade, great quantities of which were illicit. One particular estimate is that five-sixths of the vital molasses imports of Rhode Island were smuggled; another, perhaps exaggerated, puts the proportion of all the imports of the colonies which were smuggled as high as a half. Thus many colonists were not merely cramped and irritated by the Navigation Acts but had become dependent on trade which evaded them. This was to have grave consequences when the central government began to try and set its house in order and enforce its own edicts.

The grievances of the colonists, of course, differed, reflecting in particular the differences between the geographical sections. The Southern colonies, dependent primarily on the great staple crops produced by slave labour on plantations, were likely especially to resent the restriction of their market to Britain. Some elements in the middle colonies (New York, New Jersey and Pennsylvania), which lived principally by farming and by the export of grain, as well as by maritime trade, might feel most hindered, in what could become a rapidly diversifying economy, by the restriction of local manufactures. The New England colonies, with their less fertile land, and their shipbuilding, seafaring and fishing, might be most infuriated by the complex regulations concerning overseas trade. Inhabitants of the West would experience most acutely the shortage of money and most feel the need of simple and cheap manufactured goods, which could as things stood only come from far-off Britain. But some groups in every part of the colonies, despite the already remarkable prosperity, had by the end of the colonial period considerable economic grievances against the British government.

Thus by 1763, after only a century and a half since the first foundations, the American colonies had come to thrive in a manner perhaps till then unmatched in history. It was clear that there were no longer serious obstacles, either from the Indians or the European powers, to the westward expansion of what Tocqueville later called 'the Anglo-Americans', except the obstacles (sometimes formidable) of nature itself – and the rewards of overcoming these were extraordinary. The occupation of the great fertile valley of the Mississippi was to be one of the most important events in the development of the western world in the next 100 years. But that it was to be possible was not due solely to the existence of this vast, virtually unpopulated land, immensely rich in natural resources: it was also due to the toughness, energy, enterprise and political and economic skill of the people of the colonies, all of which were already visible. The environment – environments would be a better description – of America had already done its task; working on an immigrant stock, drawn perhaps for the most part from among more vigorous elements in the population of Britain and Western Europe (because the willingness to face the hazards of the enterprise constituted in itself a sort of process of natural selection), the 'great frontier' had produced a distinctive people, speaking a common language and economically strong, as well as in many respects socially and politically mature. They were rapidly becoming conscious of that strength and that maturity. In the famous description by Crèvecoeur, 'A European, when he . . . arrives . . . alters his scale . . . He begins to feel the effects of a sort of resurrection; . . . his heart involuntarily swells and glows; this first swell inspires him with those new thoughts which constitute an American . . . What a change indeed! It is in consequence of that change that he becomes an American.'

Some of the main traits in the American character were even now apparent. Whether a New England merchant or a gentleman planter from the South, the American was economically acquisitive, business-like, and pragmatic: he who conquers a wilderness can never forget that the first necessity of life is to earn one's daily bread. He was, however, a church-goer and a believer, but he did not think of this as in any way incompatible with acquiring treasure on earth: he perhaps better than anyone else exemplified the association of Protestantism with the rise of capitalism. He was, as for example in New York, New Jersey and Pennsylvania, tolerant from the necessities of his circumstances, from habit, and from lack of interest in the theological differences around which intolerance had crystallised in the past; he happily accepted the Anglican church in Virginia and called it Episcopal, although it had no bishops. He prized knowledge and education highly, but the education he most wanted was elementary and the knowledge he most valued was useful – America's ablest and most respected scientist was the utilitarian Franklin; there were by the Revolution nine degree-giving colleges in the colonies (to England's two), all closely geared to the daily needs of society; and the newspaper and the practical manual were the chief products of the printing presses. He had found it essential to be a master of many trades, and his ideal was the unspecialised man: a lawyer turned his hand to all the branches of the law, and every frontier farmer had to be a soldier. He had rapidly learnt that he must discard many of the useless customs, habits, ideas and institutions of the time-calcified European society which he had left; he was impatient of titles and inequalities, of social pretensions, of outmoded and inefficient instruments of government. Though his institutions were cast in the European mould, he had become adept in governing and fertile in political expedients, and he was often and increasingly egalitarian and radical; he felt well able to manage his own affairs, and from this it was but a short step to wishing to govern himself. He was above all resolute, quick in action and furiously energetic: this was the first and greatest lesson of the frontier. Thus when he did come to desire the independence of America, he had the strength and determination to establish it.

Chapter 3

The American Revolution

THE AMERICAN War of Independence, to use the old British title, has been significantly renamed the American Revolution by American historians. This revolution, which was of profound importance for the future of mankind, was fundamentally the result of the process by which the American colonies had outgrown the tutelage of the mother country. The New World had not only produced a distinct and strong American society, it had bred in it a notably independent and levelling spirit. If the British government had been sufficiently flexible and enlightened it might have adjusted itself for a period to America's needs and demands; then with the coming, in not much more than a quarter of a century, of the steam-ship and locomotive, it might have been possible to find some form of imperial solution to the problem of governing at a distance of 3,000 miles and more. Such a solution might have been federal, like the American constitution, or permissive, like the British Commonwealth. But this was not destined to be, for the English system was in fact rigid, narrow and inefficient.

Ironically, the first occasion of friction arose out of a British government effort, rare at this time, to manage the colonies more efficiently. Under pressure from the English landed gentry, who paid the bulk of British taxation, and impressed by the cost of the Seven Years War and of the extreme inefficiency of the colonial fiscal system, Prime Minister Grenville determined to reform the imperial administration, including the customs. In 1764 the Sugar Act was passed; this actually lowered the duty on foreign molasses imported into the colonies, but the main purpose was to see that it was efficiently collected. This measure, which had some other provisions, was intended to be the beginning of the general extirpation of smuggling (which had increased rather than diminished during the war) and it thus struck at the very roots of the livelihood of many New Englanders, who had become dependent on the West Indies trade in sugar and rum. Though most colonists resented the increasing corruption of the customs service because it seemed to presage the wholesale introduction of governmental 'influence' such as had undermined political institutions in the mother country, this attempt at reform aroused even deeper fears that heavy taxes, imposed in this way without their consent, might undermine their whole standard of living.

It is natural that the struggle which now began, and which twelve years later produced the American Declaration of Independence, should have centred constantly upon the question of taxation, in the same manner as had its English domestic predecessor in the seventeenth century. Taxation is the point at which government impinges most directly, and often painfully, on the people's economic existence, which is to most of them the fundamental aspect of their lives. Arguments from Britain, however accurate, that the colonies were not contributing their fair share, even to the cost of their own defence (it was estimated that the *per capita* public debt of the colonies amounted to 18 shillings, that of the mother country to £18), made little headway in the face of this basic financial interest. *Per contra*, colonial complaints made little impression on the Englishmen whose pockets were, they themselves felt, being drained by the cost of maintaining the colonies. Accordingly, despite the vigorous though peaceful protests of American merchants against the Sugar Act, it was followed in the next year by the Stamp Act, which affected other classes besides the merchants, such as printers and lawyers.

The outcry against this new tax was much fiercer, and was accompanied by considerable disorders, which were exacerbated rather than discouraged by the threat of force which seemed implicit in the passage, at almost the same time, of the Quartering Act more fully providing for the compulsory quartering of soldiers in the colonies. This brought to the fore the fact that the colonists, unlike the government at home, now saw little need for a substantial army in America. Representatives of nine of the colonies assembled at New York, in the Stamp Act Congress, and protested against this taxation 'without consent'. The protests were supported by economic sanctions, a voluntary agreement among the colonists not to buy British goods until the Stamp Act was repealed. This was effective enough to persuade the other British economic interest of comparable influence to the landed gentry, the merchants, to bring heavy pressure to bear on the new British government of Lord Rockingham to repeal the Act. This was done in 1766, but it was accompanied by the passage of the Declaratory Act, asserting the full legislative sovereignty of the British Parliament, which included the power to tax the colonies. This was largely ignored amidst the colonial rejoicing, except perhaps by the lawyers, but it was highly significant, for it had lifted the dispute beyond that of mere taxation, and had raised the fundamental issue of principle – what exactly was the relationship of Britain with the colonies? When the practical conflict intensified, events began to push the majority on each side of the Atlantic to directly opposite views.

Britons, having in the seventeenth century established their freedom through Parliamentary sovereignty, had come to accept with little protest the increasingly unrepresentative nature of the House of Commons, partly from lethargy and partly because they valued stability so highly after the disorders of the Civil War. With the rise of Cabinet government, they also began to place, often without realising it, more and more emphasis on the unrestricted sovereignty of Parliament; to this day the 'Queen in Parliament' is legally absolutely sovereign in Britain. Americans not only knew that they were not really represented at all in the British Parliament (and tended to be contemptuous of the idea that even the British were 'virtually' represented there, although most of them had no vote), they felt that their own assemblies, in which they were fairly well represented, ought to exercise the same powers over them as Parliament did over Britain. Views differed – and altered – as to the extent to which Parliament had a general supervisory function for the whole empire, but in the end most Americans came to believe that it ought to have no power to legislate for the colonies. For a period some of them put forward a view indistinguishable from the present theory of the British Commonwealth – that the Crown was the only link between the equal parts of the empire. But the process by which the King became, and was accepted as, a constitutional monarch with exceedingly limited powers had not yet gone far enough in England for this idea to be agreeable either to him or his subjects. In the end, therefore, the two countries (though each had substantial minorities in more or less strong disagreement and opposition) found themselves in irreconcilable conflict: the British were determined to assert their sovereignty, the Americans their independence.

Underlying this clash there was also a fundamental difference, to be of great consequence in American history, as to the proper powers of government. Against the emerging British doctrine of legislative omnicompetence and sovereignty, the Americans held strongly to what was in fact a more traditional English view of the seventeenth century, that the law is sovereign. They generally agreed with James Harington who had written in 1656, 'Government is the Empire of Laws, and not of Men.' Accordingly they tended to think of the constitution in terms of immutable Natural Law and a static

Social Contract (in which most Englishmen had ceased to believe), to think of it as something more fundamental than the acts of the legislature. This is what the American, James Otis, meant when he declared, 'An act against the Constitution is void.' This belief was greatly strengthened by their necessary antipathy to the British view that, as Van Tyne has argued, 'no taxation without representation' meant 'no taxation without Parliament'. The British doctrine was beginning to conceive of the evolution of political institutions, so that Lord Mansfield wrote that the Constitution 'has always been in a moving state, either gaining or losing something'. By contrast, Samuel Adams wrote, 'In all free states the Constitution is fixed.' This pre-conception is at the very root of American constitutional development.

But the dispute had to intensify greatly before these theoretical, but basic, disagreements became clear. In 1766 the Rockingham ministry was, somewhat uncertainly, in the saddle, and there seemed a chance that the policy of its ablest (if junior) member, Edmund Burke, might be continued; it was that of conciliation, of complying with the American spirit as necessary. As he put it, 'The question with me is, not whether you have a right to render your people miserable, but whether it is not your interest to make them happy.' But very few of his contemporaries were magnanimous enough to take this view, or even to see that it would pay them far better to surrender the right to exact a revenue than to lose the colonies altogether; and in any case Rockingham was succeeded in 1766 by a new government led by the great Chatham. Because of his reputation in America, his deep sympathy with the American demand that they should not be taxed without being represented, and even his desire to reform the House of Commons itself, there seemed again some hope that a solution might be found. Some compromise would perhaps have been possible which allowed Parliament to regulate imperial trade, collecting revenue incidentally arising therefrom, but which gave to colonial assemblies the power to levy their own taxes as they had done in fact in the past; the practical problem was that, even in time of war, they had only done so with the greatest reluctance. In any event the protracted melancholic illness of Chatham prevented such a possibility, and what became in due course the Grafton ministry was soon dominated by the clever but shallow Chancellor of the Exchequer, Charles Townshend.

Taking advantage of the confusion arising from the general colonial acceptance of the need for the regulation of imperial trade from Westminster, he tried once more to raise a revenue, not by an 'internal' tax like the Stamp Act, but by 'external' taxes, or customs duties, on a number of colonial imports, including tea. The reception in America of the Townshend Acts (which also tackled once more the problem of enforcing all the Navigation Acts) made it clear that the colonists would not willingly accept any legislation which had as its intention the raising of a revenue in America. They believed with some justice that this opened the way for unlimited and ruinous possibilities of exaction by the home government. Economic sanctions were once more organised and were effective enough to result in the repeal in 1770 of all the Townshend duties except that on tea.

Though a lull in the conflict now appeared, other causes of friction beside taxation were not lacking. Ever since 1763 the West, and especially the South-West where settlement had overtopped the Appalachians, had had a deep grievance over the attempts of the imperial government to organise the occupation of the newly acquired western lands in such a way as to avoid undue trouble with the Indians. A proclamation of that year had for the moment prohibited settlement west of the mountains, and though it was quite ineffective in view of the strength of the westward movement of the pioneer population, it hit land speculators hard and also struck a most sensitive nerve in the American make-up. So did a later attempt of the imperial government to settle its Canadian difficulties, by the Quebec Act of 1774, which incorporated much of the territory of the North-West in the province of Quebec; this renewal of an apparent threat to free westward expansion was not made any more popular, especially in New England, by the fact that it offended American Protestant sensibilities through its wise and necessary official extension of religious toleration to the Roman Catholics of French Canada. Furthermore, American dissenting opinion was deeply disturbed by a contemporary proposal to establish an American episcopacy in the colonies.

All sections of the colonies now had growing grievances against the home government, but feeling ran highest in the mercantile areas, especially in the North-East. The New York Assembly had been threatened with suspension as early as 1767 for failing to implement the Quartering Act; the 'Boston Massacre', in which five Americans from a provocative mob had been shot by panicked British soldiers, had occurred in 1770; and in 1772 friction in Rhode Island between merchants and customs officers culminated in the burning of the revenue cutter, *Gaspee*. In this year Boston inaugurated the system of Committees of Correspondence between dissident elements throughout the colonies, which was to provide the framework of the revolutionary movement.

Meanwhile in Britain Lord North, a Prime Minister far more sub-servient than his predecessors to (and more sympathetic with) the narrow and now highly indignant views of King George III, had come into office. In 1773, to alleviate the financial difficulties of the East India Company, his government gave it a monopoly of tea in the colonies by allowing it to ship its large stocks at a low rate of duty; the extent to which the struggle had now passed beyond the economic stage and become a highly emotional political conflict is clear from the fact that almost all the colonists refused to buy the tea, although it was priced lower than tea had ever been before. When a party of patriots in Boston, disguised as Indians, boarded ships carrying the tea and threw it into the harbour, Parliament replied in 1774 by passing the 'Coercive' Acts. There is little doubt that it was supported in this firm stand by the majority of Britons.

In September 1774 representatives from all the colonies except Georgia assembled at Philadelphia in the First Continental Con-gress. Efforts, led by Joseph Galloway of Pennsylvania, to reach a compromise, through a system which would give Parliament's powers over the colonies to a Grand Council of all of them, failed of acceptance there (as it would almost certainly have done in Britain), and the Congress organised a 'Continental Association' to cut off all economic intercourse with the mother country. It supported Massa-chusetts in its opposition to the 'Intolerable Acts', which had among other things closed the port of Boston. Local committees began actively to prepare for resistance almost everywhere in the colonies, and by the beginning of 1775 extra-legal bodies were acting as governments in ten of the states. On 19 April in that year fighting began at Lexington and Concord near Boston. Even if that first shot was not at the time, as the famous phrase had it, heard round the world, the war which it began was to have vital effects upon the whole future of humanity.

The Second Continental Congress met on 10 May 1775. On 6 July it issued a 'Declaration of Causes of Taking up Arms', and when tentative efforts to patch up an agreement had been made by each side and rejected, opinion in the colonies steadily hardened. This process was speeded by the publication in January 1776 of Tom Paine's powerful pamphlet *Common Sense* which advocated a total and final breach. On 4 July 1776 the Congress at Philadelphia adopted the Declaration of Independence, which was largely written by a brilliant young Virginian, Thomas Jefferson.

It immediately based America's claims on what were intended to be the highest and most indestructible grounds.

'We hold these truths to be self-evident, that all men are created equal, that they are endowed by their Creator with certain unalienable Rights, that among these are Life, Liberty and the pursuit of Happiness. That to secure these rights, Governments are instituted among Men, deriving their just powers from the consent of the governed, That whenever any Form of Government becomes destructive of these ends, it is the Right of the People to alter or to abolish it, and to institute new Government, laying its foundation on such principles and organising its powers in such form, as to them seem likely to effect their Safety and Happiness.'

This was not only a justification for the declaration that the 'United Colonies are, and of Right ought to be Free and Independent States', it was also a clear public affirmation of certain universal human rights. Though many Americans at that time were not prepared to accept that the Declaration necessitated full democracy in practice, it clearly seemed – to very many Americans then, as to anyone who reads it today – to imply that all men ought to enjoy certain equal rights, including that of self-government. In other words the Declaration of Independence, though primarily concerned to assert the rights of Americans against Britons, also in a very real sense committed the United States irrevocably to the cause of democracy. However great, from time to time, the failings of the American system of government in practice, the powerful influence of this ideal has never been absent from the life of the United States.

In the war which followed the outbreak of fighting in 1775, the Americans suffered from a number of severe difficulties. They had no regular army and little military experience. George Washington, the ablest and most experienced of the colonial soldiers, was appointed commander-in-chief; he was with the greatest difficulty able to maintain an army in being throughout the war in the face of widespread apathy and growing weariness, and he seldom had as many as 10,000 'continental' veterans as a nucleus. The short-term militia on which, apart from even more evanescent local volunteers, he had to rely to swell his ranks, never numbered as many as 20,000 in any one battle. Equipment was woefully lacking, and much of what there was had to be bought from overseas. By contrast the British had some 15,000 regulars and 30,000 German (called Hessian) mercenaries, both well armed, as well as a number of 'Tory' and Indian irregulars. At sea the colonists could do little more than prove a nuisance to the British fleet by the attacks of their privateers on British commerce.

The financial condition of the Americans always seemed parlous; Congress had to rely principally on funds provided by the separate states, which lived up to their pre-war record of intense reluctance to vote supplies, and on the issue of Continental paper currency. This depreciated so rapidly in value that in 1780 it was recognised as having sunk to one-fortieth of its specie value, and efforts to hold it here failed dismally, as the phrase 'not worth a Continental', which was current well into the nineteenth century, graphically demonstrates. This chaotic situation was not uncharacteristic of the lack of effective central direction of the war, which an inexperienced Congress of state representatives and its committees was singularly ill-fitted to wage efficiently. In fact only Washington, with his courage, perseverance, integrity and common-sense ability, provided the leadership which perhaps alone made victory possible. Like William the Silent of the Netherlands two centuries before (whom he so much resembled in his situation and character) he fully deserved the recognition he later received as the 'father of his country'.

But the patriots did also enjoy some substantial advantages. There was a real backbone of ardent determination among the supporters of the revolutionary cause, who established sufficient control over public opinion in America to force something approaching 100,000 Tories into exile. In Britain by contrast there was not only considerable lukewarmness but also open Parliamentary opposition to the war, which grew increasingly formidable as the struggle dragged on. Furthermore, American inefficiency was far more than matched by that of the British government, which was dilatory, inflexible, unimaginative and complacent, so that no decisive military effort was made soon enough and each attempt at reconciliation came too late. The very American lack of unity, too, became a sort of military advantage, for there was no single centre where the British could strike a mortal blow; New York was important but not vital, and the capture of Philadelphia, the seat of Congress, was far from decisive. Finally, Britain had enormously extended, and very slow and uncertain, lines of communication across the ocean, so that her vastly greater wealth and population could never be brought effectively to bear.

Above all, she was unable to prevent the rebellion from becoming an international war. The French still smarted from the humiliating defeat they had suffered at British hands in the Seven Years War, and in February 1778 the intense efforts of the American envoys in

France, led by Benjamin Franklin, were rewarded by her entry into
the struggle, followed by that of Spain in the next year. Fears of
British sea power, and resentment at its use to restrict neutral commerce, resulted both in Holland's participation in the war in 1780
and in the subsequent formation of the hostile Armed Neutrality of
the Northern powers of Europe to protect their trade against Britain.
The French not only provided for the Americans a popular symbol
of support in the person of the Marquis de Lafayette in 1777, but
sent an army of 6,000 men under Rochambeau in 1780; in addition
they furnished supplies and arms, as well as a large part of the
$7 million in specie which the Americans obtained from abroad.
Perhaps their most important contribution of all was, for brief but
vital periods in 1780 and 1781, to break Britain's indispensable
control of the seas off the United States. Thus by 1782 when the
North ministry was replaced by that of Rockingham, which began
peace negotiations with America, Britain was fighting a full-scale
war with three of the major European powers, and had become far
more concerned to win this than to reassert her control over the
United States.

But even when fighting the colonies alone the British had not been
able to gain – or even effectively to summon their energies for – a
decisive triumph. General Gage's initial but expensive victory at
Bunker Hill on 17 June 1776 outside Boston was followed less than
a year later by the evacuation of the city by his successor, General
Howe. The latter's brother, Admiral Howe, landed unopposed on
Staten Island near New York city in July 1776, and in the succeeding
months the British forces pushed slowly south, defeating Washington
at Long Island and White Plains, but the American army was able
to strike back at Trenton. General Howe, moving his army by sea
and defeating Washington again at Brandywine Creek, captured
Philadelphia in September 1777, but meanwhile the tide had turned
in the north.

There, in late 1775 American forces had temporarily captured
Montreal, and a gallant attempt under Benedict Arnold (later to
become in American legend the supreme embodiment of treachery,
first by giving information to Britain and finally by changing sides)
to take Quebec had only just failed, but their retreat in the spring of
1776 prepared the way for the first disastrous British defeat. A
grandiose plan for an attack by General Burgoyne down the
Champlain route from Canada, and a junction with the British
forces from New York at Albany, thus cutting off New England from
the other rebellious areas, failed totally through lack of co-ordination and of military realism: Howe, at sea on his way to Phila-

delphia, sent no troops from New York and 'Gentleman Johnny' Burgoyne proved grossly over-confident. At Saratoga he surrendered his whole remaining force of 5,000 men to General Gates on 17 October 1777. This American victory was probably the final factor in bringing France into the war.

During the winter of 1777-8 Washington was still just able, in conditions of great hardship, to keep his army in being at Valley Forge, while British peace overtures came to nothing, and so their new Commander, Clinton, evacuated Philadelphia and retired to New York in the summer of 1778. A successful British campaign, launched by sea in the Deep South under Clinton in 1780, was followed in the next year by further not unsuccessful fighting against the Americans by Cornwallis, whom Clinton had left in command in the South when he returned to New York. But once again this could not be a conclusive blow, and the two British commanders were at odds with one another about the next steps, while Cornwallis remained, with 7,000 men, in occupation of Yorktown on Chesapeake Bay. The French admiral De Grasse then appeared with twenty warships off the Virginia coast, a sufficient force to prevent the relief or evacuation of Cornwallis: Washington, advised by Rochambeau, had seen his opportunity and, leaving Clinton covered by a small force in New York, marched swiftly to invest Yorktown with 16,000 French and American troops. On 19 October 1781 Cornwallis surrendered, and the British bands fittingly expressed their sense both of the importance of their defeat and of the blow their old world superiority had suffered by playing, as they marched out to surrender, the tune called 'The World Turned Upside Down.' It was indeed never really to be the same European world again.

Lord North is said to have received the news of Yorktown like a bullet in the chest, but it was not until the passage by the House of Commons of a motion renouncing all further efforts to subjugate the thirteen colonies that, in March 1782, he was able to prevail on the King to allow him to resign. In the protracted negotiations which ensued the American commissioners (Franklin, John Adams, Jay and Laurens) certainly gave no foundation for the later American myth of the naïve United States diplomat outsmarted at every turn by unscrupulous British wiles; they showed themselves prepared if necessary to make a separate peace with Britain, though in fact the actual American-British treaty of 1782 did not come technically into effect until the conclusion of the Peace of Paris between Britain and France in 1783, while Franklin was able to restore enough Franco-American good feeling to obtain a loan of 6 million livres from

France. The actual terms of the treaty were much more favourable to the United States than most Americans had dared to hope.

She obtained broadly a boundary across the top of New England and thence along the St. Lawrence and through the Great Lakes in the north, down the Mississippi in the west, and, very approximately, a border with Florida running along the 31st parallel in the south. There were great ambiguities in the boundary line (largely as a result of geographical ignorance), especially in New England, in the area between the Great Lakes and the source of the Mississippi, and in Florida, but the last was to prove much less troublesome than the others, since Britain also ceded East and West Florida to Spain, now a weak power, in 1783. The terms also granted the United States certain fishing rights, important to New England, off the coasts of British North America, while the West benefited from the clause guaranteeing mutual free navigation of the Mississippi. Britain extracted two articles from the Americans, one allowing British creditors to try to get payment of their debts in America, the other recommending to the several states the restoration of Loyalists' property. An ambitious proposal put forward by the United States delegates for virtual Anglo-American free trade, though sympathetically received by liberal Englishmen like Shelburne and Fox, unhappily failed to gain the support of conservative British mercantilist opinion, and all that remained of it in the end was an expression of intention to negotiate a subsequent Anglo-American commercial treaty. Above all, the first Article of the peace recognised the United States to be 'free, sovereign and independent States'.

Chapter 4

The Confederation and the Constitution

AMERICA HAD gained her freedom and a great patrimony, but she faced grave problems. Not the least of these was whether the thirteen states did in fact constitute a nation: they were certainly a confederacy rather than a union, officially styled 'The United States of America', and were significantly known, in abbreviation, not as the 'U.S.,' but as the 'U. states,' each state, as J. R. Pole has written, 'retaining an emphatic individuality.' This question was in a sense to remain unresolved until the Civil War settled it once and for all, although the full inauguration of the Constitution in 1789 constituted a giant leap towards unity. But in 1783 the much more tenuous 'Articles of Confederation,' which had been finally signed two years earlier, alone bound the thirteen states institutionally together.

The weakness of the single chamber Congress, which was really the sole federal authority, reflected the widespread suspicion not only of any government stronger than those of the separate states, but also of any strong government whatsoever: as Tom Paine, Englishman though he was by origin, had put it, 'Government, even in its best state, is but a necessary evil; in its worst state, an intolerable one.' All decisions of consequence required the support of seven of the state delegations to Congress; decisions on war and peace, foreign treaties, requisitions of money from the states (the sole method of taxation), the issue of currency and the raising of loans, had to have nine positive state votes (so that abstentions often acted as a veto); and amendment of the Articles needed unanimous consent. The authority of Congress was not exercised directly on individuals but through the states, and there was no power to coerce a recalcitrant state; given the traditional and powerful American dislike of voting taxes even in their respective states (whose governments their peoples so effectively controlled), the fiscal powers of the government of the Confederation were totally inadequate. The popular belief in the need to protect fundamental natural rights by insisting on state sovereignty against the encroachment of central government found expression in the fact that the Articles

51

were a written constitution, exceedingly difficult to amend.

On the other hand, the United States had conducted a victorious war, and they had not merely carried on the day-to-day affairs of government (limited in scope in the eighteenth century anywhere in the Western world), but they had at least one act of real statesmenship to their credit. Chiefly owing, it is true, to the obstinacy of Maryland, which refused to ratify the Articles until the claims of the separate states to lands west of the Ohio River had been largely surrendered to the federal government, the whole future development of the West was in the hands of Congress. That the new states which were to grow up there would be the wards of the whole nation was to be of profound importance to American unity. The Ordinances of 1785 and 1787 both laid the foundation of the system of individual land sale and settlement and also outlined the procedure by which territories would be organised under the aegis of Congress until such time as they should be ready to apply for full and equal membership of the union as States. And though the predominant power in America lay in the hands of the separate state governments, which had been created, by active popular consent of the governed, out of the old colonies during the course of the war, the form of these constitutions demonstrated that to a very considerable degree they had common political ideas, such as the rule of law and the need, if liberty was to be preserved, for the separation of the legislative, executive and judicial powers. Their common fund of political experience had produced a real sentiment of American nationalism; tempered by such trials as Valley Forge, their patriotism transcended its local origins.

As was natural, this national feeling was strongest among the more prosperous and better educated, and they were the class with most reason to be dissatisfied with the ineffectiveness of the Confederate government, in what used to be called by American historians the 'critical period' following the war. This conflict had left the usual legacy of economic depression and social disorder. The post-war recession was intensified by the flooding of the American market with a huge back-log of cheap British manufactured goods. The currency situation, too, which was already difficult, became increasingly chaotic; large quantities of paper money were issued in various forms by seven states in 1786. (This was a long-standing and respectable tradition in America in time of need). Six states, it is true, did not depart significantly from fiscal orthodoxy, but one of these was Massachusetts, and it was there that in 1786 a rural revolt, led by Captain Shays, broke out against the state government when it demanded the payment of taxes in specie, which was in very short supply, especially in Western areas. Though Shays' Rebellion was easily put down, it added to the already potent alarm of the well-to-do in the country as a whole. They feared that the tide of radicalism, which had swept the states during the war, would undermine all property rights. They also shared a more widespread fear of violence and the collapse of all law and order, though this may have been without real justification.

Hamstrung by its lack of powers, Congress could take no effective measures to alleviate the economic distress. It could not impose currency stabilisation, let alone uniformity, on the states (though it took steps to put its own in order), and it could not raise anything like the revenue needed to service its debts and carry on the barest minimum of government activity. In particular, it could not impose a tariff either for revenue or to protect such domestic industries as did exist against British competitition. The attempts of several of the states to do what Congress could not do only rendered the situation more confused, for in their efforts to raise revenue for themselves and to protect their own industries, they began to build customs barriers against each other, thus underlining the fissiparous tendencies which were increasing in this vacuum of national power.

This weakness also extended into the political sphere; State governments began to squabble with one another, and some not only had their own militias but actually built their own navies. Finally, it became more and more clear that Congress was incapable of conducting an adequate foreign policy, and a number of grave diplomatic problems, especially with Britain, seemed to threaten the very future of the infant nation. This aroused its new-found and vigorous patriotism, which began increasingly to find expression in a demand for the fundamental revision of the Articles of Confederation.

Arising from consideration, at a meeting at Annapolis in 1786, of the very limited question of the need of Maryland, Virginia and Pennsylvania to reach an understanding about navigation of the Potomac River, Congress was eventually persuaded, largely by conservative opinion (in the person of Washington and such men as Alexander Hamilton of New York and James Madison of Virginia), to authorise a convention of representatives from all the states to amend the Articles of Confederation. They met at Philadelphia in May 1787, and, under the dignified presidency of Washington, soon determined to produce a totally new constitution. This was a vital step: it was indeed, though its objects were rather conservative than radical, a fulfilment of the American Revolution. The states had all, even in the press of war, established new governments; they had almost all done so in some fashion which based them firmly on popular consent, and the legislatures of two of them, Massachusetts and New Hampshire, had actually summoned special representative bodies, called conventions, and had submitted the constitutions which these framed to the voters for ratification. This constitutional procedure, one of America's most important contributions to the practice of free government, accorded well with the general contemporary conviction, arising from the doctrines of Natural Law and Social Contract, that, if the powers of governments were to be restrained, written constitutions, more fundamental than the normal acts of the legislature and more difficult to alter, must be created by special processes peculiarly designed to gain and to demonstrate the support of the people. (Written constitutions also fitted well into the tradition of colonial charters and church covenants.) It was significant that the convention method was the one Congress was induced to adopt, for it was to make easier the by-passing of the State governments which exclusively dominated the government of the Confederation.

That this was what would be done was made clear when the Convention decided, in line with the arguments of George Mason of Virginia, to submit the Constitution, not to the state legislatures, but to conventions of the people in the states; the former, he said, 'are the mere creatures of their state Constitutions, and cannot be greater than their creators . . . Whither then must we resort? To the people with whom all power remains that has not been given up in the Constitution derived from them.' In this respect the motives of the members of the Convention might seem merely to be a continuation of the root-and-branch liberalism which had been in the ascendant for the past decade. The revolutionary ferment had worked not merely against the British connection, but also against many traditional limitations on democratic and popular control of government. A mass of commercial and industrial restrictions had disappeared in the Revolution. Many states also abolished entails, quitrents, primogeniture and titles of nobility; disestablished their churches; and moved in the direction of manhood suffrage by allowing most (in some states almost all) taxpayers to vote. In a number of states, such as Pennsylvania, this radical tide rose very high. But in fact the conservative forces which predominated in the Convention, as John Adams – a supporter of the new popular procedures – observed, had regarded these as 'new, strange, and terrible doctrines'. Washington himself wrote, 'Mankind, when left to themselves, are unfit for their own government.' How did this paradox arise?

Love of liberty had in the Revolution been largely indistinguishable from fear of tyranny, and especially the arbitrary rule of a distant government (that of George III). As a result, such powers as were reluctantly delegated by the people to the authorities were kept as far as possible under their immediate control in their states. The powers of the state executives, and even legislatures (which were on the whole strengthened at the expense of the other branches in this period), were severely restricted not only by written overriding constitutions but by deliberately balancing these powers against one another and against the judiciary, while the Articles of Confederation were, as we have seen, under the absolute control of the states. Yet in fact, of course, the overall government in Westminster had always been present from the first foundations, and had, indeed, been almost the sole link between the individual colonies, whose own efforts at devising a comprehensive system of co-operation, like that of the Albany Congress of 1754, had all failed. Without the successors of this 'federal' authority of Westminster, the Congress and its Commander-in-Chief, the War of Independence could never have been won. It seemed clear to conservatives in 1787, and rightly so, that the United States would probably not remain a nation at all, let alone become a great one (as her people, almost without exception, desired) unless the authority of the federal government was much strengthened. This they were determined to do, but they accepted, some with reluctance, the necessity of popular ratification, not only in order to thwart the vested interests of the states, but also because they recognised that even a republic, in which they believed (as opposed to a democracy in which many of them did not), had, for urgent and practical as well as moral and theoretical reasons, to be based directly on the consent of the people of the United States.

Thus in order to gain unquestionable ratification of a new form of national government, whose increased powers many of the most ardent lovers of liberty gravely mistrusted, its conservative advocates had to put it to the touch of a popular, if not democratic, decision 'to win or lose it all'. This was of great significance for the future of free government in America and throughout the world, for it meant that all the major elements in the political life of the United States had now accepted the essential process of continuous free popular government through the polls. From this stemmed in considerable degree the vital development of democratic government in the whole Anglo-American community, as opposed to the reliance on tradition and force which still and for long prevailed elsewhere, including most of Europe. At the same time, as compared with the cautious and evolutionary approach of the British to political change, the necessary formulation, in one breath so-to-speak, of a complete blue-print of government for what was in due course to become one of the greatest nations on earth imparted to the American people a penchant for, almost a tradition of, great and sweeping changes in, and broad and radical concepts of human government. (They have, it is true, not greatly modified the Constitution, but they have innovated radically at state level, and in the outside world the League of Nations and the United Nations would have been very different without it.) The Constitution represented a great step forward, even though it seemed to many at the time a leap in the dark; it was so successful that it enabled W. E. Gladstone to declare at the height of Britain's power in the nineteenth century, that 'as the British constitution is the most subtle organism which has proceeded from progressive history, so the American constitution is the most wonderful work ever struck off at a given time by the brain and purpose of man.'

The ratification of the Constitution was also to signalise the emergence of modern federalism, which was in essence an American invention. Confederations existed, and had existed, elsewhere, in response to variations in race, language or geography, but in none did the central as well as the local governments have effective power, and in none were these powers not only of equal authority within their own spheres but also equally derived from direct popular support. The most striking and novel demonstration of this fact was that both State and Federal governments had immediate jurisdiction over and applied their power directly to the individual. Neither was the agent of the other: the citizen was directly subject to each.

The ratification of the Constitution, however, was not to be easy, let alone a foregone conclusion. It was decided that the document would come into effect when nine out of the thirteen states had ratified it, and as soon as the Convention's work was done, by 17 September 1787, a prolonged, urgent and grave national debate (generally speaking on a plane altogether worthy of the event) was conducted in the states on the issue of ratification. The first exposition of the case put forward by the supporters of the Constitution, in what came to be known as *The Federalist* papers (chiefly by Hamilton and Madison), is a classic of political science, but some of its opponents, such as Patrick Henry of Virginia, were men at that time of equal fame. As the Federalists had anticipated, it was swiftly ratified in five states; then, as they had hoped, ratification followed in four more doubtful ones between 6 February 1788, when Massachusetts voted in favour, and 21 June, when New Hampshire's adhesion brought the Constitution into operation. But even so, it might have been a very ineffective instrument without the great and geographically crucial states of Virginia and New York; the former in fact ratified only three days after New Hampshire, and, largely as a result, New York followed in July. North Carolina did not join till 1789, and Rhode Island till 1790, long after the new government had been inaugurated with Washington as President.

Nor had the actual deliberations of the Convention been swift or simple, lasting as they did through four trying months of the Philadelphia summer. But to have carried them to a successful conclusion at all was a considerable achievement, and to have brought forth a document which has remained in a quite remarkably unaltered form the basis of American national political life, from that day to this, almost justifies Jefferson's description of the Convention as an 'assemblage of demi-gods.' Since 1789 the Constitution has only had twenty-four amendments, and the first ten of these, known as the Bill of Rights, were passed all together in 1791; they further clarified and guaranteed the rights of individual citizens, as had been promised by supporters of the Constitution to those still apprehensive that a strong government might imperil their liberties. The Constitution, for all its failings, enables the United States to claim with reason that, except for the Civil War, the American people have the oldest tradition of broadly democratic self-government in the world (older even than that of Britain). That classically simple and elegant document, on display for all the world to see in the National Archives in Washington, was 'the artifact of a generation of political masters'. Few if any other eras could have produced a set of men sufficiently learned yet enlightened, idealistic yet practical, emancipated yet experienced, to devise in a few months a form of government which has been capable of adaptation to the rapidly changing needs of such a society – one that grew from a predominantly agricultural population of less than 4 million people, inhabiting a part of the eastern seaboard of North America, at the birth of the republic, to a great industrial society of well over 180 millions, stretching from ocean to ocean, which is the United States today.

Perhaps the most important element in this achievement, and one which was to remain a vital and dominant strain in American life, was its pragmatism, for the Convention was able to complete its work only by a series of essential compromises.

The fundamental compromise was between those who wished, like Hamilton, to create as strong and centralised an American national government as possible, and those who wished to preserve the maximum of state autonomy. This question of individual viewpoint early became associated with a cleavage between the large and the small states, embodied on the one hand in the 'Virginia plan' for a quite new system headed by a powerful legislature with representation proportionate to state population and hence strength, and on the other hand in the counter-plan of New Jersey for mere amendments to the Articles of Confederation, giving Congress somewhat more power. This jealous split between large and small states, which dominated proceedings for about two months, was settled by the compromise which gave all states equal representation in the Senate with two members, but made representation in the larger House of Representatives proportionate to population. (The House, according to the apportionment based on the 1790 census, had 106 members; by 1910 it had risen to 435 where it stands at present, reapportionment being in effect automatic on the recommendation of the Census Bureau.) Curiously enough, the large state *v.* small state issue has never again been a real one in American politics, which is not only a tribute to the solution reached but evidence of the nationalising effect, in itself, of such a dramatic *tour de force* as the formation of a new supra-state political structure like the Constitution. But one of the reasons why the Constitution endowed the Union government with as much power as it did was that, by and large, its most violent opponents, such as Patrick Henry, were not in the Convention at all, for it tended to be more representative of conservative opinion, which on the whole favoured a stronger national authority.

In the same way, the body was on the whole one of prosperous rather than poor men, and, though they had widely different individual economic notions and financial interests, they naturally showed a preference for measures which would protect property. Though too much has been made by historians, led by Charles Beard, of the idea that the fifty-five members of the convention were moved primarily by narrow economic motives (and especially by the financial self-interest of those of their number who owned government securities), there can be little doubt that many of them included in their objectives prevention of the erosion of capital values by the inflationary paper money issued in such large quantities in some states such as Rhode Island. It is also unquestionable that the poorer classes, who produced agricultural goods and who might, if they were not literally and exclusively subsistence farmers, profit most from a continuing monetary inflation, were not strongly represented in the Convention. Not only was this in the nature of things, but it is also probable that the conservative elements threatened by inflation were stronger in the East, which has on the whole been more strongly entrenched in American politics than such rural areas as the West. Thus the Constitution gave Congress the power to regulate foreign and inter-state commerce, to tax, to borrow money, to 'coin Money' and to regulate its value, but it prohibited differentials and duties of any kind in inter-state commerce and forbade states to 'coin Money; emit Bills of Credit; make any Thing but gold and silver Coin a Tender in Payment of Debts; pass any . . . Law impairing the Obligation of Contracts.'

The third basic cleavage which it was necessary to settle by compromise in the Convention was between two of the great sections of the country, both of which were strongly represented at Philadelphia, the North and the South; in the end this compromise was to prove unable to stand the test of time. The debates show that the basic difference between the agricultural South, producing for export great staple crops by Negro slave labour, often on large plantations, and a North of yeomen farmers (living largely by subsistence agriculture) and of maritime traders, who were soon to branch out into industry proper, was already apparent. Delegates from the Deep South, indeed, were already expressing the passionate conviction, which was to dominate the whole South by the time of the Civil War, that the permanent continuation of Negro slavery was essential to their existence. Opinion in the North was increasingly suspicious of the slavery system (Massachusetts and Vermont having already abolished it), and especially of the African slave trade, while enlightened men in the Upper South such as Washington, Jefferson, and Madison had the gravest misgivings about it and hoped that it might in due course die out. The bitter question in the Convention was whether Negro slaves (the vast majority of the 757,000 Negroes in the United States in 1790 being in servitude in the South) were to count in the apportionment of representation, and it was solved by the most obviously artificial of the compromises; under it each slave (the actual word was studiously eschewed in the Constitution) was counted as three-fifths of a person for this purpose and (the *quid pro quo* exacted from the South) for that of direct taxation. The South in its turn allowed its fear of discriminatory Northern economic legislation to be allayed by the prohibition of a tariff on exports from the United States, of which it produced the great bulk. It also managed to get the abolition of the slave trade forbidden, but only until 1808, when in fact it was abolished. Finally, the return of fugitive slaves to their masters by other states to which they had escaped was guaranteed in the Constitution.

Once the nature of the bicameral legislature had been agreed, there was little doubt that the Federal authority would, as was coming to be the case in almost all the states, be divided between it and an executive (as well as judicial) branch. (There was at first some feeling against a single Chief Executive.) This was in part by inheritance from, and analogy with, the British system of King, of Lords and Commons, and of an independent judiciary (the Constitution based itself directly on the vital British precedent when laying down that judges 'shall hold their Offices during good behaviour'). But the recent British developments in the direction of cabinet responsibility in practice – as opposed to theory – were even less clearly understood in America than they were in Britain, so that members of the legislature were forbidden while in Congress to hold any civil office of the United States. Nevertheless, in some respects the American political system, even up to the present day, has remained similar to the British form of government as it operated in the eighteenth century, before the rise of the modern party system. The separation of the powers had also in part come to be regarded, especially since the Revolution, as the only sure safeguard of liberty, in the manner suggested by Montesquieu. Of course the separation was not complete; the need for the President's assent to legislation – that is, his real power of veto in all cases where a two-thirds majority could not be found in each House – was one example of an exception, and another was the requirement of a two-thirds majority in the Senate for the ratification of all treaties made by the President. But it was deliberately made sufficiently complete to render positive governmental action very difficult unless a wide spectrum of agreement existed between the branches of the government.

Thus the federal judiciary, headed by the Supreme Court (which was the final court of appeal), not only specifically received an original jurisdiction which included cases between the States and cases to which the United States was a party, but it also assumed the basic and profoundly important right to interpret the Constitution itself. This was, it is true, a sort of legislative function, but it certainly emphasised the separation of powers and was to prove a potent instrument for checking the power of the legislature. Whether or not this was intended in the Convention, it is arguable that any fundamental written constitution, which is antecedent to the legislature (whose power is derived solely from it), needs interpretation, and that this can best be done by the judiciary. But this power of invalidating legislation, of 'judicial review', though it may frustrate legislative tyranny – rather as the Constitution may protect the rights of the individual against the tyranny of the majority – undeniably has had very frequently the result of limiting the effective activity of the federal government. This has become increasingly clear to us in the twentieth century, but it is vital to realise that there is, deeply embedded not only in the American political system but also in American political ideas and traditions, a primal belief that it is better to run the risk of ineffective government rather than the danger of governmental despotism.

This conviction has of course weakened with the passage of the years, but it is extraordinarily difficult for peoples to throw off long-standing preconceptions, especially those acquired in the traumatic days of their birth as nations. Burke in a frequently quoted passage had declared that the American love of liberty in large degree resulted from the fact that they took their bias from the hands of the English at a time when, in the seventeenth century, the latters' adoration of their freedom was fiercest: the era of the American Revolution had continued, and emphasised, this bias.

Nor was this underlying conviction purely political, or even social; the publication of Adam Smith's *Wealth of Nations* had coincided with the Declaration of Independence, and the Revolution had abruptly, *ipso facto*, abolished the whole machinery of British imperial mercantilism. The full powers of economic control which West-minster had claimed to exercise were not given to the new Federal government and some of them were also denied by the Constitution to the States. The state governments (especially where influenced by the New England communitarian tradition) did play a vital econo-mic role none the less (in 'internal improvements' of communications for example) and the Constitution did confer very substantial economic powers on the federal government, as we have seen (such as the issue of money and the regulation of inter-state commerce); but they were not fully deployed, let alone reinforced in practice, until the twentieth century. In a sense the Revolution did for the United States what it took years of painful political controversy and protracted legislation to achieve in Britain – a dismantling of the formidable apparatus of traditional European state economic inter-ference. This, fortified by the practical circumstances of a new society in a dispersed and virgin land, led to a marked degree of individual economic initiative, and even to a considerable accep-tance by some – not including Alexander Hamilton – of the theoreti-cal doctrines of the rising *laissez-faire* school of classical economics, at least in domestic affairs (the tariff was another matter). The effects of this coincidence, for such in some degree it was, of the formation of the Constitution with the rise of economic individual-ism (so natural a growth in any case in America), are still visible today in some of the instinctively unfavourable responses of many Americans to direct, and especially positive, government economic action, if not in the whole American capitalist ethos.

But, thoroughly as the idea of the balance of governmental powers
was embodied in the Constitution, the will of those in the Convention who wished to create an effective federal authority did prevail
sufficiently to allow the growth of one of the greatest of the world's
bodies politic; America remained for the best part of a century a
union of states rather than a consolidated nation state, but after the
Civil War its unity was sufficient to enable it to absorb the huge
masses of immigrants – more than 36 million between 1850 and
1945 – who poured into the land. And even before the great sectional split between North and South, the really essential powers to
govern the country did exist. In a negative sense this was ensured by
the very considerable limitations imposed on the power of the States
by the Constitution; apart from the economic restrictions noted
above, the States were forbidden without the consent of Congress to
'keep troops, or Ships of War in time of Peace, enter into any Agreement or Compact with another State, or with a foreign Power, or
engage in War, unless actually invaded, or in such imminent
Danger as will not admit of delay.' The States were also enjoined to
give 'Full Faith and Credit . . . to the Public Acts, Records and
judicial proceedings' of each other.

In a positive sense, apart from the powers already enumerated,
the Congress was given authority to declare war and to maintain
armed force, to 'establish Post offices and Post Roads', to 'establish
an uniform Rule of Naturalisation', to grant patents and protect
copyrights, and to rule the 'Seat of Government', which was in due
course to be established in the District of Columbia. Above all, when
in due time the climate of opinion became favourable, that part of
the first clause of Section 8 of Article I which gave Congress power to
tax in order to 'provide for the . . . general Welfare of the United
States' was to prove an enormous reservoir of Federal power, as was
the concluding passage of the same section which gave Congress
power 'To make all Laws which shall be necessary and proper for
carrying into Execution the foregoing Powers, and all other Powers
vested by this Constitution in the Government of the United States,
or in any Department or Officer thereof.'

The President was empowered to appoint, 'with the Advice and
Consent of the Senate', officers of the United States, civil and mili-
tary; to give Congress 'from time to time . . . Information of the
State of the Union and recommend to their Consideration such
Measures as he shall judge necessary and expedient'; and to call
Congress into special session 'on extraordinary Occasions' (regular
annual sessions being prescribed by the Constitution). His treaty-
making power and duty of receiving ambassadors were to give him

authority to conduct a comprehensive and vigorous foreign policy. He was also made Commander-in-Chief of the armed forces, from which source a huge authority was in time to flow.

One other fundamental division split the Convention, as well as the country: though almost everybody feared the encroachments of government, and especially the federal government, on their freedom, by no means everyone believed in full democracy. The Declaration of Independence did constitute a real and deeply felt, albeit theoretical, commitment to ultimate democratic government, and radical forces in some of the states had gone a considerable distance towards implementing it in practice. But the conservatives, who were strong at Philadelphia, inherited deep traditional fears of unrestrained popular rule. Hamilton, who was an extreme exponent of this point of view, said in the Convention, 'The people are turbulent, and changing; they seldom judge or determine right', and accordingly desired a far stronger national government than the Constitution actually created, in order that it could more effectively control this *hoi polloi*. This point of view was not necessarily either sheerly reactionary or very unreasonable, for in a half century Tocqueville and John Stuart Mill were both to express concern that the full democracy by then established in the United States had substituted for the tyranny of the despot the tyranny of the majority. A man like John Adams, deeply devoted to liberty, already apprehended this possibility, and in fact that same separation of the powers was in the end to prove a salutary protection against this new popular threat to individual liberty also.

Here too the conservatives appeared to get their way. The members of the Senate were to be appointed by the legislatures of the states for a six-year term (one third of them to retire every two years), so that no direct popular participation was involved and the Senate was expected to be somewhat insulated from the passions of the masses. This element was only given relatively free play in the elections of members of the House of Representatives, but these Congressmen, as they came to be called, were elected for only two years, which meant in the long run that the House was not only much weaker than the British House of Commons, but in many respects than the Senate itself, since the latter was a continuing body and its members had much greater political security and hence influence. The stipulation, for example, that money bills must originate in the House, which was directly drawn from British practice, did not give it anything like the exclusive financial power enjoyed by the House of Commons, because the Senate, itself a representative body (unlike the House of Lords), made the fullest use of its power of amending bills for raising revenue equally with all other bills.

Furthermore the Constitution merely laid down that electors of members of the House of Representatives 'in each state shall have the qualifications requisite for Electors of the most numerous branch of the State Legislature.' In other words, the suffrage for members of the House was to be the same as that for the equivalent body in each state, and thus varied considerably. The extent of it at this time is a matter of much complexity and some doubt, but though most of the states had property qualifications for the vote, these were chiefly based on land, ownership of which was sufficiently widespread to allow something which in practice approached manhood suffrage in a number of states. This largely democratic situation was to some extent modified by the existence in many states of substantial (and in a few cases very substantial) property qualifications for office-holding, for example for state senator or governor.

But the place where the most elaborate procedures were created to protect the federal government from the direct influence of the 'turbulent mob', as a contemporary phrase went, was in the election of the President and Vice-President, the latter being chief presiding officer of the Senate and the successor of the President in case of his 'Removal . . . from Office, or his Death, Resignation or Inability to discharge the Powers and Duties' of his office. So elaborate were these provisions that they failed to function satisfactorily and had to be altered by constitutional amendment in 1804, but even by that time it is clear to the historian that they were not going to work at all, even in their revised form, in the way intended, constituting indeed a classic example of the best laid constitutional plans that 'gang aft a-gley'. But it is also an example of the remarkable capacity of a free society to adapt an inflexible paper procedure to its own uses. The Americans' political genius, indeed, has shown itself as much in making unwritten modifications to the practice of their Constitution as in producing the document in the first place. The system was one of indirect election of the President and Vice-President, designed to ensure a cool, sober and reflective choice, but by the election of 1800 it had become apparent that Presidential elections were to be distinctly popular and indeed spectacularly ritualistic in character, and they have continued to be the most democratic and intensely fought of American political campaigns. (For some time to come, it is true, popular participation in government in many areas was still much limited by indifference and by continued acceptance of a 'deferential' society, as well as by other factors). What is more, it had also become clear that political parties (and normally two major ones) had come to stay, as an integral part of Presidential elections as well as of American political life as a whole, although the idea of party government had, as in contemporary Britain, been deliberately scouted, in fact repudiated, by the Philadelphia Convention.

As the system soon began to work, parties operated on a nation-wide basis, to choose and support candidates for the two offices, every four years; at first the elections took place on different days in different states but in recent times they have come to be held on a single day in November. (Thus every fourth year since 1796 a Presidential election has taken place, as well as an election of the whole House and one-third of the Senate, to say nothing of an increasing number of officials in various states.) Technically in a Presidential election the people are not voting for President or Vice-President, but for State Electors who will choose both of them. In fact, however, the party candidates for State Elector are already pledged to vote for their party's candidates for the two posts, so that their role is a purely formal one, and the public thinks of itself as voting for the President directly. In addition, it has become the un-written but virtually inviolable practice that whichever party wins the election in each state takes all the State's Electors, who are, according to the Constitution, to be 'equal to the whole Number of Senators and Representatives to which the State may be entitled in the Congress.' Thus the state of Nevada in 1964 had 3 Electors, since it had 1 Congressman and 2 Senators, the state of New York 43 (41 plus 2). This procedure of election through the States can pro-duce anomalies; thus in 1888 President Harrison was elected by 233 to 168 electoral votes, although his opponent Cleveland had 5,540,309 popular votes to Harrison's 5,439,853. But the system works, and has the merit of producing a definite decision, however close the contest may be, as it was for example in 1960. It is, never-theless, a strange outcome of a system carefully devised to guard the choice of the Chief Executive from the fever of popular participation. But it is evidence of the extreme political skill of the American people that they have thus been able to adapt their necessarily somewhat rigid constitutional structure to the enormous changes in the life of the world and of their own nation in the last century and three-quarters.

The Founding Fathers, seeing their written constitution as embodying fundamental law and protecting basic rights, made it very difficult to alter (and who, in view of the strains set up by, for example, mass immigration into the United States, can be confident that they were wrong? Could an unwritten constitution like the British, dependent so much on the political habits which long homogeneity make easy, have withstood those strains so well?).

'This Constitution, and the Laws of the United States which shall be made in Pursuance thereof; and all Treaties made, or which shall be made, under the Authority of the United States, shall be the supreme Law of the Land; and the Judges in every State shall be bound thereby, any Thing in the Constitution or Laws of any State to the Contrary notwithstanding.' Two alternative procedures were laid down for amending it; the first, which has never yet been used, provided for the calling of a convention like that of Philadelphia to propose amendments, on the application of the legislatures of two-thirds of the states; the second one provides for proposals for amendment to be passed by two-thirds of both Houses of Congress. But in either event the amendments must be 'ratified by the Legislatures of three fourths of the several states, or by Conventions in three fourths thereof, as the one or the other Mode of Ratification may be proposed by the Congress.' Many amendments have been called for, but very much fewer have been chosen for ratification by three-quarters of the states.

Nevertheless, the delegates, as they departed from Philadelphia (or at least as they saw the Constitution come into effect), could reflect with satisfaction that they had completed a work which was to go far to justify the preamble they had written for the document. 'We the People of the United States, in Order to form a more perfect Union, establish Justice, insure domestic Tranquility, provide for the common defence, promote the general Welfare, and secure the Blessings of Liberty to ourselves and our Posterity, do ordain and establish this Constitution for the United States of America.'

Chapter 5

The New Government

THE CONSTITUTION, for all its merits, was only a skeleton: in an operation almost without precedent the new government had to put flesh on its bones. This was made easier by the fact that fifty-four members of the 1st Congress had been in the Philadelphia Convention or in one of the state ratifying conventions, and that all save seven had advocated ratification. The continuous presence of Washington as President for two terms (the second undertaken reluctantly) greatly aided this continuity: his contribution as the first President was almost as important as that he made as Commander-in-Chief during the war. Because exercised with such dignity and restraint, his decisive role, especially in choosing between the policies of Hamilton and Jefferson, has sometimes been under-estimated. It is often said that the United States is an elective kingship (though Washington kept some state, proposals to go any further, even by conferring on him the title of 'His Elective Highness', were soon swept away) and certainly the long-term trend of the American political system has been towards giving a man elected for four years broader and deeper powers to govern during that term. But Washington's moderate common-sense saw to it that in these first days – of whose vital precedent-making character he was well aware – a wise path was taken between establishing executive functions and co-operating as fully as possible with the elected representatives of the people in Congress.

Indeed he, in common with most contemporaries, expected – and desired – to work more closely with the Senate than turned out to be practicable; although small enough in numbers (twenty-two only at first) it declined to become a sort of privy council, and after one unfortunate attempt to take the Vice-President's position in the chair, in order to take its advice on an Indian Treaty, Washington (and his successors after him) made his treaties first and merely submitted them to the Senate for ratification when signed, though he did continue his practice of presenting Messages in person to Congress. In the same way, Hamilton's wish as Secretary of the Treasury to promote co-operation between the executive departments and the legislature by reporting his recommended measures to the House in person came to nought, largely through the opposition of Jefferson, himself Secretary at the State Department, and Madison, who was a leader in the House. One result was that the Cabinet of the President and his executive officers (whose meetings had not even been provided for in the Constitution) came to be of considerable importance, and they developed no real sense of being responsible to any authority except the President himself. Washington's first Cabinet was representative of different political viewpoints (incarnate in its dominating personalities, Hamilton and Jefferson) and also of different sectional interests (containing, for example, two Northerners and two Southerners); though the latter practice of balancing the sections (for instance, Western and Eastern) has remained, Washington had decided by 1795 that he would not 'bring a man into any office of consequence knowingly, whose political tenets are adverse to the measures which the general government are pursuing.'

Washington did, however, adhere to his view that legislation was the function of Congress, and was reluctant even to use his veto power, though he did so when he deemed it necessary. Nevertheless his administration exercised vigorous leadership. Congress had early passed bills creating the State, Treasury and War Departments, and then a federal Judiciary Act organising thirteen district courts, four circuit courts, and a Supreme Court of six members, the last empowered to review state courts' decisions as to the constitutionality of statutes, which was an important step towards the full doctrine of judicial review. Under Madison's leadership, a tariff ranging from 5 to 15 per cent *ad valorem* was adopted, both for revenue and for the protection and stimulation of certain domestic manufactures, such as iron, glass and hemp. Hamilton, a brilliant and assertive young man of illegitimate birth, originally from the West Indies, who had had a fine war record, partly as A.D.C. to Washington, and had married into a wealthy New York family, was a firm believer not only in a strong government, but in America's inevitable future as a great commercial and industrial nation somewhat on the British pattern. Desiring positive federal action to promote these objectives, he took the initiative for the administration by urging successfully upon Congress in 1790 the assumption, at their face value by the new government, of all the old state debts (as well, which was generally accepted, as those of the Congress of the Confederation), the establishment of a central Bank of the United States, the organisation of the national currency, and the setting up of a United States mint. His aim was, not only to promote economic development, but also to strengthen the national government by giving the moneyed interests who would profit thereby a vital stake in the now established order. There can be little doubt that this Burkean programme did have an important effect of just this kind.

But it was not implemented without a struggle (particularly over who was to be paid, the present holder or the original purchaser of the national securities) and his second famous series of proposals – the Report on Manufactures of December 1791, which advocated the development and protection of American industry, especially by a high tariff – were not accepted. The chief opposition came from his fellow Cabinet member, Jefferson, and also from Madison. Jefferson, a tall mild-mannered Virginian, born in the then frontier foothills of the Appalachians, had, if not as commanding an intellect as Hamilton, a more speculative and far-reaching (and some would say deeper) mind and a pen even more luminous than Hamilton's was powerful. If the New Yorker was the soldier in political life, Jefferson was the scholar, and a pre-eminent master of the art of politics: if their personalities were contrasted, their views were even more so, for Jefferson was above all a lover of liberty rather than authority, a son of the eighteenth-century enlightenment with a profound instinctive belief in the possibilities of human progress in America. But the vision of the United States which he saw as he looked out over the warm Virginia countryside – from the ingenious home he built to his own plans on his little Blue Ridge mountain top – was not one of teeming cities and bustling commercial activity (the areas and agents, as he believed, of human corruption), but of a republic of yeoman farmers, devoted to freedom in a society of self-governing equals and deriving a modest plenty from the tilling of the abundant soil. If Hamilton was in essence a mercantilist, facing eastward over the sea lanes of trade, Jefferson was in a sense a Physiocrat, surveying the seemingly illimitable and fertile West, which stretched out towards the setting sun. In dramatic, even symbolic, form, this personal antithesis embodied two contrary, deep, and profoundly important currents in the stream of American life; and if in the end, as inevitably as he had supposed, it was to be Hamilton's America that was to triumph, the industrial colossus with its riches and might was always to be redeemed by the spirit of Jefferson, which pierced through the trappings of power to individuals who, within the limits imposed by a common humanity, remained at once seemingly simple, fundamentally friendly and remarkably free.

Jefferson lost the first round, but characteristically obtained for his action a *quid pro quo* for Hamilton's funding of State debts, the establishment of the federal capital in the District of Columbia, on the Potomac river between Virginia and Maryland, and not within the corrupting confines (as he thought them) of the North. Fortified by the trenchant, indeed violent, agrarianism of a man like John Taylor of Caroline County, Virginia, the Jeffersonians were able to block for many years in a spirit of economic *laissez-faire* the state protection of industry which Hamilton sought, but in the end the heirs of Hamilton were bound to triumph, as Jefferson himself admitted when he said in 1816, 'Experience has taught me that manufactures are now as necessary to our independence as to our comfort.' But from this conflict in the first four years of the Republic there sprang the 'first' political party system in the United States, and in a sense anywhere in the world; the Federalists were strong in the North-East, the Democratic Republicans, as they came to be called, in the South and West. (They were the predecessors in a real sense of the Jacksonian Democrats – although their successor, John Quincy Adams, was Jackson's chief opponent – and I shall for the sake of clarity and convenience take the somewhat unusual course of referring to them as Democrats.) Despite Washington's warning in his Farewell Address against 'the baneful effects of the spirit of party', despite the fact that the national parties always tended to remain mere election coalitions of local parties, despite the lack very frequently in later years of real issues of principle such as these, parties were to remain a persistent and indispensable feature of American political life.

There was no Presidential contest in 1792, but already the para-phernalia of local party machinery and the apparatus of opposed party presses, as well as incipient party caucuses both in the Congress and at the State level, had begun to make their appearance. All Washington's efforts to keep Hamilton and Jefferson in double-harness (and even to keep their animosity within bounds) proved unavailing, and he allowed Jefferson to resign, primarily over foreign affairs, on the last day of 1793. The President's views were distinctly closer to those of Hamilton, but the latter also resigned, partly for financial reasons, at the beginning of 1795. Both men now devoted themselves much more fully to political organisation, while the increasing passions of party found expression in the views of the arch-Federalist, Fisher Ames, when he withdrew from national politics in 1797: 'The efficiency of government is reduced to a mini-mum – the proneness of a popular body to usurpation is already advancing to its maximum.' All the old Federalist fears of demo-cracy, which had been allayed by the Constitution, reached a new height as a result of the belief that Jefferson was proposing to let loose a flood of New World Jacobinism. The panic found an expression verging on the absurd in the excessive military measures taken by the government, under Hamilton's inspiration, to crush the so-called Whisky Rebellion – a violent Western revolt against the new excise imposed on what was not merely the favourite beverage but the most convenient cash crop of the rural back-country.

In the election of 1796, Jefferson was just beaten for the Presidency by John Adams, a Federalist much less 'High' than Hamilton and not on good terms with him, but, under the system as it then operated, Jefferson became Vice-President. The Federalists now gave full rein to their alarm at what they saw, in nightmare colours, as the subversive Jacobin doctrines of their Democratic opponents; as President Timothy Dwight of Yale apostrophised, in a manner worthy of Burke, 'Shall our sons become the disciples of Voltaire, and the dragoons of Marat; or our daughters the concubines of the Illuminati?' In very much the same fashion (and deliberately so) as the Younger Pitt's government in Britain, they passed in 1798 a series of measures, known as the Alien and Sedition Acts, which restricted certain activities categorised as seditious, such as writing anything 'false, scandalous and malicious' against the government of the United States, impeding the operation of any federal law, or advising an 'unlawful assembly, or combination'. They also made the process of naturalisation much more difficult, and took certain powers for the deportation of enemy aliens. Adams was at best a luke-warm supporter of the measures, and this attempt by the High Federalists to affix the label of disloyalty to the Democratic Republicans backfired. Adams increasingly dissociated himself from extreme Federalism, especially in foreign policy where he halted the trend towards war with France; and as a result of this Federalist split and the public reaction against the vindictive prosecutions of Democrats under the repressive legislation, as well as the heavy cost of federal war preparations, the latter decisively triumphed in the Presidential election of 1800. The confusion in the electoral machinery resulted in the decision between two Republican candidates, Jefferson and Aaron Burr, being taken – in effect by the Federalists – in the House of Representatives, and largely as a result of Hamilton's opposition to Burr, Jefferson became President.

But this retribution against the Federalists, albeit they had acted on the still near-universal theory that party opposition was by definition treasonable, did not come before their actions had foreshadowed, in ominous fashion, those sectional cleavages which were long to be the gravest political problem of the United States. Washington had wisely warned in his Farewell Address, 'In contemplating the causes which may disturb our union it occurs as matter of serious concern that any ground should have been furnished for characterising parties by *geographical* discriminations – *Northern* and *Southern*, *Atlantic* and *Western*.' The Federalists had become increasingly dependent solely on the support of the mercantile North-East, and Southern and Western communities tended to be strongly Democratic.

But the danger of disunity found expression at another, and more strictly constitutional, level in a series of Resolutions formally passed by the State legislatures of Virginia and Kentucky in 1798–9. These not merely protested against the Alien and Sedition Acts, but declared them to be unconstitutional because they violated the Bill of Rights. The nature of the American federal structure not only accommodates itself to great geographical diversity (which is its great merit, and perhaps the only way of reconciling order with liberty in a continental nation), but does so by giving State and Federal authority independent powers and equally valid rights within their respective spheres: especially in the early days of this 'Union of States', the common phrase 'the sovereign State of' Virginia or Kentucky or Massachusetts was no idle one. Thus from the very beginning there developed the doctrine of State Rights, which any minority which thought its vital interests threatened, would tend to utilise to protect itself. At this stage these two States went no further than to take advantage of the fact that there was no certainty as to whose was the last word in deciding what legislation is or is not in accordance with the fundamental law of the Constitution (Congress, the Supreme Court, the Executive, or the States), but before long, in different circumstances, States were to advance the ultimate and totally disruptive argument that in case their truly vital interests were attacked they had the actual right of secession from the United States.

The dangerous implications of the Resolutions were concealed by the Democratic victory, and the moderation of Jefferson in due course made the Federalist phantasmagoria of American Jacobinism look absurd; he declared in his Inaugural Address, 'We are all Republicans, we are all Federalists.' But though Federalist rule ended in disarray and Adams left Washington a disappointed man, the first ruling party of America had done the state good service by inaugurating the republic and strengthening both its central government and its financial structure. And Adams, in one of his final acts, left an enduring – and to the Democrats irritating – bequest to his successor by appointing his last Secretary of State, John Marshall,

Chief Justice of the Supreme Court. Marshall was a Virginian, a staunch Federalist and an exceedingly able lawyer and statesman, and for thirty-five years he used (as Adams had realised he would) his proper domination of the Supreme Court, in a series of remarkable decisions, to fortify and stabilise the authority of the federal government, and especially the Supreme Court itself.

As early as 1803 in *Marbury* v. *Madison*, he established the right of the Court to invalidate Acts of Congress in conflict with the Constitution. Much later in *M'Culloch* v. *Maryland* (1819) he went further, and, with his eyes on what he regarded as the perils of State Rights, asserted in effect the power of the Court to annul Acts of States contrary to the Constitution, the exact antithesis of the 'nullification' idea suggested in the Kentucky Resolutions. Almost as important, this judgement attacked the Democratic doctrine, known as 'strict construction', which denied to the federal government any powers not specifically granted to it in the Constitution; instead he advanced the much broader proposition, 'Let the end be legitimate, let it be within the scope of the Constitution, and all means which are appropriate, which are plainly adapted to that end, which are not prohibited, but consist with the letter and spirit of the Constitution, are constitutional.' In other judgements he buttressed the rights of property even against government action, which was a legacy of less certain value. Jefferson came to hate his cousin, Marshall, and to fear 'the consolidation of our government by the noiseless and therefore unalarming instrumentality of the Supreme Court', but even at the height of his political power his efforts to destroy this formidable bastion of Federalism, by asserting Congressional control over the Supreme Court, failed; and well into the second Administration of President Jackson, Marshall continued to preside over the Court and to render it, as Bryce said, 'the living voice of the Constitution.'

Federalists had dreaded, and some Republicans had anticipated, that Jefferson's inauguration would mark a political and even social revolution, but in fact his policies did not differ nearly as much as many had expected from those of Adams. Some Federalist legislation was repealed (such as the Naturalisation Act and all excise levies) but the main structure of executive power, the judicial system and the national bank were not affected, while the consolidated debt continued to be honoured and the tariff was retained for revenue purposes. Nor did Jefferson permit as much Democratic vengefulness as many desired, so that there were only 164 changes in 334 federal offices during his first term; and not many of the posts the Federalists had created for their friends, at the last minute of their period in office, were abolished. In fact his administration was in many respects inactive, of set purpose, for he and his followers on the whole fervently believed that he who governs least governs best. Albert Gallatin was an effective Secretary of the Treasury, who was able to rely solely on land sales, customs, and postal services for revenue because of strict economy in government; drastic reductions in the civil and especially military and naval departments enabled much of the government's income to be devoted to paying off the national debt. There was quite as much corruption over land sales as in the Federalist era, and state banks were chartered freely. The chief change was that government policies, as for example in taxation, tended to favour agrarian interests, rather than those of commerce and industry which the Hamiltonians had fostered.

But Jefferson increasingly came to be aware, as he enjoyed the responsibilities of supreme office, that the powers of the federal government were fully needed. Indeed, in the greatest coup of his Presidency, the unexpected purchase of the whole of the huge territory of Louisiana (which was as big again as the entire United States) from Napoleon in 1803, he knowingly threw his constitutional inhibitions overboard and acted under the very broadest construction of the Constitution. The prospect of acquiring 865,000 square miles of territory, much of it to prove magnificent, for approximately 8 cents an acre, was altogether too much, and rightly so, for the political scruples of a man with Jefferson's fertile imagination and deep faith in the destiny of the United States. As a child of the frontier the West always fascinated him; and he sent out the remarkable exploring expedition of Lewis and Clark which, between 1804 and 1806, crossed the whole of the new territory, and beyond, to the Pacific Ocean. Some Federalists, on the other hand, fearful of the disorganising influence of this vast frontier, agreed with Fisher Ames when he declared that the country had some limits when the Mississippi was its boundary, but that 'Now, by adding an unmeasured world beyond that river, we rush like a comet into infinite space.' But even Jefferson tended to think of the Rocky Mountains as a natural boundary for the United States, though characteristically he had a vague vision of the rest of the sub-continent occupied by Americans organised in friendly but independent sister-republics.

For Jefferson's genius operated on three levels. The summits were bathed in the misty glow of his sanguine sentiments; the middle tier was one in which rational and theoretical considerations hedged political authority about with restrictions and limitations; but at bottom he was a consummate practical politician, who got his way by often devious methods, which his opponents regarded as crafty or even as occasionally savouring of sharp practice. His effect on the constitutional development of the United States during his eight years as President (and during the succeeding sixteen years in office of his friends and close neighbours at Monticello, Madison and James Monroe) was profound, and all these three traits of the statesman are perceptible in his influence. His hopeful, humane and high idealism made an inestimable contribution to the smooth development of American democracy, to the fundamental fact that the United States really was to be a government of the people, although it did also impart an element of naïveté or impracticality to America's polity, especially perhaps in foreign affairs. His belief in strict limitation of government power, too, did much to let loose the intense energies of the mass of individual Americans, which have been one of the essential means of their success in exploiting their vast domain, but it did also gravely weaken the authority of the executive arm, which was the decisive and dynamic arm, of the government. But because of his own extraordinary political skill, he was able to get much of his own way with the Congress (if not with the Supreme Court). When, however, the wand of the magician was no longer in Washington, his able but much less practical and subtle successors found it hard to operate the constitutional machine with any real pretence at efficiency.

This was precisely what John Marshall had predicted; 'Mr. Jefferson,' he said, 'appears to me to be a man who will embody himself with the House of Representatives. By weakening the office of President, he will increase his personal power. He will diminish his responsibility, sap the fundamental principles of government, and become the leader of that party which is about to constitute the majority of the legislature.' Federalist efforts to associate the executive closely and openly with the legislature had failed, and had been replaced by the caucus system of Congressional leadership, but this had not weakened the power and initiative of the Presidency. A caucus was (and is) a meeting of party leaders, and especially at this time of the Congressional representatives of the party, particularly to nominate party candidates for the Presidency. The Jeffersonians adopted the caucus system and Jefferson's personal prestige for a long time enabled him to get executive policies implemented, but these vital processes now tended to be covert (he discontinued, for example, the practice of addressing Congress in person); the Democrats in general believed that government initiative should lie in the Congress, and Jefferson himself professed his belief that the President should 'inform . . . the legislative judgement, . . . carry that judgement into faithful execution'. Jefferson got his way because he was also the leader (even manager) of his party, which controlled the legislature – and all subsequent successful American Presidents have had to combine these two roles – but he did severe damage to the smooth functioning of the Constitution by undermining the inherent, open and proper authority which the Executive had been developing.

For the Congress, and particularly the House (which was still seen as very much the dominating chamber, like the House of Commons), was singularly ill-fitted, even as legislatures go, to initiate policy. It did make serious efforts to equip itself to perform this function, as James Bryce pointed out, by dividing 'the unwieldy multitude into small bodies capable of dealing with particular subjects' – that is to say by creating the committee system, which is a vital part of congressional procedure. Select Committees appointed for particular *ad hoc* purposes expire with the Congress that set them up (Joint Committees are appointed to resolve differences in legislation between House and Senate and occasionally to consider policy jointly), and so the heart of the machinery is the Standing Committees, which are automatically re-formed at the beginning of each new Congress. At first few of them were set up by the House (only one in the First Congress – that on elections), and none by the Senate; the House Committee on Ways and Means, which was formed in 1796 to deal with national finances and which was to become and to remain one of the most influential of all Congressional Committees, was only the fifth to come into existence. Significantly, under Jefferson and Madison they proliferated with great rapidity. The Senate did not begin to set up committees until 1816 (when it had grown to thirty-six members), but they increased rapidly in number thereafter. The Senate evolved a system of appointing members to committees in party caucus, but the House came to invest this vital power in the Speaker of the House, its presiding officer but essentially a party figure. Both processes indicate how vital party organisation had become, and although straight and strict party votes in Congress are exceedingly rare, they are almost invariable at the opening sessions when Standing Committees are organised, so that the majority party ensures it has a majority on every committee. In time the power of Standing Committees, and their sub-committees, and the chairmen of both, came to be very extensive, especially in a negative way (by blocking legislation), and appointments tended to be by strict seniority, so that experience, but also caution and conservatism, had great weight.

During his first term Jefferson operated the system very successfully, and his overwhelming triumph in the election of 1804 seemed to augur as well for his second, especially as a duel in that year between Burr and Hamilton, in which the latter was killed, at one blow removed his oldest Federalist opponent and completed the discredit of his chief Democratic rival. But in fact, as was to happen again in American history to parties which are excessively strong in Congress, the Democrats became divided against one another, and, led by the violent and eccentric but brilliant John Randolph of Roanoke, Virginia, a State Rights faction which disapproved of the strength of Administration leadership and its broad construction of the Constitution, began to attack the President. But more and more, public attention became focused on foreign policy, and on the increasingly unhappy sequence of events which was to lead, at the end of Madison's first term, to the War of 1812. But things had become bad enough by the time of Madison's election in 1808 for Jefferson to quit Washington with relief for his home near Charlottesville (where he was to spend the many years remaining to him in planning and building the University of Virginia). In the election the Republicans retained control of Congress, but the Federalists made sweeping gains; considering, however, the condition to which the foreign policy of Jefferson, and Madison as his Secretary of State, had reduced the economy of the country by the date of the election, this was a remarkable tribute to the hold which the Jeffersonians had established over the country. The truth was that, however grim foreign affairs might be, much of the United States and especially the ever-expanding West, was in a very real sense isolated from the affairs of the outside world: the American people were in time to become fully aware of the fact and to take full advantage of it. But this process of cutting their ties with Europe and facing resolutely west would in the end take more than thirty years after independence to complete.

Chapter 6

New World and Old, 1783-1814

THE TREATY of Paris had left the United States with a huge territory but a number of vexed diplomatic questions, which it proved at first unable to solve because the weakness of the Confederate government was even more conspicuous in external than in internal affairs. America had two close neighbours, her powerful ex-enemy Britain and her weak ex-ally Spain. British North America hedged her in to the north and the British West Indies were commercially vital to her, and especially to New England. Along her entire southern and western border ran the lands of Spain – East and West Florida and the huge Louisiana territory, including New Orleans and the mouth of the Mississippi, which was daily becoming more indispensable to the commerce of the expanding West. The problem of defining clearly the boundaries laid down in the 1783 Treaty was rendered more acute by Britain's refusal to evacuate certain north-west military posts in American territory until the provision permitting British creditors to collect debts owed to them in the United States was implemented. The Canadian fur trade – its hunters ranging far into the west – and Britain's consequent relations with Indian tribes hostile to the advance of the American frontier aroused the enmity of Americans, and encouraged the British to hold on to the posts in case the American federation broke up. The failure of the United States to settle with Spain the question of the south-western border and of the navigation of the Mississippi mouth (which was closed by Spain from 1784–8 and at which duties were still exacted on commerce thereafter) led to the first of a number of plans, or conspiracies, by Americans, to set up some sort of state in the west, possibly under Spanish protection but certainly independent of the United States. Few things show more clearly the growing strength of the westward movement in America than this willingness, if necessary, to sacrifice the tie with the United States to it.

With the inauguration of the new government, however, the survival of the United States soon became more obviously assured, and one of the greatest Federalist achievements was the settlement by two important treaties of a number of fundamental issues in foreign relations. For this most of the credit must go to Washington, who saw that solutions on these lines were vital to the young republic. Though it was negotiated with a debilitated Spain, the Pinckney Treaty of 1795 was exceedingly important for the future of the United States, since it clarified the boundary in the south-west, granted the right of deposit of goods at the mouth of the Mississippi, and above all guaranteed to Americans free navigation of the river, which was recognised as the boundary with Louisiana above the 31st parallel.

Much more complex and, because she was America's only powerful neighbour, quite as important, was the settlement with Britain. The policy which resulted in this has been called by its historian, Bradford Perkins, 'the first rapprochement'; after the War of Independence there was a deliberate drawing together on both sides, especially in view of Federalist feelings in favour of the British system of government, which were greatly intensified as a result of their growing horror of Jacobinism after the outbreak of the French Revolution in 1789. Enthusiastic Democratic support for France, on the other hand, centred for a while around the figure of 'Citizen' Genêt, the Minister to the United States sent by the new French government in 1793, who became so foolishly involved in domestic affairs that Washington demanded his recall in 1793 (though it was characteristic both of the French Revolution and of the American way of life that he thought discretion the better part of valour and spent the rest of his life as a private citizen in the United States).

When war broke out between France and Britain in 1793, Washington had to decide whether he would consider the treaty of 1778 with France still valid; he decided in effect in favour of neutrality, although he did not use the word, but enjoined, in the so-called Neutrality Proclamation of 1793, 'a conduct friendly and impartial toward the belligerent powers'. In fact Congress passed a neutrality law in 1794, and in his Farewell Address the President was almost to sanctify the American policy of neutrality as well as of isolation: 'The great rule for us in regard to foreign nations is, in extending our commercial relations to have with them as little *political* connection as possible . . . Europe has a set of primary interests which to us have none or a very remote relation . . . Why forego the advantages of so peculiar a situation? . . . It is our true policy to steer clear of permanent alliances with any portion of the foreign world . . .'

The United States now found itself the world's leading maritime neutral, successfully bent on expanding its commerce with both belligerents and with other nations as rapidly as possible. The

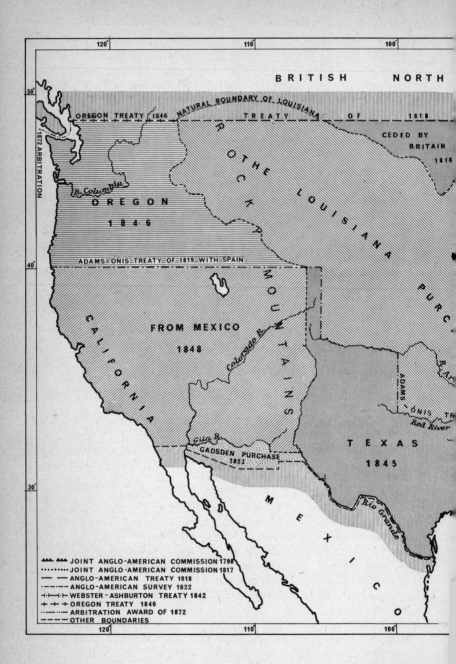

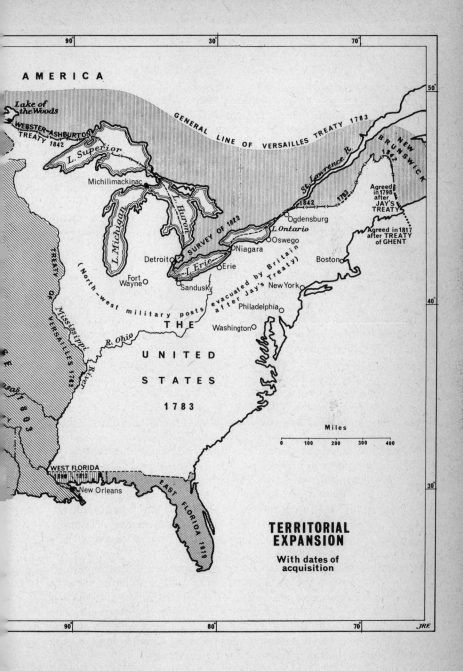

90°   **30°**   **70°**

50°

A M E R I C A

Lake of the Woods

WEBSTER-ASHBURTON
TREATY 1842

GENERAL LINE OF VERSAILLES TREATY 1783

L. Superior

St. Lawrence R.

NEW BRUNSWICK 1842

1793

Agreed in 1798 after JAY'S TREATY

Michilimackinac

SURVEY OF 1822

L. Huron

1842

Agreed in 1817 after TREATY of GHENT

L. Michigan

Ogdensburg

L. Ontario

Oswego

Detroit

Niagara

L. Erie

Erie

Boston

Fort Wayne

Sandusky

New York

(North-west military posts evacuated by Britain after Jay's Treaty)

Philadelphia

T H E

Washington

R. Ohio

U N I T E D

S T A T E S

1 7 8 3

TREATY OF VERSAILLES 1783 Mississippi River

Purchase 1803

Miles

0   100   200   300   400

WEST FLORIDA

New Orleans

EAST FLORIDA 1819

40°

30°

TERRITORIAL
EXPANSION

With dates of acquisition

90°   **80°**   **70°**   JRF.

interest of France, and even more of Britain which controlled, as well as depended on, the seas, was to restrict as far as possible the trade of neutrals with the enemy. This direct, if in a sense tripartite, clash of interests was to dominate the foreign relations of the United States during the scarcely interrupted twenty-two years of war which followed. But despite these incipient difficulties, President Washington was determined to improve relations with Britain. The result was the treaty negotiated by John Jay, his special envoy, in London in 1794, probably the most unpopular treaty in American history. It only passed the Senate, after a bitter debate in secret executive session, by the narrowest margin possible, because of the determined support of Washington, who was characteristically undeterred by the outburst of popular wrath which greeted it. In retrospect the treaty seems less unsatisfactory than it did in the emotional atmosphere of the time.

Though some of its commercial clauses on the vital West India trade were so unfavourable that the Senate rejected them outright, others did lay the foundations of extensive Anglo-American trade between the two homelands (and even of United States trade with the British East Indies); the basic difficulty was that in an age when the free-trade ideas of Adam Smith had only made a few converts in Britain, the United States had by gaining her independence been automatically shut out of the closed mercantile system of the British Empire. This, given the traditional pattern of American Atlantic and Caribbean commerce, was a grave commercial handicap, but in fact local concessions in the British West Indies kept the traffic alive until the coming of free trade in Britain, beginning in the 1820s, solved the problem by doing away with the tariff barriers. No really effective provisions about neutral maritime rights were included in the treaty, but joint commissions were set up which both adjudicated a mutual settlement of long outstanding claims (with a financial balance heavily in America's favour) and also settled one of the main border disputes; this mode of arbitration by joint commission not only set an important precedent in Anglo-American relations – which was followed in a series of Anglo-American agreements between 1814 and 1822 – but in the whole history of international diplomacy. Finally, and much the most important, Britain now at length evacuated the forts in the west, where a more vigorous American government policy had subdued the Indians and opened virtually the whole of the present state of Ohio to settlement. The two essential needs of the United States in the foreign policy of these formative years were to unlock the Mississippi and to open up the west, and these things Washington achieved.

Partly as a result of the anger of the French at Jay's Treaty, partly of Federalist Anglophilia, American relations with the Directory in France now steadily deteriorated, and, as a result of its seizures of American shipping carrying British goods, a state of undeclared war developed between the United States and the French, whom many Americans believed to be aiming at world domination. Negotiations in 1797 proved abortive and America seemed on the brink of becoming an open ally of Britain, but President Adams – to the chagrin of the High Federalists – held back, and in 1800 an agreement was signed with the newly established régime of Bonaparte, which ensured peace and formally abrogated the Franco-American treaty of alliance of 1778. In any case the crisis might have passed, for a transitory peace was made between Britain and France in 1802. Adams, by the time he left office, had restrained his followers and averted the war which a number of them wanted with France: Jefferson and Madison were not to succeed so well in preventing the war with Britain which many of the Democrats sought.

It was by degrees born in upon the Jeffersonians that, even if France had ever been a democracy, she had under Napoleon become an increasingly aggressive dictatorship; and his acquisition of the Louisiana territory from Spain placed a formidable potential enemy on America's western border. News reached Jefferson in Washington late in 1802 of the suspension of the right of deposit at New Orleans, and the President began to contemplate a revolution in his foreign policy; he even wrote that 'we must marry ourselves to the British fleet and nation.' But the Purchase, by removing the French threat, allowed him to revert to a policy of neutrality, and with the renewal of war between Britain and France in 1803 the problems of neutral maritime rights appeared again in greater force than before, and augmented persistently until the coming of war between Britain and the United States in 1812. Yet the situation was, as one American remarked, a 'triangular', or 'prismatic' one; on the face of it there was little to choose between Britain and France in their attitude to the United States. Why then was it with the former that America slid unchecked into war?

It was partly that, as the same observer continued, he could not understand 'fighting three armies together. One against two on the same side, is no new thing, sir, but three against each other is a perfect novelty.' Though the United States ought perhaps in logic to have fought both at once, this was hardly practicable, and yet her frustration reached such a point that in a sense she had to fight someone. This was partly because, though the Democrats ceased to be pro-

French, they did not cease to be anti-British; Jefferson never really stopped believing, as he once put it, that the British nation, and above all others its King and his ministers, hated America. There were certainly grounds for believing this of George Canning, British Foreign Secretary during a critical part of this period, for his attitude towards the United States was almost as arrogant as that of the Minister he sent to Washington in 1809, F. J. Jackson, whose conduct was so intolerable that the Administration soon refused to hold any further communication with him. This tendency among British Tories to treat the United States as if it were still a colony, or at least a rude uncultivated society, naturally tended to produce among many Americans (and not only Democrats) an emotional reaction such as did not exist in the case of France.

This was especially true of one issue which was perhaps the most important one, emotionally, in heightening tension between the two peoples – impressment. The British navy's traditional, if crude and inequitable, method of conscripting seamen was impressment, or the naval press gang, which shanghaied sailors not merely in British seaports, but off merchant vessels at sea. Her need for sailors during the war became steadily more desperate, and as the years passed and conditions of service in the British navy remained exceedingly bad, desertion became an increasing problem, especially desertion to American ships, where of course it was easy for deserters to claim that they were in fact American citizens. (Though it never became an overt issue, there did underlie this actual situation the fundamental fact that the British government, like virtually all governments at this date, refused to recognise the right of a British subject to renounce his allegiance by naturalisation in another country, which obviously struck at the roots of America's being.) As a result, British naval vessels constantly exercised what their government never ceased to claim as a right, that of impressing British sailors off American merchant ships.

Unfortunately, they frequently exercised it – and it was galling enough to American sensibilities in any case – in an overbearing and unscrupulous manner, by seizing seamen who genuinely were Americans; there were many American cases of the most severe hardship resulting from the practice, although of course there were also cases in which American captains were far from reluctant to keep their own ships fully manned at the expense of a lie or two to protect British deserters. The British government, however, never claimed the right to visit and search American ships of war, and it was the totally unwarranted seizure in 1807 of a number of British navy deserters from the United States naval vessel the *Chesapeake*, at the cost of twenty serious American casualties, that first brought the countries to the brink of war. Jefferson was still in the White House and he was, whatever his feelings about Britain, a deep lover of peace; his moderate and sensible measures in the crisis were principally responsible for averting war at that time. A long delayed diplomatic settlement of this particular incident was reached late in 1811, but the impressment issue was never resolved, for the truth was that Britain's naval strength was literally vital to her continued existence, and even more to any hope of victory, in her mortal struggle with Napoleon, and she would not surrender any instrument of sea power which helped her to keep her fleets in being. Impressment continued to be 'a running sore' which poisoned Anglo-American relations right up to 1812.

But it was not on the impressment issue alone that the United States went to war, nor yet for solely emotional reasons, though there was a broad sense in which the War of 1812 was, as it has been called, the second war of American independence, a final assertion of the dignity of the United States and its liberation from European ties and Old World presumption. Such an assertion of national honour was not so necessary against France as against Britain, which was after all – and long remained in myth though not in reality – America's national enemy number one. But the final reason why it was with Britain that the United States went to war was that, because of her sea power and the existence of British North America, it was Britain which weighed much the more heavily on American rights and ambitions; France had no territorial contact with America and Britain controlled the seas between them, and it was largely because of this that it was with Britain that America's war was fought.

Of the two other, and more concrete, causes of the conflict, much the more complex and less obviously profitable to the United States was that of neutral commercial rights. With the details of the manifold arguments in international law raised by the British to restrict American trade with France, and by the Americans to enlarge their ever more profitable commerce with French-controlled Europe, we need not concern ourselves, for in fact, as is almost always so, belligerent and neutral produced the arguments which suited their case; and the two belligerents soon, step by step, abandoned all pretence of traditional legality in favour of reprisals. Thus to Napoleon's 'continental system', embodied in the Berlin and Milan Decrees, Britain replied with her Orders-in-Council, but both were attempts to strangle the enemy economically (and incidentally strengthen oneself) by cutting down his commerce as drastically as possible. The trade of the neutrals (and the United States, whose trade grew by leaps and bounds in response to the demands of war and the reduction in British and other competition, was the neutral with most at stake) suffered accordingly.

But the United States did not suffer in silence, and indeed was far from inactive in endeavouring to protect her rights. There was no real possibility of an armed alliance of neutral states, such as that formed by the northern European powers in the Revolutionary War to protect their interests, since more and more neutral nations were conquered by Napoleon or became belligerents, and in any case Jefferson was temperamentally opposed to the use of armed force. Indeed, such was his dislike of it and his liking for government economy, that under his administration the military, and especially naval, forces of the United States were allowed to reach what many considered to be a dangerously low ebb. But he did believe that, in an adaption of the non-importation agreements used by the colonists with such effect against the British in the first stages of the American Revolution, he had a weapon almost as effective as war or the threat of it; in a way this was the first international use of economic sanctions unbacked by military force, which was to play so large, and ineffectual, a part in the attempts of Woodrow Wilson's League of Nations to maintain world peace in the 1930s.

It was a political invention not untypical of one strain in the American character, and very typical of one side of Jefferson's personality; it believed in the supreme importance of the cash nexus, and it had in it a pronounced vein of idealism, which bordered at times on the simple. The idea of some leading Democrats, that the withdrawal of their trade from the belligerents, particularly Britain, would bring great nations, locked in a life and death struggle, to heel by economic pressure alone was distinctly naïve. In internal affairs, especially when the government desired rather to stop taking positive actions than to enact definite policies, this ingenuous strain in Jeffersonianism could do no great harm, protected as the United States was by her size, resources and remoteness; America could afford the luxury of such domestic enthusiasms as pantisocracy and prohibition. But in the ruthless, troubled arena of international affairs, and America's relations with 'the ancient world' and its 'agonising spasms of infuriated man' (as Jefferson himself called them), the Administration's panacea of applying commercial sanctions to Britain and France was a fiasco. The Embargo policy, as it was called, went through a number of different manifestations, all of which were almost equally unsuccessful; and most of them did American interests much more damage than those of the belligerents. Both Canning and Napoleon had the measure of the efforts of

Madison to play off Britain against France, and the severe economic depression produced in the United States, both on the seaboard (especially in New England) and in the tobacco-growing areas of the South, by these experiments, led to discontent which found some expression in the growing clamour for war.

But the chief vocal demand for war came, as a number of historians have pointed out, not from the South, and certainly not from the North-East, but from the West. Though in his War Message to Congress in 1812 Madison mentioned only one western cause of war, the hostility of the Indian tribes supported by British fur-trade interests, there was a powerful American sentiment in the West for the conquest of Canada. There is little doubt that the influence of the young 'War Hawks' in the Twelfth Congress, under the leadership of Henry Clay as Speaker, was a vital factor; they expressed the growing chauvinism of the generation which was in due course not only to espouse the idea that it was the 'Manifest Destiny' of the United States to occupy the whole sub-continent, as far as the Pacific Ocean, but also to put it into execution. The victory of William Henry Harrison over the Indian tribes at Tippecanoe in 1811 formed a focus for their enthusiasm.

There were some laudable efforts to prevent the accelerating drift into war in the ten years after 1803. In fact, two treaties were negotiated, either one of which might well have prevented it; one was the Pinckney-Monroe agreement, signed by Jefferson's envoys in London on New Year's Eve, 1806, but it was not even submitted by Jefferson to the Senate on the ground that it did not contain a British repudiation of the right of impressment. *Per contra*, a British Minister sent to Washington (by a short-lived Whig ministry under Charles James Fox which was friendly to the United States), David Erskine, signed an agreement in 1809, but it was equally unceremoniously repudiated by Canning; and the trend to war was resumed. It has always been held as a great historical irony (to be impossible later, in the era of the transatlantic telegraph) that it had become clear in London just before America declared war in 1812 that the most offensive of the Orders-in-Council would be repealed almost at once. The war, however, was not caused by the blockade alone, but by this potent combination of factors, maritime, western and emotional.

The two countries had drifted into the war, and in some sort it would be true to say that they drifted out of it again, for it was a stalemate if ever there was one. American forces singularly failed to make any real progress in their ambitious efforts to conquer Canada, but their tenuous and isolated naval forces gave the Royal Navy a shock or two. A British force's temporary capture in 1814 of Washington (where they burned the predecessor of the present White House as well as the Capitol) was more than outweighed by a disastrous defeat of their regular troops (for reasons of military stupidity very similar to those which decimated their ranks at Bunker Hill in 1775) by General Andrew Jackson at New Orleans in the next year. (This American victory, to add a final bizarre touch, was fought after peace had been signed but before the news of it had reached America).

Well might one American history call it 'a futile and unnecessary war', for the Treaty of Ghent, which terminated it in December 1814, in fact contained no mention at all of any of the important causes of the war, impressment, neutral rights or American westward expansion. In fact it merely ended hostilities and restored the *status quo*. But it also continued and improved upon the use of the joint commission, for the adjudication or arbitration of border disputes, which had been inaugurated in Jay's Treaty. Seldom has a war been so inconclusive, but in such cases it is frequently the result that it is shortly renewed; the Treaty of Ghent had exactly the opposite effect, for at the date when this book is published, in 1964, the United States and Britain will be celebrating 150 years of mutual peace. For the American people the war was a kind of catharsis which purged them of many of their feelings about, and some of their connections with, the mother country: for the British it was a salutary lesson which taught them that the United States was a state which must be reckoned with and might one day before long become a Great Power.

But though internationally indecisive, the war was far from having no domestic results or ultimate implications in foreign policy. For what is interesting was the reason why America made such a bad showing. Admittedly there was no comparison between British and American power, especially at sea, for Britain was much larger in population and vastly stronger economically, but until 1814 she was in the last throes of a desperate struggle in Europe, while the United States (as the War of American Independence had shown) had all the strategic advantages. One reason for America's lack of military success was her unpreparedness, but far more important were her internal divisions. While there might be some enthusiasm for the war in the West, and acceptance of it in the South, it was bitterly resented in the North-East. Indeed, by an odd paradox, a war fought ostensibly and chiefly to protect the maritime interests and trade of the United States, was hated, indeed repudiated, by the very section which conducted by far the greatest proportion of that commerce.

New England lived by her traditional mercantile connection with Britain, and detested and denounced the Embargo as a sectional and party policy; her merchants would very much sooner have continued their trade, even though it was subject to irritating and even undignified British restrictions, and in fact they were doing pretty well despite the blockade. Such an attitude came naturally to this Anglophile centre of Federalist feeling, and it hardened rather than weakened with the coming of war. Some New England sea captains sailed their vessels under the British flag for the duration of the war, and many others, sailing under the Stars and Stripes, continued to supply the British enemy through its whole course (very much in the way that their forefathers had evaded their taxes and supplied the French in the wars of the eighteenth century). The disaffection, however, went further than this and took on a constitutional form which cast ominous shadows forward upon the future of the Union.

In the Virginia and Kentucky Resolves (1798) a Southern and Democratic section had carried their protest against Federalist New England measures to the point of suggesting State nullification of federal actions; the Federalists themselves now went much further and suggested secession from the Union in protest against this Southern Democratic war. In 1814 they summoned a Convention of disaffected States to Hartford, Connecticut, and official delegates from Massachusetts, Connecticut and Rhode Island assembled there in December 1814 with unofficial representatives from Vermont and New Hampshire. They took no decisive action, but passed a number of threatening resolutions, which resulted in nothing but Democratic ridicule when the news of peace arrived. In fact, the treasonable attitude of many New Englanders produced a strong reaction in the rest of the country and was probably decisive in causing the decline of the Federalist party, which rapidly faded from the national scene. The immediate effect of the war, despite this sectional cleavage, was to arouse national patriotism further, especially perhaps in the West; it found particular expression in the hero legend of Andrew Jackson. The expansionist fever, which sought its outlet in the ambitions of Manifest Destiny, first raised the American national temperature in this war period; this was to reach its highest pitch in the next thirty-five years. But it was almost as if the spirit of the era now opening was to be so frenetic partly because it was a way of preventing, or concealing, the sinister possibilities of sectional cleavage against which Washington had so solemnly warned and which were in the event finally to result in the Civil War.

Chapter 7

Economics and Politics

THE WAR of 1812 had had a dual effect; it aroused American nationalism to a new fervour but at the same time delivered the *coup de grace* to American entanglements with Europe. With an almost audible sigh of relief and remarkable national unanimity the people of the United States seemed to shrug off their political connection with Europe and to turn westwards to develop, with unprecedented speed and energy, the mighty and fertile valley of the Mississippi. This great area, with its superb natural water communications, which could readily be improved, lent itself remarkably to rapid development by the use of steam, first in the steamboat which revolutionised American domestic transport, and then in the railroad which continued the process. The capital for this swift growth came to some extent from the eastern seaboard but to a very considerable degree from Europe, especially Britain. It not only made possible the development of a national transport system but also of a market economy on something approaching a national scale. The great artery of these at first was the Mississippi, and it was the supreme era of New Orleans which was in the 1830s the greatest exporting port in America. These things went with and facilitated the growth of the nation's population.

In 1810 the United States Census figure was 7,239,881: by 1850 it had more than trebled, to 23,191,876. No new states were admitted between Ohio (the seventeenth) in 1803 and Louisiana in 1812, but by 1850 when California (far beyond the boundaries of the United States in 1812) was admitted, a further thirteen states had joined the Union since then. Already by 1820 the frontier of settlement had begun to cross the Mississippi and by 1840 had overflowed into Texas and was reaching out towards the distant Rocky-Mountain-boundary of the Louisiana Territory in the North-West, driving the Indians before it.

Following increasingly well-worn trails, like the Wilderness Road into Kentucky, or the Cumberland Pike to St. Louis (the only great road to the west constructed by the federal government, which terminated at Vandalia, Illinois, in 1852), the 'rolling wave of seeking men' surged out along the rivers and roads. This was the heyday of the agricultural pioneer-settler, whether he was an independent farmer on his own modest holding (producing at first largely for his own consumption), as in the north, or whether he was a planter (with a handful, or a sizeable retinue, or slaves), opening up the great Black Belt of Alabama, Mississippi and beyond to cotton cultivation, in the South. This dominant theme in American life was reflected in the two great political disputes over government support for the development of communications and over the sale or grant of public lands. The construction of highways and canals, the improvement of river and dam and harbour facilities, especially after the coming of the river steamboat, and ultimately the building of railroads were the principal interest of the West. (Steamboats began to ply on the Mississippi in the second decade of the century but full growth did not come until the thirties). Very rapid developments occurred, especially with canals and on the rivers; these were often under private enterprise, particularly east of the Appalachians, but there was a persistent and powerful demand for government support of 'internal improvements'. The phenomenal success of the Erie Canal, which was built by the State of New York to join the Hudson River to the Great Lakes, and was completed in 1825, made it the foundation of the long economic pre-eminence of New York City; it led to a great canal boom, in which almost all building through and west of the mountains was either public enterprise by the states or heavily state aided. Because they were usually costly and frequently crossed a number of state lines, State subvention of internal improvements often seemed inadequate, but regional and state rivalries made it difficult to adhere to, or even conceive, any sort of federal 'plan' for an efficient national transport system, and inhibited federal officials from supporting developments in other regions than their own. Perhaps as important was the fact that Jefferson, and more especially his successors of the 'Virginia dynasty', as well as many Jacksonian Democrats after them, characteristically had, as 'strict constructionists', constitutional scruples about Federal Government subsidies for communications which were not strictly for postal or military purposes. There were always, however, those to oppose them who favoured 'broad construction' of the constitution, and took the Hamiltonian view that the 'general welfare' clause empowered it to appropriate money for virtually anything conducive to this end which was not prohibited elsewhere in the document.

Broadly speaking, on the second question, that of public lands, Eastern creditor interests, which were strong in the Federalist party, had looked on the sale of lands at an economic price as a source of revenue for the federal government which ought not to be squandered, and as a means of deliberate development in the common interest; but, with the rise of Western influence, beginning with a bill of W. H. Harrison – first congressional delegate from the Ohio Territory – in 1800, there was a marked trend towards a policy of cheaper and more liberal grants of land. This view, which was held by most men in the West, regarded the lands as almost a birthright of every American; and by a number of acts, notably the Pre-Emption Act of 1841 which gave certain rights to 'squatters' on the public domain, this process was continued until the famous Homestead Act of 1862 granted for a nominal sum 160 acres (one quarter of a 'section' a mile square) to any adult American who would cultivate it. But after, as well as before, this date, the land speculators (from General Washington onwards) often did a very profitable business, and performed a by no means entirely anti-social and useless function by facilitating in practice the expeditious distribution of land.

The westward movement, nevertheless, was only one aspect (although the most important) of America's remarkable economic growth in these years; it was fed, for example, by an ever-rising flood of European immigrants, which, however, did little to alleviate the chronic shortage of skilled labour (a perennial American problem). The basically British stock, though the British element was still overwhelming in the whole body at the time of the Revolution, had already been diluted by French and German strains; now, especially after 1814, not only did the number of immigrants grow rapidly (to an average of around a quarter of a million a year in the two decades before the Civil War) but the non-British content greatly increased. More of these immigrants, too, (proportionate to the total) went on to farms than was to be the case later in the century, and so they fed the agricultural frontier indirectly, although making a substantial contribution to the beginnings of American industrial growth as well. They came predominantly from Northern Europe, especially Germany (and also Scandinavia, though the numbers from there did not compare with the former), but this was also the great era of Southern Catholic Irish (as opposed to Northern Protestant, often so-called 'Scots-Irish') immigration; the great majority of these went to the cities of the East, especially large commercial centres like Boston and New York, and some of them played an indispensable part as unskilled labour in the building of the railroads. For it was not only the rural produce of America which increased hand-over-fist in this period, but commerce also.

By far the most spectacular agricultural-commercial development of these years was that of the great export staples produced by slave labour on plantations – tobacco, and rice (and later sugar), and above all cotton, from the Deep South. Owing to the invention of the cotton gin – for cleaning the cotton after picking – by Eli Whitney in 1793, cotton production grew from 178,000 bales in 1810 to more than 2 million by 1850. The South specialised to such a degree in cotton cultivation that this had a markedly stimulating effect on the development of commercial agriculture in the Old North-West. Thus agriculture was one of the main bases of American commercial expansion. Indeed both America's agricultural and commercial growth was tied inextricably to the unprecedented phenomenon of the Industrial Revolution in Britain; not only did the cotton of the south and south-west supply the maw of Lancashire's mills, but British rails largely provided the tracks of the first American railroads. More than this, British capital, as we have remarked, did a great deal to open up the west so swiftly (allowing the United States to run a fairly consistently adverse international trade balance for many years); thus although resolutely isolating herself as far as possible politically from the affairs of Europe, America was still bound intimately in an economic sense to Britain. (Well into the nineteenth century, for example, New England merchants reckoned in pounds, shillings and pence). Symptomatic of the emotional difficulties of this particular Anglo-American relationship was the intense bitterness aroused among British investors by the repudiation of their debts by certain states of the Union during hard times such as those after the crash of 1837.

This Anglo-American connection was important to the South, which desired not only to sell to Britain but to import thence, this being by far the world's cheapest source of manufactured goods; and as the cotton crop swelled, so did the Deep South's support for a low tariff, indeed for as great a degree of free trade as possible. But the South actually handled almost none of its own commerce; it relied on New York and British credits made available through merchant factors, and also on the commercial and maritime skills of the North-East. Though the Federalist party never recovered from the War of 1812, the next quarter of a century was one of great New England influence in the Union. This, though it was reflected in a social and cultural pre-eminence, derived fundamentally from her commercial strength. Partly as a result, paradoxically, of the opportunities offered by the long wars which tied the hands of so many competing nations, America's maritime trade had attained by these years a position of strength relative to other nations greater than it was to reach again until well into the twentieth century; this commerce centred in the North-East, especially Boston (now at the peak of its power) and New York (which was catching up fast) : it was epitomised in the international leadership of the swift and beautiful Yankee 'clipper' ship. This trade was predominantly with Britain; in the years 1846–50 40 per cent of American imports came from Britain and 50 per cent of American exports went to the United Kingdom. This continued, far into the middle years of the century, the close traditional connection between New England and old, which found expression in the Anglophilia of many New Englanders.

In fact, however, a change was coming over the economy of New England which was to render it less complementary to, and more competitive with, that of Britain, for it was ceasing to be pre-eminently commercial and beginning to industrialise; thus the new cotton mills established in 1813 at Lowell, Massachusetts, began to compete with British imported goods in the American market, and before long in foreign markets as well at least in the cheaper and cruder lines. In due course the process of industrialisation was to accompany, if it did not cause, the relative decline of New England, as it expanded and accelerated (beyond all recognition) into the rest of the United States; but at first it fortified her position. It did, how-ever, effect a change in the attitude of the section to the tariff, which n the past their commercial interests had tended to want to keep low because a high rate of duty would have the effect of retarding the growth of international trade. Beginning in the period of the Embargo and even more the War of 1812, when necessity combined with patriotism to encourage new American industries to produce what could no longer be imported from Europe and especially Britain, industrialisation, though it was still largely regional in character and centred in the North-East, began to gather momen-tum. So did political appreciation of the need for effective tariff protection when the infant industries were subjected, after the Treaty of Ghent, to the full blast of competition from British manufactures, a huge back-log of which was 'dumped' – just as in 1783 – on the American market.

Much of the very texture of American politics in the next quarter of a century – and indeed throughout American history – was to be economic, though personalities, too, were plainly of importance in this age of Jackson, Clay, Webster and Calhoun; representation of the economic and financial interests of their constituents became the staple stuff of Congressional life. And in this era these three great economic issues, the tariff, western lands, and internal improvements, and one great financial issue, banking, dominated the politico-economic scene. Furthermore, as had already been the case in the Federalist-Democrat (as well as the Colonial) period and was to continue to be so in greater or less degree until the present day in the political system of the United States, these economic interests tended to become identified with the geographical sections. In the economic scramble to exploit the resources of the United States, and especially the West, in these decades, politics assumed the appearance of – and in great degree became – a series of changing alliances between different regional pressure groups. Thus the South with its export staples was principally concerned to keep a low tariff and minimum government expenditure; the North-East (New England and much of New York and Pennsylvania) became chiefly exercised to protect its growing industry and to prevent the syphoning off of its pool of cheap labour by the too rapid development of the frontier; the West desired mostly cheap public lands and federally supported internal improvements.

For a short time after the War of 1812, however, there was some degree of national unity on these, as on other, issues. Madison and Monroe indeed had come to accept many policies once castigated as Federalist; characteristic was the fact that in 1811 the Democrats had refused to recharter the First Bank of the United States, whereas Madison, sobered by the financial difficulties of his Administration during the war, supported the establishment of the Second Bank of the United States, which received its charter in 1816, chiefly on the ground that the nation's currency was in chaos. A more remarkable illustration of this short lived national agreement was the establishment of the first truly protective tariff in American history, that of 1816, which protected especially the cotton, wool and iron industries, imposing duties ranging from 7·5 to 30 per cent *ad valorem*. It received votes from every state except North Carolina, even including that of John C. Calhoun of South Carolina, then in an ardent nationalist phase. He went further, and proposed later in the same year a bill for internal improvements at federal expense, declaring that America's size exposed her to 'the greatest of all calamities, next to the loss of liberty, and even to that in its consequences – *disunion*'. To forestall this danger, 'Let us bind the republic together with a perfect system of roads and canals. Let us conquer space.' But this was too much for Madison's remaining Jeffersonian instincts and he vetoed the bill.

Henry Clay, another of the younger generation of leaders, believed that he could perpetuate this nationalist agreement by what he named his 'American System'. This called for a high tariff for the benefit of the East, and, with the ample resulting revenue, extensive internal improvements for the benefit of the West. He believed that the West would support it, even though his third plank was a high price for public lands, because the revenue would be spent on communications which would open up the East (and the outside world) to Western produce. Finally, he believed the Old South would go along with it because they approved of a high price for public lands, and above all, perhaps, because he himself was a slave-holder from Kentucky. This home state gave Clay a pivotal base in this period, for it was at once western and southern but sufficiently long established as a border state between North and South and West and East (on the great Ohio-Mississippi river system) not to be offensive to the North-East. Such a firm political base – like the even solider one of his contemporary and rival, Daniel Webster, in Massachusetts – is indispensable to any American statesman, and especially to Clay who (again like Webster) was throughout his political life a perennially unsuccessful candidate for the Presidency.

The national unity attained during this brief span between 1814 and about 1820 was by no means confined to economic issues, though its political aspects followed much the same pattern – that is to say, the policies of the ascendant Jeffersonians (Monroe succeeded Madison in 1817, after a smashing victory over the Federalists, and in the election of 1820 was not opposed at all) became more and more indistinguishable from those of the Federalists. The latter never recovered from the taint of treason which they acquired in the popular mind during the war, and the central position now occupied by the Administration led to the period being called 'The Era of Good Feelings'. But in many ways the unity was an illusion, or at least so transitory that it was more like the calm before the storm. Thus the fact that Monroe recognised his Secretary of State, John Quincy Adams of Massachusetts (son of the second President), as his heir-apparent looked on the surface like evidence of the lack of sectional animosity, but the bitterness of the campaign of 1824 told a different tale. And beneath the surface of the political structure there was even more bitter, frequently local and sectional, discontent with the existing system.

The answer indeed was that the appearance of national unity during Monroe's administration was bought at the price of almost total government ineffectiveness. The President was not of the stature of Madison, let alone Jefferson; and even Adams, a man of considerable intellectual ability who desired to give the country better leadership than his predecessor, appeared in the event to be a classic case of *capax imperii nisi imperasset*. In a manner not really to be found again until the first term of Dwight D. Eisenhower, Adams saw himself, not as a party leader, but as President of the whole people. Thus he had, although remaining very much a New Englander, a truly national policy and a belief in a strong and active federal government, but he had, largely because he lacked a party, no means of providing the latter or of carrying out the former. Jefferson, who so overshadowed his successors, had in fact undermined the overt powers of the Executive, as outlined in the Constitution and filled out by Washington, by stressing the paramount role of the elected Legislature, and especially the unwieldy House. But he maintained his personal ascendancy and, at least in his first term, gave the country leadership by his subtle political influence (exercised, discreetly and out of the public gaze, through such instruments as the caucus, or small group of party leaders). Madison and, even more, Monroe, however, had not the magical skill of their great predecessor, and proved unable to lead the country effectively. Moreover, even Jefferson was increasingly impotent in his second term, especially as affairs more and more became dominated by international problems. Indeed, lack of forceful Presidential guidance might be tolerable in peace-time, isolated as the United States was behind the great oceans, but it had proved singularly unfortunate for the country when the war came, and was one of the main reasons for her lack of preparedness and, consequently, success.

For a few years after the war the new patriotism it had excited helped to conceal the fundamental defects of a system which left the task of leadership to a body of more than 200 members, but by the end of Monroe's second term it was apparent that Congress was floundering ineffectually. Even the good feelings of the era could not allay the increasing sectional feeling which rose repeatedly to the surface unchecked by Presidential leadership, while localism gained an even stronger hold on the proceedings of Congress. This was, and is, a fundamental fact of American political life; in a great federation of regions with very different economic, social and political interests, the legislature is deeply concerned with the satisfaction of local needs – and rightly so. This is implicit in its structure. Senators represented their States as such, and at this time were not popularly elected but actually appointed by their State legislatures; Congressmen were elected in their States and there was an increasing tendency (made mandatory in 1842) for them to be elected by specific districts. The Constitution lays down that Senators and Representatives must be inhabitants of the state which elects them, and Congressmen usually live in or close to their district. In much greater degree than British Members of Parliament, who can (if defeated in one constituency) seek a seat elsewhere, they are totally dependent on their local political standing and organisation, and are much more responsive, therefore, to purely local demands. Hence the tradition of the 'pork barrel', legislation through which, by an immensely complex system of implicit if not explicit bargains with his fellows in Congress, a member gets economic advantages for his community – construction, for example, of a dam, or a harbour, or even a post office, improvement of a river for navigation, or in later years a pension for a serviceman or his widow and family.

In due course, with the revival of the party system and especially in periods of vigorous Presidential leadership, party ties were to do something to temper this localism, but they have never at any time been nearly as important as they came to be in Britain. Even when, much later, party Whips, and House and Senate (Majority and Minority) Leaders, came into being, members of Congress looked more, far more, for guidance to the views of their constituents than to the wishes of their party and its leaders. Thus straight party votes, which almost always occur in the House of Commons, almost never do take place in Congress, except, as we have noticed, in the vital opening days of a new session when the all-important decisions on the membership and chairmanship (and hence party control) of the manifold Committees are taken. Thus too, in recent times, the representatives of great sections, such as – perennially – the Democratic South, will frequently vote on certain measures with their conservative Republican colleagues rather than with their liberal Democratic party co-members. At the height of their effectiveness American national parties remain essentially coalitions of local interests. The national party organisations, though they have become somewhat more important in recent years, tend to hibernate between Presidential elections, and even in these the parties really cohere only as great alliances of state and local party-groupings. And at state level, too, where there are permanent party organisations, their members must retain roots (which always need nurturing) deep in their city or county. At all levels, moreover, there are multifarious state, county, city, township and ward offices, which form the vast foundations of the political superstructure, so that politicians frequently, even usually, graduate to Washington through local political offices, while either membership of the Senate or the governorship of a State can lead to the Presidency. (The latter was at one time the favoured route, but now perhaps it is the former.)

In these years of the second quarter of the nineteenth century the classic pattern of American politics showed most clearly. The sections had very diverse economic interests, which needed development in this period of national growth; staple crops in the South, commercial agriculture in the North-West, commerce and industry in the North-East. The representatives of these competing sectional interests were, and in the view of most citizens properly, expected to use their political influence to advance the development and prosperity of the regions they represented. Yet the very competition of the sections and the rapidity of economic change made action by the federal government difficult. It was much easier to get a coalition of such pressure groups against any particular measure than in favour of it, which helps to explain the 'negative' and indecisive character of federal policy. When in the same period in Britain there was an analogous struggle, over the Corn Laws, between agriculture and industry, it took the form of a conflict between town and country but less obviously between region and region. Only in such cases as severely depressed areas do occasional Members of Parliament today hearken to their local constituents rather than to the party Whips. The compactness and relative homogeneity of economic interest of Britain contrasts strikingly here with the size and diversity of the United States, and the difference is reflected in their political systems.

The causes of this vital Anglo-American difference also run deep in history. The United States federation really did spring originally from its thirteen different colonial sources, and had no influential and long background of centralising royal government really comparable with that of the mother country. Furthermore, the aristocratic British national tradition – to misapply the dictum of Sieyès – that 'confidence should arise from beneath, and power descend from above' was early replaced in the United States by a democratic spirit – and process – in which initiatives really do come up from local 'grass roots'. The revolutionary tradition in some ways strengthened a reluctance to accept national leadership, except in times of great crisis or after a prolonged public debate. The provision in the Constitution for the 'compensation' of the President and all the members of Congress (and the existence of pay for office at almost all levels of state and local government as well) early led to the creation of a class of professional politicians largely dependent on politics (and thus on their local constituents and party supporters) for a livelihood, and hence to a tendency to be concerned with local, usually fundamentally economic, matters even to the exclusion of national issues. This character the American party system has never quite lost.

Yet it was to be the renewal of party activity – what is sometimes called the rise of the 'second party system' – which was, in the hands of Martin Van Buren of New York and Andrew Jackson of Tennessee, to restore vigour to the American government. They saw (the former the more consciously, perhaps, being a professional politician *par excellence*) that only by ensuring that the President was also leader of a powerful party could dynamic leadership be exercised. It was Adams's failure to see this which made his four years of office rival even those of Monroe in ineffectiveness; so powerful did the opposition to him become and so effective the co-operation of those who were to be the Jacksonian Democrats, that in the mid-term elections of 1826 (for the first time in American history) a strong majority opposed to the President and his policies was returned to Congress. Thus Jackson, after he had been swept into the Presidency in 1828 (having been narrowly defeated in 1824, when he almost certainly had more popular support than Adams), with his coterie of advisers or 'Kitchen Cabinet', dominated his party – the modern or Jacksonian Democrat party – as fully as Jefferson had ever done, and much more autocratically. But there was, too, a most important corollary, for he also restored the prestige and the actual (and fully utilised) powers of the Presidency. Jefferson had thought of the legislature as the elected arm of the government, and the executive as existing to do its will, but in the twenty years since he had left office it had become clear beyond doubt – and it was accepted as being right and proper that this should be so – that the President was popularly elected. He had therefore a democratic mandate quite as strong as that of Congress, and one which was from the whole people, and not any particular group.

Thus he came increasingly to be accepted as the supreme embodiment of the general will of the nation. He could speak for the entire body of Americans, as well as being Head of State, Commander-in-Chief and Chief Executive. (Jackson spoke negatively as well as positively by using the veto far more freely than his predecessors). On the whole it has been when the President has exercised his powers of leadership to the full that the American system has operated most successfully. It is in this sense that he really does combine many of the functions of both the British Crown and Prime Minister, and that he has been called, not without reason, a powerful monarch elected for a term of years. This Jacksonian system restored the separation of the powers as established in the Constitution; it was – and is – recognised as necessary, even desirable, that Congress (especially the House) should represent local interests and that the Supreme Court should stand guard over the Constitution and the liberties it guarantees. At the same time the President not only has his specific powers, but represents the interests of the people of the United States as a whole, while through the party system he can give direction to government and obtain a necessary modicum of co-operation with the Senate and the House. This system, even at its best, may produce frustration (especially perhaps in foreign observers who do not fully comprehend the inbuilt and almost inevitable social and economic and sectional – quite apart from political – resistances in the United States to most courses of action proposed by a powerful central government). But it still remains true that, in many spheres, uniformity and uniform policies could only be obtained in this great sub-continental nation at a price to their liberties and freedom of action which the American people are not prepared to pay.

Chapter 8

Jacksonian Democracy

THE OUTBURST of national energy which manifested itself most forcibly in Jacksonian Democracy is a complex phenomenon, but its main impulse seems to have been the product of a fusion of popular political and economic motives which has been called by Richard M. Reinitz 'exploitive egalitarianism'. The theoretical democracy of the Declaration of Independence suddenly appeared (although the appearance of suddenness is perhaps deceptive) to take practical shape; it is as if the nation became aware of its identity and as if the people spontaneously began to grasp the powers of government which had hitherto been exercised in their name. Certainly these are the years of American resentment at the long cultural dominance of Europe (which found particular expression in a remarkable outburst of literary Anglophobia) and of an insistent, sometimes overbearing, American patriotism. And these national passions were henceforward unshakeably democratic and egalitarian.

They were also in marked degree economic in inspiration; thus the prodigious territorial aggrandisement of the United States during the next quarter of a century was in a sense seen as the exploiting, rather than the conquest, of a continent. That democracies are at first materialistic in many respects should not surprise us: earning their daily bread is the prime pre-occupation of the mass of mankind, and when they once seize full control of their own government they tend to use it if they can, to their economic advantage. Hence, for example, the competition for the chartering of corporations, both at state and national level, at this period (when, as in Britain, new forms of business organisation such as the joint stock company were being swiftly evolved). In this popular spate of individual economic effort, this scramble for material success, there were some casualties, particularly the concept of rational development of the nation's resources in an ordered fashion under some kind of temperate government control, such as was envisaged in a general way by J. Q. Adams. But it may be doubted, in the context of American democratic emotions at the same period, how real an alternative this was.

For along with equality and democracy, certain ideas of freedom, both political and economic, were also implicit in the American *credo* and found their first full expression at this time. The co-existence of abundant natural resources, of federal democratic government, and of belief in free economic individualism made the idea of any sort of 'plan' of national growth illusory. And the enormous success of the 'free-for-all' in the acquisition of territory and the generation of energy and wealth makes for scepticism that any alternative system would have been preferable, even if it had been possible. In any event, speculation is idle, for the fundamental fact of democracy is that the people do what they will with their power.

And from this time forward the American people themselves were indeed to have the decisive voice in their own affairs, for the Jacksonian revolution did not merely overthrow the old mode of Jeffersonian rule through Congress and replace it with vigorous Presidential leadership: it also overturned the whole concept of caucus government, as being in some sense secret and therefore undemocratic. Jefferson's accession to office in 1800 had gone some way towards fulfilling the democratic aspirations expressed in the Declaration of Independence, but by 1820 it was becoming clear that this was not enough for the populace, who detected – not without justice – a patrician element in the system which the later Jeffersonians had practised – a system which in the hands of some of the Federalists would have been plainly oligarchical. Jackson was depicted as 'the people's friend', and one of his close supporters, Amos Kendall, wrote of the election of 1828, 'It was a proud day for the people. General Jackson is *their own* president.' But when the more conservative elements in American life observed the wild scenes on the White House lawn at the party celebrating the inauguration of the President (who had had to take refuge in a tavern from the – in every sense of the word – spirited enthusiasm of his supporters), they were more inclined to agree with the view of an eye-witness, Mr. Justice Story, 'The reign of King "Mob" seemed triumphant.'

This democratic upsurge found expression in three main political changes. The first was the establishment of an open, democratically controlled, system for the choice of party candidates for the 'great national prize' of the Presidency, one which would not only avoid the confusion of multiple candidatures (there were four important candidates in 1824, so that once again, as in 1800–1, the final choice had to be made in the House), but which would also give full publicity to the party's choice. The latter function was of great importance, for, since nationally agreed policies were very hard to find, political parties were to be held together to a considerable degree by their drama, by the exciting show that they put on for the voters; as Herbert Agar has written, the modern presidential campaign was to be a' combination of sport, cynicism and zeal.' Indeed, in the election of William Henry Harrison in 1840, although it owed a very great deal to the bad times during the slump of 1837–9, there were probably fewer real issues than in any other presidential contest in American history, but the campaign of the 'log cabin and hard cider candidate' (run on such slogans as 'Harrison, two dollars a day, and roast beef') was such great fun that an exceptionally high number of votes was recorded.

The instrument used to choose the party candidate was the presidential nominating convention, the first important and fully-fledged one being held by the Democrats in 1832 to ensure the choice of Van Buren for Vice-Presidential running-mate with Jackson. It consisted of delegates from local party machines originally equal in number to the number of presidential electors to which the state was entitled, though it has got larger as time has gone on. The convention does also produce a party platform, but this tends to be drawn up in the way which will attract the greatest number of voters and not on the lines of policy which might be desirable in the abstract; this technique of getting as many sections and groups as possible under the 'umbrella' of the party often leads to confusing and even contradictory planks in the same platform. Hence, too, politics tended in the nineteenth century, and even later, to be more concerned with appealing to the Irish or German or Italian vote, as it might be, than with issues of principle, while minority, often regional, groups in the Democrat party protected their particular interests even in the convention itself by a procedural rule, retained until 1936, that 'two-thirds of the whole number of votes in the convention shall be necessary to constitute a choice.' This nominating system by conventions has, with minor modifications, been retained by all major parties up to the present day, and for a period spread through many levels of political life.

The presidential convention thus meets every four years to choose, and give glamour to, a candidate and to evolve a platform on which the election will be fought, but these alone would not suffice to keep a great American party together. The real cement was often found in the federal patronage, the offices to which the newly elected President could appoint his party followers – ranging from his Secretary of State to the lowliest Postmaster in the Union – and it was in this field that the second Jacksonian 'reform' took place. This was the overt adoption of the doctrine that as far as offices were concerned 'to the victor belong the spoils of the enemy'. But the 'spoils system' was held by Jacksonians to be in a real sense a reform; they declared that their dismissals of office holders prevented the perpetuation of a closed, and often corrupt, group of powerful bureaucrats, (not unlike that which resulted from the corrupt British patronage system of an earlier day) and that a sort of rotation in office was a health-giving and democratic process. This was linked with the idea that in a truly popular government almost everyone could perform the normal duties required of a public official, and in any case the actual number of dismissals was more moderate than has often been thought, amounting during Jackson's eight years to perhaps only one-fifth of those he found in office. But the hope of federal office remained a vital lubricant of the machinery of the professional politicians.

Parties, however, remain basically state organisations, and many of the 'pickings' upon which professional politicians depend for their livelihood (or much of it) exist at state and inferior levels of government. It is by such means as these that parties and their organisers survive, for example, in lean years following unsuccessful national elections. This is illustrated by the truly formidable task which faces an American elector on a Presidential election day; he will not only vote for President and Vice-President, a Representative, and nowadays perhaps a Senator, but also, it may be, for Governor of his State, State Senator, and State Representative, as well possibly as judges, district attorneys, a member of a local school board, and a host of other officials at lesser levels, right down to the clerk of the local township. Considerable conscientiousness is needed to vote with care and discrimination in such cases; hence not merely the tendency to 'vote the straight party ticket' – that is to say to vote automatically for all the candidates from a single party – but also in part the relatively low percentage of the electorate which usually votes, even in a Presidential year. (At the present day much the most important cause of low polls is discrimination against the Negro in the South.) It must never be forgotten how large even now the State looms in the life of the citizen; in James Bryce's famous words in *The American Commonwealth*: 'The State, or a local authority constituted by State statutes, registers his [an American's] birth, appoints his guardian, pays for his schooling, gives him a share in the estate of his father deceased, licenses him when he enters a trade (if it be one needing a licence), marries him, divorces him, entertains civil actions against him, declares him a bankrupt, hangs him for murder. The police that guard his house, the local boards which look after the poor, control highways, impose water rates, manage

schools – all these derive their legal powers from his State alone.'
(1893 Edition.)

It was, therefore, in this sphere that the third Jacksonian reform
took place, the democratisation and reinvigoration of State politics.
For all the new Democracy's national sweep, Democrats, especially
the conservative, often Southern, elements among them, generally
believed that the functions of the Federal government should be
strictly limited, and that positive policies should largely be left to the
States. The new opposition (i.e. anti-Jacksonian) party, the National
Republicans, formed in 1828, who later (in 1834) developed into the
broader based Whigs, to some extent tended to take a rather more
positive view of the Federal government's function and to favour
business interests and the well-to-do. (New American parties often
capitalise on their predecessors by choosing names reminiscent of
them; thus these forerunners of the Whigs – a term itself emotionally
associated with the patriotic cause in the Revolutionary Era –
included the word Republican in their name because of its Jeffersonian flavour. The Jacksonians had done it more directly and
justifiably by calling themselves Democrats, instead of Democratic
Republicans as their forerunners, Jeffersons's followers, had done.)
The Democrats continued the trend, already apparent not only in
the Revolutionary period but also in that of Jefferson, towards full
manhood suffrage throughout the Union, both in the rural areas and
in the rising cities, whose labouring classes become henceforward
steadily more important. The radical wing of 'the Democracy'
(called Loco Focos in New York) became increasingly important,
and a number of constitutional developments were devised to give
greater direct power to the people, such as the revision of state
constitutions by popular processes, the direct election of State
executives, and in an increasing number of states the election of
judges. This, the third, great popular movement in American
politics made the full dedication of the United States to democracy
clear beyond doubt. The Whigs were the successors of the Federalists but could never, like them, be non-democratic or even too
overtly inegalitarian; in fact, they strove to appear as the true
democratic heirs of Jefferson in opposition to the executive tyrant,
King Andrew.

This process of democratisation proved most potent as a binding
force of the new Democratic party; it did indeed itself constitute one
of those rare issues of principle on which a whole American national
party could unite. But though this enthusiasm lasted out Jackson's
time, it did not keep the succession to him secure and it did not

prevent differences within the party during his own presidency. But the President provided the popularity and the drama, and his chief henchman, Martin Van Buren of New York, who became Secretary of State, the extreme skill of a master of the political machine. Jackson indeed personified 'Uncle Sam' (which was coming to replace 'Brother Jonathan' – brother that is of 'John Bull' – as the popular embodiment of the United States) in this period of belligerent American patriotism. Tall and thin, forthright and choleric, he was the first great American soldier-hero after Washington; his reputation as the victor of New Orleans had been enhanced by his subsequent career as a most effective hammer of the Indians; indeed he was in a sense a characteristically American irregular soldier. These traits endeared him to the West, while his Tennessee background kept him sufficiently *persona grata* to the South, so that he could hold together these great sections in political alliance, at least for a time. He thus symbolised the dominant forces in American life in the heyday of the Mississippi River, with its constant flow of steamboat traffic binding together the North-West and the South-West.

His problems were mostly internal rather than external ones, for the westward movement was still filling out the existing territories of the United States, and was only just beginning to overflow its borders in the south-west. These domestic problems were very complex, but the General's cast of mind and will, despite his now considerable political experience, was towards simple and decisive actions; his advisers, however, especially Van Buren, managed to temper his bluntness on certain issues where this was politic. Thus in the matter of internal improvements, the administration retained Western support by spending almost twice as much money on them in its first term as that of Adams had done, while placating the South and other conservative areas by vetoing, with much éclat, a few minor measures of the same kind, such as that for the Maysville road in Kentucky which was only about sixty miles long and was entirely intra-state, not inter-state. Nor did the administration's policy over the sale of public lands, which the North-East desired to limit and which Clay rationalised by proposing that the revenue arising there-from (as well as from the high tariff) be devoted to internal improve-ments, lead directly to open conflict. But it did help to do so in-directly, because its growing support of cheaper and easier land sales pleased the West but was less alarming to New England than the increasing Southern hatred of the rising tariff.

This was indeed fundamentally much the most dangerous issue of Jackson's presidency, because it brought the whole existence of the

Union into question. In 1824 growing manufacturing interests in the North-East had (despite the opposition of traditional New England commercial influences) succeeded in obtaining the passage of a tariff which raised the level of duties from 20/25 per cent to 30/36 per cent. In 1828 after elaborate manoeuvrings, and rather unexpectedly, a much higher tariff was passed, which raised the rate of duties very sharply indeed to an average of more than 50 per cent. The South repudiated this 'Tariff of Abominations'. Calhoun, who had supported earlier tariffs as having a tendency to unite the nation, was now convinced that this was 'viciously sectional', and led his State in outright opposition, not only to the tariff, but to the authority of the federal government to make it law. (Webster from Massachusetts, *per contra*, had also reversed himself, supporting in the 1820s the tariff he had opposed in 1816.) Calhoun's powerful and cogent arguments were expressed in *The South Carolina Exposition and Protest*, which was in essence based on Jefferson's Virginia and Kentucky Resolutions of 1798, but whereas these had never got beyond the talking-stage, the obstreperous South Carolina was shortly to put its so-called Nullification Doctrine into effect. This claimed that where a majority in Congress passed legislation deemed by any State to be unconstitutional, the State could 'interpose' and 'nullify' the law in question.

At first, however, the South Carolinians were uncertain what stand the President, himself a Southerner and Westerner, would take on the issue, but as it became increasingly one not of the tariff only but of the unity of the nation, and even the very existence of the Union, it was more and more certain that the straightforward, uncomplicated and undaunted leader in the White House would come out strongly for the broad and simple construction of the constitution which he had taken a solemn oath to 'preserve, protect and defend.' During a great debate in the Senate on public lands with Robert Y. Hayne of South Carolina, Webster had set the stage for the state rights versus nationalism issue in a splendid speech concluding with the famous peroration (learned by generations of American schoolchildren), 'Liberty and Union, now and forever, one and inseparable.' Some weeks later on 13 April 1830, at a dinner arranged by Southerners sympathetic to state rights to celebrate the anniversary of Jefferson's birth, Jackson nailed his colours to the mast in one of the most dramatic scenes in American history. He rose to propose a toast, the assembly rising with him, and looked Calhoun in the eye – 'Our Union, it must be preserved.' An observer, Isaac Hill, noted that Calhoun's hand shook a little and that he spilled some of the yellow wine from his glass, but he recovered quickly and answered with another toast, 'The Union, next to our liberty, most dear.' But, as Hill remarked of Old Hickory's original toast, 'A proclamation of martial law in South Carolina, and an order to arrest Calhoun where he sat could not have come with more blinding, staggering force.'

The split robbed Calhoun of any chance he might have had of the succession to Jackson, which was to go in 1836 to Van Buren, who became Vice-President instead of Calhoun after Jackson's resounding victory over Clay in the election of 1832, but South Carolina was not mollified by the tariff passed in that year, although it reduced the levels established in 1828 broadly to those of 1824. At the same time, Westerners felt that they might get more in the matter of public lands from the administration than from the increasingly conservative South, which thus found itself more and more isolated. And within the South itself the extremists who dominated South Carolina put that state into an ever more exposed and solitary position; its legislature summoned a convention which 'nullified' the tariff, but no other state followed suit, although the Virginia and Kentucky Resolutions had vaguely envisaged states acting either singly or together to nullify acts of the federal government. On 10 December 1832 the President issued a 'Proclamation to the People of South Carolina' firmly denouncing nullification as tending to treason and the disruption of the Union, and in March next year Congress passed 'An Act further to provide the Collection of Duties on Imports', known as the Force Act. Meanwhile, however, Jackson did not shut his mind to conciliation and in Congress Clay, the 'Great Pacificator', managed to promote a compromise tariff bill, signed by the President on 2 March 1833, which provided for the gradual reduction of duties until a level of approximately 20 per cent would be reached by 1842. South Carolina nullified the Force Act, but accepted the tariff, and on that practical if theoretically untidy basis the tension died down.

But though the tariff was never again to precipitate so severe a crisis, the fatal tendency for sectional disunion to take political and constitutional shape, against which Washington had warned, had been greatly strengthened. When to the progression from the Virginia Resolves through the Hartford Convention to the Nullification storm there succeeded the most severe of all America's problems, that of Negro slavery, the outlook for the Union was to be bleak indeed. But for fifteen years sectional strife was allayed, largely by the national expansionism which reached its peak in the Mexican War and which found expression during Jackson's administration in his support of a policy towards the Indians in the West and South which amounted to ruthless resettlement or even extermination. Over this issue he supported the State of Georgia in the virtual expropriation of the Cherokee Indians, against the Supreme Court itself; it was on this occasion that he was reported to have affirmed what was tantamount in practice to the equal right of all three branches of the federal government to interpret the law and the Constitution, by declaring, 'John Marshall has made his decision. Now let him enforce it.'

The final great issue of the Jackson era, too, that of the Bank of the United States, did not take a really sectional form, though, like almost all American political questions, it had sectional aspects. The problem was on the face of it simply whether or not to recharter the Second Bank of the United States, but it was in fact one of extreme complexity. We have seen that from colonial times the question of a sufficient circulating medium, and the associated problems of banking functions and state and federal authority, had been crucial in American life. The establishment of the constitution had strengthened the credit of the United States, but banking practices had remained far from satisfactory, as was indicated by the re-creation of a Bank of the United States in 1816 after a hiatus of five years. The third president of this Second Bank of the United States, Nicholas Biddle, did much to bring some sort of uniformity to the mass of paper currency still constituted by the banknotes issued by state-chartered banks; notes were returned regularly to issuing banks for redemption. In the course of the years, Biddle, who was a man of remarkable ability and international reputation, came to occupy a position of great power, exercising as he did some of the functions of a central bank and tending to be the spokeman and leader of the creditor, chiefly business, elements in the community who favoured a stable circulating medium. Debtors still welcomed inflationary paper currency, and there was plenty of scope, especially in the West where economic development was so avidly sought, for loose banking practices by 'wildcat' banks (so-called because so isolated that only wildcats could reach them).

On the other hand, the classic antithesis of western debtor and eastern creditor is far too simple. Many farmers and frontiersmen acquired a mistrust of all banks and a suspicion of all but hard cash, which Jackson fully shared. So did many city workers. Furthermore, the commercial interests of the country, especially strong of course in the North-East, although needing a stable currency, always wanted an ample supply of credit facilities in the form of paper instruments of various kinds. And certain eastern banking interests lined up against Biddle; some state banks, for example, especially in New York and other commercial centres, objected to the ascendancy which the Second Bank of the United States gave to Philadelphia. Once again it was to prove easier to assemble an alliance of interests against the Bank and what it stood for than in favour of it, although this alliance included mutually hostile and contradictory forces such as certain banking interests and hard money fanatics. In a sense Biddle stood for rationality and a broad national interest, but he also stood for a sort of privilege, in banking and – in the minds of some of his enemies – in society and politics too. In the same way, he wanted stability and a controlled expansion of paper money, but the latter was closely associated in the public mind with the evils of instability and inflation. Nor did Biddle act politically in a tactful or wise fashion, so that Jackson was able to call on all the flourishing egalitarian instincts of his supporters in the struggle.

Although the charter of the Bank did not expire till 1836, Biddle conspired with his National-Republican friends (which did not endear him to the President) to pass a bill for recharter in 1832, at a time thought to be politically inconvenient for Jackson, who was just entering the election campaign. But they reckoned without the democratic obstinacy of the General, which was one of the secrets of his popularity. He vetoed the bill as 'dangerous to the liberties of the people' and tending to the 'prostitution of our Government to the advancement of the few at the expense of the many . . .' Handsomely sustained by the people of the United States in the election of 1832, he did not wait for the Bank to expire in four years' time but went over to the attack by placing government funds in selected state banks; deposits of the Bank of the United States shrank from $19 million in 1832 to $9 million by 1834. Biddle reacted by contracting the Bank's obligations, but the President was quite unmoved by petitions seeking relief and in due course the Bank expired as an official national organ, though it was rechartered by Pennsylvania. It was a loss to the nation, which in many respects it had served well: the vacuum which it left in the financial and economic life of the country was not to be effectively filled for more than three-quarters of a century.

Jackson's financial ideas and prejudices were simple and limited, like those of many of his countrymen (indeed the vast majority of the men of his time), but most authorities agree that the disappearance of the Bank was a pity: they are somewhat less unanimous on the next phase of the President's financial policy. The industrial cycle of boom and slump, which had begun with the industrialisation of Britain in the eighteenth century, spread also across the Atlantic, and indeed increasingly throughout the Western world; there were Anglo-American economic recessions in 1796–7, 1802–3, 1807 and 1815. The trade cycle acquired a peculiar violence in America, and especially at this time because of the rapidity of the exploitation of the western territories of the United States. There had been a fever of land speculation, reminiscent in its wildness of Britain's South Sea Bubble more than a century before, which had risen to a peak in 1818 and had collapsed in 1819; now once more it rose to a dizzy height in 1835–6. At first the Administration approved of the boom, but as the mania got out of hand, it began to impose restrictions, the most important of these being the Specie Circular of 11 July 1836, which prohibited payment for public lands in anything except coin or hard money. This reflected the other main financial conviction of the President, his dislike of soft, paper, money. At the same time, by a strange coincidence, the debt of the United States had been totally paid off, which left a Treasury surplus in January 1836 of $30 million, and Congress provided for what was in effect a hand-out of all the surplus over $5 million to the States. This added dangerously to the economic disturbance.

Such was the situation when Van Buren assumed office in 1837, and within two months the inevitable had happened and the bubble had burst. The panic was one of the worst in American history and was succeeded by one of its most severe depressions: banks suspended specie payment, nine states failed to pay the interest on their debts while two actually defaulted, and the economy, which began to revive in 1843, did not recover fully until the late 1840s. How far the Specie Circular had hastened the collapse is uncertain; it was repealed in 1838, but there was a continuing battle over the hard currency policy. Finally, the Independent, or Sub-Treasury, Act was passed in 1840, which arranged for the withdrawal of government funds from the so-called Pet Banks and their retention under direct Treasury control, where they were certainly safer. On the other hand, although the Specie Clause, which would have gone very far in the direction of hard money, was consistently voted out of the bill, it did, as the Whigs claimed, really mark an abdication by the administration of its responsibility to maintain an adequate and regular national currency; this accorded well, however, with the view of conservative and many other Democrats of the limited role which the federal government should play in the life of the country, especially its economic life. As Jackson had declared in his veto of the Bank bill, 'If it [government] would confine itself to equal protection . . . it would be an unqualified blessing.'

This negative tendency continued to prevail in domestic affairs until the Civil War, while the federal government fell increasingly under the influence of the Southern wing of the Democratic party, which itself, largely because of the emerging slavery issue, became more and more conservative. The hold of Jacksonian Democracy was temporarily broken by the depression, and in 1840 General Harrison was elected as the Whig candidate on his personal and military reputation and without any sort of platform. When he died only a few days after his Inauguration (the first President to do so in office) he was succeeded by Vice-President John Tyler of Virginia, who not only made it clear that he was not going to be merely an acting-President but very shortly broke with the majority of the Whigs and began to pursue a policy virtually indistinguishable from that of a rather conservative Democrat. From this complex political situation only three matters of importance emerged. The Independent Treasury Act was repealed and no legislation could get through Congress to replace it, so that the federal government (under a nominally Whig President) withdrew even further from its regulatory functions in the chaotic currency situation. The Pre-Emption Act of 1841 eased the system of acquiring public lands, a measure for which the West had long clamoured. In 1842 a new tariff raised levels back to the 1824 level of 30/36 per cent but a fresh attempt to distribute federal funds to the states failed of passage. The 'Whig experiment' had been very far from a success, and in 1845 the Democratic and Southern ascendancy was to be renewed, and the upward trend in the tariff reversed. In 1846 the Walker tariff began the process and in 1857 an even lower one reduced duties to well under 20 per cent.

But during the latter part of Tyler's administration, attention had concentrated increasingly on foreign affairs, and there, during the Presidency of James K. Polk of Tennessee, who narrowly defeated Clay in 1844, the eyes of America were to remain fixed until 1848.

Chapter 9

Territorial Aggrandisement, 1814–61

IN 1815, after the Treaty of Ghent, the American people seemed to turn their backs on the old world and face decisively west, and during the ensuing decades of exuberant popular nationalism they devoted themselves to the enlargement and exploration of their continental domain. The patriotic fervour of the preceding years had already resulted in a territorial rounding-off process in the South, which in many ways set the pattern of American expansionism. Even before the actual outbreak of the war, in 1810, a revolt of American inhabitants in Baton Rouge against the ineffective Spanish regime had given President Madison the chance to do what Jefferson had long wished to do and annex part of West Florida; two further bites, in 1812–13, completed the process as far as West Florida was concerned, but at the end of the war East Florida, including the great peninsula itself, remained Spanish.

Disorder on the border between Florida and the United States grew steadily worse after the war, and in 1818 General Jackson, who was in command there, took matters into his own hands. He marched into Florida, captured Pensacola, and hanged two Englishmen on the largely justified charge of inciting the Indian tribes to war. President Monroe returned the captured Spanish posts, but Jackson was far too popular to be disciplined, and it became clear that Britain, who alone could shore up the crumbling Spanish dominion in the colony in face of the widespread revolutions in Latin America, was not prepared to take issue with the United States on the matter. In 1819 therefore protracted negotiations between America and Spain ended in the Adams-Onís Treaty which in effect sold East Florida (as well as West Florida) to the United States for $5 million. The whole of the south-eastern American coastline, as far west as the Sabine-River-border of the Louisiana Purchase, now became part of the United States.

The settlement removed one source of potential friction with this particular European power, and the success by 1821 of the rebellion against her in Mexico (and other parts of Central and South America) removed the other principal one, leaving the United

States, *vis-à-vis* Latin-America, a young giant among the weak successor states of the Spanish Empire. More and more, Americans like John Quincy Adams began to see themselves as the dominant power in an isolated Western Hemisphere. The only flaw in this vision was Britain, which not only bolstered the strength of British North America but was also able by her command of the seas to break down America's isolation at will. In hard fact, it was the actual, if in a way involuntary, protection afforded to the United States by the Royal Navy's enforcement of the *Pax Britannica* throughout the nineteenth century which preserved the isolation of the American people and made possible their expansion to the shores of the Pacific Ocean.

This emerging situation of American dominance was shortly to find expression in the most interesting development of United States foreign policy in the first century and a quarter of independence, the Monroe Doctrine. This was precipitated by the problem of the recognition of the new Latin-American nations, which was accorded by the United States early in 1822. In Europe the Holy Alliance of absolutist monarchical states had grown steadily in power since the Napoleonic wars, and later in the same year Britain decisively dissociated herself from its reactionary policies. In April 1823 France invaded Spain and released King Ferdinand from the liberal constitution which the Spaniards had established. He thereupon launched a policy of tyrannical revenge; and fears were aroused in both Britain and America of intervention by the Holy Alliance, especially France, to restore Spanish rule in the Latin-American colonies.

In August, therefore, Britain's Foreign Secretary, Canning, proposed to Rush, the American Minister in London, a common Anglo-American policy on the Spanish colonies. For a time even Jefferson, in his retirement, favoured the acceptance of what looked like becoming an Anglo-American alliance, which could, as he put it, 'establish the American system, of keeping out of our land all foreign powers, of never permitting those of Europe to interfere with the affairs of our nation'. President Monroe at first inclined to this course, despite the fact that it might particularly alienate Russia, which 'dreads a connexion between the United States and Great Britain' and which had a direct interest in North America through her ownership of Alaska and her extensive claims to what is now the north-west coast of the United States. But in the end it was the view of John Quincy Adams, the Secretary of State, which prevailed, that it would be more fitting for the United States to act alone, 'to avow our principles explicitly to Russia and France, than to come in as a cock-boat in the wake of the British man-o-war', '*to make an American*

Approximate Frontier Lines at
density of population of 6 per
Square Mile

····· 1800
—·—·— 1830
—··—··— 1850
— — — 1870
shaded on populous side 1900

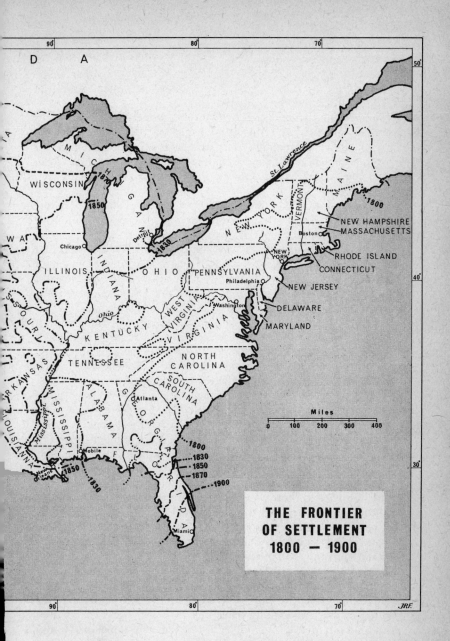

THE FRONTIER
OF SETTLEMENT
1800 — 1900

cause, and adhere inflexibly to that'. Once persuaded, President Monroe acted quite independently of Britain and included in his Seventh Annual Message to Congress on 2 December 1823 a passage which was to be of great significance in the development of American foreign policy.

The occasion, he said, 'has been judged proper for asserting, as a principle in which the rights and interests of the United States are involved, that the American continents, by the free and independent condition which they have assumed and maintain, are henceforth not to be considered as subjects for future colonisation by any European powers . . .'

He went on to observe that recently 'a great effort' had been made, in the Spanish and Portuguese revolutions in Europe, 'to improve the condition of the people of those countries, and that it appeared to be conducted with extraordinary moderation'. 'Of events in that quarter of the globe, with which we have so much intercourse and from which we derive our origin, we have always been anxious and interested spectators. The citizens of the United States cherish sentiments the most friendly in favour of the liberty and happiness of their fellow-men on that side of the Atlantic. In the wars of the European powers in matters relating to themselves we have never taken any part, nor does it comport with our policy so to do. It is only when our rights are invaded or seriously menaced that we resent injuries or make preparation for our defence.'

'With the movements in this hemisphere we are of necessity more immediately connected, and by causes which must be obvious to all enlightened and impartial observers. The political system of the allied powers [that is, of the Holy Alliance] is essentially different in this respect from that of America. This difference proceeds from that which exists in their respective Governments . . . We owe it, therefore, to candor and to the amicable relations existing between the United States and those powers to declare that we should consider any attempt on their part to extend their system to any portion of this hemisphere as dangerous to our peace and safety. With the existing colonies or dependencies of any European power we have not interfered and shall not interfere.' 'It is impossible that the allied powers should extend their political system to any portion of either continent without endangering our peace and happiness . . . It is equally impossible, therefore, that we should behold such interposition in any form with indifference.'

This famous Message not only affirmed the intention of the United States to isolate herself from what Jefferson called 'the broils of Europe', but it also announced her intention of using her power to maintain a similar isolation for the whole Western Hemisphere. There were two exceptions to this, the recognition of the colonial *status quo* (provided, he implied, that it was also recognised by European powers) and America's watchful concern for the direct effect that Europe's disturbances might have on United States interests. But in addition it demonstrated clearly, perhaps for the first time, two frequently opposed strains in American foreign policy. On the one hand, America would preserve – provided Europe's powers did not intervene – 'neutrality' in the relations between them and the Latin-American states and 'not . . . interfere in the internal concerns' of any power of Europe but '. . . consider the government *de facto* as the legitimate government for us': on the other hand, the United States could not but be devoted to their own political system – that is, democracy, or at least free government – 'under which we have enjoyed unexampled felicity'. Furthermore, it was clearly implied that Americans could not but prefer it for other nations as well as themselves, especially in the Western Hemisphere, where indeed any attempt to impose anything different would be regarded as an act unfriendly to the United States. For all the protestations of neutrality at this time, the second strain was in later years frequently to result in an American refusal to extend *de jure*, and even *de facto*, recognition to powers of whose international conduct, or sometimes political system, the government of the United States disapproved.

This then was the theory of the Monroe Doctrine, which became in a manner the core of American foreign policy, and which has in fact only been very gravely breached on two occasions in subsequent American history, by Napoleon III in Mexico in the 1860s, when the hands of the United States were tied by the Civil War, and by the Soviet Union in Cuba in the 1960s, when her hands were tied by fear of unleashing a nuclear war. But at first the Doctrine only worked in practice because, as Monroe's administration had been well aware, Britain, with her sea power, was in substantial agreement with the immediate objectives of the policy. When the President asserted, 'It is still the true policy of the United States to leave the parties to themselves, in the hope that other powers will pursue the same course', he knew that the British Government was already virtually committed not only to follow such a course itself but to ensure that others did so too. And as the nineteenth century progressed and Britain became more firmly committed to democracy, it was possible broadly to maintain this tacit agreement, though even in 1823 Britain was really excepted (and recognised to be so), since she was strongly opposed to the Holy Alliance, at which

President Monroe's Message was specifically directed. In fact, partly because the European powers had already resolved not to interfere, partly because of Britain's ascendancy, and partly because the actual power of the United States outside the North American continent was not yet commensurate with the role for which Adams and Monroe had cast her, the Monroe Doctrine as such was not heard of again, to all intents and purposes, till the Administration of President Polk more than twenty years later.

By that time the United States had greatly increased both her power and her will to use it in asserting her dominance within the Western Hemisphere, for she was in the full fervour of her belief in her Manifest Destiny, a phrase first used in *The Democratic Review* in 1845. The exact extent of this destiny was never very clear (and indeed was liable to be obscured in flights of oratory), but it almost invariably encompassed the expansion of the United States at least to its present borders, and frequently stretched over the entire Hemisphere. As J. L. Hawgood puts it, quoting John L. O'Sullivan (the coiner of the phrase), ' "The far-reaching, the boundless future will be the era of American greatness. In its magnificent domain of space and time the nation of many nations is destined to manifest the excellence of divine principles. Its floor shall be a hemisphere, its roof the firmament of the star-studded heavens." For John O'Sullivan, indeed, the sky was the only limit.' Gone certainly was the widespread belief of the 'limitationists' of the 1820s, that the Rocky Mountains formed for the United States, as Thomas Hart Benton put it at that time, 'a convenient, natural and everlasting boundary'. The fulfilment of this destiny – a destiny, in the eyes of its believers, not only of the United States but of popular government also – was to dominate the foreign policy (and, in its last ten years, the whole history) of the United States, till 1848, and even beyond.

Two powers stood in the way of this ambition, Britain and Mexico – the one strong; the other weak: the one less immediately in the way; the other, through its possession of the vast territory of the south-west as far north as the 42nd parallel, more directly in America's path. Neither nation regarded the United States and its policies in this era with equanimity or trust, but the interests of Britain were not sufficiently engaged to cause her to resist, unless the Americans refused all compromise, and she had also an expectation of American expansion which some few Britons had even begun to welcome. The dominant British opinion was probably exactly expressed by Palmerston; 'As to propitiating the Yankees by countenancing their schemes of annexation it would be like propitiating an animal of Prey by giving him one of one's travelling companions. It would increase his Desire for similar Food and spur him on to obtain it . . . There can be little doubt that in the course of Time the Anglo-Saxon race will spread far to the South in America, but it is for our Interest that this should not happen until the Swarms are prepared to separate from the Parent Hive.' Mexico might fear such an eventuality, but her interests and honour left her no alternative but to fight, even though with singularly little prospect of anything but severe defeat. On the other hand, in the end, the Anglo-American disputes which might have led to war in these years were all settled by compromise, though compromise in which for the most part the United States got what she essentially desired.

The relations of the United States with both these powers were thus principally the effect of the westward movement, which progressed with great rapidity, especially in favourable phases of the business cycle. In 1820 the frontier of settlement had scarcely reached the Mississippi; by 1840 it was approaching the 95th meridian, some 300 miles to the west; by 1860 its leading edges were across the arid plains of the supposed 'Great American Desert', almost within striking distance of the Rocky Mountains, nearly 500 miles further on, while by sea around Cape Horn and across the Central American Isthmus the lure of gold had brought a rapidly expanding population to California. The advancing tide of American migration soon spilled over into the Mexican province of Texas; these men, mostly Southerners, were at first encouraged by the Mexican government, which discovered too late that they were a formidable American, largely pro-slavery, fifth column. Early in 1836 they proclaimed their independence of Mexico, which sent a punitive expedition against them under General Santa Anna; after initial successes, in which the Alamo fortress at San Antonio was taken and its garrison massacred, it was routed by a small force of American Texans under Sam Houston at San Jacinto. The Mexicans were forced out of Texas, but refused to recognise its independence.

Neither, however, would the United States do so immediately, despite President Jackson's closeness to Houston, for Northern anti-slavery elements, largely Whig, were opposed to the recognition of this new state (which had just reversed the Mexican policy of the abolition of slavery and legally established it) – and this was an election year. When the election campaign was over, Texas was recognised by America, but constant efforts to annex the new sovereign state, which the Texans wanted, were frustrated by Northern influence until, after the election of the Democrat Polk in 1844 on a vigorous expansionist platform, the outgoing Southern

Whig President Tyler obtained a joint resolution (by simple majority vote) from both Houses of Congress – a treaty having earlier been rejected by the Senate – and issued an invitation to the vast Lone Star State to end its eight years of independence. There had been American fears, especially among Southerners, that Britain, which was now pursuing, after the abolition of slavery in the British Empire in 1833, a sort of international anti-slavery policy, would interfere in some way to frustrate the annexation of Texas, but it was not in fact in the South that Anglo-American friction in this period was most severe, but over the northern border of the United States and British North America.

Dispute had long existed over the exact boundary of Maine with New Brunswick, which in the perspective of history can be seen as an almost inevitable result of the geographical ambiguities of the early treaties, but which produced actual clashes in the area in 1838, the so-called 'Aroostook War'. This had not been the only source of friction; there had been constant trouble as a result of the efforts of the American government, especially under John Quincy Adams, to induce Britain by economic pressure to admit regular American trade with her colonies, particularly the West Indies, but the moderate and amicable policy of Jackson in the matter and the beginnings of the British trend towards free trade had finally solved this problem by 1837. More grave was the outbreak of a rebellion in that year aiming at Canadian independence of Britain. It was easily suppressed, but not before Canadian exiles and American sympathisers had angered the Canadian authorities by their un-neutral acts. The administration of Van Buren, despite the unpopularity of the course, enforced an impartial neutrality to the best of their ability, but by 1840 tension between Britain and the United States was acute.

The new Whig administration of 1841, however, and especially its Secretary of State, Daniel Webster, were determined to allay it, and he negotiated with a British envoy, Alexander Baring, Lord Ashburton (of Baring Brothers, the great banking house which dominated the vital Anglo-American trade of this era), one of the most successful of Anglo-American agreements, the Webster-Ashburton Treaty of 1842. This not only settled outstanding diplomatic differences and the Maine border dispute, but virtually defined the whole northern boundary as far west as Oregon. This territory remained, however, a bone of contention, which produced in 1844 a further crisis (almost the last of its kind) when Polk won the Presidency on the slogan, aimed at the British claim to part of Oregon, '54° 40' or fight'. Once more for a time, armed conflict seemed possible, but

British moderation and the fact that even a belligerent Democracy thought better of fighting a war on two fronts (as the Mexican war became imminent and finally broke out) led to a settlement, in the Oregon Treaty of 1846. The only serious dispute over the Canadian border which remained to be solved was to be that with Alaska, which the United States had not yet acquired.

British interference (as it was thought to be by believers in Manifest Destiny) on the Pacific coast had, because of the ubiquity of British seapower, been sufficiently influential to constitute one factor in causing the American government not to pursue the possibilities opened up by the temporary occupation by their forces of Monterey in the Mexican province of Upper California in 1842, but many Americans had not ceased to hunger with increasing pangs for this the largest bite of new territory they could yet acquire. Mexican California stood, a huge and very sparsely inhabited area, squarely in the path of America's final attainment of her present continental boundaries. Britain really had no strong interest, nor any standing, in this distant area to the south of Oregon, and the hold of the Mexican government upon it was weak. In a sense the maritime interests and activity of New England shipping and commerce in this part of the Pacific, as well as in more remote regions such as China, made her the most vitally concerned section. Contacts by land across the deserts and mountains were perhaps less important than those by sea, and almost as much of the pressure to acquire California came from the North-East as from the West of the United States.

The considerable efforts of Webster, that New Englander of New Englanders, to acquire California by negotiation failed, but President Polk was quite prepared to use other measures, and the Mexican government played into his hands by breaking off diplomatic relations with the United States when Texas entered the Union. With absurd over-confidence, in face of what was to prove America's overwhelmingly superior strength, skill and energy, Mexico began to talk of war, and there were reports of Mexican troop movements on the Rio Grande border of Texas. President Polk then, late in 1845, sent United States forces under General Zachary Taylor to the border, about the exact line of which there was a long-standing dispute between Texas and Mexico. The President showed his confidence by warning off possible European intervention with a reassertion of the Monroe Doctrine in his Annual Message to Congress on 2 December 1845; indeed he strengthened and enlarged it by declaring that 'the people of this continent alone have the right to decide their own destiny'. From this position of strength, however, the President did not respond to a Mexican threat of war by military action but made a last effort to induce the Mexicans to sell much or all of California to the United States by diplomatic pressure. On receipt of information that the Mexican government would not negotiate, the President ordered General Taylor forward to the actual line of the Rio Grande, the farthest edge of the American claim, which he reached by the end of March 1846.

Then, for more than a month, no news of what was happening on the border reached Washington, where irritated tension at this situation mounted. Finally, the impatient President took the bull by the horns and summoned a Cabinet meeting on the morning of 9 May, which, with only one dissentient, agreed to send a message to Congress asking for authorisation to use the armed forces of the United States to collect payment for certain adjudicated but un-fulfilled American financial claims against Mexico. This would have been tantamount to a war message, but in the afternoon of the same day news reached Washington that a Mexican force had crossed the Rio Grande and precipitated hostilities in the disputed tract of territory. The Cabinet was hastily reassembled in the evening, and the message was changed to one without any ambiguity of intention. It declared, 'The cup of forbearance had been exhausted even before the recent information . . . But now, after reiterated menaces, Mexico has . . . invaded our territory and shed American blood upon the American soil. She has proclaimed . . . that the two nations are now at war. As war exists . . . by the act of Mexico . . . we are called upon by every consideration of duty and patriotism to vindicate . . . the honor . . . and the interests of our country . . . I invoke the prompt action of Congress to recognise the existence of the war . . .' Many prominent Americans, such as John Quincy Adams, and even that belligerent apostle of slavery, John C. Calhoun, regarded the war with some justice as one of aggression. In the North, and especially New England, there was very bitter opposition to it.

Even this division among Americans in their support of the war did not prevent a swift and decisive American triumph, one which not only clearly demonstrated the ascendancy of the United States in the Western Hemisphere but set a pattern, began a tradition, of total American victory in war which was to be of great importance in her future history. By the late summer of 1846 virtually the whole of California and the south-west had fallen into American hands. General Taylor advanced successfully into Mexico, took Monterey, and defeated the attack of Mexican forces at Buena Vista in

February 1847. On 29 March 1847 General Winfield Scott began a successful attack by sea (aimed ultimately at Mexico City) with the capture of Vera Cruz, and by 14 September was in the Mexican capital. The Treaty of Guadalupe Hidalgo of 1848 recognised the Rio Grande border, and in effect sold New Mexico and Upper California to the United States for $18,250,000. It had added, quite apart from the huge acquisition of Oregon, well over half a million square miles to the territory of America, an extent of land nearly equal to a third of the area of the United States at the opening of Polk's Presidency.

Only one minor acquisition was needed – the 'Gadsden' purchase of a small tract of territory south of the Gila River in 1853 – to round off the present borders of the contiguous continental United States. But it was by no means certain that America's Manifest Destiny had yet been accomplished. There was a powerful party which favoured further United States expansion into Central America in the 1850s, and despite an Anglo-American treaty jointly regulating the possibility of a canal across the Central American Isthmus in 1850 (the Clayton-Bulwer Treaty) friction between them over this area continued for a number of years. It almost resulted in hostilities in 1854, but had abated by 1860. Similarly, the designs of some Americans on Cuba, chiefly Southerners desirous of gaining new slave territory, had come to naught by the beginning of the Civil War. In fact, at least until it rose from the ashes thirty years later in the new form of American Imperialism, Manifest Destiny had taken America as far as she was to go in this direction.

Despite the revival from time to time, especially just after the Civil War, of American desire to incorporate Canada in the Union, the expansion of the United States in the Western Hemisphere was indeed shortly to come to an end. This was in part due to those persistent, idealistic, elements in American life which believed that the United States, as the first great free nation, had a special duty not to indulge in 'imperialist' aggression against her weaker neighbours. It was in part due to sheer satiety from her enormous acquisitions of land during Polk's four years in office. But it was most of all the result of the ever-growing and ever-more-bitter sectional animosity between the free North and the slave South, neither of which would countenance the addition of territory that would strengthen the hand of the other. It was the seemingly remorseless approach of the Civil War which perhaps really arrested the further advance of the United States in pursuit of a more distant, and less obviously manifest destiny.

Chapter 10

Slavery and Secession

THE ENORMOUS territorial expansion of the United States, culminating in 1848, had the paradoxical effect of persistently aggravating the increasingly bitter dispute between North and South over slavery, which was the worst sectional cleavage in American history. Whenever the time came for a new western Territory, about whose future 'domestic institutions' there was any doubt, to be admitted to the Union as a State, the question whether it was to be slave or free was inevitably raised in an acute form. In 1819–21, even before the Nullification crisis of 1832, there had been an intense and ominous struggle over the admission of Missouri, one of the northernmost border States of markedly Southern character. It had eventually been admitted with slavery at the same time that Maine in the far North was admitted as a free State, but legislation was also passed laying down that the rest of the Louisiana Purchase (of which Missouri was a part) should be forever free north of the line 36° 30′, above which almost all of Missouri lay. This territorial compromise implicitly accepted that line as a division for the future between North and South, but the crisis had been grave enough greatly to alarm the aged Jefferson, who wrote, 'This momentous question, like a fire bell in the night, awakened and filled me with terror. I considered it at once as the knell of the Union.'

The funnel-like geographical shape of the Louisiana territory, however, gave much more prospect of new States to the North than to the South; this fact explained the enthusiasm of many Southern slaveholders for the acquisition of Texas, but the North managed to delay this latter accession of Southern (as well as American) strength, as we have seen, for no less than eight years. Furthermore, the Nullification crisis in the same era, though it directly concerned only the fire-eating South Carolina, went far to convince the rest of the South that the North was not to be trusted to respect their vital interests. And with the failure of the doctrine of Nullification (which Calhoun always claimed, with some reason, was essentially devised to preserve the Union by weakening it sufficiently to protect the indispensable rights of the South), the minds of many Southerners turned more and more to the extreme doctrine of secession, first seriously adumbrated by their principal opponents, the New Englanders, in the War of 1812. By the time the vast acquisitions of the Mexican War were in the offing the stage was set for the final fifteen years which were to lead to the outbreak of hostilities. This President Jackson had prophesied when he said after the Nullification dispute, the 'next pretext will be the negro, or slavery question.'

Much ink has been expended by historians over the problem of whether the conflict was inevitable or, as the contemporary phrase of W. H. Seward had it, 'irrepressible'; long before the event (just after the Missouri Compromise of 1821) J. Q. Adams had written in his diary, 'I take it for granted that the present question is a mere preamble – a title-page to a great, tragic volume.' We cannot here enter upon the profound question of inevitability in historical causation, but we must note that the causes of the struggle ran deep in the very structure and nature of American society: they were, even more certainly than those of the Revolutionary war, not 'light and transient'. The 'great American Civil War', indeed, as Winston Churchill has written, 'must upon the whole be considered the noblest and least avoidable of all the great mass-conflicts of which till then there was record.' It was fundamentally – as are all conscious (and often even unconscious) human actions, including great wars – the product of states of mind; mainly of two dominant attitudes – one, in the South, on the whole fanatical; one, in the North, on the whole unflinching. What were these two casts of thought and how did they come into being?

Since 1832 the ardent, even rabid, Southern secessionists had gradually, through the pyramidal economic and political structure of the South's plantation-slave society, gained an overwhelming initiative in, almost a control over, the policies of their States, especially in the Deep South. Moved by the increasing grip of cotton on the economy of their section they had discarded much of the valuable political tradition of men like Jefferson and Madison and come to believe, indeed openly to proclaim, that slavery was a 'positive good'; and in the inmost recesses of their minds lurked always the question, 'What else is possible but slavery?' In other words, beneath the problem of slavery lay the more fundamental one of race relations. And their fervent, if often blind, faith in the slavery system was fortified by their dependence, for their life in its broadest sense, on the great staple crops, especially cotton, and it was made more hectic by their ever-present fear (especially for their wives and children) of bloody insurrection by a Negro slave people which numbered much more than a third of the population of the whole South and which nearly equalled the white population in the cotton South.

On this state of mind the growth of anti-slavery feeling in the North, which Southerners felt to be for the most part ignorant of real conditions south of the Mason-Dixon line and which was expanding in wealth and territory a great deal faster than the South, had a drastic cumulative effect. Increasingly obstinate Northern resistance to the spread of slavery into the new territories of the west seemed to many Southerners merely a prelude to ultimate attack on the 'peculiar institution' in the Southern States themselves, especially after the North should have expanded far enough to gain the three-fourths majority of the States necessary for a constitutional amendment abolishing slavery. Already the South was coming to be outnumbered by the free States not only in the House but, after 1850, in the Senate; and, even if this terror of the subversion of their whole way of life had an element of fantasy in it, leaders as proud, as arrogant, and as bellicose as those of a South, which saw itself as a new home of knightly ardour, became determined to cut the Gordian knot and by secession to sever all connection with the North while they still had the time and the power. Such was the strain of secessionist thought in the South.

The attitude of what became by 1860 the dominant strain in the North, that of the convinced members of the Republican party, was less fanatical and perhaps less forceful, but it was to prove as firm. Striking its deepest and most nourishing roots in New England, the home in these years of a wide reforming zeal and in close contact with the heart of the world anti-slavery movement in Old England, it also had deep roots in parts of the Middle-West; this latter section had grown up entirely under the Federal government and its feeling for the Union was correspondingly strong. The Republican party had sprung into existence in the middle fifties and had as its chief bond an unwillingness to countenance the further spread of the slave system. Increasingly its members had come to believe, along with enlightened opinion in Europe, that slavery was a great moral wrong; as Lincoln put it, 'If slavery is not wrong, nothing is wrong.' Beginning around 1830 and greeted with great unpopularity even by many who ultimately became Republicans, a fanatical group of reformers which favoured the immediate and total abolition of Negro slavery came gradually, though its actual numbers were never large, to gain influence; its perhaps most extreme leader, William Lloyd Garrison, with his anti-slavery organ, *The Liberator*, declared in 1843 that the 'compact which exists between the North and the South is a covenant with death and an agreement with hell.' Thus the North, too, had its disunionists over the slavery issue.

The depth of passion of the Abolitionists was tempered in the case of more moderate Republicans by political common-sense, but Lincoln again, moderate and far from Abolitionist though he was, showed his emotion clearly enough. The sight of shackled slaves, he wrote, 'was a continued torment' to him; 'I confess I hate to see the poor creatures hunted down and caught and carried back to their stripes and unrequited toil; but I bite my lips and keep quiet.' (Northern apprehensions also arose about the trend in the South towards the suppression of civil liberties over slavery – as for example the right of petition). In practical political terms Republicans disclaimed, and sincerely, any desire to attack slavery where it existed, that is in the Southern States, but were determined to prevent its extension into the new Territories. On this latter point Lincoln was adamant; 'Entertain no proposition for a compromise in regard to the extension of slavery.' 'On that point hold firm, as with a chain of steel.' But the Republican view did not stop here; it repeatedly proclaimed its desire not only for 'a policy that looks to the prevention of it as a wrong' but also its hope for 'the time when as a wrong it may come to an end.' In Lincoln's famous phrase, the Republican party wished to rest assured that the institution was 'in the course of ultimate extinction.'

Here indeed was the real clash of wills. As Lincoln wrote to his old friend Alexander H. Stephens of Georgia, later Vice-President of the Confederacy, in December 1860: 'You think slavery is right and ought to be extended, while we think it is wrong and ought to be restricted. That, I suppose, is the nub. It certainly is the only substantial difference between us.' It was this which made many Southerners reject as utterly unreliable the official line which Republicans drew between their personal views and their stated policy of abiding by the Constitution, continuing to return fugitive slaves to their owners, and not interfering 'directly or indirectly . . . with the institution of slavery where it exists'. This, as Lincoln went on, 'I believe I have no lawful right to do . . . , and I have no inclination to do . . .' But this asseveration, solemnly repeated in his First Inaugural, rang hollow in those Southern ears which remembered the words spoken by the relatively unknown Illinois politician three years before in 1858, in the speech that brought him for the first time great national prominence. Here he deliberately eschewed an expression of personal conviction, but stated – three years before the outbreak of hostilities – his opinion as to the course which events would in fact follow. This prophecy may give some support to the idea that it was not a 'Repressible Conflict'.

'We are now far into the fifth year since a policy was initiated with the avowed object and confident promise of putting an end to slavery agitation. Under the operation of that policy, that agitation has not only not ceased, but has constantly augmented. In my opinion, it will not cease until a crisis shall have been reached and passed. "A house divided against itself cannot stand." I believe this government cannot endure permanently half slave and half free. I do not expect the Union to be dissolved; I do not expect the house to fall; but I do expect it will cease to be divided. It will become all one thing, or all the other. Either the opponents of slavery will arrest the further spread of it, and place it where the public mind shall rest in the belief that it is in the course of ultimate extinction, or its advocates will push it forward till it shall become alike lawful in all the States, old as well as new, North as well as South.'

Lincoln may have gone much too far in ascribing to the South, later in this speech, a deliberate conspiracy to extend slavery into the Northern States, but he saw with great clarity these two diametrically opposed points of view which were at first and dogmatically held only by small minorities, but which were, with seemingly irresistible force, to gain increasing control of North and South until the conflict broke out.

And in retrospect, even while the battle was at its height in 1865, Lincoln was to make an analysis of the causes of the war, in his Second Inaugural, which has not been surpassed in insight, and certainly in succinctness, by the historians. We may use it as a most convenient guide to the forces which, in the years leading to the war, so conditioned the minds of the two protagonists as both to make the conflict possible and also to sustain it for so long with such bitterness and ferocity. In this most famous of all American speeches – oration is too orotund a word for any of Lincoln's quiet yet masterly utterances – he began by casting his mind and that of his audience back to his First Inaugural, delivered in 1861; at that time

'all thoughts were anxiously directed to an impending civil war. All dreaded it, all sought to avert it. While the inaugural address was being delivered from this place, devoted altogether to *saving* the Union without war, insurgent agents were in the city seeking to *destroy* it without war – seeking to dissolve the Union and divide effects by negotiation. Both parties deprecated war, but one of them would *make* war rather than let the nation survive, and the other would *accept* war rather than let it perish, and the war came.'

It would be hard to better this account, astonishingly balanced and just for a war leader in the throes of battle. The initiative in the break up of the Union was Southern, and it was the secession of the South which was the *casus belli;* the occasion of hostilities – the legal justification as it were, for the use of military force by the Federal Government to suppress the insurrection – was this constitutional issue. As the President had once more expressed it in his First Inaugural,

'I hold that, in contemplation of universal law and of the Constitution, the Union of these States is perpetual. Perpetuity is implied, if not expressed, in the fundamental law of all national governments ... Plainly, the central idea of secession is the essence of anarchy. A majority held in restraint by constitutional checks and limitations, and always changing easily with deliberate changes of popular opinions and sentiments, is the only true sovereign of a free people.'

As he was to put it later in the year, the war is 'to demonstrate to the world that those who can fairly carry an election can also suppress a rebellion; that ballots are the rightful and peaceful successors of bullets; and that when ballots have fairly and constitutionally decided, there can be no successful appeal back to bullets.' Yet the North's attitude did play an important part in persuading the South that slavery could not indefinitely subsist within the Union. Lincoln, in a well-known public letter written in 1862, might declare, 'My paramount object in this struggle *is* to save the Union, and is *not* either to save or destroy Slavery. If I could save the Union without freeing *any* slave, I would do it; and if I could save it by freeing *all* the slaves, I would do it; and if I could do it by freeing some and leaving others alone, I would also do that.' But few Southerners could have failed to take far more account of the final sentence of the letter, 'I have here stated my purpose according to my view of *official* duty, and I intend no modification of my oft-expressed *personal* wish that all men, everywhere, could be free.'

Thus beneath the political surface, on which the reason for the war seemed to be simply the preservation of the Union, lay always the much deeper cause, the question of slavery. This Lincoln clearly recognised in the Second Inaugural, the insight of which is far superior to that of the normal state paper. He went straight on to the heart of the matter: 'One eighth of the whole population was colored slaves, not distributed generally over the Union, but localised in the southern part of it.' The institution was by now, indeed, peculiar to the Southern States, for during the first years of the Republic (in a succession ending with New Jersey in 1804) all states north of Delaware, Maryland, Virginia and Kentucky, finding slavery withering economically, had set its abolition in train; and no new slave States had come into existence north of Missouri or west of Arkansas and Texas. 'These slaves', the President continued, 'constituted a peculiar and powerful interest.' The word interest is exactly the right one, for it accurately and strongly suggests the integral part which the institution played in the economic, as well as the whole social, way of life of the South.

By 1860 there were nearly 4 million slaves in the South, and the vast majority of them were used in the production of great agricultural staples; tobacco in the Upper South, rice in South Carolina, sugar in Louisiana, and cotton, above all, almost everywhere in the Deep South. Under the unprecedented demand of the cotton industry of Lancashire, in the throes of what was very properly called the Industrial Revolution, the cotton plantations spread west through the so-called Cotton, or Black, Belt of South Carolina, Georgia, Alabama and Mississippi at a remarkable pace, and cotton production soared, as it sometimes seemed never-endingly, from £160 million in 1820 to £2,300 million in 1860, when it constituted two thirds by value of all United States exports. So rapid was the expansion that, even with the astonishing European demand, the average price sank from 15 cents a pound in the 1820s to 9 cents in the 1850s. On the other hand, the price of slaves rose from $350 in 1800 to $1,500 in 1860 for a prime field hand, so that, given Southern belief in the social and economic necessity of slavery, an ever-increasing proportion of Southern capital was tied up in slaves, although the wasteful methods of cultivation of single crops as destructive of the soil as these staples led to rapid soil exhaustion and a constant need for new territory. It was firmly believed that only Negro slaves could work effectively in the hot climate of the South.

And if slaves were to be used fully, only the relatively simple processes of staple crop cultivation in general, and cotton cultivation in particular, could be easily envisaged by the South, for the gang labour of plantations made the slaves easier to oversee and to control. The large plantation was not the general rule (though it was probably economically the most efficient unit), for only about 46,000 out of 350,000 slave owners possessed more than 20 slaves. The South, too, did still grow a high proportion of its own food. Yet so great was the economic and social strength of the planter class that it dominated the life and politics of the South. Except for some mountain areas where there were virtually no slaves, the Southerners, many of them falling into the 'poor white' class, accepted the leadership of the planter oligarchy. This was partly because in some cases their economic circumstances were so bad that they gave free rein to their race prejudice, to their belief that they had one unquestioned and unquestionable badge of superiority to their Negro competitor, their white skin. Thus much of the South was tied to the chariot wheels of the cotton slavery system, and it believed that not only its livelihood, but also its neo- or pseudo-aristocratic way of life, and even its domestic safety, were indissolubly bound up with the inviolate preservation of this nexus.

This way of life was not without its virtues, despite its feet of clay. It was in some measure leisured, it took manners and even chivalry seriously (though the latter degenerated easily into the language and practices of the duellist and the braggart), and, under a largely fantasy screen of devotion to lineage and class, it concealed, even in great degree from itself, the harsh materialism of 'the almighty dollar'. As the poet Stephen Vincent Benét saw, the South could command an extraordinary devotion,

'*Why were they all going out to war?*
He brooded a moment. It wasn't slavery,
That stale red-herring of Yankee knavery
Nor even states-rights, at least not solely,
But something so dim that it must be holy.

. . . .

Something so shrouded it must be great,
The dead men building the living State
From 'simmon-seed on a sandy bottom,
The woman South in her rivers laving
That body whiter than new-blown cotton
 And savage and sweet as wild-orange-blossom,
The dark hair streams on the barbarous bosom,
If there ever has been a land worth saving –
In Dixie land, I'll take my stand,
And live and die for Dixie!'

This belief of the South in its mode of living was not to be shaken by moral denunciations from the North, nor by prophecies of ultimate social disaster, let alone by theoretical assertions of mere economic inefficiency.

This 'peculiar and powerful interest,' the President went on, 'All knew . . . was somehow the cause of the war.' Once again it is perhaps impossible to better this simple analysis; certainly slavery was 'somehow' the fundamental cause of the Civil War.

In startling contrast to this agricultural society, so greatly dependent not only on slavery but also on the commercial facilities provided almost exclusively by the Yankees and the British, was the even more swiftly expanding but commercial and increasingly industrial section 'at the North'. The great development of canal and river steamboat traffic was succeeded by the even swifter transport revolution of the railroad; by 1860, of the nation's 31,000 miles of railway, 22,000 were in the North and West. American foreign trade, largely in Northern hands, expanded fast, and the 1850s, with the Yankee clipper ship, marked the greatest relative international strength and superiority of the American merchant marine till mid-twentieth century. Industrial expansion, chiefly in New England, New York and Pennsylvania, was unprecedented in speed and scale, especially between 1843 and 1857. In 1860 pig-iron production reached 900,000 tons and the cotton industry manufactured more than 400,000 lbs. of cloth. Even the agriculture of the North, responding to this bustling, hustling spirit of enterprise, far exceeded that of the South in efficiency, for the pace of the slave was not adapted to the modern industrial world. It was still possible to make profits from cotton cultivation, and Southern output per hand and acre also rose in this period, but economic diversification was almost certainly retarded and economic progress was certainly slower than in the North. Free labour by its nature proved very much more efficient than servile, and the slave system, to which the South seemed bound by such unbreakable social bonds (as well, paradoxically, as by the fact that staple crop cultivation was more efficient in large units for which slavery appeared indispensable), was becoming an increasing, if unrecognised or unadmitted, handicap to economic progress.

But slavery was at bottom a moral issue: 'To strengthen, perpetuate, and extend this interest was the object for which the insurgents would rend the Union even by war, while the Government claimed no right to do more than to restrict the territorial enlargement of it.' Although in his First Inaugural he had in fact gone so far as to express willingness to accept a constitutional amendment laying down 'that the Federal Government shall never interfere with the domestic institutions of the States, including that of persons held to service', Lincoln never wavered on the prevention of the spread of slavery into the West and believed that this restriction would in fact spell its inevitable doom, either by economic and moral pressure, or possibly in the fulness of time by a new constitutional amendment abolishing it once and for all. It seemed, as the Second Inaugural expressed it,

'strange that any men should dare to ask a just God's assistance in wringing their bread from the sweat of other men's faces, but let us judge not, that we be not judged . . . The Almighty has His own purposes. "Woe unto the world because of offences; for it must needs be that offences come, but woe to that man by whom the offence cometh . . ." Fondly do we hope, fervently do we pray, that this mighty scourge of war may speedily pass away. Yet, if God wills that it continue until all the wealth piled by the bondsman's two hundred and fifty years of unrequited toil shall be sunk, and until every drop of blood drawn with the lash shall be paid by another drawn with the sword, as was said three thousand years ago, so still it must be said, "The judgements of the Lord are true and righteous altogether." '

The story of the coming of the war, in the thirteen years between the Treaty of Guadalupe Hidalgo and Lincoln's Inauguration, has indeed the air of Greek tragedy in its step-by-step advance towards catastrophe. Even during the course of the Mexican War the so-called Wilmot Proviso, which would have prohibited slavery in any territory acquired from Mexico (this not being covered by the twenty-five year old Missouri Compromise), was constantly put forward by Northern members of Congress, but it did not pass the Senate. In the Presidential election of 1848 an anti-slavery party, pledged to 'free soil, free speech, free labor, and free men', nominated ex-President Van Buren, who got enough Democratic votes to let in the Whigs, although their candidate, General Zachary Taylor, as a military hero had not thought it necessary or advisable to pledge himself to any positive policies at all. When he died in 1850 he was succeeded by Millard Fillmore; neither left any signal mark, but the latter accepted the great Compromise of 1850 (as it came to be called) proposed by his friend Henry Clay of Kentucky to settle the immediate crisis over slavery which arose when California, as a result of the extremely rapid growth of its population in the gold rush of 1849, began to demand admission to the Union as a free state. So bitter was the feeling on the issue that the wheels of government faltered; it took 63 ballots to elect a Speaker of the House in 1849, and Southerners commenced actively to consider secession.

Clay enlisted the support of the other great Unionist of the Senate, Daniel Webster of Massachusetts, and against the still obdurate opposition of its third dominant member, the dying John C. Calhoun of South Carolina, he succeeded, after a long struggle, in getting through Congress the measures together constituting the Compromise of 1850. These admitted California as a free state; organised the new territories of Utah and New Mexico without any positive arrangements about slavery; abolished in the District of Columbia the internal slave trade (which still existed throughout the Southern States and was a source of great profit to the Upper South, whose surplus of slaves were constantly shipped down river to the labour-short plantations of the Deep South); and, as a sop to the South, enacted a much more stringent Fugitive Slave Bill. Though hated by extremists, both North and South, the Compromise was widely welcomed by moderate opinion, but this last effort of the older generation to save the Union which their fathers had created and which Webster had eulogised as 'a copious foundation of national, social, and personal happiness' was not to allay sectional controversy for long.

In 1852 was published the most potent of all anti-slavery tracts, Harriet Beecher Stowe's *Uncle Tom's Cabin*, and in 1854 one of the new generation, the Democrat Stephen A. Douglas of Illinois, who was Chairman of the Senate Committee on Territories, felt bound, partly for valid reasons of policy and partly from general and personal political motives, to raise once more, in the Kansas-Nebraska Act which he proposed, the whole question of slavery in the Territories. He adapted an idea which had been in some minds at the time when the Utah and New Mexico Territories were organised without any arrangements about slavery, and called it popular, or 'squatter', sovereignty, believing that this very democratic procedure of leaving the decision on slavery to each new territory and state, would prove the best method of solving the slavery question in the West once and for all. Since the Nebraska Territory was part of the Louisiana Purchase, the Bill in its original form called in question the constitutionality of the Missouri Compromise itself, and under Southern pressure Douglas amended it specifically to repeal the Compromise. It was greeted with a bitter outburst of wrath in some quarters of the North, but with Franklin Pierce of New Hampshire – a pro-Southern or 'doughface' Democrat (a 'Northern man with

Southern principles') – in the White House and with 'the Democracy' also dominant in Congress, the bill became the law of the land on 30 May 1854. Far from quieting the sectional controversy it sharply aggravated it.

It led first to the foundation and rapid growth of the Republican Party, whose one firm bond was opposition to the extension of slavery in the Territories. But enduring American parties cannot long subsist on a single issue, and the Republicans successfully appealed to many interests. The party platform in 1860 had planks not only on slavery and the Union but on the desirability of an increase in tariffs for the protection of industry, on the need for a Homestead act making western lands more freely available to the people, and on the constitutionality of internal improvements, and particularly a transcontinental railroad, financed by the Federal government. Finally, it hedged on the other great issue of the day, Nativism, a chauvinistic response to the vast flood of immigrants entering the United States, calling for 'efficient protection to the rights of all classes of citizens, whether native or naturalised.' This was typical of the practical political skill which created the machinery of the Republican party, for the nativist American or Know-Nothing Party (so called because of its secrecy – characteristic of the American love of mysterious secret societies – which caused its members when challenged to reply, 'I know nothing') had grown with astonishing rapidity in the years before the Kansas-Nebraska Act and only slowly ceased to expand even after it. But in the end the Republicans forged ahead into the place of the disappearing Whig party, and put a candidate, John C. Frémont, into the field in the Presidential election of 1856, who won 33·1 per cent of the popular vote. James Buchanan of Pennsylvania, another doughface Democrat, was elected, but with only 174 electoral votes compared to the 254 of Pierce in 1852.

Meanwhile, however, events had marched forward from the Kansas-Nebraska Act. In 1857 came the Supreme Court settlement of the case of *Dred Scott* v. *Sanford* in which a majority of the Court, led by Chief Justice Taney (a Marylander appointed by President Jackson), in a sweeping decision, declared that the Missouri Compromise had been unconstitutional and appeared to lay down that a Negro of slave ancestry could not be a citizen of the United States. This decision was greeted with rejoicing in the South (whose slave property thus appeared secure in all the Territories of the United States) and with a determination to reverse it in the North. From time to time in American history it has become necessary in the view of the majority, who cannot, as Lincoln pointed out, allow the policy of the government to be 'irrevocably fixed by decisions of the Supreme Court', to try to get the Court to reverse itself; on occasion this has been attempted by the threat of altering its composition, of 'packing' it. In this instance the questions of the powers of the Court and its rightness in the matter of slave property were to be answered amidst the cataclysm of Civil War and Reconstruction.

Most ominous of all the developments from the Kansas-Nebraska Act was the outbreak of civil war in miniature in Kansas, with the protagonists of both North and South endeavouring, through rival constitutional conventions and through violence, to gain control of the Territory and hence of the future of the emergent state – which would thus in theory be with or without slavery. Though other factors were involved and though the area was not well-suited to slavery, it was the slavery issue which gave 'Bleeding Kansas' its importance. The situation was rendered much more confused when President Buchanan espoused the Lecompton constitution favoured by Southerners without submitting the question of slavery properly to the vote of the people of Kansas. He and it were then denounced by Douglas, who was sincere in his belief in popular sovereignty and who was re-elected to the Senate from Illinois in 1858 after a keen contest with Abraham Lincoln, the Republican candidate, who made a national reputation for himself in the famous series of debates between the two men which preceded the election. In these Lincoln forced Douglas to amplify his squatter sovereignty doctrine and gave great publicity to its original inconsistency with the Dred Scott decision; most important of all, Lincoln made unmistakably clear the fact that the doctrine was totally incompatible with a moral conviction as to the evil of slavery. 'The real issue ... is the sentiment ... of one class that looks upon the institution of slavery *as a wrong*, and of another class that *does not* look upon it as a wrong.' The former 'is the sentiment of the Republican party ... from which all their propositions radiate.'

In 1859 the sporadic violence of Kansas was surpassed in the absurd but deliberate invasion of the State of Virginia by an armed band of fanatics led by the wild, unbalanced abolitionist, John Brown; the expedition had the object of freeing the slaves and precipitating an insurrection. He succeeded in seizing the Federal arsenal at Harper's Ferry, but was there captured by a force of marines under Colonel Robert E. Lee, tried for treason to the Commonwealth of Virginia, and hanged. Under the grim shadow of these events, the Republican candidate for the Presidency was elected in November 1860. His 180 electoral votes came entirely from the North and West, while those of the Democrat Breckinridge, a purely Southern candidate, came entirely from South of the Mason-Dixon line. Two moderate candidates, uncommitted on slavery, Douglas (who had 'bolted' the Democratic convention) and Bell, gained only 12 and 39 electoral votes respectively; these came from the Border States. The pattern of sectional division was complete.

In the months between the election and Lincoln's inauguration, President Buchanan took no effective steps to prevent disunion, and efforts among Congressional leaders, notably the Crittenden Compromise, to heal the rift by some form of constitutional amendment protecting slavery in the Southern states also failed. Led by South Carolina on 20 December 1860, the States of the Deep South – Mississippi, Florida, Alabama, Georgia, Louisiana and Texas – seceded, and in February, in Montgomery, Alabama, met to draft a new Confederate Constitution, which was very closely modelled on that of the United States, but specifically protected slavery. When Lincoln was inaugurated on 4 March 1861 the Confederate government was in effective control of its whole territory, except one or two Federal forts, including Fort Sumter, on its island in Charleston harbour. For just over a month Lincoln delayed a decision on whether to relieve the garrison, although the supplies of the Fort were running out. Then on 6 April the President seized the nettle and ordered a relief expedition to sail. As a result of orders from President Davis of the Confederacy to prevent the reinforcement of the fort, if absolutely necessary by force, at 4.30 a.m. on 12th April 1861 General Beauregard, in command of the insurgent forces at Charleston, fired on Fort Sumter. The Civil War had begun.

The Civil War

O N 15TH APRIL Lincoln called for 75,000 volunteers to put down combinations 'too powerful to be suppressed by the ordinary course of judicial proceedings', and shortly there-after Virginia, North Carolina, Tennessee, and Arkansas, border states which were to suffer most from the war and in which com-promise sentiment had been strongest, reluctantly followed the Deep South into the Confederacy. By pursuing a moderate policy, especially on the slavery question, the President held the remaining border states, four of which were slave, within the Union, though they (as well as Tennessee and Arkansas) were bitterly divided within themselves, while Kentucky for a period actually maintained its neutrality. The upper and western portion of Virginia refused to accept secession and remained in the Union as the new and separate State of West Virginia.

As has so often been the case in great modern wars, 'Neither party expected for the war the magnitude or the duration which', as Lincoln put it, it in the end 'attained': he initially called for militia service of only three months. In fact the war was to last for almost exactly four years, and to inflict some one million casualties on the American people.

The eleven states of the Confederacy numbered approximately $5\frac{1}{2}$ million whites and $3\frac{1}{2}$ million slaves: the twenty-three states remaining in the Union had a population of about 22 million. Aided by modern industrial methods, ranging from the railroads which were so vital for Northern victory to the canning of food to feed the troops, the governments fielded armies larger than in any war before that date. Deaths numbered more than 600,000 (about 360,000 in the North and 260,000 in the South): these, in a total American population of approximately 31 million, represented an ordeal comparable to the three-quarters of a million deaths suffered by Great Britain in the First World War, when its population was somewhat over 40 million. The American losses have only been exceeded in the Second World War and the Union casualty rate (that of the Confederacy was even higher) was, in proportion to population, over six times that of the years 1941–45. The War between the States, as the South called it, lies, indeed, like a great chasm across the course of American history.

The North started the war with substantial advantages. Not only did it greatly outnumber the Confederacy and vastly exceed it in size and resources, but it had a far stronger commercial and industrial base; and, as had been – and was to be – increasingly the case throughout modern history, technology based on industrial resources was to be one of the decisive factors in bringing victory in battle. (It was in a sense technologically the first of modern wars, with a great increase in fire power, both by shell and rifle, which gave the North a special advantage accruing from its technical supremacy). Probably between $1\frac{1}{2}$ and 2 million men, all much better equipped and armed than their opponents, passed through the ranks of the Union Armies, compared with 600,000 to 1 million in those of the South. The Federal government was able to raise some $3 billion (American billions of 1,000 million each) in taxes and loans for the conduct of the war, compared with $2 billion in the Confederacy, whose infinitely graver inflation meant that this sum was really considerably lower than it appears. The Confederacy, moreover, was much more dependent on foreign industry for the purchase of arms and equipment than was the industrial North. Though the Army of the United States lost many officers to the Confederate forces, and virtually all its bases and much equipment in the South, it did start the war as, after a fashion, an army in being and did not have to be created from scratch like that of its enemies. (The Negro, too, made an appreciable contribution, as soldier and labourer, to the Northern cause.) Even more important in some respects was the possession of the Navy, which expanded swiftly because virtually all the ship-building facilities of the nation were in the North; by the end of the war the blockade of the coastline of the South, though never complete, was without question a decisive factor in starving the Confederate armies of the supplies they desperately needed and gave the Union a tightening stranglehold over the exports upon which the South so greatly relied for its economic strength. To many historians it has seemed almost the principal cause of the defeat of the South.

On the other hand, the South was not without some advantages. The structure of Southern society produced an officer class accustomed to command and full of supremely self-confident martial ardour, while its tough yeomen proved a hardy, indeed indomitable, soldiery, who bore the physical hardships of a gruelling war with fortitude and remarkable loyalty. Until disillusioned by the blockade and the wariness of the European powers in committing themselves, they believed that they had, in 'King Cotton', an economic lever of crucial importance with which to force France, and more especially Britain, to enter the war (or at least to recognise the Confederate government) in order to ensure the supplies of cotton vital to British and French industry, and even, as it was thought, to their whole national economies. Above all, the South had only to wage a defensive war, and could do so on interior lines, which gave her a great strategic advantage: she just had to hold out until the North wearied, whereas the Union armies had the much more formidable task of reconquering every inch of Southern territory.

The vital question, therefore, always remained whether the North would persevere till the bitter end. In this Lincoln played an indispensable part, for his resolution never failed, even when it looked for a time as if he might not be re-elected in 1864; his Democratic opponent in that election, General George B. McClellan, sometimes gave an appearance of considerably less determination than the President to fight to a finish whatever the cost. Jefferson Davis, who had been elected President of the Confederate States, though a man of much narrower vision, was equally determined, and had had professional military experience in the Mexican War, but this led him to interfere too much in the detailed conduct of military operations. Lincoln, on the other hand, though he had great difficulty in finding what he called 'fighting generals', and so perhaps altered his commanders too frequently (beginning with the dismissal of the able but cautious McClellan), showed a strong fundamental grasp of the strategy of the war. On the whole, the military commanders of the South were superior to their opposite numbers, but, though no Union general probably approached the upright and noble Southern hero, Robert E. Lee, in capacity or in the love of his soldiers, the final Northern commander, Ulysses S. Grant, displayed a remarkable and unflinching, even brutal, moral courage in fighting doggedly through to victory in the face of casualties perhaps unprecedented in the history of war. The war was, indeed, a demonstration, conclusive for those with eyes to see, of the political resolution and fighting qualities of the American people, but the fact that the Northern victory was in the main one of numbers and material superiority left a powerful imprint on American military habits and modes of thought from that time forward.

This is not to underestimate the importance of morale; however great the margin of Northern superiority in strength, its will might have failed at any time, as Confederate leaders hoped it would. And both sides had difficulties of morale, though those of the North seemed on the surface the more serious. At the political level there was a persistent and vocal Democratic opposition which was far from enthusiastic about the fratricidal conflict, so that even a man like Clement L. Vallandigham, condemned by court-martial for declaring disloyal opinions with the object of weakening the government, received while in exile the Democratic nomination for governor of Ohio. Lukewarmness to the war was widespread; resentment of 'the draft', or conscription, led in New York City in July 1863 to riots so bloody that probably at least 500 people were killed in the course of them; in the Border states, naturally, but also in the middle-west, especially along the Ohio Valley where many people were of Southern extraction, 'Copperheadism', or sympathy to the Southern cause, and actual treason to the Union (centring in secret societies like the Knights of the Golden Circle) flourished. The Federal government, too, was divided against itself almost as much in war as in peace; Lincoln in some respects mistrusted Congress as a war instrument and it did not meet in special session until nearly three months after Fort Sumter. The powers of the Executive – in particular the President's 'war powers' as Commander-in-Chief – were, therefore, expanded to the limit during the struggle, and the President as a result also had to maintain a running fight with the Supreme Court on such issues as the powers of army commanders over civilians under martial law. In the end, however, the influence of the Federal government, and above all of the President, was greatly enhanced by the outcome of the conflict.

Outright Southern treason to the new Confederacy was much more rare. Perhaps most remarkable was the complete absence of slave insurrections, when the vast majority of able-bodied whites were away at the front, though increasing numbers of slaves did flee to the Union forces. On the other hand, the political and constitutional difficulties of the Confederate government were perhaps worse than those of Washington; the Confederate Constitution not only protected slavery but also, as the artifact of secessionists, State Rights. Its preamble declared 'We, the people of the Confederate States, each State acting in its sovereign and independent capacity . . .', and from the first, despite the exigencies of war, the States jealously guarded their prerogatives. The governors of North Carolina and Georgia, especially, hindered the war effort to an extraordinary degree by their assertion of their rights, so that, for example, large quantities of arms and equipment were hoarded for the use of the State militias when the Confederate armies were shoe-less and ill-armed. This inbuilt tendency to disunion found its extreme personal expression in the bitter conflict which arose towards the end of the war between President Davis and his own Vice-President, Alexander H. Stephens.

None the less, Southern morale on the surface at least was astonishingly good. There did in fact arise during the ante-bellum period, and even more during the war itself, what really amounted to a new Southern nationalism, which at the popular level was invoked by a song like 'Dixie' and which at all levels enabled the Confederacy to fight so long and so well. It was this which misled many foreigners, such as Gladstone, who declared, in a notorious speech in 1862 which seemed to call for recognition of the Confederacy, 'there is no doubt that Jefferson Davis and other leaders of the South have made an army; they are making, it appears, a navy; and they have made what is more than either, they have made a nation.' Europeans, too, were inclined to see only a gallant South fighting for its nationhood, like Poland or Italy, and even to think of the Confederacy as guarding, rather than undermining, individual freedom. Indeed the arguments of Jefferson Davis read very similarly to those of John Stuart Mill on *Liberty*; and so liberal a man as Lord Acton could write to Lee after the war: 'I saw in State Rights the only availing check upon the absolutism of the sovereign will, and secession filled me with hope, not as the destruction but as the redemption of Democracy.' This undoubtedly gave some moral strength to Southern arms. But – it was the constant tenor of Lincoln's thought – what was the right for which the South fought? At bottom it was the right to keep Negro slaves. This involved the Confederacy in a fundamental political, and all Southerners in a fundamental psychological, contradiction, which at the very end of the war found expression in the bizarre proposal, long advocated by the Confederate Secretary of State, Judah P. Benjamin, for the emancipation of slaves who would join the Confederate Army, and even for the total abolition of slavery. How far this deep moral dilemma – still present in a somewhat milder form in the South a century later – weakened Southern resolution and how far it gave it a desperate determination would be hard indeed to determine.

But unquestionably, by contrast, a certain conviction, a faith in its own rectitude fortified the will of the North. In 1861 Lincoln put it once again, as he so often did, better than anyone else:

'And this issue embraces more than the fate of these United States. It presents to the whole family of man the question whether a constitutional republic or democracy – a government of the people by the same people – can or cannot maintain its territorial integrity against its own domestic foes . . . It forces us to ask: Is there in all republics this inherent and fatal weakness? Must a government, of necessity, be too strong for the liberties of its own people, or too weak to maintain its own existence?'

More than this, slavery was incompatible with the principles of the Declaration of Independence on which the nation was founded, and the war, which had been caused by the Republican policy of preventing its spread, was in the fullest sense a war for democracy:

'This is essentially a people's contest. On the side of the Union it is a struggle for maintaining in the world that form and substance of government whose leading object is to elevate the condition of men – to lift artificial weights from all shoulders; to clear the paths of laudable pursuit for all; to afford all an unfettered start, and a fair chance in the race of life.'

For all his hatred of slavery the President, cautious by nature, never forgot his deep doubts about the integration of the Negro, nor his understanding of the difficulties of the slaveholder, nor the fact that there were still some slaveholding States (with more than 3 million citizens) within the Union. He continually pressed upon them and upon Congress, but without effect, plans for compensated emancipation of the slaves in the Union, but was also under constant pressure from the Radical wing of his own party to take more drastic steps. Carefully, in 1862, as the situation on the battle fronts improved, he prepared, strictly as a military measure under his war powers, the Emancipation Proclamation, which declared that, as from 1 January 1863, 'all persons held as slaves within any State or designated part of a State the people whereof shall then be in rebellion against the United States shall be then, thenceforward, and forever free.' Though, at the moment it came into effect, it freed not a single slave, it was widely welcomed abroad and revivified Northern faith, and as the Union armies ground forward into the South they automatically put, as Lincoln had foreseen, an irrevocable end to Negro slavery in the United States. Certain Union border States took measures against slavery before the end of the war, but the ultimate *coup de grâce* was delivered by the Thirteenth Amendment, which was finally declared in force by Secretary of State William H. Seward on 18 December 1865. 'Neither slavery nor involuntary servitude, except as a punishment for crime whereof the party shall have been duly convicted, shall exist within the United States, or any place subject to their jurisdiction.'

Yet this was a war, and its outcome depended upon battle. This remained true also for foreign intervention, on which the Confederacy set such store. Right at the beginning of the war Britain recognised, over the protests of the Union, the belligerency of the South, but she never went so far as to recognise the Confederate government. Nor did either she or France ever come to the point of imminently considering actual intervention in the conflict, though she became embroiled with Washington in such disputes as that over the construction of the Confederate commerce raider, *Alabama*, and though Napoleon III even took the opportunity of defying the Monroe Doctrine by direct intervention in the affairs of Mexico. Whenever there arose in the British Cabinet a sentiment in favour of intervention, prompted by the grave economic results of the lack of cotton for Lancashire's mills (and in some quarters by an aristocratic feeling for the Southern oligarchy, though this was balanced, despite economic harships resulting from the war, by liberal and working-class sympathy for the North), Prime Minister Palmerston's eyes always turned to the military scene. And slow though the progress of the blue-uniformed 'Federals' might seem, the grey Confederates were never able to triumph spectacularly enough on the field of battle to break the Northern will to win.

The pace of the war was so slow at first because of the unpreparedness of both sides, and the sharp defeat of the Union armies south of Washington in the first real, if small-scale, clash of the war at Bull Run helped to make General McClellan, who was shortly put in command of the Army of the Potomac, even more cautious than he was by nature. Lee reckoned him his most formidable opponent, but Lincoln tried a succession of generals (including McClellan himself once more) before finally putting Grant – whose victories in the West caused Lincoln to say to all his denigrators, 'I can't spare this man; he fights' – in supreme command of all the armies of the United States in March 1864. His great opponent, Lee, had since 1862 been in command of the Army of Virginia, where the bulk of the forces of both sides had been concentrated from the beginning. This recognised the fact that Washington and Richmond, the two capitals (Richmond had become Confederate capital in 1861), were both close to the front line in this area. It is uncertain how conclusive, in these two wide federations, the capture of either would have been, but it dictated the general strategy of the North, which soon became clear. This was to hammer away, or at least to hold firm, in dense fighting here on the left in Virginia, while conducting a vast encircling movement on the right, in the far-away region of the Mississippi.

Thus while a series of relatively indecisive battles took place in the East, culminating in that at Antietam in September 1862 between Lee and the restored McClellan which was 'a defeat for both armies', the Union fought first to capture or hold Missouri, Kentucky and Tennessee and then to master the Mississippi, thus detaching the South-West from the South. To this end naval forces under Admiral Farragut had captured New Orleans at its mouth in 1862 and had begun to work up the river. By the summer of 1863, following Grant's decisive and brilliant capture of Vicksburg, the objective was achieved, and, as Lincoln said, 'The Father of Waters once more flows unvexed to the sea.' Meanwhile, in the East, at Fredericksburg and Chancellorsville Lee had superbly beaten Burnside and Hooker respectively, but his enterprising bid for a decisive victory by the invasion of Pennsylvania was foiled by the stubborn and skilful defence of the Union armies under a new commander, General Meade, in the greatest battle of the Civil War, at Gettysburg, in July 1863. The Union, however, showed its habitual failure to press its advantage after battle, and Lee retired in good order. But Grant, now commanding all the armies of the West, raised the siege of Chattanooga in November and the Confederates were driven out of Tennessee; with his elevation to the newly restored rank of Lieutenant-General and his consequent move to Virginia in the spring, the stage was set for the final phase of the war.

In May 1864 the Army of the Potomac crossed the Rapidan with the object of destroying the Army of Virginia, and with unbreakable determination Grant forced Lee, despite a brilliantly conducted defensive, to move back to the outskirts of Richmond in a six weeks campaign of unprecedented ferocity. Despite Lee's use of trenches and breastworks (to a degree not equalled until the First World War) the numbers and fire power engaged in the prolonged battles of the Wilderness and Cold Harbor were so great that his losses were very heavy, but those of the Union were much worse, amounting to 50,000 men. At the same time in the West General William Tecumseh Sherman started out from Chattanooga towards Atlanta, Georgia, which he finally captured on 1 September. Despite the continued existence in his rear, until its defeat in mid-December, of a formidable Confederate force, Sherman decided to cut loose from his communications to conduct the long-planned march to the sea which would cut the heart of the Confederacy in two. Despite the misgivings of both Grant and Lincoln (who expressed himself 'anxious, if not fearful'), he set off for Savannah with 60,000 men on 10 November. By 20 December he had reached it and turned north into South and North Carolina; by April he had reached Raleigh,

N.C. His deliberate, but controlled, devastation of a broad swathe of country on either side of his route, as he went (in the words of one of the most famous of Union songs) 'Marching through Georgia', brought the realities of war home, as had been intended, to the central strongholds of Confederate loyalty.

So when the end came in Virginia, resistance collapsed almost at once throughout the whole of the South. In fact, despite the dogged resolution of Grant's ceaseless hammering at the Army of Virginia, Sherman's march towards its rear was one of the most potent factors in forcing Lee to loosen his hold on Richmond. Grant had proved unable to oust the Confederates from Petersburg, the southern bastion of the city, in the summer of 1864 and had settled down to a systematic and gruelling siege throughout the long winter months. By April 1865, however, Lee was forced by lack of food to abandon the defence of the Confederate capital, but as soon as his ragged army of 28,000 men moved out it began to disintegrate. On 9 April 1865 at Appomatox Court House Lee, a proud, courteous and immaculate figure to the last, personally surrendered his 13,000 troops to a gracious, mud-bespattered and dishevelled Grant, who was dressed in a uniform scarcely distinguishable from that of a private.

The war had profound effects upon the history of the United States; it has indeed been called the Second American Revolution. It left the usual legacy of war – devastation and poverty – but because the great preponderance of the fighting had taken place in the defeated section, this burden was vastly greater in the South, whose Confederate government, of course, totally disappeared (along with its entire currency and financial apparatus) and whose State governments were bankrupt. The physical destruction in the war areas was enormous.

The North, on the other hand, though it suffered a price infla-tion of perhaps about 100 per cent from 1861–5 (partly because of the issue of $450 million of inconvertible paper currency, the Greenbacks, whose descendants are still in use) and was to foot in the end an enormous pensions bill, proved astonishingly able to liquidate its liabilities; the growth of the far west, for instance, had in fact continued even while the gigantic struggle went on in the east. One of the principal means by which money was raised for the war was the tariff. As soon as the low-tariff Southern members of Congress had left that body, the Morrill Tariff of 1861 sharply raised duties, and this trend continued so that by the end of the war rates averaged 47 per cent – more than twice those of 1857. Though initiated for revenue, these increases naturally suited the book of many industrial interests, and were to be maintained, indeed increased, in the post-war years. There can be little doubt that they greatly aided the rapid growth of America's (still relatively) infant industries; the war had also led in all probability to some acceleration in the development of a satisfactory domestic capital market, for $2,621 million was raised by loans compared with $667 million by taxes; and there was a decrease in the country's dependence on Europe. Such measures as the National Banking Acts and the Act of 1865 which drove state bank notes out of circulation by laying a 10 per cent tax on them greatly improved the financial structure of the United States. The conventional thesis of the historians has been that the war greatly stimulated American industrialisation, and though this view may have underestimated pre-war development, there seems little doubt that, given the inevitable warping effects of the unbalanced demand and the labour shortage of the war years, industrial growth continued at a rate which allowed a remarkable upsurge as soon as hostilities ceased. So great was the resilience of the economy that even the South recovered swiftly and was beginning to industrialise within a remarkably few years.

The bitter emotional aftermath of the war was far less easily remedied. It finally ensured the triumph of the way of life of the North and West. In concrete terms, it abolished slavery and preserved the Union. It had also certain secondary effects; the Union was not merely conserved, it was greatly strengthened, so that from this second revolution, perhaps for the first time, a modern nation emerged; the power of the Federal government, and especially in the end of the President within that government, was to show itself greatly enhanced. In more poetic terms, those of Benét in *John Brown's Body*, the Northern victory buried the Old South,

> 'Bury the bygone South.
> Bury the minstrel with the honey-mouth,
> Bury the broadsword virtues of the clan,
> Bury the unmachined, the planter's pride,
> The courtesy and the bitter arrogance,
> The pistol-hearted horsemen who could ride
> Like jolly centaurs under the hot stars.
> Bury the whip, bury the branding-bars,
> Bury the unjust thing
> That some tamed into mercy, being wise,
> But could not starve the tiger from its eyes
> Or make it feed where beasts of mercy feed.

Bury the fiddle-music and the dance,
The sick magnolias of the false romance
And all the chivalry that went to seed
Before its ripening.

And with these things, bury the purple dream
Of the America we have not been,
The tropic empire, seeking the warm sea,
The last foray of aristocracy
Based not on dollars or initiative
Or any blood for what that blood was worth
But on a certain code, a manner of birth,
A certain manner of knowing how to live,
The pastoral rebellion of the earth
Against machines, against the Age of Steam,
The Hamiltonian extremes against the Franklin mean,
The genius of the land
Against the metal hand,
The great, slave-driven bark,
Full-oared upon the dark,
With gilded figurehead,
With fetters for the crew
And spices for the few,
The passion that is dead,
The pomp we never knew,
Bury this too.'

The ghost of the Old South, however, was not to be so easily laid and has never ceased to haunt the affairs of the United States; even the New South which emerged in the twentieth century was to be an exceedingly awkward spectre for the American body politic. On 9 April 1865 the formidable task of reconstruction, physical and moral, lay before the President: six days later he was dead. The Union, America, Democracy, had a martyr whose legend was indeed to show that the blood of martyrs can be as much the seed of freedom and self-government as of the church. We cannot tell how different the history of Reconstruction would have been if Lincoln had not been assassinated, nor easily assess how much the circumstances of his death at the climax of his long travail of war have imparted a halo of sanctity to the last phase of his life. We can only say of his policy, his intentions, towards the defeated South that they are (to adapt his own words, used in a quite different connection, to the working-men of Manchester who made such sacrifices in support

of the Northern cause) 'an instance of sublime Christian heroism
which has not been surpassed in any age or in any country.'

He put his policy in its finest and most famous form in the last
paragraph of his Second Inaugural, delivered somewhat over a
month before the end of the war. His sentiments elevate this political
utterance to a level far above politics: they raise Abraham Lincoln
from statesmanship to sainthood.

> 'With malice toward none, with charity for all, with firmness in
> the right as God gives us to see the right, let us strive on to finish
> the work we are in, to bind up the nation's wounds, to care for
> him who shall have borne the battle and for his widow and his
> orphan, to do all which may achieve and cherish a just and
> lasting peace among ourselves and with all nations.'

Chapter 12

Reconstruction

THE PRACTICAL problems of Reconstruction were none the less intractable, as Lincoln had foreseen even before the war began; he said in his First Inaugural, 'We cannot remove our respective sections from each other, nor build an impassable wall between them . . . They cannot but remain face to face, and intercourse, either amicable or hostile, must continue between them . . . Suppose you go to war, . . . when, after much loss on both sides, . . . you cease fighting, the identical old questions as to terms of intercourse are again upon you.' This fact was always in Lincoln's mind during the course of the war, and his approach to the problem was characteristically enlightened, moderate and pragmatic. The war had abolished slavery and preserved the Union: it did not determine what the new status of the more than $3\frac{1}{2}$ million Negroes in the South was to be, nor how the relationship of the seceded states to the Union was to be renewed. These were the two key questions of Reconstruction, made all the more difficult to answer by the bitterness of the war, both North and South.

The practical problem of the relationship of the seceded areas to the Union was raised, even before the Emancipation Proclamation, by the capture of New Orleans in April 1862. General Ben Butler of Massachusetts, a stormy petrel in American politics, who was in command there, urged on the President an amnesty for all who would take a simple oath of allegiance to the Union, for the Confiscation Act of July in that year specifically allowed the President the power of amnesty. 11,000 citizens took the oath and in February 1863 elected two representatives, who were seated in Congress until the end of the session in March; though Tennessee had had some representation in the first two years of the war, this Louisiana incident remained unique, but it set the tone for Lincoln's essentially *ad hoc* proposals to get the seceded states once more, as quickly as might be, into their 'proper practical relation with the Union'.

On 8 December 1863 the President moved nearer to a comprehensive policy with his Proclamation of Amnesty and Reconstruction, issued in his capacity as Commander-in-Chief. It proposed to grant recognition to any state government set up by persons, who had been pardoned after taking an oath to support 'the constitution of the United States and the Union of the States', when they numbered one-tenth of the votes cast in the election of 1860. Radical Republican critics considered that his concern for reconciliation with the white South would be at the expense of the Negro race, but he replied that if the ex-slaves were pushed forward too fast their rights would ultimately be slower in coming. He suggested to the Governor of Louisiana in March 1864 that the franchise be granted to 'some of the coloured people . . . – as, for instance, the very intelligent, and especially those who have fought gallantly in our ranks.' He later commended the new constitution there as 'better for the poor black man than we have in Illinois', but his policy of hastening slowly was increasingly attacked by the left-wing of his own party, who were moved partly by vindictiveness against the enemy, partly by a genuine idealistic concern for the Negro, and also, before long, partly by a desire to preserve the ascendancy of the Republican party by controlling the South through the use of the Negro vote.

This strange mixture of hatred of the South and charity towards the Negro, of moral idealism and political cynicism, of patriotism and party addiction, was exactly personified in the leader who was to dominate Congress (earning the soubriquet 'The Great Commoner') until his death in 1868, Thaddeus Stevens. He regarded the ex-Confederate states bluntly as conquered provinces on which the righteous will of the North should be ruthlessly imposed. In July 1864 the Radicals got through Congress the Wade-Davis bill, which demanded a majority of white male citizens, who would take the 'ironclad' oath that they had never voluntarily borne arms against the United States or aided those in rebellion, before recognition of a new government. Lincoln 'pocket-vetoed' the bill (let it lapse without his signature on the adjournment of Congress) and continued on his way under his war powers. To Radical Republican dislike of his leniency to Confederates this added a growing legislative mistrust of the burgeoning power of the Executive, already grown to formidable proportions through the exigencies of war. At the same time, with his customary tact, the President made it clear that he was not wedded to any particular scheme of Reconstruction and that, although he privately remarked that he was glad Congress was going to adjourn till December, in this process the legislature must play a vital part.

His successor, Andrew Johnson, had none of Lincoln's flexibility, let alone political genius, but was an industrious, self-made, self-educated, courageous, and obstinately opinionated man. His loyalty to the Union (despite his Democratic Tennessee origins, he repeatedly declared that 'Treason is a crime and crime must be punished. Treason must be made infamous and traitors impoverished') was unquestionable, and he had always detested the Southern oligarchy. This fact, and his support of the ordinary yeoman farmer of the South, especially from the uplands, against the planters – in what he believed to be true Jacksonian, Tennessee, fashion – led the Radicals to think him their man. Such was not the case, for in the event he very closely followed the lines of Lincoln's policy, probably long after the master, with his deeply sensitive *tact des choses possibles*, would have modified it. Both Arkansas and Tennessee had fulfilled the President's ten per cent requirements, but Congress, which was now in recess until December 1865, had refused to recognise either government. Undeterred, Johnson issued on 29 May 1865 an amnesty proclamation which was on the whole even milder than his predecessor's had been, and he began to use the pardoning power very generously. On the same day, despite the attitude of Congress over Tennessee and Arkansas, he issued a proclamation of reconstruction for North Carolina on the same lines, and even advanced in effect the dogmatic, characteristically Jacksonian, orthodox State-Rights argument that Congress had no power to interfere with the functions that 'the people of the . . . States . . . have rightfully exercized from the origin of the Government to the present time.'

With Congress still out of the way, the President pushed on his scheme of Reconstruction with vigour, to the increasing pleasure of the South, and by December all the one-time Confederate States except Texas had new governments, largely dominated by ex-Confederate leaders. Some of these governments unwisely went much too far during the process of establishing control of their States and increasingly alienated Northern opinion. Thus they complained about the presence of Federal, especially coloured, troops, although by the end of 1866 only a skeleton force was to be left in the South; some State constitutional conventions even prevaricated (until sharply reminded by the President) over his few essential demands for readmission – repudiation of secession, of slavery and of the Confederate debt; most States, above all, enacted the so-called Black Codes, which so rigorously controlled the Negroes (who might indeed have constituted, like Elizabethan vagrants, a real problem of social order) that they looked like a covert re-introduction of something not too different from slavery. The last fact especially aroused the ire of the North at this time; in the famous phrase of the Chicago *Tribune*, Northerners would turn the State of

Mississippi into a 'frog-pond' before they would permit the black
codes to 'disgrace one foot of soil in which the bones of our soldiers
sleep and over which the flag of freedom waves.' Yet as a recent historian puts it, the codes 'forecast, to a remarkable degree, the future
attitude of former Confederates toward the place of the Negro in the
South' – an attitude in which Northerners were before long to
acquiesce. Nevertheless, these State governments of Presidential
Reconstruction remained in operation for considerable periods, and
by 18 December eight of them had ratified the Thirteenth Amendment abolishing slavery, thus bringing it into effect. What is more,
they began the reconstruction of the South and, in some spheres such
as that of free public education for whites, were beneficent inno-
vators. Their virtues were not to alter their fate when Congress reassembled on 4 December 1865.

Yet this fate was not pre-ordained, for, well organised though the
Radicals were, Congress still contained a strong Presidential (largely
Democratic) group, and a moderate uncommitted majority,
including such an influential man as William Pitt Fessenden of
Maine; this might have made a compromise between Johnson and
Stevens possible had it not been for the President's almost obsessively
rigid policy. The Radicals seized the initiative at once by refusing
even to allow the names of the waiting representatives of the ex-
Confederate states to be included in the customary opening roll call,
let alone seating them. Congress then immediately set up a virtually
unprecedented body, the Joint Committee of Fifteen (9 from the
House, 6 from the Senate; 12 Republicans, 3 Democrats), which was
in effect to control the whole process of Congressional Reconstruction, and to be increasingly dominated by the Radicals. This phase
of American history was more than an episode in the aftermath of
war: it marked the first and only real attempt in American history
on the part of the legislature to seize and retain the initiative in
government. This move in the direction of legislative sovereignty
was in accord with the growing nationalism of the period, both in
America and Europe, and for a time looked like being a serious
threat to the cherished doctrine of the separation of powers. This
became more and more obvious as the split between the President
and the Republicans as a whole (as well as just the Radicals)
widened.

Early in 1866 the President vetoed a bill to extend the life of the
Freedmen's Bureau, a war-time relief agency which did good work
for both Negro and white but which was to become increasingly a
Republican instrument for sustaining the party vote among the
Negroes of the South; in March he also vetoed a Civil Rights Act

which reversed the Dred Scott decision of nine years before by extending citizenship to 'all persons born in the United States . . . of every race and colour' and guaranteeing them 'full and equal benefit of all laws and proceedings for the security of person and property.' Both Acts were later passed over the veto (still a fairly unusual procedure), but it was clear that any legislation might be reversed by another Congress or in the Courts. Therefore in April 1866 the Joint Committee on Reconstruction proposed what was to become the Fourteenth Amendment. The Thirteenth had merely abolished slavery (a pre-requisite of the admission by the President of any state reconstructed under his auspices,) but the Radicals went much farther in the Fourteenth, ratification of which in its turn was made a condition of recognition by Congress, and moderate opinion in that body hardened in its favour during the summer when further serious disorders broke out in the South (in New Orleans on 30 July some 34 Negroes and 4 whites were killed in rioting).

The President, however, obdurately clung to his policy of insisting on the legality of the Southern governments, and, in what came to be called his notorious 'swing around the circle' before the Congressional elections of 1866, took to the hustings – he was proud of his rough-and-tumble stump speaking – in a series of speeches which did much to lower his prestige. The Radicals made considerable gains in the vital elections (which ensured them the two-thirds of both houses necessary to impose their will), despite a Johnson-sponsored National Union Convention at Philadelphia in which the Massachusetts and South Carolina delegates entered arm in arm; this Radical triumph was largely because the President's policy seemed even to moderate Northerners more and more dominated by a South which was in its turn dominated by what W. J. Cash called the 'great captains' of the Confederacy. Johnson's dislike of the oligarchy of the pre-war South seemed to wane and he became steadily reconciled to the old-line Southern leaders. It was precisely these men whom the Radicals hated because they believed that this class had been responsible for the war and might do great harm again if left in power. The President made his position clear when he met the second session of Congress with an even more obstinate Message. Thus encouraged, ten Southern States rejected the Fourteenth Amendment by early 1867. The Congressional majority then made clear their determination to coerce the South into the acceptance and implementation of the Amendment by setting out upon what 'Hudibras' Butler would have called a 'godly thorough reformation' of all the ex-Confederate states.

In January 1867 Congress had resolved to meet in March instead of the customary December – in other words to remain in virtually continuous session. In an Act of 2 March the whole South was divided into five military districts, the commanding generals of which were to supervise the election of new constitutional conventions in each state, in which only adult males not disfranchised for rebellion were to participate. When a majority of qualified persons had ratified the constitution proposed for each state by its convention and Congress had approved it, and when the state had ratified the Fourteenth Amendment, it could be readmitted to the Union by Congress. On the same day the Tenure of Office Act prohibited the President from dismissing Cabinet Officers without Senate approval (they had always had to be approved on appointment) and the Command of the Army Act required the President to issue all military orders through the General of the Army. During the summer three further reconstruction acts fortified these, one specifying that a majority of the votes actually cast were necessary to ratify a new constitution, instead of a majority of registered voters, since the Alabamans had defeated theirs by the simple device of registering but not voting. The President's Jacksonian belief in the inviolable rights of the States now directly confronted a Radical majority in Congress coming close to a revolutionary imposition not only of legislative supremacy, but even of something like Cabinet responsibility. The last hope of the constitutional conservatives disappeared when the Supreme Court declined to intervene – in the view of J. G. Randall 'evaded fundamental decisions touching reconstruction' – in *Mississippi* v. *Johnson* and *Georgia* v. *Stanton*, but to make assurance doubly sure, in *Ex Parte McCardle*, when it looked as if the Court might interfere, Congress deliberately removed the jurisdiction of the Court while the case was *sub judice*.

The South was stunned by this re-introduction of military rule, this return of the hated blue soldiers marching back into its self-governing States: not so the President, who took heart from Democratic gains in the state elections of 1867 and denounced Negro suffrage (except on the most limited scale) with new vigour in a Message to Congress in December. Talk of impeachment had been heard for some time, but on 9 December the House of Representatives voted against it. On 21 February, 1688, however, the President defied the Tenure of Office Act by dismissing Secretary of War Stanton without the consent of the Senate, and on the 24th, for the first and so far the only time in American history, the House launched proceedings with a resolution that 'Andrew Johnson, President of the United States, be impeached for high crimes and misdemeanours in office.' The vote was a triumph for the ailing

Thaddeus Stevens, who led the attack. The impeachment was plainly political, and the impeachment managers overplayed their hand. Though himself radical, Chief Justice Chase presided over the Senate, acting in its judicial capacity, with great fairness, and there was an undoubted public reaction against the Radicals. Despite intense pressure on the minority, on 16 and 26 May amidst tremendous suspense, impeachment failed by one vote to gain the necessary two-thirds majority. This decisively put an end to the possibility of a total change in the American constitutional structure of divided powers, and ultimately confirmed the system of Presidential leadership as evolved under Jackson and strengthened under Lincoln. Stevens died in mid-August proclaiming 'The Country is going to the devil', but Congressional reconstruction continued. By the completion of registration in ten former Confederate States in 1868, there were 600,000 white and 700,000 Negro voters, and by the end of July the Fourteenth Amendment had been ratified by the necessary three-quarters of the states.

This amendment was the foundation stone of Congressional Reconstruction. Its key provision ran, 'All persons born or naturalised in the United States . . . are citizens of the United States and of the State wherein they reside. No State shall make or enforce any law which shall abridge the privileges or immunities of citizens of the United States; nor shall any State deprive any person of life, liberty or property, without due process of law; nor deny to any person within its jurisdiction the equal protection of the laws.' If the right to vote was improperly denied in any state, the basis of its representation was to be proportionately reduced and certain categories of rebel were excluded from office except when permitted by a two-thirds vote of both Houses, but this did not work well, especially as President Johnson continued to pardon on a wholesale scale. When the sectional balance in the election of General Grant as President in 1868 had driven home how important to the Republicans the Negro vote in the South was, the Fifteenth Amendment was put through. It merely gave Congress power to enforce by appropriate legislation its one simple provision, 'The right of citizens of the United States to vote shall not be denied or abridged by the United States or by any State on account of race, color, or previous condition of servitude'.

Grant had 214 electoral votes to 80 for his Democratic opponent, but only a 300,000 popular majority in a poll of $5\frac{3}{4}$ million; his election was won to the noise of strident Republican appeals to patriots to support the party that had saved the Union and won the war, to the accompaniment of what came to be called the waving of the bloody shirt. The Radicals had, however, gained an acquiescent, indeed gullible, President, and were pretty firmly in the saddle for his term of office. Meanwhile, in the South, Tennessee alone had been restored to the Union in 1866. The first reconstructed state to be admitted was Arkansas on 22 June 1868, and North Carolina, South Carolina, Louisiana, Alabama and Florida followed three days later. Others – Mississippi, Texas and Georgia – proved more obstreperous (Georgia, for example, expelling all Negroes from the new legislature in September), and so were not admitted until 1870. In Virginia, on the other hand, conservative, anti-Republican, forces gained control of the State in October 1868, long before her readmission in January 1870. Conservatives gained control at the same time in Tennessee. Setting aside Virginia, which really avoided Radical Reconstruction altogether, the traditional view of these Republican régimes in the South has been that they were hopelessly corrupt and incompetent. How true is this?

They derived their support from three main groups; first, the Negroes – nearly all freedmen, most of whom were illiterate but with a sprinkling of educated leaders, such as lawyers and ministers, who not only attained a number of State offices but sent members to the Federal House of Representatives and even to the Senate; second, Northerners who went South, opprobriously dubbed 'carpet-baggers', although their motives ranged from the highest idealism (in the case for example of many teachers) through honest political and economic ambition to a vulture-like eye for the pickings to be had in the 'prostrate' South; and third, those with the worst name of all, renegade Southerners or 'scalawags', some of whom were concerned only with the main chance but others of whom were genuinely converted to Northern ideas or believed it necessary now to co-operate with the Federal government, that is, the Congress. It is hard to assess the relative strength of these groups but the stereotype of the monolithic Negro rule of Black Reconstruction is plainly inaccurate, for the Negroes were in a clear majority in only one of the state conventions (South Carolina).

What is more, the constitutions made by these conventions on the whole stood the test of time well, although they were not enacted without travail. All the states eventually incorporated universal male suffrage to comply with Congressional requirements, but there was a sterner battle over universal, free, public primary education, centring on the question of racially mixed schools. These were not widespread in the North in this era, although ardently desired everywhere by the Negroes, who had a passionate wish for education in general, and in the South only South Carolina and Louisiana were unequivocally integrationist and only unreconstructed Tennessee overtly segregationist. The cost of schools was great and taxation understandably unpopular in the circumstances of post-war poverty, but all the states emerged with public systems of education (in which the pre-war South had been very deficient) open to members of both races, at a time when compulsory education was not yet the universal order of the day in the Western world. The same cry of extravagance was raised against other expenditures by the states, as, for example, on pensions and certain rudimentary welfare services, none of which had been undertaken by Southern states before the war. The cost of physical reconstruction – of railroads, for example – and of economic rehabilitation (about which there was relatively little disagreement) was huge, and inflation made it much greater, so that it is scarcely surprising that the debt of Alabama, for instance, was not only much larger than before the war but rose from $8,355,000 in 1869 to $25,503,000 in 1874.

There is no doubt that there was much extravagance and corruption. The traditional histories of the period quote plenty of examples such as the vote of $1,000 to the Speaker of the South Carolina legislature after he was said to have lost that sum in a horse race; heavy expenses were charged to the public by public servants, many of whom were of course new to the temptations of office; there was widespread corruption in railroad construction, in North Carolina and Georgia for example. But corruption has been endemic in American politics (with inflated expenses there – as elsewhere – far from unknown) and reached an unprecedented pitch in the United States as a whole in these post-war years. In the not unusual psychological reaction against the horrors of this first of modern wars, there was an ostentatious materialism, a pursuit of pleasure, and a relaxation of traditional moral standards which justified Mark Twain's title of 'The Gilded Age'. The hectic pursuit of the 'Almighty Dollar' seemed well nigh universal: it was the age of the Crédit Mobilier scandal in Congress and the period during which Boss Tweed of New York robbed the city, it was alleged, of $100,000,000. It was not to be expected that Radical Reconstruction governments in the South, most of whose members (especially the newly freed Negroes) were inexperienced and under-educated, would be models of probity or paragons of efficiency, particularly in view of the bitter passions which were the legacy of slavery and war; but they were not without redeeming virtues and were certainly by no means as bad as they were subsequently painted by early twentieth-century historians.

This process of denigration, indeed, began during Reconstruction itself, as an integral part of the Conservative white supremacist drive to regain control of their state governments. It early became clear that Republican rule in the South could for the foreseeable future only be maintained by the Negro vote, the stupendous task of organising which was performed by such bodies as the Union League. These taught the coloured people their political rights and duties (a highly necessary operation), or, according to the point of view, 'voted' the freedmen like 'herds of senseless cattle': in fact, they 'got out the vote' in very much the manner in which this task was performed for ignorant immigrants by the political 'machines' in the great Northern cities. Undesirable though it might be, it was not unnatural that some Federal government employees in such agencies as the Freedmen's Bureau should be active in Republican politics, and that the League, like so many organisations in American life with its tradition of frontier violence, should have been involved sometimes in the use of threats and force. Thus it became one of the main pretexts for the rapid rise of white (at first conspiratorial and underground) societies, such as the Klu Klux Klan and the Knights of the White Camellia, employing much more, and much more overt, violence for the overthrow of the 'Black Republican' régimes. Believing far more profoundly in white supremacy than in free and orderly government, as most ex-Confederates did, Democrats in the South would argue that no other course was open to them; and so violence and terror, directed primarily at the uneducated and superstitious Negro by those who spoke with the master's voice of traditional authority, swiftly increased.

Some Republican state governments tried to protect themselves by legislation against the societies, like that of Governor Brownlow in Tennessee in 1868, but the Grand Wizard's order to his Invisible Empire of the K.K.K. to dissolve in 1869 only made it more invisible; others, like that of Governor Powell Clayton of Arkansas in 1868, declared martial law in affected areas; yet others, as in Florida in the same year, began to organise local militias, often largely Negro, even though these were still forbidden by Federal law. In March 1869, under heavy pressure from Republican governments in the South, Congress decided to permit these militias, which were then organised in almost all the Southern states; in other words, it was now plain that reconstruction could only be maintained in many places by the use of military force, and in the end this had to mean by Federal military power. In fact, however, once the military governors had set up the new governments, the process of withdrawing Federal troops began once more, as in Virginia, where the number sank from 1,112 in November 1869 to 315 by 1871; by 1876, outside the regular Federal military installations, there were only remnants of soldiery in South Carolina, Louisiana and Florida, which were the last three states to see the overthrow of Republican rule. This does illustrate clearly the fundamental and real dilemma, in a free society like the United States, of maintaining Republican, Negro-based, governments in face of the determination of an effective and disciplined white political force, backed by the threat and sometimes the reality of violence, to regain Democratic control in their States. What it meant was that the Congressional reconstruction of the 'late insurrectionary states' could only be continued as long as it was enforced by the military power of a Federal government determined to maintain Negro suffrage in the South.

And the truth was that, although Congress acted vigorously in 1870 and 1871 with three Enforcement Acts (the last of which empowered the President to suspend habeas corpus and proclaim martial law), the heart began to go out of this Northern interference in a South whose white majority was more and more resolved to overthrow 'scalawag', 'carpet bag', and above all 'Negro', rule. The fundamental fact was that the passions engendered in the war, both hatred against the Southern Whites (so pronounced, for example, in a man like Stevens) and high idealism to enfranchise the Negro (so central to the career of one like Charles Sumner), waned as time passed. This was especially so in the latter case, for the coloured man was not enfranchised, nor in the process of being enfranchised, everywhere in the North, and he did not have social equality anywhere in the North. This decreased willingness to maintain expensive and painful intervention in the South was fortified by the materialistic ethos of America in these years; one side of the coin was a laudable business desire to develop the South economically, which could best be done in alliance with the white Conservatives, and the other was the augmenting corruption of life during the Presidency of Grant, which was not merely apparent among the financiers (such as Jay Gould and James Fisk whose effort to corner gold culminated in the Black Friday panic of 24 September 1869) but also among politicians very close to the White House (such as the President's Private Secretary Orville E. Babcock, who was indicted, though acquitted, in the notorious Whisky Ring scandal).

Though the President was personally not corrupt, this odious environment caused a revolt against 'Grantism' – that of the 'Liberal Republicans' led by Carl Schurz and others – within his own party in 1870. This movement, by a significant paradox since it came from the idealistic wing of the Republicans, became pledged to the restoration of amity with the white South, and its sole Presidential candidate (the unsuitable Horace Greeley in 1872) was endorsed by the Democrats; he only captured six Southern and Border states, and General Grant – and the bloody shirt – even carried enough Republicans into both Houses to give the party once again a two-thirds majority, but the President and his supporters themselves were tiring of disciplining their unruly ex-enemies. He used the pardoning power with growing liberality and intervened with increasing reluctance; by 1874 he refused to send Federal troops to support the Republican government of Adelbert Ames in Mississippi, because he believed that the great majority of the public were, as he said, 'ready now to condemn any interference on the part of the government.' Even the Supreme Court, recovering at last from the decline into which it had sunk after the Dred Scott decision fifteen years before, began to show some signs of invalidating a number of Radical measures, and in 1874 the Democrats won the Congressional elections and controlled the House for the first time since the war.

Meanwhile the Conservatives maintained relentless pressure in the South. In 1871 they won control in Georgia, in 1873 in Texas, in 1874 in Arkansas and Alabama. By controlled but open threats of force, the 'Mississippi Plan,' they gained that State in 1875, leaving only three states, South Carolina, Louisiana and Florida in Republican hands. In 1876, in the really crucial contest, Wade Hampton, Confederate general and the best type of Southern Conservative, backed by his highly disciplined 'redshirts' or 'rifle clubs', claimed victory in the South Carolina gubernatorial elections, as also did his counterparts in Louisiana and Florida. But in all three states, the Republicans also asserted that they had won, and this was characteristic of the uncertainty over the Presidential election in the country as a whole. At first it seemed a clear victory for the Democratic reform Governor of New York, Samuel J. Tilden, but by using their control over the State canvassing boards (which determine election disputes), in these three states and in Oregon, the Republicans were able to claim that their candidate, Rutherford B. Hayes of Ohio, would be elected by 185 electoral votes to 184. When Congress met, the issue was still undecided and it even began to look to some as if it might lead once more to national bloodshed. A special commission of 15 members (5 Democrats from the House, 5 Republicans from the Senate, and 5 members of the Supreme Court) at the very last minute, by a strict party vote, declared Hayes elected on 2 March 1877. He was inaugurated on 5 March,

Tilden accepted this unsavoury situation with dignity, and there was no second civil war.

More, however, was involved than a mere party victory: the white Democratic South as a whole accepted it as part of a tacit compromise, which had been emerging for some time, by which the North ceased to try to impose its will in the Southern States. The outward and visible signs of this bargain were the withdrawal of Federal troops from South Carolina on 10 April 1877 and the accession of Wade Hampton to office on the one hand, and the Southern acceptance of President Hayes on the other. The inward and less immediately visible meaning was that the Republicans consented to white supremacy in the domestic affairs of the South, while the South, not as ready for a showdown as, apparently, were their Northern Democratic allies (whom they described as 'invincible in peace, invisible in war'), prepared to ally itself with the increasingly powerful and increasingly Republican Big Business of the North, in order to renew its economic expansion. On both sides of the Mason-Dixon line there was a strong desire to return to what was on a later occasion to be described as 'normalcy'.

The long-term result of Conservative 'redemption' was the re-establishment of absolute white supremacy and the remarkable phenomenon of the Solid South, ruled by governments drawn exclusively from the Democratic party; this unique one-party system in the South made a mockery of democracy as far as the Negro was concerned, thus totally undoing the work of Radical Reconstruction. It did not happen all at once, but when finally accomplished exclusive white dominion was to endure at least until the middle of the twentieth century. The full re-entry of the South into national politics through the Democratic party took place against a background of rapid growth in Southern agriculture, commerce and industry which came to be called the 'rise of the New South', but the Confederacy was not emotionally re-integrated with the Union until the united patriotic fervour apparent at the time of the Spanish-American War of 1898. The Negroes of the South naturally felt in 1876 that they had been betrayed by the party of Lincoln, but their own leaders, especially Booker T. Washington, with his autobiography *Up from Slavery* (1901), came to accept the situation and humbly to preach education for the Negro as the necessary means of earning his full rights in society. In fact many Negroes continued to vote (and occasionally to hold office) in the South for twenty years after Reconstruction.

The 'Redeemers', who now dominated Southern politics, were at first mistrustful of the masses, white as well as black, although the former were on the whole ready to follow these successors of the old Southern oligarchy, who were most of them genuinely less racist than their followers and in some cases even tended to think of racialism as a bar to economic development. The economic cleavage between these conservative capitalists and the poorer whites became in time deeper and more deeply felt, and the former were better able to bid for Negro support – even for the Negro vote such as it was. Then, for a brief period with the rise of a genuinely radical social and economic movement – Populism – in the South as well as elsewhere, there seemed a real possibility of a class alliance between Negro and poor white led by Tom Watson of Georgia. This opposition, however, so frightened the conservatives and ran so flat contrary to the deepest anti-Negro feelings of the mass of the whites, that both sets of 'Caucasians' turned together upon the coloured population of the South and fully implemented white supremacy. This is exemplified in the career of the radical 'Pitchfork' Ben Tillman of South Carolina. Thus, in 1892, a key Populist year, there were 162 lynchings in the South, the highest number for any year, but violence declined as rigid segregationalist policies were enacted. There had been segregation earlier but the full force of Jim Crow was not felt till the 1890s, when it was put into operation on two fronts. Politically the Negroes were deprived of power by such devices as poll taxes which they could not afford, literacy tests they could not pass, and more open forms of discrimination, such as the notorious 'grandfather' clause, which enfranchised any person whose grandfather had voted; socially, the Negro was ruthlessly set apart, by segregation in public transportation, restaurants, toilet facilities and all the rest. Finally, after the Supreme Court ruling in *Plessy* v. *Ferguson* in 1896 that separate facilities for coloured people, if of equal quality, were not illegal in transportation, segregation was imposed in the most vital field of all – education. By 1910 the Negro had been effectively disfranchised in eight states and Jim Crow prevailed in every walk of Southern life.

Thus at the beginning of the twentieth century the situation of the Negroes was scarcely, if at all, better than under the Black Codes at the time of Presidential Reconstruction. The efforts, the cost, the additional bitterness produced by ten years of Radical Reconstruction had, it seems, accomplished nothing, for the Fourteenth and Fifteenth Amendments had really become, as far as the Negro was concerned, dead letters. One cannot for this reason accept the idea that the Radicals were profoundly wise, any more than the idea that Andrew Johnson's policy, however rigidly and thus ineptly applied, was wholly misguided: the President wanted to go too fast for public opinion in one direction, the rehabilitation and even democratisation of the white South; his opponents wanted to go too fast for the facts and for public opinion in the other direction, full Negro enfranchisement. Always for the true statesman there is the basic problem of reconciling the ideally right with the practically possible, and one cannot but wonder whether Lincoln alone, with his flexible policy of hastening slowly, truly understood the question. At any rate, it is interesting to recall the words of his very last public address, on 11 April 1865, which, even though probably extemporaneous, clearly shows the direction in which his thoughts tended:

'By these recent successes, the reinauguration of the national authority – reconstruction – . . . is pressed much more closely upon our attention. It is fraught with great difficulty. Unlike a case of war between independent nations, *there is no authorised organ for us to treat with* . . . We simply must begin with and mould from disorganized and discordant elements . . .

Let us all join in doing the acts necessary to restore the proper practical relations between these States and the Union . . . The amount of constituency, so to speak, on which the Louisiana government rests, would be more satisfactory to all if it contained fifty thousand, or thirty thousand, or even twenty thousand, instead of twelve thousand, as it does. It is also unsatisfactory to some that the elective franchise is not given to the colored man. I would myself prefer that it were now conferred on the very intelligent, and on those who serve our cause as soldiers. Still, the question is not whether the Louisiana government, as it stands, is quite all that is desirable. The question is, Will it be wiser to take it as it is and help to improve it, or to reject and disperse it? . . .

These twelve thousand persons are . . . fully committed to the Union and to perpetuate freedom in the State . . . Now, if we reject and spurn them . . . [w]e, in fact, say to the white man: You are worthless or worse . . . To the blacks we say: This cup of liberty which these, your old masters, held to your lips, we will dash from you, and leave you to the chances of gathering the spilled and scattered contents in some vague and undefined when, where, and how . . .

If . . . we sustain the new government of Louisiana . . . [w]e encourage the . . . twelve thousand to adhere to their work, and argue for it, . . . and fight for it . . . and ripen it to a complete success. The colored man, too, . . . is inspired . . . to the same end

. . . Concede that the new government of Louisiana is only to what it should be as the egg is to the fowl, we shall sooner have the fowl by hatching the egg than by smashing it . . .

What has been said of Louisiana will apply to other States . . .'

Chapter 13

Industrial America

BY 1877 the United States was on the threshold of modern industrial greatness. In the half-century after the Civil War she grew steadily more self-dependent economically, and her commercial and financial ties with Europe became relatively weaker, so that, for example, in 1913 Britain sent only 9 per cent of her exports to the United States and these made up only 15 per cent of the latter's total imports. Whatever the economic effects of the Civil War itself, there is no possible doubt whatever of the prodigious industrial development of America by the early twentieth century. National Income rose from $4 billion in 1859 to $25½ billion in 1910, and the proportion of this contributed by manufacturing rose from 12 per cent to 21 per cent in the same period. During the years 1850–1910, too, the size of manufacturing units increased rapidly; the average production of American industrial establishments multiplied about twelve times, and their average capitalisation about sixteen times. By the beginning of World War I America had become the world's leading industrial power.

This industrial growth was widely spread in every sense. It expanded out of New England and the Middle States, and into the Middle-West and even the South; the economic centre of gravity of the country as well as its 'population centre' moved steadily west. Early industries like textiles and pottery developed further; coal and iron production grew beyond recognition (in 1860 the U.S. produced less than 1 million tons of pig iron: by 1920 she produced 35 million and was the world's foremost steel maker); and totally new industries like mineral oil and electricity sprang up. One of the most huge and swiftly growing industries, the railroads, was also an indispensable instrument for the expansion of all the rest. In 1865 there were 35,000 miles of railroad in the United States, chiefly in the North (in whose victory this was a crucial factor): in 1900 there were 200,000 miles, spread throughout the entire country – more than in all of Europe. The supreme achievement was the transcontinental railroads, which were only made possible by large-scale aid from the Federal government in the form of vast land grants and – at first – of direct loans. (Between 1862 and 1872 the Federal government granted 200 million acres and $64½ million, while State and local authorities were also generous.) By 1893 five transcontinental railroads were in operation. The first was completed in 1869; it was built from both ends at once, the Union Pacific from Iowa and the Central Pacific from California, and the two met amidst scenes of wild enthusiasm at Promontory Point, Utah. The railroads were of great psychological as well as economic importance; as J. Potter writes, 'The nation's success story thrived on success and the trans-continental railroad could be regarded as the greatest engineering achievement of all time. What Drake and the Elizabethan sea-dogs did for English superiority complexes, Congress, engineers, and Chinese and Irish labourers did for the American faith in the inevitability of material progress when they planned and completed the first railroad across the continent.'

The railroads were the chief agency for the exploitation of the far west; before the war it had mainly been settled by sea, for traditional overland methods of transport, such as the wagon train and the pony express, were either too slow and cumbersome or too limited in scale to be commerically effective. In 1870 the line of the frontier had not reached the hundredth meridian, (except for patches of settlement in Colorado, Utah, California and Oregon) although almost everywhere it was over the ninety-fifth: twenty years later only three states, apart from Alaska and Hawaii, remained to be admitted to the Union. As F. J. Turner noted, in 1890 the Superintendent of the Census reported, 'up to and including 1880 the country had a frontier of settlement, but at present the unsettled area has been so broken into by isolated bodies of settlement that there can hardly be said to be a frontier line.' This marked the crucial phase of the closing of the frontier, and this termination (albeit in no sense abrupt) of what had been a continuous condition of American life since the first foundations nearly 300 years before was bound to have effects of great consequence.

The final westward rush was considerably assisted by the Homestead Act of 1862, for by the close of the century 80 million acres of homesteads had been granted by the Federal government, but about 100 million had also been acquired by speculators, so that a great deal of the best land had to be bought. In any event, farm acreage increased from 407 million in 1860 to 878 million in 1910, while the population of the trans-Mississippi West rose from 6,877,000 in 1870 to 16,775,000 in 1890. This speed of development was all the more remarkable in view of the striking and adverse change in the character of the land roughly west of the ninety-eighth meridian, for it became increasingly arid and largely devoid of timber except in the mountains, so that, for instance, the log-cabin was replaced by the much less satisfactory sod-hut. In the East it was possible for a farmer to make a living off 160, or even 80, acres: in the West it was often impossible on 320 acres. So the farm migration had serious setbacks; these were postponed by the much better (i.e. wetter) than average weather cycle from 1878–86, when extensive settlement in unsuitable areas took place, but the disastrous summer droughts and winter blizzards of the succeeding ten years brought about actual retrogression in places, as witness the doleful legend on returning wagons (which had gone out inscribed 'Kansas or bust'), 'In God we trusted, in Kansas we busted.'

The grave and novel agricultural problems arising from these conditions were to be overcome to a considerable extent by two means. The first was an ultimate change in government philosophy concerning the scope of desirable interference in the economic life of the country – away, that is, from the dominant doctrine of *laissez-faire*; but so embedded was this in the American mind and so encouraged by the extraordinary successes of contemporary industrial capitalism, that the alteration was very slow in coming in some spheres. The necessity for change is most clearly demonstrated in the history of irrigation, which is both the only real answer to lack of rainfall and also virtually impossible without state control, or something very like it. It is highly significant that the first successful practitioners of large-scale irrigation in the Western world were the Mormon settlers of Utah; the genius of their leader, Brigham Young, in their remarkable trek in search of religious freedom to the shores of the Great Salt Lake, and the unusual powers of the 'Church of Jesus Christ of the Latter-day Saints' placed absolute control of the vital waters of the Wasatch Range in the hands of the authorities, and this alone made possible the communal planning necessary in modern irrigation. In time the States, and, much more important, the Federal government, began to develop the massive water conservation schemes, for power as well as irrigation, which are still being fast augmented today. In due course, too, the attention of the Federal government was to turn, especially under Theodore Roosevelt, to the need for programmes of conservation of other resources, especially timber. Much earlier, the government had supported agricultural research and education; the U.S. Department of Agriculture was formed in 1862, and in the same year the Morrill Land Grant Act, in a step probably unprecedented in any nation, provided for Federal support of agricultural education by the establishment of land-grant colleges.

But the most immediate and important means by which agriculture developed in these years, new farming techniques, sprang much more directly from the parallel industrial growth of the United States and were much more in accord with its spirit of free enterprise. The joint result of the westward movement and the application of industrial techniques to agriculture was a vast expansion in farm production, which rose from $1¼ million in 1859 to $5½ billion in 1910. In the latter year 11½ million persons were employed in agriculture (the highest ever), but these constituted a lower proportion of the American labour force than at any previous date; similarly, agricultural production constituted only 21 per cent of national income in 1910 as opposed to 30 per cent in 1859. This was chiefly due, in all probability, to mechanisation. The Civil War had exacerbated the chronic American shortage of labour and stimulated mechanical inventions like the McCormick reaper, so that the estimated total value of farm implements and machines at the time of the war had risen fourteenfold by 1920. Thus it has been estimated that if the two million agricultural workers in six western states in 1880 had shelled their corn by hand, on the edge of a shovel, as had been done in the 1830's, the entire body of them would have taken 110 days to shell the corn they produced. The original horse machines were during the period replaced by steam, and then gasoline and electric, ones.

Farming efficiency was also improved by better breeding methods for livestock, by the development of superior strains of plants, by the production of chemical fertilisers, and by more research into diseases and pests. These changes were general, but had much more effect in some areas than in others. The South, for example, defeated and conservative, poor and illiterate, and with its consuming race problem, was much slower than other sections to benefit. In the West further new methods helped to overcome the special problems of the region – artesian wells that of water shortage and barbed wire that of the lack of timber for fencing. In certain cases (as still today in, for instance, the citrus fruit production of California and Florida) technological and geographical circumstances dictated highly specialised agricultural development. The most notable example was the Cattle Kingdom of the Western plains, the habitat of the cowboy for about twenty years after the Civil War, where the cattle lived on the open ranges before being driven the long distances to railhead, as, for instance, on the famous Chisholm Trail from Texas to Abilene in Kansas. In time, enclosure, closer settlement and the ramification of the railroads, as well as further new techniques such as canning and above all refrigeration, brought this romantic era to an end – in reality if not in myth and in the minds of the youthful (both old and young) the world over. Thus the production of meat was able to keep pace with that of cereals and raw materials, and agricultural production rose from $1½ million in 1859 to $5½ million in 1910. This was made possible by, but also made possible, the even greater industrial expansion: it fed the cities and supplied the factories.

Yet, despite this, many farmers, especially in the West, did not prosper to the same extent as did (with the exception of the periods of deep depression) many of their industrial counterparts. Between 1873 and 1895 in fact agricultural production increased at a greater rate than industrial output; there was therefore substantial overproduction and prices fell. Thus it was typical that wheat, from $1·05 a bushel in 1870, reached its nadir (in the whole history of the United States) of 49 cents in 1894. To make the matter worse the competition of new lands just coming into production in Australasia, Canada and South America meant that the surplus could not be profitably exported, and furthermore, international prices, which were falling, increasingly dictated the domestic price, so that the whole problem of planning production on a single farm became more difficult at the same time that it was becoming more complex technologically. The tariff, far from being a help, simply forced the unfortunate farmer to pay more for his manufactured goods. Finally, immigration and the legend of the frontier helped to maintain a persistent land boom in the trans-Mississippi West, and by 1886 this had become a speculative frenzy, while the persistent demand for mortgages kept rates of interest constantly rising. By 1890 there were as many mortgages in Kansas, Nebraska, Minnesota and the Dakotas as there were families, and between 1880 and 1900 the number of farmers who did not own their farms at all rose from a quarter to a third of the whole; farm failures led to the collapse of the mortgage system and a drop even in land prices. The farmer, in the Cotton Belt as well as on the Plains, had been the victim of both rising costs and falling prices for his commodities, for his transport was (in large part necessarily) dear and he had difficulties in switching crops quickly; when in 1893 industrial slump was added to drought, erosion, frost, flood and locusts and the like, his situation seemed without hope. But soon the tide turned; higher rainfall years began again in 1897; the American population began to match farm acreage better, and so over-supply diminished; prices for both produce and land rose; and the relation between income and fixed charges improved. American agriculture indeed entered, for the first time for thirty years, a prolonged period of prosperity which was to continue nearly to the First World War.

What really saved the farmer was the swelling domestic market, truly national for the first time with the coming of the railroads. In fact his position was in the long run improved by one of the commanding features of this period, the 'rise of the city'. It transformed the United States from a predominantly farming – almost Jeffersonian – nation to one in which by 1920 more than half the people lived in cities, and especially great cities. Thus by 1900 there were more than thirty-six cities with populations over 100,000. This growth of urban centres was made possible not merely by the development of industry and the expansion of agriculture itself, but also by mass migration.

The population of the United States nearly trebled in fifty years, from 31½ million in 1860 to almost 92 million in 1910; between 1850 and 1909 immigration added the astonishing total of approximately 25 millions and, in the peak year (1907) alone, reached the fantastic figure of 1,284,349 immigrants. The full effects of this development on agriculture were only felt in the new century, and during its first decade immigration reached its all-time peak. Immigrants did not only help to consume, but to produce, for they provided a huge pool of unskilled labour, without which industrial expansion could never have proceeded so fast. Skilled labour, recruited from the ranks of older immigrant and native American stocks, did not object to this flood of newcomers so long as industrial growth continued and lifted them up the economic ladder with it. A growing proportion of immigrants went to the cities, and, being drawn increasingly from South and East Europe, many were probably less literate and educated than some of their predecessors from Germany and Scandinavia, though their economic absorption was scarcely such a problem as that of the Irish in mid-century. Their rootlessness, however, added to the difficulties of this unprecedented problem of urbanisation, which raised the proportion of the American people living in cities from 15 per cent in 1850 to 46 per cent in 1910. The problem was, of course, world-wide but was peculiarly novel in the United States (where in 1800 only one person in ten lived in a town of more than 1,000 inhabitants) and also grew peculiarly fast there (in 1831 Chicago was a tiny trading post, but by 1900 had 1,700,000 citizens). The city, naturally, with its augmenting amenities of all kinds for better living, was far from an unmixed evil, as can most readily be seen by a glance at the obverse of the coin, the poor and harsh, even sometimes degraded and desperate, conditions of life on the farm, especially in the South and the West. Nevertheless the political and social problems in these new urban agglomerations –

transportation, housing, sanitation, amenities, crime – were certainly formidable.

They were in their nature not readily, if at all, soluble by any other agency than government, which was as reluctant to extend its power to grapple with them in the city as it was in the country. In practice, it is true, business men were willing enough to accept such things as land grants and tariff protection from the Federal government, in violation of classical extremes of *laissez-faire* but they violently rejected any suggestion that their activities should be regulated by the government. Individual enterprise, indeed, ('unhindered' by the state) in which American belief had never been weak, understandably attracted an even more passionate faith among many Americans as a result of its almost incredible contemporary feats in industry: this was the epoch in which Horatio Alger's heroes, rising from rags to riches by their own unaided efforts, became the cynosure of American boyhood. Fact was even stranger than fiction, to take just one instance, in the career of the penniless Scotch immigrant, Andrew Carnegie, who rose from a bobbin boy to become the greatest steel master in America, owning more than 50 per cent of the $160 million of capital stock of his giant firm in 1900. Small wonder that faith in individual enterprise, which seemed so splendidly to deliver the practical goods, was deep and persuasive.

Laissez-faire also acquired much theoretical support in these years. Even such an exponent of the intervention of government by a high tariff as the economist-sociologist, Henry Carey, had believed, in the words of his biographer, in a 'dog-eat-dog individual competition within national boundaries.' Social Darwinism now preached the survival of the fittest in society as well as nature, and was taken to imply a ruthless individualism; in William Graham Sumner, the political economist, American capitalism, with its overwhelming primary emphasis on the sanctity of property, found a popular, if not perhaps very profound, prophet. More than this, so widespread did the doctrine become that it dominated the judiciary and the Supreme Court itself, in these days of Mr. Justice Field. Turning to this purpose the Fourteenth Amendment – 'nor shall any State deprive any person of life, liberty *or property*, [my italics] without due process of law' – much of the apparatus of Federal law came to support the non-intervention of the government in economic affairs. This was what led Mr. Justice Holmes (himself an admirer of the greatest exponent of Social Darwinism) to remark that 'the fourteenth amendment does not enact Mr. Herbert Spencer's Social Statics.' *Laissez-faire* was thus an even more unchallenged doctrine in the late nineteenth century in the United States than in the United Kingdom.

Even the nascent labour movement, in contrast with that of Europe, had very largely to accept industrial capitalism on pretty much these, the industrial captains' own, terms; certainly labour relations in these years were a Darwinian jungle. The Homestead strike of 1892 ended in a pitched battle between the steel workers and a strike-breaking force from the Pinkerton detective agency, but the warlike victory availed labour little, for an attempt by a young anarchist to assassinate the President of the Carnegie Company, Henry C. Frick, alienated public sympathy and state militia broke the strike. The Pullman Car Company strike in 1894 was perhaps the gravest in American history, being finally broken by Federal troops dispatched by President Cleveland at the behest of his Attorney-General, Richard Olney, against the wishes of the Governor of Illinois. In 1900 the Industrial Commission concluded that strikes and lock-outs were far more prevalent in America than in other industrialised countries, and this remained so for many years to come. In the face of mass immigration, it was feared that similar violence was spreading into the political arena: in the Haymarket Riot of 1886 in Chicago seven police officers were killed by a bomb and more than sixty people injured, mostly police; and this was ascribed to anarchists and foreign agitators.

What was interesting was the reluctance of labour to use its political power to call in the state to aid it; the first great labour movement in American history, that of the Knights of Labor under Terence V. Powderly, which flourished in the seventies and eighties, was a diffuse and over-ambitious attempt to bring all the workers of the nation under one umbrella. It suffered, like all early American labour organisations, from the fact that the country was still more than half rural, with the farmers not only (for the most part) property owners but deeply suspicious of anything rooted in the 'wicked cities', from which no good could come. Marxism and socialism were less weak at this time, when the proportion of foreign born in the United States was at its height, than at any subsequent period – in the presidential election of 1912 Eugene V. Debs, the Socialist candidate, polled nearly 5 per cent of the ballots cast – but they never appealed to more than a very small minority. Characteristically, the first really successful labour movement in the United States was the essentially practical American Federation of Labor, a national federation of craft unions formed in 1886, which fell in time almost completely under the control of its first president, Samuel Gompers. In the end it came to confine its activities largely to the improvement of wages and working conditions in each industry, though at first it had made certain political demands and still had such things as the eight-hour day in its economic platform in 1918. Above all it eschewed revolutionary, and even radical, politics; in other words labour tended tacitly to accept for many years the basic belief of industrial capitalism that the state should not interfere unnecessarily with the free play of the 'natural' forces of the economy, but insisted that in each industry labour should be recognised as one of these forces.

In the end, indeed, liberal intellectual protest against the economic system in some directions outran that of labour, while the most insistent voice of dissent was that of the farmers. For before long, despite the actual productive triumphs of industry, the system began to arouse deep misgivings, not merely on account of its quite unprecedented and alarming scale, as well as its ruthlessness, but also because of its tendency to concentrate enormous wealth and power in a few hands, and in fact to move towards the quasi-absolute power of monopoly. The contrast between the ostentatious and conspicuous consumption – Thorstein Veblen published the *Theory of the Leisure Class* in 1904 – of the newly rich and the condition (albeit better than elsewhere) of the urban masses called attention to this, but what began to offend even some traditionalist Americans was that it made a mockery of democratic equality of opportunity and ran counter to the cherished doctrines of free enterprise of even the supporters of the system. Thus in 1901 Carnegie, by selling his own steel holdings, made possible the completion of the great edifice of the United States Steel Corporation, dominated by J. P. Morgan, the banker; this probably avoided an economic war of the nine main existing steel producers. U.S. Steel had a capitalisation of $1,400,000,000 (a quarter of the total estimated national wealth of the United States in 1800) and by 1924 was producing half the pig-iron and rails and nearly all the barbed and fencing wire in the United States. Yet Carnegie was a very human being and a founder of modern philanthropy: the impact of the career of John D. Rockefeller on the public mind brought him much closer to the image of the 'robber barons' of this early industrial era.

Carnegie had consolidated his industry vertically in the first instance, so that he came to control all the processes of steel production – ore, shipping, railroads, coke, steel, by-products. Rockefeller with his Standard Oil Company, formed in 1870, at first expanded horizontally, that is by ruthless cut-throat competition which drove many of his competitors out of business, so that he nearly established something like a total monopoly of the oil industry. (By the end of the century, however, new fields at home and abroad were lessening the firm's hold.) With no doubt unconscious irony, the legal form in which monopolies of this kind operated utilised the traditional concept of the 'trust', which had not only a beneficent sound but a vagueness which helped to evade the growing criticism. Stockholders of twenty-seven companies, covering all branches of oil production, made over their holdings to three trustees to 'hold, control and manage' for the exclusive benefit of the persons named in the agreement. When the pace of competition with the trust drove out small rivals, it was claimed that efficiency was keeping prices down, but there is little doubt that the monopolistic tendencies of the trusts enabled them later on to increase their profits and to exercise appreciable power over prices, especially before 1900.

But consolidation must not be confused with monopoly, nor enormous corporations with trusts: bigness alone is not necessarily bad, for a few giants can compete effectively with one another, and there also grew up the 'countervailing power' of the great distributive agencies (Woolworth's developed in the 1880s and Sears Roebuck, the mail order firm, in the 1890s). The increasing scale of American industry also owed much to the development of scientific management in these years, for in truth the vast expansion of American business enterprises in the nineteenth century arose from two contradictory forces, one of firms expanding to improve efficiency, the other of firms expanding to destroy competitors, thus for a while eliminating the need for greater efficiency. The huge size of the American market; the tremendous resources of the subcontinent; the energetic drive of business; the skill of the American people; and the freedom, combined with a modicum of order, of the American political system led to the unprecedented development of mass production by the first decade of the twentieth century, especially in the new automobile industry.

Despite the growing outcry against trusts and monopolies, which was far louder than any counterpart in Europe (home of cartels in the early twentieth century), the financial needs of industrial growth put more and more power in the hands of the financiers; the proportion of national income devoted to investment rose to a peak of 16 per cent from 1889–98, and as a result the national product increased 25 per cent from 1899–1908. Indeed, some industrial leaders began to lose control to these 'finance capitalists' around the turn of the century, though others (like Rockefeller) converted themselves from 'production' to 'paper' men. Here the typical figure was J. Pierpont Morgan of New York, who had first entered industry to salvage railroad lines in difficulties, beginning in 1879 with the New York Central, of which he became a Director. This pattern was reinforced by the ability to supply new money for expansion, and in the end his part in U.S. Steel gave him a dominating position; thenceforward, as it was said, in any board of which he was a member, where J. P. Morgan sat was the head of the table. This greater power he used responsibly, unlike some of his predecessors (such as Jay Gould), and American industry gained a great deal from the channelling of long-term capital to it; the money probably did much to speed rationalisation and the establishment of expensive new industries like electricity. Careers such as his led to an ultimate national tendency towards consolidation between different industries, the final stage of finance capitalism; Cochran and Miller write, by '1907 a few financial titans like Morgan, Rockefeller, Baker, Stillman, Schiff, Warburg, the Guggenheims and Ryan had gained dominant positions in the directorates of most of the key enterprises in the land.'

It was not only economic power that they wielded, for they had great influence over the whole life of the United States; some contemporaries believed, and were followed in the belief by a generation of historians, that, in the words of Morison and Commager (in one of the most influential short histories of the United States, published in 1937), 'Politics was largely a Punch and Judy show, but though the puppets and even the voices changed, the hands that held the strings were the same. Business ran politics, and politics was a branch of business.' The 'titular leaders', the politicians, were sometimes manipulated by these 'real rulers', but more often all that was necessary was to insist that the good old rule – that the Federal government keep its hands off – be applied; the States were all too frequently powerless, even if willing, to intervene because the massive new industries were not only protected by the courts under the Fourteenth Amendment, but far outran the physical jurisdiction of the States and had in many cases financial and political strength superior to that of the State governments. Even in the spheres where the responsibilities of the government were clear and incontrovertible, business interests often got their way in the late nineteenth century, though 'business' was never a monolithic force and was often divided as to what it wanted. Thus, despite real efforts by President Cleveland to lower tariffs and despite what appears to the European the anomaly of a huge budget surplus in the 1880s (which seemed to many a standing invitation to 'extravagance of the pork barrel and pension grab variety'), the

McKinley tariff of 1890 made protective duties for industry higher and more comprehensive than ever before. Similarly, almost unnoticed because of the relative cheapness of silver at the time, the United States had in 1873 demonetised silver and undertaken to redeem its obligations in gold, thus conforming to the dominant international custom, led by Britain, of maintaining the gold standard, which pleased many in business. The silver question, of which we shall hear more, was a new one, but the 'Greenback' movement, pledged to prevent the deflationary currency policy of withdrawing the paper money issued during the war, was in the accepted American political tradition and was much more successful; it halted the process of currency deflation, and the green dollar bills, made redeemable in gold, remained in circulation, largely because Greenbackism was a farmers' movement which was able to muster a million votes in the elections of 1878.

It was not until the new century that the voice of urban protest became really insistent; the late nineteenth was the heyday of the political 'machines', especially in the cities, and of the professional politicians who ran them or depended on them – those who lived by, and moved and had their being in, politics – Conkling, Platt and Hill of New York; Randall, Cameron and Quay of Pennsylvania; Hanna, Foraker and Brice of Ohio. Because there 'were no clearly defined issues between the major parties', during 'this period the electorate played a game of blind man's buff. Never before had American politics been so intellectually bankrupt.' Since there were no apparent moral issues, the customary American political appeal to economic interest in all branches of politics was strengthened; this went on in the very core of political life with the intensification of the Jacksonian 'spoils system' in the distribution of political office. The severity of this problem is dramatised by the fact that President Garfield was assassinated by a disappointed officer seeker in 1881; his predecessor Hayes had stood out against corruption and his successor, Chester A. Arthur, himself a machine politician, rather surprisingly (it is a tribute to the intense moral effect of the White House upon its occupants) supported the passage of the Pendleton Civil Service Reform Bill. This began a long process of reform, so that a start was made with entry by competitive examination and so that by the 1920s some 60 per cent of Federal civil servants (300,000 out of 500,000) enjoyed security of tenure. In 1936 the figure was some 500,000 out of 800,000, and at the present time about 90 per cent of Federal employees fall into this category. A far richer source of Federal, especially Republican, patronage was the granting in the end of virtually universal pensions to veterans of the

Civil War; and even the Democrat Cleveland was able to do little to staunch this flow of money from the public purse.

It was not, however, only in this very public way that political support could be purchased. At a time when social services at any level of government were virtually unknown, the herds of immigrants in the great urban centres – bewildered, often ignorant of the language, totally untutored in politics – were sitting targets for the political machines; a vote was a very cheap price to pay for a bucket of coal in winter distress, perhaps a little extra food at Christmas, and above all a job when unemployed. Nor was this only a base contrivance, for the real humanity of many a 'ward politician' led often to a lifetime of political loyalty, and could be the beginnings of an education in the difficult arts of democracy. The appeal was not only material: the machines appealed, too, to the national blocs of immigrant votes; sticking close, naturally, to their fellow countrymen in their new homes, sometimes clannish by nature like the Irish, whole cities acquired a racial character (there were, it was said, more Poles in Buffalo than in any city in the world except Warsaw). The 'play' for the 'immigrant vote'– the German vote in Milwaukee, the Italian vote in New York, and the Jewish vote in a number of places – was a game played at the highest political level. It is never quite clear how effective it was in gaining actual support for political parties, but it was one of the few ways in which a consciousness of the outside world entered the political life of the United States in the late nineteenth century. Behind, for instance, the frequent and passionate Anglophobia of American politics at this time there often lay the political feelings, and skill, of the Irish, who, because partly of their knowledge of English (as well as the English), early came to exercise great influence in such bodies as the trades unions and the Roman Catholic Church.

Essentially, however, in political as well as economic life, America was in these years remarkably isolated from international affairs; and during this separation from the outside world became a power so great that inevitably her strength would soon have broken the bonds of her isolation. By mid-century her economy had reached what W. W. Rostow has called the take-off point, and by 1910, despite the industrial cycle of booms and slumps (such as the desperate depression of 1873), it was not only in full flight but had become in many ways the foremost in the world. The dependence of the United States on European investment had declined rapidly, though she was till a net debtor nation; in 1914 American investment abroad amounted to $3½ billion compared with just over $7 billion of foreign capital invested in America. But she had long been a 'mature debtor' nation, whose visible balance of trade had only been adverse in seven years between 1870 and 1900, and had never been unfavourable since that time. It only needed the cataclysm of the First World War to make her the world's greatest international creditor.

Chapter 14

Populism and Progressivism

N OT ONLY WAS the United States politically isolated from the rest of the world in the late nineteenth century, but its administrations, democratic though they might be in theory, were in a sense isolated from some increasingly potent elements of American public opinion at home. The domination of wealth and the corrupt tone of public life, especially where numbers were greatest, in the big cities, meant that the American people – inhibited also by the *laissez-faire* doctrines which seemed to have made possible the staggering, if unequally distributed, growth in the productivity of the nation – were slow to use the political power which their democracy gave them to remedy abuses and to employ the power of the state to better the relative economic condition of large sections of the population. Partly because the phenomenon of industrialism, despite the English experience, was so strange and so genuinely difficult to comprehend, even the most vigorous national leader to hold the Presidency between 1877 and 1901, Grover Cleveland, merely scraped the surface of the problem, except perhaps in his ultimately unavailing efforts to lower the level of the tariff. But in time (as was probably inevitable in a world where, to some extent impelled by the logic of events, socialist and Marxist ideas of state ownership – and, a *fortiori*, control – of industry and of the economy were rising high enough to lap even the distant shores of the land of the free) growing American discontent led to the assertion of the power of the Federal government in the social and economic life of the United States.

Nor must the degree of *laissez-faire*, even at this date, be exaggerated, for some States were soon active in economic regulation, while the Federal government itself was early under pressure in the spheres where it had inevitable economic functions to perform, such as the regulation of the currency. In the election of 1880 General James Baird Weaver ran as a Greenback candidate, not without success in the country areas; the farmers, who were strongest in the West and South, were indeed to form the hard core of political protest for the next twenty years, thus illustrating once more the powerful tendency in American political life for issues of principle to be inextricably associated with the support of the various geographical sections. Jacksonian Democracy had been, as was natural in an agricultural society, overwhelmingly rural; this new popular movement, which culminated in the formation of the Populist party, although it made serious efforts to appeal to the great new urban areas, was still fundamentally a farmers' affair.

Indeed, as for a period in the history of Britain half a century before, these years in America can perhaps be best understood in terms of the rivalry between the country and the mushrooming cities. Populist propaganda might be redolent of something which sounded like the class war ('From the . . . prolific womb of government injustice we breed two classes – tramps and millionaires', declared the 1892 Platform) and might cry out to the workers of the cities in the same manifesto ('That the Union of labor forces of the United States this day consummated shall be permanent and perpetual . . . The interests of rural and civil labor are the same. . .') but little real urban support was, or was likely to be, forthcoming, on grounds of principle, for a party whose Presidential candidate four years later – and for that period its foremost leader – William Jennings Bryan, was to declare, 'the great cities rest upon our broad and fertile prairies. Burn down your cities and leave our farms, and your cities will spring up again as if by magic; but destroy our farms and the grass will grow in the streets of every city in the country.' As Samuel Gompers saw, 'composed, as the People's Party is, mainly of *employing* farmers without any regard to the interests of the *employed* farmers of the country districts or the mechanics and laborers of the industrial centres', it could not become a workingmen's party. Not until the coming of what was called Progressivism, in the era of Theodore Roosevelt and Woodrow Wilson, was the industrialisation of the United States to result in the actual rise of a powerful urban radical movement.

Populism thus arose out of the farmer's grievances. But, though it had a Jeffersonian air, its problems derived from the fact that farming had now become a commercial, almost industrial, enterprise; as Carl N. Degler has phrased it, 'Populism was at once the last gasp of the agrarian myth and the coming of age of the farmer as businessman.' It set the twentieth-century pattern of a farm bloc looking always to government for practical aid. The chief farm grievance was the decline of prices, due both to overproduction and foreign competition and also to what the farmers regarded as the artificial barriers to the sale of their products in the expanding industrial areas. They resented especially the barrier of the railroad mono-

polies, at whose mercy they were; they considered railroad practices, such as differential rates and free passes, inequitable, but
though these were levied largely at the expense of the farming communities, it was perhaps as much an inevitable result of distance and
dispersal as of the unfair use of their monopoly position by the railroad companies. In the West the burden of farm debt made these
difficulties immense, and in the South, where special post-war
conditions of lack of capital had led to the by-now deep rooted
practices of share-cropping and the crop-lien system, the extent of
the indebtedness of farmers, both white and black, was even worse.
This was also a period of deflation, with a steady rise in the value of
money, so that the burden of debt increased; this deflation was
almost, if not quite, as much the result of currency policy as of excess
of agricultural supply, for, despite the rapid expansion of the
economy, there was no corresponding expansion of the circulating
medium. The shortage of currency was alleviated by the growth of
the use of bank accounts and cheques, but this did not keep pace
with economic development, and the overall shortage in money
supply remained grave; indeed there was some contraction of the
almost $2 million of currency which had been in circulation in
1865. It was for this reason that the issue of bimetallism came to
supersede the problem of the Greenbacks and that it became the
main plank in the Populist platform; but in the long run much the
most important aspect of the movement was that it saw and believed
(thus continuing an important American tradition) that currency
was not an act of God but an act of state, and demanded that the
government act in such a way as to suit the interests of the impoverished farmer.

The demonetisation of silver – the 'crime of '73' – had taken place
at almost exactly the moment when it would have become profitable,
on the old bimetallic basis of the currency, to sell silver to the
government; in fact the Act of 1873 had simply made no provision
for the coinage of silver dollars, but the great silver-producing
interests of the American West, centring in the region around
Colorado, depicted it as a crime of the eastern financiers, whom the
farmers deeply mistrusted, and of the British supporters of the gold
standard, which appealed widely to Anglophobe elements in
American life. This conjunction of a vested economic interest –
silver production – and deep farm discontent with the contracting
currency, both of which were strongest in the plains of the West, is
a classic example of sectionalism in the politics of the United States,
and it gave an intense impulse to the clamorous demand for the
free and unlimited coinage of silver at a ratio of 16 to 1 of gold,

which was in a sense to dominate American radical thought for the next twenty years. In 1878 the silver men gained, over President Hayes's veto, the Bland-Allison Act, under which the government had to purchase a minimum of $2 million of silver a month, but this did not appreciably increase the per capita currency in circulation. Silver production continued to increase (from $36 million in 1873 to $57 million by 1890) and in 1889–90 six new Western States were admitted to the Union, so that the silver bloc became extremely powerful in the Senate. In 1890 the Sherman Silver Purchase Act laid down that the government must buy 4½ million ounces of silver a month with Treasury notes, redeemable in gold or silver, 'it being the established policy of the United States to maintain the two metals on a parity with each other upon the present ratio.'

This was neither the gold standard nor the free and unlimited coinage of silver, but it seemed to contribute to the constant drain on the gold reserves of the Federal government which developed during the slump of 1893. Cleveland's belief in gold led him to insist to a special session of Congress in 1893 on the repeal of the Sherman law as the only remedy for this government insolvency, but the accomplishment of the repeal in October irretrievably split the Democratic Party before the election of 1896, in which free silver became the key, if not the sole, popular issue. In fact, this curious theme soon disappeared from the national scene, at least until the Great Depression, with the steady growth, in succeeding years, of the world production of gold (from $100 million in 1890 to $300 million in 1899). In 1900 the United States quietly went fully on the gold standard, although the American government to this day in effect subsidises the silver industry, and silver dollars still circulate in the West. But bimetallism may perhaps be seen in a different light after our further half-century of experience with the industrial cycle; there appears to be a case for arguing that the dominant gold standard – bullionist – concept of money was already quite inadequate and that in the deep depression which began in 1893 the freer coinage of silver might well have been a way of promoting re-expansion, even at the price of inflation.

The excessive concentration on the silver issue was unfortunate for the many other causes that the Populists had at heart, some of them springing from the second main root of Populism, the farmers' organisations – principally the Patrons of Husbandry, or Granges, which flourished in the 1870s and the Farmers' Alliances which succeeded them in the 1880s. Though the Granges were ostensibly non-political, they were influential in efforts by the farmers to control the grosser railroad abuses and they formed a number of farmers' co-operatives which were not very successful; the North West Alliance and the Southern Alliance were overtly political and became a leading element in the Populist movement. But meanwhile the embattled farmers had had a few successes, as for example in the control of railroads within their borders by such states as Kansas and Illinois, whose legislation was broadly upheld by the Supreme Court (in the so-called Granger cases of 1876), 'when private property is affected with a public interest.' In the next decade, however, the climate of opinion changed, with the rise of industrialism and Social Darwinism, and in the late 1880s the Court virtually reversed itself and in effect invalidated State regulation. Nevertheless, political pressure did not relax, and in 1887 Congress passed the Interstate Commerce Act which prohibited certain practices and also set up the first modern American federal administrative regulatory agency, the Interstate Commerce Commission. This body was intended to undertake continuous supervision of the railroad industry, in which the traditional idea of competition as an automatic regulator of prices and restraint upon monopoly was now plainly implausible. But the idea was so novel that the Court still continued to review cases, almost always deciding against the Commission, and by 1898 this agency itself confessed its failure.

The People's party was actually formed in 1891; its forerunners were the Granges and the Alliances, the Greenbackers and free silverites, the Knights of Labor and a number of other and more esoteric groups. In 1892 they ran Weaver as their candidate, and he received thirty-two electoral votes, the first third-party candidate to break into the Electoral College since the Civil War. He did best on the whole where his ticket was 'fused' with that of the Democrats, and this fusion sentiment developed rapidly, so that when in 1896 the Democratic Party, their convention swept by the silverite enthusiasm evoked in a famous speech by the young William Jennings Bryan of Nebraska, nominated the latter as their candidate, the Populist convention had little option but to follow suit. But they showed their independence by rejecting the conservative Democrat Sewall of Maine for the Vice-Presidential nomination, and choosing the radical Tom Watson of Georgia. Bryan fought the Republican William McKinley in one of the fiercest of presidential campaigns, but he concentrated excessively on the silver issue which had aroused such passion among his followers, as he had done in his convention peroration; 'we will answer their demand for a gold standard by saying to them: You shall not press down upon the brow of labor this crown of thorns, you shall not crucify mankind upon a cross of gold.' In large part as a result, he was defeated by

7 to 6½ million votes, and this in a real sense marked the end, not only of an effective Populist party, but also of an era, in which the United States had been a predominantly agricultural nation: it signalised in a manner the final triumph of Hamilton over Jefferson.

Populism, however, though it followed the classic pattern for the failure of American third parties, absorption by one of the big two, can by no means be accounted a total failure, although not very many Populists attained office even at State level and those who did jeft a meagre legislative and administrative legacy. It may be better ludged by its effect on the subsequent political history of the United States; and this, basically because the Populists followed the advice of one of their most vigorous leaders, Mary Ellen Lease, 'to raise less corn and more hell', was very considerable. The declared Populist aims of 1892 can be considered as the first modern political programme in the United States. It demanded, among other things, (1) an increase in the circulating medium to $50 per head, (2) the graduated income tax, (3) government ownership of railroads, telephones and telegraphs, (4) effective labour organisation and an eight hour day, (5) the restriction of immigration, (6) the prohibition of alien land ownership, (7) post office savings banks, (8) a single Presidential term, (9) the Australian (or official, as well as secret) ballot, (10) the direct popular election of Senators (instead of their appointment by State legislatures), (11) the referendum and the initiative (or referendum on popular rather than governmental initiative), and (12) government credit for farmers. Of these there has been no progress in the direction of only one, (6); there has been very limited progress in the direction of (3), by increasing regulation of railroads, and some progress in the direction of (8), by the restriction of the President to two terms in office; and there has been very substantial progress in the direction of (1) and (4), as well as (11) (these electoral procedures exist in many states). All the remainder, (5), (7), (9) and (12), and also (2) and (10), have been fully implemented – the last two by constitutional amendment. This was a remarkable achievement, and is to be explained in great degree by the fact that the Elisha of Progressivism was ready and waiting to assume the cloak of the Populist Elijah.

Thus as Eric Goldman expressed it in 1952, in 'many fundamentals progressivism continued Populism'; this was not only because Populism had had a number of forward-looking policies, but also because Progressivism was at bottom in the same liberal, democratic American tradition. But it was primarily urban rather than rural in character. As Degler has it seven years later, 'Though

the Progressives were overwhelmingly city men and dealing with
urban problems, they espoused ideals developed in an earlier and
rural period of the nation's history . . . Progressivism . . . against the
backdrop of an earlier era of American thought was but a latter-day
Jeffersonianism.' It was, too, a somewhat more amorphous movement than the People's Party, for the Progressive Party of 1912 did
not get the support of many – even most – genuine progressives, and
that of 1948 was chiefly concerned with the very different issue of
foreign policy. Yet in a real sense the 'New Nationalism' of Theodore
Roosevelt in 1912 was more 'progressive' than the 'New Freedom'
for which his victorious opponent, Woodrow Wilson, then stood, for
the essence of the continuity between Populism and Progressivism
lay in the willingness of both to extend the sphere of government
action to benefit the majority. Indeed in a number of respects, as
witness the career of the Socialist Mayor of Milwaukee, Emil
Seidel, some Progressives were prepared to go much farther in
strengthening the hand of government, against the will of *laissez-
faire* doctrinaires, than the considerable distance their successors
have actually gone. This was perhaps mainly because of the dramatic
extremes of ostentatious wealth and – by American standards –
grinding poverty in these raw early days of industrialism. But, like
Asquithian Liberalism, and for the most part Fabianism, in Britain
(and also like the farmers' movements which preceded it in America),
Progressivism was largely middle class in composition; it was predominantly the party of the small business man, although it appealed
rather more successfully than Populism to the urban working class.

Progressives were concerned with the whole spectrum of abuses
and anomalies and social problems facing the United States (as they
have mostly faced all other emerging industrial societies) – poverty,
disease, the concentration of economic power in a few hands, the
industrial cycle of boom and slump; they were particularly concerned about political corruption, conservation of natural resources,
slum conditions, crime, child labour, impure food, and vice,
especially in the great cities. Because administrative action required
honest and efficient governments, they continued the Populist
demands for the purification and democratisation of politics, laying
more emphasis on anti-trust action (for the quite broadly drawn
Sherman Anti-Trust Act of 1890 was very weakly executed) and
specifically demanding women's rights, which followed Populist
practice rather than theory. Their advance-guard consisted of the
journalists, authors and investigators – the so-called 'muckrakers' –
who, in a succession of scalding works, directed the attention of the
American people to the evils of the era.

So wide and varied were the men and opinions with the label Progressive that almost the only way of defining the term is by a 'little list'. Some had moved on from Populism, like the journalist Ignatius Donnelly; the Utopian Socialist Edward Bellamy with his famous *Looking Backward* (1888); and the highly influential Henry George, whose *Progress and Poverty* (1879) demanded the re-creation of free opportunity by a single tax on land rent and who, in effect, attacked the roots of Social Darwinism by pointing out that man, unlike the beasts, could alter the environment in which he lived and deeply influence the struggle for survival. Some were drawn from the churches, like Walter Rauschenbusch with his *Christianity and Social Crisis*, and Father John Augustine Ryan; or from the Universities, like the economist Richard T. Ely (characteristically, from Johns Hopkins and the University of Wisconsin). Some were lawyers, like Oliver Wendell Holmes, Roscoe Pound, Dean of the Harvard Law School, and Louis Brandeis; or like Clarence Darrow, Ben Lindsey, founder of the system of juvenile courts, and J. P. Altgeld, Governor of Illinois and author of *Our Penal Machinery and Its Victims*. Some were historians like the great Charles A. Beard, and Ida M. Tarbell with her *History of the Standard Oil Company*; political scientists like Algie M. Simons; anthropologists like the anti-racist Franz Boas; sociologists like Edward A. Ross with his *Sin and Society*; or philosophers like John Dewey, the powerful figure associated with philosophic Pragmatism. Others were journalists, who were numerous and important; Jacob Riis with *How the Other Half Lives*, William Allen White with *A Certain Rich Man*, Henry Demarest Lloyd, who inaugurated muckraking in *Wealth against Commonwealth* (1894), and Lincoln Steffens, greatest of the muckrakers, with his *Shame of the Cities*. Yet others were novelists – some of the most striking in American literature – Hamlin Garland, Upton Sinclair, Stephen Crane, Frank Norris, and Theodore Dreiser.

In politics below the Federal level two figures might be singled out as symbolic of the Progressives; Tom Johnson, a Henry Georgeite, who was reforming Mayor of Cleveland, Ohio, from 1901–9 and the leader of the city reform movement in the United States, which evolved new plans for the efficient conduct of municipal affairs, like the 'city manager' and 'city commission' schemes to take administration 'out of politics' and put it in the hands of 'efficient organisers', such as men who had started their careers in business. Robert M. La Follette Sr. not only was to State government what Johnson was to City, but was the Grand Old Man of Progressivism, whose long career in the pioneer progressive state of Wisconsin most fully embodied the spirit and aims of the movement. It was in the states

in fact that the Progressives achieved most, at least at first. By the
First World War 20 states (mostly in the West) had the initiative and
referendum and 10 the recall, by which elected officials could be
forced by petition to face the electorate before the expiration of their
normal fixed term in office. By 1914 all states but 1 had regulations
concerning the age, and often conditions, of child labour, and 11 had
votes for women; widespread State support of the aged was beginning, and by 1920 all but 5 had adopted accident insurance systems,
while there were corrupt practices Acts in most states. La Follette
had been elected Governor of Wisconsin in 1900, but in 1906 he
moved to the Senate in Washington, just when Progressive ideas
were beginning to have real effect at the Federal level.

Characteristic was the growth of the primary election system,
operating through the States but deeply affecting national politics.
It arose at bottom because the open convention method of selecting
party candidates to run for office – ironically, like the closed caucus
system before it – came to fall more and more into the hands of the
professional (including many machine) politicians, largely as a
result of the cumbersome size and relative infrequency of conventions. Since professionals tended always to be identified with the
status quo, it was radicals and reformers who pressed for the 'only
democratic' system of choosing party candidates to run for office, the
'direct' primary election (as opposed to the old, simple primary to
choose electors to nominate party candidates). In the Southern
States, where victory in the Democratic primary election was tantamount to final election, because Republicans were virtually never
elected, the primary became of the first importance and was often
a genuine battlefield between radical and conservative policies; thus
even in the monolithic, one-party system of the South real contests
of principle (except on the race question), can take place, which is,
as Sir Denis Brogan has pointed out, a tribute to the extraordinary
political ingenuity of the American people.

They showed this ingenuity, too, in the general development of
the primary system, from its exclusive control by the parties (when
it proved almost if not quite as liable to fall into corrupt or at least
'professional' hands as the convention system) to its public control
by the State, which could ensure fair practices. Indeed, in their
search for democratic processes, they went so far as to abolish in
certain states even the requirement that those voting in party
primaries should be members of that party; the 'closed' direct
primary, in which only Democrats could vote in the Democratic
primary and only Republicans in the Republican, was also found to
be susceptible to professional influence, even when organised by the

State, and so, for example, at one time in California and Washington, the 'open' primary replaced it, under which the voter could vote in either party primary. The candidate, too, in California could then 'cross-file', and win (as Governor Earl Warren was wont to do before he became Chief Justice) both Democratic and Republican nominations in the primaries – which are, as it were, 'heats' – and then in effect run against himself in the 'finals' – and, naturally, be elected without difficulty! It is in such extreme cases as these 'blanket' or 'free-for-all' primaries that the zeal of the American people for reform seems to have led them to give excessively free rein to their remarkable ingenuity. By 1916, at any rate, all save three states had some form of direct primary, but recently their number has declined notably. The convention system still prevails to-day in the great quadrennial Presidential nominating conventions of the parties, though the delegates to these are sometimes bound by the results of preliminary primaries in certain states.

The first President to be markedly influenced by Progressive ideas was Theodore Roosevelt, and he was a leader of dynamic quality. Able, ebullient, priding himself on his physical toughness, and with a resolution that merged into ruthlessness, he was a 'gentleman', Harvard-educated and with a real knowledge both of biology and of history, especially naval history and the history of the West, of which he had practical experience. But in his nearly two terms in the White House (he succeeded President McKinley after his assassination in 1901) his specific accomplishments in domestic policy were limited, although, as in his previous career – for example as Governor of New York – he proved an excellent administrator, and did much to encourage the idea of an increase in executive power, especially in economic affairs. He managed in the Hepburn Act of 1906 to get the Interstate Commerce Commission endowed with effective control over railroad rates, thus setting a pattern of continuing Federal administrative regulation for many spheres; he inaugurated efficient Federal control of drugs and food purity; he promoted, for example in the District of Columbia, legislation on workmen's compensation, on child labour and on factory inspection; and he intervened, with beneficial results for labor, in the bitter anthracite strike of 1902. But, though he denounced 'malefactors of great wealth' and believed firmly 'that all corporations engaged in inter-state commerce should be under the supervision of the national government,' he in fact achieved less in the Courts in the way of actual anti-trust decisions than his less belligerent and increasingly conservative successor, William Howard Taft.

His real domestic importance (and his chief enduring impact on America was probably in foreign policy, where perhaps his heart really was also) lay in the change which he effected in public opinion about politics. His achievement in liberalising, even if to a limited degree, his own Republican party, which had become increasingly the party of the Right, was considerable, but perhaps more remarkable was the change he wrought, by his example, in the tone and ability of American politicians, and especially of American Presidents. The greatest British student of American affairs, James Bryce, wrote in his masterpiece *The American Commonwealth*, published in 1888, a chapter entitled 'Why Great Men are Not Chosen Presidents', and gave as his principal reason that the best men in the community despised politics. No man did more to change that than 'T.R.'. And partly because, as J. M. Blum writes, he 'was by personality incapable of believing that his best activity was his least activity', that his role should be 'exclusively that of an umpire', he rode the reforming wave in the direction of increasing Federal power, even if he did not create it. And his concrete monuments of political reform would very probably have been greater if he had succeeded in his bid to return to power in 1912.

In 1909 Taft had succeeded him with his blessing, but some disillusion with what he regarded as the new President's weakness and subservience to the conservatives, and a growing restlessness under the spur of his own still youthful and vigorous personal ambition led him to stand against Taft as a Progressive in the election of 1912 when he failed to get the Republican nomination. He had come to accept more and more the necessity of increased government control amidst the great wealth of modern industrial society; he espoused in particular the ideas put forward by Herbert Croly in his *Promise of American Life*, and the 'Square Deal', as he called the programme of his Progressive Party in 1912, went much farther in this direction than he had gone before. This 'Bull Moose' campaign, which T.R. launched with the characteristic sentiment, 'We stand at Armageddon, and we battle for the Lord', aroused enormous enthusiasm among his followers. But the orthodox Republicans, who had always mistrusted him (Mark Hanna, the *alter ego* of McKinley, had greeted the accession of this 'wild man' eleven years before with the words, 'Now look, that damned cowboy is President of the United States'), were not to be won over, and Taft's 3 million votes ensured that Roosevelt with 4 million had let in the Democrat Woodrow Wilson with 6 million.

The measure of T.R.'s radicalism by 1912 is that the platform of this first Democratic President since Cleveland, the 'New Freedom', was in many respects more conservative than the New Nationalism of his Progressive opponents, most of whom were drawn from Republican ranks. Wilson's career, like T.R.'s, was to end in disappointment, but this was to be over international affairs, while his reforms in domestic policy were to be of far greater significance than those of Roosevelt, who, however, left in foreign relations the great legacy of a first-class navy and the Panama Canal. The two men did, however, despite this similarity of career, present a remarkable contrast in character, although Wilson, too, was a gentlemen, a scholar, and a statesman of commanding political ability. But he was a don and a pedagogue, inescapably the professor in politics; his practical political experience – one term as Governor of the little state of New Jersey – was very limited, but his trained mind had long mastered the constitutional and political problems of the United States, on which he was a leading authority. He had in fact deeply studied British constitutional practice, and believed that dynamic presidential leadership should give direction and a sense of legislative responsibility to Congress. He was essentially the moralist, often the didactic moralist, in political life. Roosevelt had believed in power, though he used it in the cause of morality: Wilson believed, as befitted the offspring of a line of Presbyterian ministers, that morality was itself a source, indeed the chief source, of power in human affairs. He characteristically talked of the 'imprudent wilfulness' of T. R. and himself declared, 'The force of America is the force of moral principle.' Finally, whereas T.R. was overtly and warmly emotional in his dealings with men, whom he saw as individuals, Wilson was aloof, and even cold, and had few intimates, saying, 'I have a sense of power in dealing with men collectively which I do not always feel in dealing with them singly.'

It was not, perhaps, surprising that his views at first tended to be conservative, for he was a Virginian and hence, as a Southerner, necessarily a Democrat, while on the race issue, for instance, he never adopted a truly liberal attitude. What was remarkable was that his political development while in office was increasingly progressive. (In this move from right to left he greatly resembled Gladstone, who was such a hero of his that he had had a portrait of him over his desk at the age of sixteen.) Yet it would be a serious oversimplification to relegate the New Freedom to the realms of reaction because it was reluctant to accept the necessity of 'Big' Business. The New Nationalism was a novel and positive Hamiltonian policy of guiding and controlling modern industrialism, out of which such prodigious economic blessings could and did flow. The New Freedom was a traditional and negative Jeffersonian policy of mistrusting monopoly (and even industrialism itself in some degree) and using the power of the Federal government to restrain it and to restore the strength of 'the little man' who had been the backbone of the American economy in the past. It was not unnatural that, when the spirit of Progressivism had affected both parties, the Republican party, which was *par excellence* that of industry, should more readily accept the phenomenon, whereas the Democrats, the heirs of Jackson and Bryan, should attempt at first, Canute-like, to stem the tide.

But within these limits Wilson was a vigorous reformer from his first inauguration. He transformed the constitutional scene by pushing through the most comprehensive legislative programme since the birth of the Republic; this he achieved by constant pressure, even actual attendance, on Congress. (He revived the practice, which had lapsed since President John Adams, of addressing it in person.) His first great, and very necessary, reform was the traditional Democratic one of the tariff; with the newly passed Sixteenth Amendment legalising the income tax, he was able in the Underwood Tariff of 1913 to achieve a striking and long-overdue reduction in the overall rates from 40 to 26 per cent and a considerable extension of the free list. More important, perhaps, and certainly more of an innovation, which showed the power of the progressives, was the sweeping reform of the banking system in the Federal Reserve Act of December 1913. This started as a bill simply to reform public banking, but ended by vastly extending government control; it established twelve privately controlled Federal Reserve Banks, but these were regulated in the public interest by the Federal Reserve Board, and it constituted the best attempt yet to give the country a sound yet flexible currency, along with a system for mobilising banking reserves in case of financial stringency.

During the next three years the President came increasingly under the influence of the liberal lawyer, Louis D. Brandeis, whom he was to appoint to the Supreme Court in 1916, but he still thought at first along his accustomed lines and resisted measures inspired by the New Nationalism. Thus he refused to support a bill granting long-term agricultural credits, although a provision allowing short-term ones had been put in the Federal Reserve Act; and, most significant, the Clayton Anti-Trust Bill of 1914 deliberately did not at first include a clause setting up a powerful Federal trade commission of the kind favoured by Roosevelt. But during the year Brandeis adopted the idea and the President came decisively to support it, so that the Clayton Act and a Federal Trade Commission Act were passed in the fall of 1914. The Commission showed a new acceptance by the President of the idea of co-operating with industry; so much

so that when the anti-Trust programme was softened in the circumstances of the 1914 economic depression, many of his radical
supporters thought that he had 'gone over to business.' The most
vital step, however, was taken by the President on the eve of the
election of 1916 when the Republicans were re-united and it became
clear that he could only win by attracting a substantial number of
Progressive votes. In what appeared a deliberate course of action,
he behaved like a politician as well as an intellectual convert, and
led Congress into the most fundamental Progressive legislation to
date.

Bills were passed authorising long-term rural credits, establishing
workmen's compensation for Federal employees, and forbidding the
shipment in inter-state commerce of goods manufactured in whole or
in part by children under the age of fourteen, or under the age of
sixteen working more than eight hours a day. The last-named Act,
although held unconstitutional by the Supreme Court some years
later, demonstrates very clearly the general potentialities of flexibility
even in the relatively rigid American constitution. Such interference with the 'natural laws' of economics ran flat counter to the
legal manifestations of Social Darwinism which had long dominated
the judiciary and much of the public mind. The powerlessness, on
the face of it, of the Federal government to intervene in this matter
which was so clearly within the jurisdiction of the states was evaded
by the use of the clause in the Constitution which grants to Congress
the power 'To regulate Commerce with foreign Nations, and among
the several States' – and fewer and fewer goods did not at some time
cross a State line. Similarly, the Federal Aid to Highways Act
supplemented state and local with Federal funds for the construction
of highways, thus avoiding doubts as to the constitutionality of
direct action, or expenditure, for such purposes by the Federal
government. During succeeding years this Federal policy of 'matching' local funds was to be one of the most potent instruments for the
extension of Washington's power. By using such means as these it
was not necessary for Progressive legislators to rely on favourable
judicial interpretation of the 'general welfare' clauses of the Constitution, which are to be found in the preamble and, more specifically
important in law, in Section 8 of Article I, authorising Congress to
lay taxes to 'provide for the . . . general Welfare of the United
States'.

To cap his policy, in September 1916, just before the election, the
President intervened decisively on the side of labour in a crisis
threatening the railroad industry, and urged through Congress the
Adamson Act establishing an eight-hour day on all interstate rail-

roads, thus averting the disaster of a national railway strike. These and other measures had their effect in the very closely fought campaign. At first, on election night, it looked as if Charles Evans Hughes, the Republican candidate, had been elected, but when the results from the West came in Wilson had a popular majority of 9,129,606 to 8,538,221 and an electoral majority of 23. He took the mass of Progressive votes and perhaps 300,000 from the Socialists: it was a classic Democratic triumph of the South and West, *plus* just enough urban labour votes to make the difference between victory, and defeat as in 1896. But domestic issues had by no means exclusively dominated the attention of the electorate. The President had also fought on the slogan, 'He kept us out of war.' Within less than a month of his Inauguration the United States was in fact at war with Germany.

Chapter 15

American Isolation and
Anglo-American Friendship, 1861–1914

W HEN THE Civil War began the South pinned much of its
hope on the intervention of France and, more especially,
Great Britain, or at least on their recognition of the
Confederate government, with all the incalculable effects which
such a step might have had. This objective the able Confederate
Secretary of State, Judah P. Benjamin, pertinaciously pursued. The
basis of the overweaning confidence of the Confederates, which
actually led them at first to impose an embargo on the export of
cotton, was best expressed by Senator Hammond of South Carolina
even before secession; 'What would happen if no cotton were
furnished for three years? . . . England would topple headlong and
carry the whole civilized world with her save the South. No, you
dare not make war on cotton . . . Cotton is King.' In fact Britain did
not intervene. Economic distress in Lancashire was made more
bearable by working-class sympathy for the Northern cause, the
cause of anti-slavery and democracy, while upper-class feeling for
the kindred 'aristocracy' of the South never gained control of the
British government's actions.

Palmerston as Prime Minister, despite the seeming willingness of
some of his Cabinet, such as Gladstone, to recognise the Confederacy, was in the end always guided by the military situation, and,
because the North continued to fight, never went beyond the
British government's original and necessary recognition of Southern
belligerency, as opposed to legitimacy, even by offering mediation.
There were a number of naval incidents, largely arising from the
blockade, and two grave crises; the *Trent* affair in 1861, settled by
the Union's return to Britain of two Confederate 'Commissioners'
who had been seized from the British ship of that name on the high
seas, and the *Alabama* case, in which what amounted to the negli-
gence of Lord John Russell as Foreign Secretary allowed this commerce raider, built in Britain, to join the Confederate navy in 1862
and do very great damage to Northern shipping during the rest of

the war. In the general operation of the blockade, which became steadily more effective as the war went on, friction with Britain was considerable, but paradoxically the customary roles of the two countries were completely reversed. The Union, instead of being the world's greatest maritime neutral as in the French wars, was now the leading belligerent, while Britain was in the unaccustomed part of the principal neutral. Thus there was, as usual, Anglo-American conflict over maritime rights, but each side is to be found quoting the precedents more normally heard on the lips of the other. This was not to be without importance when the war situation reverted to the norm of British belligerent, and American neutral, status in 1914.

The Emperor Napoleon III, too, did not in fact offer to mediate, although he considered it quite as seriously as the British government did, nor did he actually intervene in the struggle. But he did something almost as galling to Americans' pride when, taking advantage of their preoccupation with the Civil War, he interfered, for motives of Bonapartist 'glory', in the domestic affairs of Mexico. At the request of a Mexican 'Assembly of Notables', he imposed the rule of the 'Emperor' Maximilian of Hapsburg on a largely unwilling people by force of arms. This not only directly violated the Monroe Doctrine, but touched the very tender spot of American anti-imperialist sentiment. As soon as the war was over, Secretary of State Seward began to apply growing diplomatic pressure to Napoleon (who was finding his expedition very expensive, and increasingly unpopular in France) and this corresponded with the guerilla pressure maintained by the Mexican republican leader Juarez. In November 1865 Seward informed Napoleon that his intervention was 'disallowable and impracticable' and by 1867 the last French soldier had been withdrawn, leaving the well-meaning Maximilian to the fate which he obstinately chose before a Mexican firing-squad, despite the efforts of the Powers (in which Seward joined) to save him. As soon as the hands of the United States ceased to be tied, she had decisively reinforced the Monroe Doctrine as well as her isolation from European affairs.

This isolation, however, as before the Civil War, was marred still by the impingement of Britain on the life of the American continent. In the first flush of Northern military strength and confidence after the war, there was a revival of American desire to annex Britain's largest group of colonies, British North America, and this was augmented when Secretary Seward executed his greatest coup by negotiating the purchase of the vast territory of Alaska from Russia in 1867 for $7 million, an accomplishment obviously of profound significance from the perspective of mid-twentieth century. Senator

Sumner, Chairman of the powerful Senate Foreign Relations Committee, called it 'A visible step in the occupation of the whole North American continent.' During 1866 illicit raids on Canada from the United States by the Irish Fenian Brotherhood (desirous of attacking the British Empire anywhere they could) assumed formidable if not dangerous proportions, but American annexationism, not for the first time, produced exactly the opposite effect to what it intended, by strengthening Canadian fears, and the consequent movement towards Confederation in the separate, self-governing, colonies of British North America. Largely as a result of this threat from its giant neighbour, the Dominion of Canada came into existence with the British North America Act of 1867, comprising at first the provinces of Quebec, Ontario, New Brunswick and Nova Scotia.

But United States opinion still hoped that distant British Columbia might, somehow or other, come within the magic circle of the American Union, thus joining the State of Washington to Alaska and preventing a Canada stretching from the Atlantic clear to the Pacific seaboard. Meanwhile Anglo-American relations were also bedevilled by American claims for compensation from the British government for the depredations of the *Alabama* in the war. In a transparent effort to persuade Britain, in effect, to barter Canada's future for the settlement of these claims, by persuading the British North American Provinces to enter the Union, Sumner added to the 'direct' claims for reparation what came to be called the 'indirect' claims, for the payment of compensation by Britain to the United States for the whole cost of the period by which the actions of the *Alabama* had, in the American view, lengthened the war – an astronomical sum. The ambitions of the Johnson and Grant administrations, albeit unsuccessful (and the latter, to his credit, opposed by Sumner), to acquire the Danish Virgin Islands and Santo Domingo in the Caribbean as American bases, did seem to raise the possibility of a new, and more powerful, wave of sentiment like that of Manifest Destiny in the American people. In fact, however, the acquisition of Alaska was to prove its last great manifestation for many years.

Touchy as the Anglo-American situation was, Britain firmly refused to exercise any pressure on Canada to join the Union, although she would not in all probability have opposed it; and in 1870 Manitoba (despite the close links of its Red River colony with Minnesota), and in 1871 British Columbia, joined the Canadian Confederation, which thus became a continental nation. The United States was to continue permanently to have an independent neighbour on her northern border. At the same time, the now long established tradition of Anglo-American negotiation and arbitration was proving too strong to be broken by the *Alabama* claims, which were submitted to arbitration under the Treaty of Washington of 1871. The Geneva arbitral tribunal, through the individual action of the American delegate, Charles Francis Adams (worthy son and grandson of Presidents of the United States), dropped the indirect claims, which Britain would – perhaps could – never have paid, but in 1872 awarded the United States $15,500,000 for the British government's lack of due diligence. To his credit, after some soul-searching, Prime Minister Gladstone accepted the award, and paid the sum by a cheque which still hangs framed in the Foreign Office as a tribute to the greatest of Anglo-American (and even world) arbitrations.

The Washington Treaty also settled a number of other issues outstanding between the two, or rather three, countries, but these, like the dispute over the fisheries between Canada and the United States, were of minor importance, and chiefly of Canadian concern. The treaty thus set the tone for the next two decades of American foreign policy, in which there were few issues and those there were almost entirely confined to the Western Hemisphere. For American isolation, which was now at its height, had never extended to intra-hemisphere affairs; indeed during this period the umbrella of American policy began to bring the whole of Latin-America more fully under its shadow. This was chiefly the work of James G. Blaine; in his two periods as Secretary of State, he enunciated the doctrine of positive Pan-Americanism. This envisaged a sort of 'elder sister' relationship, as T. A. Bailey points out, between Washington and Latin-America, which was to be principally economic in character. The much publicised First International American Conference of 1889 resulted only in a few bilateral reciprocity agreements, encouraging the exchange of Latin-American raw materials for United States industrial products, and in the ultimate formation of the Pan-American Union, but it did set in train a long series of events which is still in motion today, in the era of Castroism.

From non-American, and especially European, affairs the isolation of the United States in the years after 1872 was remarkably complete. In 1889 Henry Cabot Lodge wrote, 'our relations with foreign nations today fill but a slight place in American politics, and excite generally only a languid interest.' Economically, American dependence on European, and particularly British, capital and commerce decreased rapidly as the industrial self-sufficiency of the United States grew apace, and politically the most serious issue that could be mustered was that over sealing rights in the Bering Sea.

But this isolation could not last long, for the conditions that made it possible were breaking down under the impact of the swift process of Western industrialisation and scientific development, which was revolutionising throughout the earth the speed and quantity of communications by sea as well as by land; the steam-engine had come fully into its own, the telegraph was being followed by the telephone and would be succeeded by the radio, and popular newspapers would soon inaugurate the era of mass communication. This breakdown of American isolation was only a part, if the most important part, of a world process – the shrinking of the globe and the filling of its open spaces. The isolationism of American diplomacy began before long to react to these fundamental forces.

This process was from one point of view a seemingly violent contraction of the international scene, by which the nations found themselves being jostled with unprecedented force by those around them: from the opposite point of view, it was an extraordinary acceleration in the rate at which a number of nations grew in population and powers of destruction. It was this process of expansion, hitherto absorbed within the huge North American continent ('empty' – save for the Indians), which became first apparent in the history of the United States, for by the end of the nineteenth century America was fairly launched upon its only real phase of colonial expansion. This era of American Imperialism, although with some justice dubbed a 'great aberration' by one distinguished American diplomatic historian, S. F. Bemis, was obviously in a sense a continuation of the westward movement and of Manifest Destiny; as Frank Norris wrote, with the license of the novelist, 'On the 1st May, 1898, a gun was fired in the bay of Manila and, in response, the skirmish line crossed the Pacific, still pushing the frontier before it.' It was no coincidence that the continental frontier was declared 'closed' in 1890.

The roots of American Imperialism were varied. One was the sheer strength of industrial America, which 'is capable', as Bryce wrote, 'if she chooses, of quickly calling into being a vast fleet and a vast army. Her wealth and power has in it something almost alarming.' A particular aspect of this was her desire for new markets; her foreign trade doubled between 1870 and 1890. Another was the application of Social Darwinism to foreign as well as domestic development; the idea of the survival of the fittest led to the notion, common also in Britain, of the superiority of the Teutonic, or at least Anglo-Saxon, race, and hence to belief in the rectitude of imperialism. It was the Americans whom Kipling, writing to a Kansas editor, exhorted to

> 'Take up the White Man's burden —
> Ye dare not stoop to less —
> Nor call too loud on Freedom
> To cloke your weariness.'

Imperialist sentiment, strongest among Republicans, had become a serious factor in American politics by the 1890s, though there was always the traditional counter-strain of anti-imperialism. Henry Cabot Lodge could write, in a famous article:

> 'From the Rio Grande to the Arctic Ocean there should be but one flag and one country . . . In the interests of our commerce . . . we should build the Nicaragua canal, and for the protection of that canal and for the sake of our commercial supremacy in the Pacific, we should control the Hawaiian islands and maintain our influence in Samoa . . . [T]he island of Cuba . . . will become a necessity . . . The tendency of modern times is toward consolidation . . . The great nations are rapidly absorbing for their future expansion and their present defence all the waste places of the earth. It is a movement which makes for civilization and the advancement of the race. As one of the great nations of the world the United States must not fall out of the line of march.'

Symptoms of this sentiment had in fact begun to become apparent much earlier in the century. The United States took the initiative, from 1853 onwards, in opening Japan to the West, and had made a commercial treaty with China even before that, in 1844. More specific was her interest in a naval base in Samoa, which became a tripartite protectorate of America, Germany and Britain in 1889, and was to be finally divided between the first two in 1899. Much more important was Hawaii, with which America had from the beginning closer relations than any other power, (largely because she was geographically nearer), and with which she made reciprocity agreements in 1875 and 1887, giving her exclusive right to the splendid naval base of Pearl Harbour. In the early 1890s it was perhaps only the opposition of President Cleveland, a convinced anti-colonialist, which prevented the American advocates of outright annexation of Hawaii from getting their way, which they finally did in July 1898, in the wave of patriotic enthusiasm engendered by the Spanish-American War of that year.

This war was the strongest manifestation of American imperialist feeling. The United States had always been deeply concerned about – and from time to time covetous of – Spain's most important remaining colony in the Western Hemisphere, the island of Cuba, which lay a mere ninety miles off the coast of Florida. A long series of revolts against the largely corrupt and inefficient Spanish colonial régime culminated in the protracted Cuban rebellion which began in 1895, and, though the attitude of Washington was studiously correct, there was a rising tide of American popular resentment against Spain. This sentiment had in it both a genuine strain of anti-colonialist sympathy for the Cuban people (W. J. Bryan, for example, volunteered for military service when the war came), and an antithetical strain of jingoistic American imperialism. The latter was whipped up by the great power of the yellow press, particularly the *New York Journal* of William Randolph Hearst and the *New York World* of Joseph Pulitzer, and national passions reached such a pitch against this affront to liberty on the very doorstep of the world's greatest democracy that a belated Spanish willingness to move in the direction of granting Cuban autonomy did not allay it. Then, in a still mysterious episode, the United States battleship *Maine*, on an ostensibly 'friendly' and perhaps necessary mission to Cuba, sank in Havana harbour on 15 February as the result of an explosion, with the loss of 250 American lives. Whatever the cause – whether, as seems most likely, a Cuban act of provocation or even an internal accident – the American public were immediately and irrationally convinced of Spanish guilt. To the popular cry of 'Remember the Maine', Congress declared war on 25 April.

So overwhelming was American superiority, despite her lack of preparedness, that the war – fought in, and at sea around, Cuba and the Spanish Pacific colony of the Philippines – was over in less than four months. By the Treaty of Paris what was left of the four-centuries-old Spanish Empire was partitioned. Cuba was granted independence, but the United States, by treaty with the Cuban government, gained the important naval base of Guantánamo and, by the so-called Platt Amendment, very broad rights of direct interference in the domestic affairs of the island. The Spanish colonies of Puerto Rico in the Caribbean and Guam in the Marianas were ceded outright to the United States, and after much soul-searching (genuinely deep in many quarters) America in effect purchased her first, and only, great overseas colony, the Philippines, for $20 million.

It was this seeming foundation of an American colonial Empire which made the struggle for ratification of the Treaty in the Senate so bitter; it was eventually passed by the margin – narrow in view of the need for the two-thirds majority – of fifty-seven votes to twenty-seven. In fact rebellion against American rule, led by the Philippine patriot Emilio Aguinaldo, began almost before the new colonial régime had been established. But America's possessions in the Pacific were now formidable; she had annexed the Midway Islands in 1867, and was to gain Wake Island in 1900 and Swain's Island in 1925.

The main condition of America's swift and total defeat of Spain had been the non-intervention of other powers, and much European opinion had tended to be sympathetic towards the Spanish monarchy. That the United States was left alone in the ring with her weak opponent was largely the result of the positively friendly policy of the British government towards America. Superficially, this might seem a surprising attitude on the part of the 'greatest Empire the world had ever seen' towards the growing imperialism of her one-time colony. It was at first sight, too, all the more remarkable because, in an outburst of traditional Anglophobia, American governmental and popular bellicosity over a long standing and not very important Anglo-Venezuelan boundary dispute had (in response to a self-satisfied and stupid British failure to understand the depth of American feeling on this Western hemisphere issue) brought the two great nations to the verge of conflict in 1896. When faced with the actual prospect of war, governmental and public opinion on both sides of the Atlantic had undergone a swift change, a settlement had been reached, and the tropical thunderstorm soon gave way to clearer skies. At this superficial level it was certainly true that the Venezuela crisis taught both countries the salutary lesson that good relations between them needed to be carefully nurtured.

But though there was a definite and partly deliberate change of diplomatic policy on both sides, there was also going on beneath the surface of events a profoundly important international movement, which L. M. Gelber called 'The Rise of Anglo-American Friendship'. This was what Bismark, who died in 1898 before the process had fully begun, meant when he said that 'the supreme fact of the nineteenth century was that Britain and the United States spoke the same language'; and the Anglo-American entente which developed during the next twenty years was to be perhaps the commanding international fact of the first half of the twentieth century. This development had deep roots in the life of the two peoples, and these had been nourished by the twenty-five peaceful Anglo-American years which followed the Treaty of Washington of 1871, though the development had been obscured by the persistence of traditional currents of Anglophobia.

Although trans-Atlantic economic bonds were loosened during this period, the broader and basic ties, of common legal institutions, common social habits and a common concern for freedom, persisted, and became in many ways stronger and more self-conscious. The British Reform Act of 1867, a vital step towards democracy, had owed much to the victory of the Northern cause in the Civil War, and by the time of that of 1884 Britain was beginning to assume a fully democratic aspect, which did a great deal to draw the two peoples together. Even divisions in the two countries came to have a paradoxically binding effect. The Republican ascendancy from 1897 onwards coincided with the Conservative supremacy in Britain, and the two shared a common 'Anglo-Saxon' imperialist sentiment, so that instead of acting as a rival when the United States emerged as a world power, Britain not only ensured by her friendly neutrality and her paramount sea-power a free hand for the Americans at the time of the Spanish-American War, but actively encouraged them to acquire colonial possessions when they had won. *Per contra* the Republican Administration resisted anti-imperialist demands for American assistance to the little Boer republic during the war between it and the mighty British Empire from 1899–1902. Likewise, pro-Boer feeling in Britain evoked sympathy in liberal American circles, and there was to be much in common, as Colonel House pointed out, between the great Liberal governments of 1906–16 and the Democratic Administration of Woodrow Wilson.

These trends were deliberately, and in some cases ardently, encouraged at all levels. There was, for instance, increasing mutual travel (and in wealthy circles intermarriage), and organisations like the English-Speaking Union were formed at this time specifically to foster Anglo-American friendship. Both great British parties came to vie with one another in their persistent courtship of the United States, and, though the American response was, on the whole, cooler, highly influential leaders like John Hay (who was promoted from his very successful embassy in London to be Secretary of State during the crucial period from 1898–1905) were profoundly Anglophile. Even the fact that both were great sea-powers – the United States Navy, negligible before 1890, rose to be the second fleet in the world by 1906 – was capable of uniting rather than of dividing them, for the great theorist of sea power and advocate of American naval expansion, Admiral Alfred Thayer Mahan, was not only a powerful advocate of Anglo-American co-operation, but even more of a hero in Britain than in America. That this was possible owed much to the fact that the United States shared to a remarkable degree the growing British apprehension about the alarming military, and especially naval, potentialities and political attitudes of Imperial Germany. Britain was increasingly conscious of her diplomatic isolation and was willing both to ally herself formally with Japan and informally with France and also to draw just as close to the United States as America's fears of what Jefferson called 'entangling', and Washington – more cautiously – 'permanent', alliances would let her. (Washington, though denouncing 'artificial ties', excepted 'temporary alliances for extraordinary emergencies'.) This was to produce within a few years the striking spectacle of the dominant power of the nineteenth century, Britain, peacefully handing over her maritime supremacy and international ascendancy to her chief rival, America.

The course of the Anglo-American relationship, however, was still not all smooth sailing. In the Far East Britain accepted with a good grace the leadership which Hay rather surprisingly seized by his Open Door policy designed to 'bring about permanent safety and peace to China, preserve Chinese territorial and administrative entity, protect all rights guaranteed to friendly powers . . . , and safeguard for the world the principle of equal and impartial trade with all parts of the Chinese empire.' But the growing desire of the United States, with her rapidly expanding navy, to build a canal across the Central American Isthmus, and to keep it under her own exclusive control (which ran contrary to the Clayton-Bulwer Treaty of 1850), combined with an American-Canadian dispute over the Alaska boundary to produce an Anglo-American crisis in 1899. Both issues were resolved, in large part because Theodore Roosevelt, who succeeded McKinley two years later but who was very influential before this as Vice-President in the Senate, showed clearly to Britain the determination of the dominant Republicans to get their way. An unsatisfactory Anglo-American agreement negotiated by Hay in 1900, granting the United States the right to build only a 'neutralised' canal (as envisaged in the Clayton-Bulwer treaty), was not acceptable to the Senate, and was replaced by the Hay-Pauncefote Treaty of 1901, which gave America the exclusive right to 'police' – which was taken to include the right to fortify and defend – any Isthmian Canal which she built. Similarly, the Alaska boundary dispute was settled in 1903 by an arbitration in which the casting vote of the British representative was in favour of the American point of view (which T.R. had made it plain he would enforce in any case), and against the Canadian. This caused great ill-feeling in

Canada, but it preserved that Anglo-American friendship from which Canada had more than any nation to gain.

Roosevelt was the fullest embodiment of the new imperialistic American feeling; indeed he took America in some respects farther than many, perhaps most, of his countrymen wished in the direction of world power. Yet he never failed for want of popular support and was always careful, as he said, 'never' to 'take a step in foreign policy unless I am assured that I shall be able eventually to carry out my will by force.' He, more than any President, was responsible for building up the naval power of the United States; as he declared, 'I believe in power.' His other boast, 'Speak softly and carry a big stick, you will go far', was only half-practised, for he did not under-estimate the diplomatic effect of loud and angry words. Nor was he more scrupulous in his international actions than was the custom of the day when he felt that America's vital interests were at stake. Thus he resolved to build the canal, as soon as Britain, the only power which could conceivably interfere, had signed the Hay-Pauncefote Treaty, and when the Congress of Colombia unwisely rejected the Panama Canal agreement which the Colombian negotiator, Herrán, had signed with Secretary of State Hay in 1903, Roosevelt acted ruthlessly. He encouraged a revolution (within less than three months) against Colombia by the province of Panama, made sure by the presence of an American naval force that it would succeed, immediately recognised the new Government, and twelve days later signed a new canal treaty with this novel Republic of Panama. The treaty granted to the United States 'in perpetuity the use, occupa-tion and control' of a ten-miles-wide zone of land across the Isthmus, these 'rights, power and authority' to be exercised by the United States as 'if it were the sovereign of the territory.' In return America would pay $10 million down and $250,000 a year. The Senate approved the treaty by sixty-six votes to fourteen in February 1904 and Panama soon did so too. Despite considerable engineering diffi-culties, the Canal was completed by 1914. T.R. wrote the epitaph of the affair when he characteristically declared later, 'I am interested in the Panama Canal because I started it. If I had followed con-ventional . . . methods . . . the debate would have been going on yet, but I took the canal zone and let Congress debate, and while the debate goes on the canal does also.' The debate continued till 1921 when a substantial indemnity was paid to Colombia.

His attitude over the Canal was the most extreme example of his general policy towards Latin America. He was, naturally, a resolute supporter of the Monroe Doctrine, but he did not believe that the United States should prevent the collection, for example, of international debts owed by defaulting Latin-American governments. A statement to this effect made early in his presidency, that America should 'let the European country spank' any Latin-American one which 'misbehaves', resulted in a joint Anglo-German blockade of Venezuela in 1902–3, and caused the President to think again. Germany – the figure of Kaiser Wilhelm II became at this time extremely unpopular with the American public – reluctantly withdrew under American pressure (Britain had done so much earlier), and in 1904 T.R. enunciated what became known as the Roosevelt Corollary to the Monroe Doctrine. 'Chronic wrongdoing . . . may in America, as elsewhere, ultimately require intervention by some civilized nation, and in the Western Hemisphere the adherence of the United States to the Monroe Doctrine may force the United States, however reluctantly, in flagrant cases of such wrongdoing or impotence, to the exercise of an international police power.' This power successive American administrations were to wield, often with little reluctance, for nearly thirty years.

Within the hemisphere American public opinion could usually be counted upon to support the President's activity in foreign affairs. When he wandered further afield, there was considerable dissent. There was little open opposition to his mediation in the Russo-Japanese War, which was ended by the Treaty of Portsmouth, New Hampshire, in 1905, for it was successful. There was already, too, a growing American suspicion of the rising power of the Japanese Empire, although friction was allayed for many years, partly through the influence of Britain, Japan's ally. More remarkable, in the perspective of history, was Roosevelt's intervention (the exact effectiveness of which is uncertain) in European affairs at the time of the Conference of Algeciras in 1906; this, more than with the case of Japan, was the result of the President's personal ambition to cut a figure, as well as accomplishing something, on the wide stage of international affairs. It was entirely typical of the man that one of the last acts of his Presidency in foreign policy was to order the round-the-world prestige voyage of the now huge United States fleet, which was carried out in 1907.

Under his more placid successor, Taft, there was, despite growing American financial interests overseas, a pronounced ebb in the tide of American participation in world affairs, a distinct return towards the normality of isolation in the policies of the Government and the attitude of the people. In 1912 Henry Adams could write, 'Today's Boston newspaper, twelve pages, contained not one allusion or item regarding the outside world.' The fever of American Imperialism had run its course; Taft, as Governor-General, had already set the

Philippines on the road towards independence. When, in the cataclysm of World War I, America was to re-enter the arena, it
was not – far from it – any longer as a result of an inward desire for
expansion, but of the remorseless pressures which the conflict brought
to bear on her destiny from the outside, from the other, warring,
nations of the world.

Chapter 16

War and Peace, 1914–21

THE TREND towards a renewal of American isolation which had set in under Taft was at first accelerated by Wilson, who was personally isolationist and who reacted strongly against the so-called 'dollar diplomacy' of his predecessor's Secretary of State, Philander C. Knox; this the new President regarded as subservient to American financial interests. From the first he adopted a strong moral tone in international affairs, asserting, 'It is a very perilous thing to determine the foreign policy of a nation in terms of material interest.' This tone came out clearly in the only two notable foreign problems during his first year of office – both having their origin in the Western Hemisphere – the Mexican revolution which established Victoriano Huerta in power and led to the murder of his democratic predecessor, and the tolls imposed by Congress on foreign but not American shipping going through the Panama Canal, contrary to the spirit if not the letter of the Hay-Pauncefote treaty.

Wilson, who in fact probably intervened more in Latin-American affairs (specifically, in Mexico, Haiti, the Dominican Republic and Cuba) than any modern President, refused to recognise the Huerta government on the highest moral grounds, declaring characteristically that the United States must 'teach the South American republics to elect good men'. Britain, whose navy was newly interested in Mexican oil, took a different stand, and this clash was magnified by the ill-will arising over the Panama tolls. Wilson, however, was as unbending with what he believed to be wrong in his own country's policies as with those of his foreign opponents, and recommended to Congress in equally characteristic terms the amendment of the tolls legislation: 'We are too big, too powerful, too self-respecting a nation to interpret with a too strained or refined reading the words of our own promises just because we have power enough to give us leave to read them as we please. The large thing to do is the only thing we can afford to do, a voluntary withdrawal from a position everywhere questioned and misunderstood.' Britain executed a *volte-face* over Mexico, and Huerta in due course went into exile; though it was by no means the end of the President's Latin-American troubles, it terminated the Anglo-American tension. Wilson had behaved with magnamimous rectitude, but the settlement, as, alas, so often in international affairs, looked to some observers more like a 'deal' than a victory for the new international morality. But in any event, America's relations with Britain, the foreign power with which she was and had been in the past most intimately involved, were, partly because of the long ambassadorship of Lord Bryce in Washington, happily and unprecedentedly free of unsettled questions when the First World War broke out in Europe in the summer of 1914.

This great maelstrom was ineluctably to drag the United States into its vortex (as had the French Wars a century earlier) despite all the efforts of Wilson, like Madison before him, to maintain American neutrality. The President was profoundly suspicious of German autocracy and militarism and not without deep feelings for Britain, which he knew well; but he hated war, feared for the unity of his country if war came, and had a full measure of the instinctive American mistrust of the insidious yet deadly pull of the old world's affairs. Nevertheless he conceived it as his stern duty to maintain America's full rights in international law, and this produced inevitable friction with the belligerents. The question was, with which side, if either, would a decisive breach come?

The United States had reverted to her customary role of the world's greatest neutral after her belligerent status in the Civil War and the short-lived war with Spain, but now the situation was transformed because her power was so huge that, though (to her credit) she was entirely without territorial ambitions outside her existing borders, she in fact held the balance of power not only in Europe but in the world as a whole. It was to be rendered more confused by the fact that Wilson, appealing to powerful, inbred American sentiments, rejected 'balance of power politics' and was the prophet of a new doctrine of international morality. He and his only close associate, Colonel Edward M. House, sought constantly to mediate in the struggle, and for a long time considered seriously the armed imposition by America of terms of peace; the President in his mind's eye seemed to behold the New World emerging in righteousness, like a god from the machine, to enforce peace upon the iniquitous warring peoples of the Old. This led to considerable misunderstanding on the part of the Allied nations, but in the end hard facts prevailed and the United States became engaged as a belligerent against Imperial Germany. Yet it was because her rights, especially her maritime rights as a neutral, were assaulted that she entered the war, not because it became apparent to her that a victory of the

Central Powers would constitute a mortal threat not merely to her liberty but to her very existence, as was to become clear to the American people in the Second World War.

Thus it remained possible for many Americans to regard their part in the war as a 'great crusade' to 'make the world safe for democracy.' The President, having tried in vain to isolate the United States from the contamination of the war, went to the other extreme once his country was involved and preached a thorough-going internationalism, which took shape in his ardently pursued and cherished project, the League of Nations. This noble call to prevent future wars 'for all mankind' had a very wide appeal, not only in America but in Europe, where Wilson was the hero of liberals in almost every country. But this did not mean that he cordially embraced the actual leaders of the Allied governments; he was not, the British Ambassador in Washington was to write, 'a belligerent among other belligerents, but something apart'. Aloofness was inherent in his decision that the United States would not become an Allied, but an Associated, Power, which was not bound, for example, by the secret treaties made in the first years of the war by the European governments. America would see to it that there was a peace of justice when victory had been won; the President came to Europe when it had been won, in the words of Winston Churchill, 'to chasten the Allies' as well as 'to chastise the Germans.'

On 4 August 1914 the President issued a proclamation calling for neutrality 'in thought as well as in action'. It was very soon to prove difficult enough in the latter, let alone in the former, for friction over maritime rights began with Britain almost at once. The basic problem was closely analogous to that of 1812; belligerent Britain wanted in her blockade to restrict neutral trade as severely as possible, the neutral United States naturally wished to extend it as widely as possible. But the technical details were very different, for with the coming of the modern warship the whole technique of blockade had to change, although international law had not done so, despite serious Anglo-American efforts to get international agreement on this and other issues during the period of the Hague Peace Conferences at the turn of the century. Other things had changed radically, too, and from the point of view of Anglo-American relations, for the better. Britain now desperately needed American industrial products, as well as raw materials, for the conduct of the war, and this meant that a vast expansion of American trade with the Allies compensated for the German trade o which their blockade effectively deprived the United States. Indeed the stimulus which the quadrupling of her commerce with Europe between 1914 and 1916 gave to the American economy was chiefly responsible for curing the recession from which the country was suffering when the war broke out in Europe. All the same, as Britain strengthened and extended her choking hold on German trade, by new naval control measures, by extending the contraband list, and by other devices, tension with the United States tended to increase sharply.

Politically too, however, the situation had altered markedly since 1812, for now Anglo-American relations were at bottom better than they had ever been; what is more, the Liberal government of Britain was fully aware of the paramount necessity of avoiding a breach with the new American leviathan. As Sir Edward Grey put it, 'Blockade of Germany was essential to the victory of the Allies, but the ill-will of the United States meant their certain defeat . . . It was better . . . to carry on the war without blockade, if need be, than to incur a break with the United States about contraband and thereby deprive the Allies of the resources necessary to carry on the war at all or with any chance of success. The object of diplomacy, therefore, was to secure the maximum of blockade that could be enforced without a rupture with the United States.' Thus, for example, the urgent Allied decision (because of the invention of the explosive, gun-cotton) to add cotton, along with copper and rubber, to the traditional contraband list was delayed until American cotton production had by 1915 climbed out of the depression; and when it was put into effect Britain agreed to buy enough to keep the price stable at 10 cents a pound. Nevertheless, Wilson in 1916 felt so strongly about the British blockade that he declared to House, 'I am, I must admit, about at the end of my patience with Great Britain and the Allies . . . I am seriously considering asking Congress to authorize me to prohibit loans and restrict exportations to the Allies . . . Can we any longer endure their intolerable course?' Why then did not history repeat itself and America slide into war with the world's greatest naval power, which impinged so heavily on her freedom of trade?

Americans of isolationist inclinations were later – especially in the 1930s – to argue that she was too closely bound to Britain by her ever-growing financial and economic stake in Allied victory to do other than ensure that it took place, but purely economic motives are not as crudely powerful as that in the foreign policy of a free country, where it is the voter who may be called upon to die in modern war. Moreover there is no evidence that the President or his colleagues were specifically influenced by such motives; indeed it would have been quite alien to Wilson's character. The real reason why 1917 did not repeat 1812 is not far to seek. Not only was there no emotional Anglo-American issue such as impressment, but there was an even more potent one between Germany and the United States – the submarine campaign. The German Navy, unable to prevent the British blockade or conclusively to defeat the Royal Navy, felt compelled to resort to unrestricted use of their large and growing fleet of the recently developed submarines. On 4 February 1915, despite the reluctance of the German Chancellor, Bethmann-Hollweg, Germany declared virtually unrestricted submarine warfare in a zone around the British Isles. On 10 February Wilson in a stern note held the 'Imperial German Government to a strict accountability for' the results of the policy. The ruthless nature of this was shown by the sinkings which soon began, especially that of the *Lusitania* on 17 May, which was attacked without warning and sank in eighteen minutes with the loss of 1198 lives, including 129 children and babies; 128 of the dead were Americans. American anger grew and after the sinking of the *Sussex* in similar circumstances in March, 1916, the President sent a note threatening the final severing of diplomatic relations unless the Imperial German Government 'should now immediately declare and effect an abandonment of its present methods of submarine warfare.'

The civilian element in Berlin prevailed upon the Kaiser to call off the campaign, but not for long. By the end of the year the military had convinced the German government that it could win the war in Europe before America would, or could, intervene effectively, and on 31 January the resumption of virtually unrestricted submarine warfare was declared. How crucial this issue was is demonstrated by the fact that, only nine days before, the President had issued the last of his appeals to both sides for 'a peace without victory'. There were still, as there had been since 1914, vocal anti-war and pro-German elements in America, but T.R. castigated them as 'hyphenated' Americans and Wilson wrote to one of them – an unfortunate citizen who threatened not to vote for him in 1916 – 'I would feel deeply mortified to have you or anybody like you vote for me. Since you have access to many disloyal Americans and I have not I will ask you to convey this message to them'. Such an accord between these two leaders, who so disliked one another, illustrates the speed with which anti-German feeling in the democratic and deeply humanitarian United States rose; it soon swamped American irritation with the Allied blockade and even traditional feelings of Anglophobia. As Senator Henry Cabot Lodge put it, his 'heart was more moved by the thought of a drowned baby than an unsold bale of cotton.'

Once the German government had resolved that the submarine campaign was indispensable to bring Britain to her knees, given the President's almost legalistic determination not to abate in the least measure America's full maritime rights of trade and travel, the outcome was inevitable. That the campaign was in fact a grievous infringement on these rights is shown by the extraordinary terms of its renewal at the beginning of 1917. The German government announced that it would sink on sight all ships found in a large zone around the British Isles and in the Mediterranean, with the sole exception of one American steamship each week to and from Falmouth in Cornwall, this vessel to travel only on a definite route and with very elaborate markings. No great nation at that time, especially one as hostile as America to what it believed to be, with some justice, German bellicosity and authoritarianism, could have accepted such terms. But it was with a heavy heart that the President, at least, took the ultimate step, and called upon Congress to 'accept the status of belligerent which has thus been thrust upon it.' The declaration of war, which on 6 April passed the Senate by 82 votes to 6, and the House by 373 to 50, marked the end of an era for America. The President declared, 'God helping her, she can do no other', but, unavoidable as it might be, it was the final conclusive step in a process which he himself had described a few weeks earlier in his second Inaugural Address; 'matters lying outside our own life as a nation and over which we had no control, . . . despite our wish to keep free of them, have drawn us more and more irresistibly into their own current and influence.'

America's entry into the war, if it did not prevent the retreat of the Allies before the great German offensive of March 1918, sealed the fate of Germany, for, contrary to the fears of some observers who did not understand the strain of 'Thorough' in the American character, the United States was resolved, as the President put it, to 'spend the whole force of the nation' to win the war. Typical was the rapid establishment of close Anglo-American naval co-operation, and the acceptance by the United States government of Allied blockade practices of which it had recently been complaining bitterly. Much more important was the demonstration which the United States now for the first time gave to the world of the enormous strength that she could generate when wholeheartedly determined to do so. Through active Congressional support of the President's vigorous leadership and his wide use of the Presidential war power, America rapidly began to create a formidable military machine. The Administration, chiefly through a series of boards (such as that of War Industries) under a Council for National Defence, gained broad and unprecedented powers to requisition supplies, to fix the prices of these, to take possession of industry and transport as necessary, and to license imports. Both industry and labour co-operated closely with the government, and the aid of the latter was especially valuable over the imposition of conscription in the Selective Service Act of 18 May 1917. Serious efforts were also made to mobilise public opinion, and in this sphere some Americans believed that the government went much too far; the Sedition Act of 1918, for instance, which gave a pretty free run to the steam-roller of American patriotism, and which resulted in interference with, and even suppression of, a number of newspapers as well as some police arrogance, seem to critics to hark back to the Alien and Sedition Acts of 1798 and to point forward to the McCarthyism of the 1950s.

But all in all the mobilisation of America's physical and moral resources was highly effective. It was financed (to a total of $40 billion) by very heavy taxation, which avoided the excessive inflation of the Civil War, as well as by vast loans, through which $21½ billion were raised on stringent terms, epitomised in the slogan, 'Buy till it hurts'. Armed forces of more than 4 millions were raised, including upwards of 3 million in the army; ¾ million of these latter, under the command of General Pershing, reached France by June 1918, and a further 1 million by October, though, in contrast with the terrible losses of the Civil War, less than 120,000 Americans were to die and only somewhat over 200,000 to be wounded in the war. The refusal of the American government to engage its troops piecemeal, under Allied command, during the desperate fighting of early 1918 did not mean that it was opposed to unified direction of the war. In fact it inspired the setting up of a number of international economic co-ordinating agencies, such as the War Purchases and Finance Council, and, after the disastrous defeat of the Italians at Caporetto in October 1917, supported the establishment on the political level of the Supreme War Council of the nations with forces fighting on the Western Front. It had from the first pressed for unified military command, which was established under Marshal Foch in 1918. In the offensive launched by him, which led to victory in November, the American army played an important role. All this marked an exceedingly intimate collaboration for a merely 'Associated' power, but it resulted from the logic of events and from the American sense of efficiency.

It was this, as well as the scale of American industry, which made possible her remarkable productive performance. By centrally directed rationalisation of production (types of pocket-knife were reduced from 6,000 to 140), by economy of materials (new regulations for the making of corsets saved 8,000 tons of steel annually!), by the elimination of waste (much food was saved by such devices as 'Meatless Tuesdays') and by overall planning (as, for example, in the operation of the railroads), such feats were achieved as the increase of the available shipping from 1 to 10 million tons and the export, (under the control of Herbert Hoover) in 1918, of approximately three times the normal quantity of food. This extraordinary output had a drastic and fundamental effect on the international economic position of the United States. During 1917–18 the United States government, in response to the appeals of the Allies, whose dollar resources were almost exhausted, began a series of direct loans to the European governments. This method of subsidy was to be the cause of great trouble later, but the huge total of $10 billion lent was a tribute to America's economic pre-eminence. By the end of the war she had, for the first time, become not merely a creditor nation but by far the world's largest one. In 1919 she was a creditor to the tune of $3,700 million, with $7 billion invested abroad, as opposed to $3,300 million of foreign investment in the United States. This fact was a measure of the financial effect of the war and was also markedly to influence the subsequent economic history of the Western world.

The power of America gave her undisputed leadership in the last months of the war. On 8 January 1918 the President, in his famous Fourteen Points speech, had called for a 'just and stable peace', and the conditions he specified provided a magnificent propaganda weapon in the camp of the enemy, so that it was on this basis and to Wilson that the Germans applied for an armistice on 3 October 1918. He called for the end of 'secret' diplomacy; the 'removal, so far as possible, of all economic barriers' between the nations; the reduction of 'national armaments'; the restoration of her conquests by Germany; the application of the general principle of what came to be called the self-determination of peoples (in particular the 'autonomous development' of those of Austria-Hungary, as well as Poland and the Balkans); a 'free . . . and absolutely impartial adjustment of all colonial claims', in which 'the interests of the populations concerned must have equal weight with the equitable claims of the government whose title is to be determined'; and 'absolute freedom of navigation upon the seas.' But to liberals throughout the world, and especially in Britain, the greatest appeal of the President's programme lay in his call for 'a general association of nations' to afford 'mutual guarantees of political independence and territorial integrity to great and small states alike.'

The British government was opposed to the doctrine of the Freedom of the Seas in this form (and some of its Conservative elements had reservations about the colonies and the League) but was in very general agreement, as Prime Minister Lloyd George declared, with the Fourteen Points. France, under the leadership of the 'Tiger', Georges Clemenceau, was deeply sceptical about what he considered the totally unrealistic idealism of this Anglo-Saxon project for a League of Nations. These men, with Wilson, dominated the Council of Four (which included Italy), and the Council guided the negotiations of the international conference in Paris which assembled in January 1919 to draw up what was to be called the Treaty of Versailles.

The United Kingdom, however, was not the only nation with divisions of opinion about the form the peace should take, for in fact the United States was much more seriously divided than the British government, despite the seemingly overwhelming international prestige of the President. His forceful use of his powers as Chief Executive and Commander-in-Chief in the war had increasingly aroused the hostility of the legislative arm, and in the Congressional elections of 1918 the Republicans had gained control of both the House of Representatives and the Senate. When peace came, party and factional bitterness broke out with even greater intensity, and this was made worse by the President's action in taking his domestic opponents so little into his confidence that the American delegation which went to Europe contained no single one of them. And Wilson, by going to Paris in person, cut himself off from public opinion at home and was too closely involved when dubious decisions were made in the heat of negotiations. Domestic opposition centred chiefly upon what many Republicans regarded as the unbalanced idealism of the League of Nations, with its automatic and total involvement of the United States in the affairs of all the world. It became clear during February 1919 that, as a Senate 'Round Robin' put it, 'the constitution of the League of Nations in the form now proposed' would be very unlikely to get the necessary votes in that body, although Theodore Roosevelt had gone too far when he had characteristically declared some time before, 'Mr. Wilson and his fourteen points and his four supplementary points and his five complementary points and all his utterances every which way have ceased to have any shadow of right to be accepted as expressive of the will of the American people.'

But the moral force of the President's policy had great effect both

at home and abroad, although this was lessened by the concessions
he had to make to the 'realism' of certain of the Allies, especially the
French. He resisted the erosion of his high principles stubbornly, but
he had to grant, among other things, Allied reparations against
Germany (though not an indemnity) and the right of the Allies to
occupy her Rhineland territory for fifteen years. This was the minimum that Clemenceau would take, and even this was acceptable to
him only because it was accompanied by an Anglo-American.
promise of a treaty pledging military aid to France in case of un-
provoked attack upon her by Germany. This highly entangling
alliance in fact was never even reported out by the Senate committee, and since the British had made their guarantee conditional
on the American, France was in the event left with only the flabby
protection of the League of Nations, in which she had no real faith
whatever. Nevertheless the President did rise from the peace table
with the Covenant of the League virtually intact.

He had, in a belated effort to conciliate the opposition at home,
himself obtained certain modifications in it, such as one safeguarding
the Monroe Doctrine, and he returned to the United States to open
a strenuous campaign by which he firmly believed that the American
people would be aroused to support America's participation in the
total international commitment which the League constituted. But
he was stricken in the midst of his speech-making tour by an illness
which left him partially paralysed, if – as it in due course appeared –
intellectually sound. This in practice ended any real hope of the full
acceptance of the League, which could possibly have gained the
necessary votes in the immediate aftermath of the peace conference.
It still remained possible, however, that it might have been accepted,
(as the so-called Reservationists in the Senate led by Henry Cabot
Lodge said they wanted) with certain amendments, such as that
which required Congressional approval of any American obligation
arising from the maintenance of the territorial integrity of America's
fellow nations in the League. Another Senate group, the 'Irreconcilables' led by William E. Borah of Idaho, were totally opposed to
the League with or without reservations, but it is pretty plain that,
if the President had encouraged his supporters to accept an essential
modicum of amendment, the required two-thirds majority could
have been obtained, and that the other powers would then have
accepted the changes with a reasonably good grace.

This, Wilson – his natural obstinacy perhaps increased by his
stroke and accentuated by the invalid's isolation upon which his
young wife insisted – absolutely refused to do, and as a result a hard
core of loyal Democrats, chiefly from the Solid South, persisted in

voting only for the Treaty and nothing but the Treaty and against any reservations whatsoever. Some Democrats, who put the importance of even a weakened League above their loyalty to their eminent party chief, after five months of consideration in the Senate, voted (in the fifth and final vote) in favour of the Treaty with a modified League, but their forty-nine yeas against the thirty-five nays cast by a seemingly unholy alliance of Wilsonian Democrats and Republic Irreconcilables fell short of the necessary two-thirds. The defeat of the Democratic candidate, on a platform with a pro-League plank, in the Presidential Election of 1920 confirmed that the Treaty was irrevocably lost. The United States never entered the League of Nations and the Congress ended the war by unilateral action. The depth of the feeling which had now, with the fading memory of the war and the waning of idealism which accompanied it, developed among the American people against this all-embracing international experiment is best illustrated by the fact that for the next twenty years there was in the United States well-nigh universal acceptance of the decision not to enter the League, even by Democrats who, like Franklin D. Roosevelt (the Vice-Presidential candidate in 1920), had been ardent supporters of Wilson. It needed the Second World War finally to convince the Americans that they could not escape what Jefferson had called 'the throes and convulsions of the ancient world.'

Chapter 17

Boom and Depression

Historians have recently questioned the accuracy and adequacy of the term 'isolationism' to describe the policies of the United States government after Versailles, but there can be little doubt that it fairly depicts the prevailing mood of the American people, who perhaps for the last but certainly not for the first time turned with revulsion from the 'broils' of Europe. For this Winston Churchill was to castigate his mother's people, along with his father's, saying 'Nor can the United States escape the censure of history.' But he did not fail to observe that this American reaction against European involvement had a positive as well as a negative side, and went on, 'Absorbed in their own affairs and all the abounding interests, activities and accidents of a free community, they simply gaped at the vast changes which were taking place in Europe, and imagined they were no concern of theirs.' Whereas in the nineteenth century after the Treaty of Ghent, they had turned their fierce vigour to the conquest of the great West, now their restless energies went into the creation of an economic boom which, through a combination of their rich resources and the new techniques of mass production, produced commodities on a scale and at a speed unprecedented in the history of man.

This superabundant vitality overflowed into all branches of life, almost as if the confines of the United States were too limited to contain it. For this reason Andrew Sinclair has given to the twenties, which had 'an urge towards excess which has made this nation great in a small time, and has left little room for moderation', the name 'The Era of Excess'. There is indeed a strain not only of lack of restraint and of violence but of eccentricity, even 'crackpotism', which runs through American life at this as well as at other times. No modern people has been, for example, so prolific in new religions and religious sects; they produced two large religions in the nineteenth century, Mormonism and Christian Science, and innumerable small ones in the course of their history, ranging from the snake-embracing 'Rattlers' of Tennessee to the followers of Aimée Semple Macpherson with her Los Angeles Temple.

This dearth of moderation and abundance of zeal amongst some Americans has complex causes. Fanaticism is a powerful aid to emigration, as it was with many of the Pilgrim Fathers and their New England Zion; this spirit was kept alive by the ever-moving frontier, which, even after it closed, left a residue in, for instance, such zany Far Western phenomena as the Social Credit and the California 'ham and eggs' movements; and, perhaps above all, the belief in liberty, which has made so enormously valuable a contribution to the development of mankind, has left the American gate wide open to innovation. Whereas Britain's moderation, with her tightly knit and homogeneous society and her paternalistic government, is the result of her now long-standing tradition of the middle way, America's pragmatic but usually successful pursuit of compromise seems often to be through the tension of opposites pulling against one another within the more capacious and hence looser, but at the same time more rigid, framework of the Constitution of the United States.

Sometimes, however, a 'far-out' group, even one from the lunatic-fringe, is able to sway public opinion, to capture the machinery of state governments, and to strike for control of the Federal government, like the anti-immigrant, nativist, 'Know-Nothing' movement before the Civil War. But only once has such a zealous band succeeded in passing an amendment to the constitution; this was the Eighteenth, which in 1919 prohibited 'the manufacture, sale or transportation of intoxicating liquors within . . . the United States.' The Volstead Act implementing the amendment defined these as containing over one half of one per cent of alcohol.

Prohibition was the result of an extraordinary combination of circumstances, though the movement was as old as the 'Maine liquor law' of 1851. It had deep grass roots in the fundamentalist Protestantism of the South and Middle-West, and was the last fling of country against town in the Populist tradition; it had close psychological links with Puritan morality and its overwhelming sense of sin; it flourished on the actual excesses of individual drinking, chiefly of easily produced and transported hard liquor, amidst the traditional hardships of the frontier and the new ones of urban industrial society; it waxed through the genuine idealism of the movement and its hatred of the real evils of drink and of the crime and vice which were often associated with the saloon (against which the spearhead of the attack was launched, and which in fact never returned in its old form after repeal); and it gained its victory through the coincidence of two related facts, the call for efficiency in the First World War and the coming of votes for women, who constituted the true heart of the prohibition movement. Feminism swept the states in the early twentieth century and culminated in the Nineteenth Amendment, guaranteeing universal suffrage, which was passed only eighteen months after the Eighteenth (Prohibition) Amendment.

The latter was but one manifestation of the spirit of excess, though the most important. Another example, following on the anti-German hysteria of the war years, was the onset in the early twenties of the first of America's 'Red scares' against the Communism which seemed such a threat to stable society after the Bolshevik Revolution in Russia. This found much expression through official agencies, but it was general anti-foreign sentiment which led to a rebirth of the Ku Klux Klan during the war and to its spread from the South to the Middle-West; at its peak in 1924 it probably had more than four million members, who wanted to keep not merely 'niggers', but also Catholics and Jews and other 'foreigners', 'in their place'. These forces approved of, though they did not initiate, the drastic restriction of immigration which was finally imposed by the Federal government in 1924. This Act, which had the support of labour (increasingly apprehensive of unskilled competition from the immigrant) and which set the pattern for future policy, cut immigration to 150,000 a year and did it in such a way as to reduce to a minimum the proportion constituted by 'new' immigrants from south and east Europe (and, *a fortiori*, from outside Europe), as opposed to the 'old American' stock. This vital change in policy was to have results as profoundly important – and as difficult to assess precisely – as the closing of the frontier a quarter of a century earlier. The reasons for the step were understandable and, sooner or later, some form of restriction was seemingly inevitable, but it foreclosed an era of high American idealism, epitomised in the Statue of Liberty and its inscription by Emma Lazarus:

> 'Give me your tired, your poor,
> Your huddled masses yearning to breathe free,
> The wretched refuse of your teeming shore,
> Send these, the homeless, tempest-tossed, to me:
> I lift my lamp beside the golden door.'

This ever-open door had had its disadvantages. It had made the task of creating an American national tradition out of constantly changing ingredients a very hard one. It had contributed to periodic upsurges of a sometimes alarming pressure to social and political conformity (though the degree of liberty enjoyed by minorities in

America – with, for example, their own language newspapers – far exceeded that enjoyed by most central European immigrants at home). It had necessitated in a sense the extreme inflexibility of, and immense reverence for, the ark of the American covenant, the written constitution. It had encouraged the sometimes excessively exclusive emphasis on what T.R. called '100 per cent Americanism'. But it had peopled the American sub-continent at a prodigious pace; it had helped to lead to a new dimension of economic progress for humanity; and it had triumphantly aided the creation of an American patriotism which, despite its aberrations, was dedicated to the freedom of men everywhere. Few indeed are those among the nearly 200 million Americans – immigrants or descendants of immigrants every one – who would forego or renounce their heritage.

Certainly in the twenties the people of the United States seemed to live life to the full, and to throw off much of what many of them were coming to look on as the stuffy inheritance of the nineteenth century. They led the way in the full emancipation of women, which found expression in lipstick, cigarette-smoking and the short skirt; they began to take up Freud and to relax further the conventions of relations between the sexes; they developed the popular tabloid press, the widespread use of radio, and their pre-eminence in the new world of the film, associated indelibly with the name of Holly-wood; and out of the depth of the Negro American's being came jazz, which was within a generation to dominate the popular musical taste of mankind. In a broad sense, and in many ways a very healthy one, these years in America marked the coming of the world's first popular democracy of taste and manners. But they could not yet live down the old Adam, for they were still, as they (in common with the rest of humanity) had so often been before, torn between the excessive polarity of their public moral pretensions and their individual private desires. Prohibition, to take the principal example, just could not work, and by 1929 there were some 219,000 'speak-easies' for the consumption of illicit 'bootlegged' liquor in the United States, which was not far from the total number of saloons which had existed in 1919. This was what G. K. Chesterton put in his usual paradoxical way, 'The Americans may go mad when they make laws, but they recover their reason when they disobey them.' Bootlegging, 'the respectable crime', became Big Business, for liquor would sell in America for ten times its Canadian value, and it was said that in 1928 a single Philadelphia bank had 9\frac{1}{2}$ million of bootleggers' money.

The political scientist, however, can see all too clearly the bad results of this schizophrenia of theory and practice in America, which has, in the words of Walter Lippmann, the 'strongest laws and the weakest government of any highly civilized people.' Prohibition not only augmented, through the rise of organised gangsterdom (under such men as Al Capone), the American tradition of violence both in crime and law-enforcement, but brought all law into disrespect and gave corruption a renewed, sometimes increased, hold on the legal system and on politics. It became a veritable cancer on the body politic, which repeal itself could not wholly eradicate, for many of those who had thriven on illegal booze moved over into other rackets, such as gambling, and even into some of the labour organisations which were to grow so swiftly in power in the early days of the New Deal. One American journalist, before the Twenty-first Amendment repealed the Eighteenth in 1933, summed up American history in eleven words, 'Columbus, Washington, Lincoln, Volstead, Two flights up and ask for Gus.'

These excesses were made possible, however, by the real and dramatic growth of America's economy. In 1919 there had been 6 million automobiles in the country, by 1929 there were 27 million; typical of the development of labour-saving machines was the rise in annual output of refrigerators from 27,000 in 1923 to 755,000 in 1928; and production of electricity grew from 43 billion k.w.h. in 1920 to 96 billion in 1929. Total realised national income was $60 million in 1918 and $89 million by 1928, while *per capita* income increased from $651 to $745 in the same period. Huge investment in industry and increased expenditure on research, as well as the spread of scientific business management, led to unprecedented industrial development and innovation, so that labour productivity in manufacturing increased 35 per cent from 1922 to 1925.

But this expansion was unevenly distributed throughout the economy. Though there were real estate booms in Florida and California, farmers did poorly (particularly in the South and parts of the Middle West) and even industrial New England fared badly. Wheat and cotton farming, mining, and long-established industries like textiles and ship building were all relatively weak, and even in decline, at the very height of the boom. There was increased public expenditure on roads (concrete mileage multiplied more than sevenfold in the decade after the war), and on such social services as education, libraries and hospitals, but in general government intervention in the economic life of the nation was kept to a minimum by a recrudescence of unvarnished *laissez-faire* beliefs and above all by the virtually unchallenged ascendancy of Big Business during the twenties. In a sense the dominant Republican party, seeking what President Harding called a return to 'normalcy', reverted to an attitude of co-operation with, indeed reverence for, business interests such as it had displayed before the era of Theodore Roosevelt. 'The Business of America', declared President Coolidge to an approving electorate in 1925, 'is Business'.

Labour, by contrast, lost much of the ground which it had gained during the war years; weakened by internal rivalries, such as that between Gompers and his young rival John L. Lewis, the A.F.L. sank from 4 to 3 million members by 1929. The Courts once more began to deliver judgements hostile to labour and to utilise the injunction against its interests. On the other hand, the open shop and 'company unions' flourished, while 'welfare capitalism' was genuinely active in such projects as employee stock ownership and voluntary group insurance.

In another way, too, there was a reversion to pre-Roosevelt Republicanism, in the marked trend towards the consolidation of business. By 1930 two-thirds of the electrical power of America was controlled by six groups and even the number of American banks was reduced by a third between 1921 and 1931. The great giants with which we are familiar today had benefited from the financial and economic policies of the Republican administrations; now firms like General Motors and (largest of all) the American Telephone and Telegraph Company come to occupy the centre of the stage.

But though the general tone of business was on the whole good, this intimate association of business with government was in some ways reminiscent of the Gilded Age (which followed the other, and for America, greater war) in the degree of corruption in politics at both state, as well as city, and federal levels; it showed itself in a wide range of cases, from that of James J. Walker, a Tammany Mayor of New York City accused of corrupt practices at the end of the decade to the Teapot Dome oil scandal in the Federal government at the beginning. In the latter the infection came closer to President Harding than it had done to any occupant of the White House since Grant.

No breath of scandal touched Harding's successors, Coolidge and Hoover, but they both, especially perhaps Hoover, had a full share of the later nineteenth century's confidence in the future of American business. Drastic government economy and regressive tax reductions in the upper income levels were deliberately pursued in order to release capital for private investment. This confidence, fully evident in the Republican election triumph of 1928, was shared by most Americans to a remarkable degree, and so the real economic expansion of these years began to assume the guise of the greatest boom of all time, the most striking and at the same time dangerous manifestation of which was on the stock market. The American people, partly perhaps because of their addiction to publicity and proneness to exaggeration, had more than once in their history shown the heights to which they could carry speculative frenzy, as for example in the great land boom culminating in 1837. They were not, however, forewarned, even by the bursting of the Florida land investment bubble in 1926; and the irrational element which is present in financial speculation in every country – deriving from the gambling instinct, the universal gullibility and the wishful delusions of mankind – led the investment mania of many Americans in these years to outstrip the actual economic base of the United States to an extraordinary extent.

The overweening confidence of the great boom expressed itself at two levels. There were grave defects in the financial super-structure, and also serious underlying weaknesses in the economic foundations; and when the former toppled it soon laid bare the latter, which then steadily and increasingly manifested themselves over the years from 1929–33. The procedures of the American stock exchanges at this time had inbuilt perils, particularly that of allowing speculators to 'buy on margin', i.e. to purchase stock for as little as 10 per cent down. This produced a phenomenon known as leverage, by which (especially in the case of investment trusts) with constantly rising prices one set of securities, as yet unpaid for, was used to buy another, different, set, and these to 'purchase' still another, and so on, until the stock market had ceased to be a mechanism for financing economic life and had become a means of speculation – that is to say, unless one was possessed of very special skills, of gambling. As share prices continued to rise over the years, men came to think of this as a kind of law of nature, and, as if hypnotised, to ignore the widening gulf between their paper fantasy and economic reality. When apprehension did begin, many thought that they would be able to get out in time, but few actually did so. Finally, all who were still 'in' found themselves so heavily committed that they were terrified to check the rise, and so continued, through mutual reassurance (by a process which Professor Galbraith has called 'incantation') to ascend to still dizzier heights, and thus to an even more terrible fall when the inevitable debacle came.

Early in the 1920s a day on which 1 million shares were traded on the New York Stock Exchange was very rare, by October and November 1929 this figure was reached every day; during 1927

577 million shares changed hands, by 1929 the total was 1,125 million. Prices of stock rose in a similar fashion; between March 1928 and September 1929, for instance, Montgomery Ward (the mail order firm) rose from 132 to 466, and in the 12 months following September 1928 a group of 30 industrial stocks rose on average from 241 to 381. Traditionally, the price of a stock should be 10 times its annual earnings: now it was some 50 times. The ascent, of course, was never regular; nor was the descent to be so.

The rot set in on Saturday 19 October. Thursday 24 October, when 13 million shares changed hands, was the first of the appalling days, the worst of which – the most fearful in the history of the New York Stock Exchange – was Tuesday 29 October when 16 million shares were traded. All efforts to halt the collapse for more than a few days proved unavailing, and a series of sickening slumps and remorseless declines had brought the market to its nadir by the summer of 1932. On 28 October 1929 the Industrial Average of the stock market published by the *New York Times* had stood at 350; by 13 November it had sunk to 224; by 8 July 1932 it stood at 58. On 3 September 1929 U.S. Steel had been 262 and General Motors 73; on 8 July 1932 they had dropped to 22 and 8 respectively. Investment trusts, which were especially involved in speculation, fared worst; United Founders, which had stood at 70 *dollars* had sunk in the same period to 50 *cents*.

But long before this, serious symptoms of disease had become apparent also in the fundamentals of the economy; the cyclical pattern of overproduction was ending in the seemingly unavoidable contraction. During November 1929 there was a general check to business activity, and in the succeeding three years conditions worsened on a scale, if not in a way, unprecedented in the history of the American industrial cycle. Wholesale prices dropped persistently until they were down to something like a third, and more than 3,500 banks failed; national wealth was reckoned to be reduced to three-quarters and national income to two-thirds of its 1929 value. Industrial production declined by nearly a half and retail trade by a third. Foreign commerce was even worse; exports had been $5 million in 1929 and were $1½ million in 1932. Wages in industry were down correspondingly; Pittsburgh steel workers earned in 1932 half of what they had got three years earlier; workers in Southern mills were on less than $2 a day, and in New York shopgirls were sometimes earning the incredible wage of $3 a week. Unemployment, the great bane of the free enterprise system and supreme index of economic ill-health, rose from some 2 million in

1929 to 4½ million in 1930 and by 1933 had reached the terrible figure of 13 million. The agricultural recession, which had begun much earlier, deepened fast, and it was worse hit by the now rapid spread of world-wide economic depression and the consequent contraction of foreign trade. What Churchill called the Economic Blizzard had spread out from Wall Street and engulfed all mankind.

For America, with her prodigious economic development, had come, to an extent which few realised and which she was herself most reluctant to admit, to dominate the economies of the world. The United States had emerged from the war as the greatest creditor nation, but her debtors, who had mostly become so because of and during the war, could only survive and repay these huge debts if they could earn the international exchange they needed for the purpose, and this in the end plainly had to be done principally by exporting to America. The similar position in international commerce which Britain, on a smaller scale, had occupied after the Napoleonic wars had been made tenable by her unprecedented adoption of virtually complete free trade in mid-nineteenth century, for this had enabled her debtors to trade with her. The United States had now been a high tariff country for many years, and with the Republicans and Big Business in control, she took an exactly opposite course, and returned with enthusiasm to the anti-Democratic, pre-Wilsonian policy of raising her customs duties even higher. The Fordney-McCumber tariff of 1922 was the highest to date, and when the slump came the first reaction of the government was to pass the even more protectionist Smoot-Hawley measure of 1930, despite a remarkably united protest from many American economists. This merely exacerbated the situation of United States agriculture, which could only be readily helped by exports, and these the countries of Europe could not buy if they could not export manufactured goods to the United States. Even less could the peoples of the world buy American industrial goods, so that American industry could not find in exports an escape from the declining domestic market. Thus the cold mantle of the greatest depression in history fell upon the peoples of the world, among whom the Americans, partly because their expectations in the euphoria of 1928 had been so high, certainly did not suffer least.

What had gone wrong? Professor J. K. Galbraith suggests certain causes of the crisis. First, very uneven distribution of national income, with 5 per cent of the population having a third of all personal income; this portion was naturally spent predominantly on luxuries and capital investment. This led to a failure to maintain consumer demand (there was, for instance, a decline in house, as opposed to business, building) and to an excessive expansion of industrial plant and hence to over-supply and the saturation of the market; the situation was exacerbated by the close association of the wealthy with stock market speculation, so that there was a hideous contraction of income after the crash. Second, corporate structure was weak, particularly in investment trusts. Third, banking practices were faulty, and the banks too heavily involved in the speculative mania, with the result that there was an epidemic of failures which had a very grave psychological effect. Fourth, economists on the whole were far from wise before the event, and the tone of the stock exchange was poor, with a higher than usual proportion of confidence-men and swindlers taking advantage of the fever (Richard Whitney, President of the Exchange in the early thirties, was arrested for larceny in 1938). But, ironically to English eyes, perhaps the salient weakness was in the apparently healthy state of America's foreign balance.

Export trade depended on the absorption of her credit balance, as we have seen, and this was as high as $1 billion in 1928. It had been covered in the recent past in two principal ways. In the early 1920s it was done to a considerable extent by gold, which flooded to America in unheard-of quantities; by the middle of the decade this flow had been checked, but the second means still continued, that of American loans abroad, mostly to foreign governments and municipalities, particularly in Germany and South America (both about as bad bets for investment in some ways as the more fanciful internal speculations). This lending abroad continued in the years of the stock market boom, despite the attractions of home investment, but once the crash came, overseas loans stopped abruptly for lack of funds and gold once more rushed in, so that when their limited supplies of gold ran out foreign countries could only fall back on exports, which were inhibited by the tariff. Accordingly, European governments defaulted on their war debts, American exports tumbled, and then the financial crisis began in Central Europe. But this was by no means all the fault of the United States. Thus, for example, the return of Britain, led by Churchill as Chancellor of the Exchequer, to the gold standard in 1925 at $4·86 to the pound led to a long series of exchange crises there; the Governor of the Bank of England and other European bankers accordingly persuaded the Federal Reserve Board to try and improve the situation by lowering government interest rates in the United States in 1927, but this in effect left the American public with even more money for investment in such things as industrial shares, which was probably a very potent factor in promoting the stock market boom.

President Hoover was, therefore, not far wrong when he ascribed the slump to international causes; in fact, there is a school of thought today which believes that this diagnosis was more nearly right than that of his successor, with its heavy, almost exclusive, emphasis on domestic factors. It was in any case characteristic of his background in international economic affairs (as organiser of relief to Europe after the war, for instance), and led him to hope most from the moratorium on war debt payments which he arranged in 1931. But by this time, the depression was far too deep for such a measure to have much effect, and the same was true of the internal steps he was prepared to take to deal with the crisis. The failure was indeed one of imagination. Despite the almost constant downward trend through all but the first six months of his four years in the White House, he – engineer that he was – along with his colleagues, was unable to see the depression except in the framework of conventional American business life. They could not but believe that if Americans remained true to the 'rugged individualism' which – it was a Republican Article of faith, however much it was myth rather than reality – had made America great, the depression, severe as it was, would pass as others had done. They applied the remedy accepted by finance capitalism outside as well as in the United States – ruthless cuts, indeed extreme parsimony, in government expenditure. But it soon became clear that actual poverty now existed on a scale which far exceeded the capacity of private enterprise to cure, or even of charity to alleviate.

The President did then take some vigorous, but still strictly limited, action. The Farm Relief Act of 1929 encouraged farmers' co-operatives; taxation was reduced in 1930 (which was later to prove good Keynesian doctrine); public works were expanded, though on a quite inadequate scale; and a Home Loans Act was intended to aid mortgagees in difficulties. Some of his measures foreshadowed the New Deal, especially the Reconstruction Finance Corporation, whose loans saved many an American business. But perhaps the most valid indictment of his policy was his refusal to accept a number of much more radical measures which were adumbrated by the Congress. This failure of executive leadership, which again marked a reversion to pre-Theodore Roosevelt Republicanism, was chiefly the result of the *laissez-faire* tradition of old-line Republicanism. In particular it can be seen in the fixation of financiers on balancing the budget (thus no deficit spending) at home and on maintaining the gold standard (thus no stimulating devaluation) abroad. As Professor Galbraith writes, 'Rejection of both fiscal and monetary policy amounted precisely to a rejection of all affirmative government policy.' So the gloom and darkness of depression, psychological as well as economic, settled deeper and deeper over the land.

Chapter 18

The New Deal

I T IS DOUBTFUL whether any modern democratic government
going to the polls can survive a catastrophic economic depression, and in the presidential election of 1932 it seemed inevitable
that Hoover, although he had won in 1928 by the huge majority of
444 to 87 electoral votes (being the first post-Reconstruction
Republican to break seriously into the Solid South), would be
defeated by almost any Democratic candidate. In fact his opponent,
Franklin Delano Roosevelt, Governor of New York, was described
by so perceptive and experienced a commentator as Walter
Lippmann as 'an agreeable man who, without any important
qualifications for the office, wants to be President.' The American
people showed, as they were to do on three subsequent occasions
(for Roosevelt overthrew the long-standing convention against
more than two Presidential terms), that they thought differently;
they elected him in November by 472 votes to 59. Although this was
a slightly lower percentage of the whole vote than Hoover had got in
1928, he had a popular plurality of over 7 million votes and took
42 states. The Democrats captured the Senate by 59 to 37 and the
House by 312 to 123.

Thus began the presidential career of the remarkable man who
was to dominate the history of the United States for a longer period
than perhaps any American had done. He was in many ways a
complex character, so that a close political associate, the blunt
Harold L. Ickes, declared, 'I cannot come to grips with him.'
His immense charm went with an occasionally perceptible personal
streak of what Americans call 'meanness' ('spite' is perhaps our
nearest equivalent); his great powers of decision and his infinite
patience sometimes alternated with procrastination and what
looked like an excessive subtlety; he was an episcopalian gentleman
with progressive, in rare instances almost socialistic, ideas, and a
wife whose increasingly reformist views on social questions kept him
in touch with the 'forgotten men', and women, of America. But he
stood squarely in the radical tradition of Jefferson, Jackson and
Wilson, and he restored to the Democratic party an ascendancy it

had not enjoyed since before the Civil War, by welding the workers (especially, to use that highly significant American term, the 'under-privileged') of both city and country for the first time into a really effective voting force.

Yet he was essentially a pragmatist, not wedded indissolubly to a particular political or economic programme and ready to try any course of action which showed promise of results. Perhaps the most acute judgement, quoted by his biographer J. M. Burns, is that of Oliver Wendell Holmes, after meeting F.D.R. when the great Justice was 92: 'A second-class intellect. But a first-class tempera-ment.' And politically it was the temperament that provided the often irresistible magnetism, from the moment when in his dramatic and unprecedented personal acceptance of the Democratic nomina-tion at the Chicago Convention in 1932 he declared, 'I pledge you, I pledge myself, to a new deal for the American people.' His hold upon that people came at bottom from his warmth – which was perhaps increased by his sufferings during the poliomyelitis which left him a permanent cripple – and from his willingness to use at the dictates of his heart all the power that the Federal government could acquire. (This also explained the deep hostility with which many of his opponents regarded him). As he once said, 'the immortal Dante tells us that divine justice weighs the sins of the cold-blooded and the sins of the warm-hearted in different scales. Better the occasional faults of a Government that lives in a spirit of charity than the consistent omissions of a Government frozen in the ice of its own indifference.' One of the common people explained his power and wrote his epitaph: 'Roosevelt is the only President who ever cared for people like us.'

The Democratic platform on which he had been elected was cautious and conservative, even ambiguous, though dominated by the economic crisis except for its espousal of the repeal of prohibi-tion. In the three months between the election and Inauguration Day the situation continued to deteriorate, despite more desperate efforts by Hoover to halt the decline. Farm and other prices sank further, as did factory production; unemployment rose to almost 15 million; and so many banks failed that two-thirds of them were closed by state action throughout the country on the eve of 4 March. It was perhaps the most dramatic Inaugural scene in American history, even including 1861. Putting into practice the idea he had uttered earlier, that the Presidency is 'pre-eminently a place of moral leadership' (his distant cousin, T.R., had, equally charac-teristically, once called it a 'bully pulpit'), the President, asserting that 'the only thing we have to fear is fear itself – nameless, unreasoning, unjustified terror', called 'for action, and action now.' He gave vent to his conviction of the bankruptcy of the old financial order, 'The money changers have fled from their high seats in the temple of our civilisation', a sentiment in the straight Populist tradition. He went on to express the hope that normal constitutional means of action would suffice, but declared that if they did not, he would not hesitate to 'recommend the measures that a stricken Nation in the midst of a stricken world may require . . . I shall [in that event] ask the Congress for . . . broad Executive power to wage a war against the emergency, as great as the power that would be given to me if we were in fact invaded by a foreign foe.'

Action did indeed follow. As his biographer writes, 'It *was* like a war'; and appropriately enough they called the first three months of his Administration 'The 100 Days'. The hectic activity of the New Deal era also in fact recalled the First World War and the unheard-of scale of intervention by the Federal government during that crisis in almost all branches of economic life. Rather as Wilson had built on the precedents created by Lincoln for the exercise of the war power by the President and Commander-in-Chief, so F.D.R. was able to attempt all he did because of the popular consciousness that so many such things had been done in the previous national emergency. He and his advisers also used, if not perhaps always consciously, European precedents for government action in defiance of *laissez-faire* traditions; as one American remarked 'the British statute book was raided on a wholesale scale' by the New Deal. The huge extension of the powers and functions of the Federal government during these years is vividly illustrated not only by the proliferation of agencies of administration and by the increase in the number of Federal civil servants from some half a million in 1933 to 850,000 in 1938 (and to 3 million in 1943 during the war, remaining at some $2\frac{1}{2}$ million today), but also by the vast expansion of the mere physical plant of government in Washington D.C., which was now to grow for the first time into a great metropolis.

The eyes of the nation were, to a degree previously unknown in time of peace, focused on the national capital on 4 March 1933, and the drama did not disappoint them. The President immediately proclaimed a 'bank holiday' and checked withdrawals of gold and silver; he then called Congress into special session on 9 March (the earliest possible date in the pre-airline age), on which day, in a quite unprecedented burst of speed, both Houses passed an Act giving the President emergency powers over banking and currency which he signed at 9 pm that evening. Next day he asked for wide powers to effect economies in government spending, and, despite some Congressional defections under organised pressure from pension groups, got them five days later. Even a call on the 12 March for an amendment to the Volstead Act permitting the manufacture and sale of beer and light wines was answered by the 16th. And he maintained his momentum in the ensuing weeks in a way quite new to American government even in time of war.

On 16 March he asked for the most far-reaching agricultural bill in American history aimed at raising farm prices and agricultural purchasing power; the Agricultural Adjustment Act (AAA) was signed in mid-May. On 21 March he proposed a Civilian Conservation Corps (CCC) to put 250,000 young unemployed men to work by the early summer; it was passed by voice vote ten days later. On the same day, in a complete break with Hoover's policy, he requested Federal grants to the states for direct unemployment relief, and Congress swiftly passed the Federal Emergency Relief Act (FERA) by large majorities. The increasingly favoured method of Federal influence over the states was used in FERA, by promising to 'match' every $3 produced by a state with $1 from Washington, thus stimulating the states to action and aiding them in it while largely avoiding the issues of constitutionality. Congress also made $500 million available to the Reconstruction Finance Corporation (RFC), created under the Republicans. Further measures, passed by June, included one giving power to the Interstate Commerce Commission to supervise the stock market, one creating a Home Owners Loan Corporation, and another including emergency railroad legislation and extending ICC control.

Most drastic in the short term was the National Industrial Recovery Act, setting up the National Recovery Administration (NRA); this envisaged an expenditure of more than $3 billion on public works and set up machinery for 'a great cooperative movement throughout all industry in order to obtain wide re-employment, to shorten the working week, to pay a decent wage . . . and to prevent unfair competition and disastrous overproduction.' It was passed almost intact despite some radical opposition to a bill which gave so much power to business as well as the Federal government. Most important, perhaps, in the long run was the creation of the Tennessee Valley Authority (TVA), authorised to develop the navigability of the river and its hydro-electric potential, using the public power so produced as a yardstick by which to measure the efficiency of private utilities. This was one of the most unpopular of Roosevelt's measures with business (his 1940 presidential opponent Wendell Willkie was president of a great utility company), but one of the most far-sighted; it was nothing less than a revolutionary concept, the development of the valley and its resources, both human and material, as a whole. It was 'national planning for a complete river watershed.'

Thus ended the 100 Days; it was an extraordinary legislative achievement and it was the President's. He veritably seemed, as an admirer called him, 'the Andrew Jackson of the Twentieth Century, championing the rights of the people.' How successful he was to be in effecting a permanent cure of the body economic remained to be seen.

The great psychological effect of this rush distracted attention from the fact that Roosevelt was playing his favourite political and administrative game of riding a number of different horses – or advisers – at the same time. In practice this often meant, in one of his favourite sayings, to put holders of antithetical or differing views 'in a room together and tell them no lunch until they agree', thus nicely leaving the final decision in the hands of the President. It could be criticised as excessively pragmatic and as producing just some kind of agreed action rather than the right action – or even the deeply considered action – in the same way that his tendency to avoid political and personal conflicts by by-passing established offices and office-holders could be held to result in an excessive proliferation of new governmental agencies and considerable administrative confusion and inefficiency. But at a deeper level, it was, in the American sense, truly democratic; it was an effort, as F.D.R. himself put it, 'to find among many discordant elements that unity of purpose that is best for the Nation as a whole.' He did thus make during his first term (looking at it another way), a real attempt to be President of all the people. By dynamic leadership of his great majorities in Congress, he got during this term more action out of the legislative arm to attempt to grapple with the great crisis than any other President has ever done. Despite his growing unpopularity with some of the business community, he commanded very wide support indeed in the nation at large.

The difficulties arising from his economic pragmatism, nevertheless, can be seen in his treatment of the London International Economic Conference which met in the summer. His delegation was divided between the orthodox low-tariff views of the Secretary of State, Cordell Hull of Tennessee, and those of Raymond Moley, a presidential adviser with much more radical instructions from the President. The nations at the Conference were moving in the direction of a vague formula to reassure the countries still on the gold standard and to try to limit the variations of the dollar when

Roosevelt sent a 'bombshell' in the form of a personal message denouncing the 'old fetishes of the so-called international bankers'; he made it clear that he was determined to raise American domestic price levels by currency manipulation and not to reduce tariffs by international arrangement. This administered a severe and perhaps worth-while shock to orthodox international finance and killed the conference, but John Maynard Keynes, emerging since the publication of his *Treatise on Money* in 1930 as a new economic prophet (and one tending to gain more honour in America than in his own country), declared, 'President Roosevelt is magnificently right.' Despite this potent judgement, there are economic historians today who incline to believe that the promotion of international trade (by, among other things, the reduction of trade barriers) might have been an equal, if not superior, method of climbing out of the slump.

But Roosevelt was understandably resolved on independent national action, which at least he could be reasonably sure of getting and which pleased his still predominently isolationist New Deal followers; by mid-January 1934 the United States was off the gold standard and the dollar had been devalued by just about 40 per cent. The Gold Reserve Act of 30 January at last gave some real control of the United States currency to the government. There was also, not surprisingly with a Democratic government, an inflationary – and probably salutary – silver content in the Act, declaring that it was the policy of the United States to raise the proportion of silver in the American monetary stock to a quarter of the whole. This was soon recognised as a concession to the silver bloc, and in the end the Silver Purchase Act of 1939 was bluntly to authorise the purchase of all new domestically mined silver at nearly double the world's prevailing price. But the President, whose personal background in finance was orthodox, did not easily give up his attempt to restore the temple of the money-changers 'to the ancient truths'. Characteristic was the Glass-Steagall Banking Act of 1 June 1933, Glass being conservative and Steagall suspicious of banking orthodoxy; it brought the American credit structure to a greater degree under the control of the Federal Reserve Board, which was given power to check speculative credit expansion by the banks, and created the Federal Deposit Insurance Corporation to insure the deposits of small banks. In 1934 the Securities and Exchange Commission (SEC) was set up to regulate the stock exchanges.

There were further developments in the New Deal in succeeding months, such as the replacement of FERA in 1935 by a new Works Progress Administration (WPA) under Harry L. Hopkins (not to be confused with the Public Works Administration – or PWA! – scrupulously administered by the 'old curmudgeon', Harold Ickes, at the Department of the Interior); WPA employed some 2 million Americans annually until the war on everything from road building to theatrical performances. Other extensions of the role and powers of the Federal government included the Federal Communications Commission (FCC) and the Civil Aeronautics Authority (CAA), but perhaps the most influential programme economically was that under the AAA, organised by Henry A. Wallace as Secretary of Agriculture. Its objective was to raise agricultural returns to a 'level that will give agricultural commodities a purchasing power with respect to articles farmers buy equivalent to the purchasing power of agricultural commodities in the base period August 1909–July 1914.' Farmers could, for example, get a government subsidy by controlling their production of staples; other such government-supported schemes, which were complicated but mostly operated by the farmers themselves, had marked social as well as economic effects, especially in the South. Severe droughts in 1934 and 1936, creating the Great Dust Bowl of the Plains, made the task of agricultural resuscitation even more difficult.

But the most dramatic manifestation of the New Deal was the National Recovery Administration (NRA), under its flamboyant head General Hugh Johnson. So headlong was the pace of this attempt to organise co-operative measures in industry under the supervision of the state that it was scarcely under his control, let alone that of the Administration. Its biggest project was to develop industrial codes of fair competition, which it did for 500 industries. (Its first was for cotton, where it laid down a forty hour week, abolished child labour, and enjoined a minimum wage of $12 or $13.) But it became more and more paper-ridden and top heavy (it issued some 11,000 administrative orders in a matter of months) and seemed to favour monopoly, so that it was increasingly attacked from the left, while, although NIRA's famous clause 7(a) gave unprecedented protection to the processes of collective bargaining, labour came to believe that NRA as a whole handicapped them in the normal operation of those processes. By 1935 it was coming to look more and more – the metaphor is apt – like a white elephant.

These massive extensions of Federal power, through the extra-ordinary ascendancy of the President over Congress, had yet to reckon with the third arm, for the Supreme Court speaks last although it does not necessarily have the final word. The bench was very conservative in 1936, its Justices having an average age of seventy-one; the Chief Justice, Charles Evans Hughes, was a moderate of great ability, but only 3 of its 9 members were liberals. It began cautiously, but in May 1935 declared the whole of NRA unconstitutional; this may have been a secret relief to some members of the Administration, but the invalidation of the vital AAA in January next year was much more grave. A Soil Conservation and Domestic Allotment Act was rushed through in February (and in 1938 a much more carefully considered AAA was to reach the statute book) but it was now clear that the Supreme Court was a potential threat to the whole New Deal programme. Further conservative decisions followed, culminating in the invalidation of a New York State minimum wage law on 1 June 1936, which was an attack even on the powers of the States to take remedial economic and social action.

In pursuit of his policies and in preparation for the forthcoming presidential election, Roosevelt stepped up his pressure on Congress for further action, and thus found himself, when the campaign opened, in a decidedly radical posture. There was a growing bitterness in business opposition to 'that cripple in the White House', fundamentally perhaps because he had undermined the self-esteem of those who had but recently offered the American people a new heaven and new earth on business principles – only to find themselves faced (in a classic example of *hubris*) with what seemed to that people like utter national ruin. In fact, F.D.R. was far from the socialist his enemies called him; rather did the New Deal, perhaps, save the American capitalist system by its energetic and persistent empiricism. But it was much too radical for business. Not however for the mass of the population. In a quite unparalleled victory, Roosevelt in the 1936 election carried every state except Maine and Vermont (523 to 8 electoral votes) with a popular majority of 27 million to 16 million. His enormous majorities in Congress, 334–89 and 75–17, made him appear invincible, but no Era of Good Feelings followed this seeming extinction of the Republican party; indeed, the President himself was to suffer a minor case of *hubris*.

In great secrecy and with excessive subtlety (especially since the Democratic platform had talked openly of constitutional amendment) Roosevelt planned a flank attack upon the conservatism of the Supreme Court. He promoted a bill laying down that for every Supreme Court justice who failed to quit the bench within six months of reaching the age of seventy the President was empowered to appoint a new member of the Court, up to a total of six additional justices (that is, of 15 in all). But the plan misfired. Despite the huge Democratic majorities in Congress, it failed to get the necessary upport, partly because the attempt to avoid the cumbersomes mechanism of constitutional amendment was so transparent that it looked almost Machiavellian, and partly because it ran counter to the deep American veneration, despite all its failings, for the Supreme Court. The people of the United States have few foci of allegiance and political emotion; there are very few trappings of state except the flag ('Old Glory', which is daily saluted in most American classrooms, inspires a deep sense of loyalty), and the Presidency is a political office, and indeed a party prize, which is deliberately kept civilian and almost devoid of outward show. The solemn black robes of the nine Supreme Court justices may lack the scarlet and the display of British law, but the hold of the court on the respect of the people is powerful.

More than that, it embodies perhaps more than anything else their almost instinctive feeling for the Constitution, the American holy of holies. And because of the deep-rooted suspicion of governmental power, even as late as the 1930s, the threat to the balance of the Constitution seemed even more grave because of the very prestige and the apparent strength of the President on the eve of his election triumph. Chief Justice Hughes, though saying 'If they want me to preside over a convention, I can do it', fought back quietly but effectively, and the legislation did not pass. The attempt, however, shook up the Court, which not only began to change its composition through voluntary retirement but, even before the new appointments produced a New Deal majority, started to take a more liberal line. However, the rebuff to the President was not a happy augury for his second term, and indeed as the sense of urgency abated a not unfamiliar pattern in American politics began to emerge. The tension between the White House and Capitol Hill grew, and the Democratic majorities proved too overwhelming, and broke their backs. The strongly conservative, mostly Southern and so-called Bourbon, element in the Democratic party began more and more frequently to align itself with conservative Republicanism in opposition to the President's radical demands. For these he now had to fight hard, and by no means always with success.

Unfortunately, the need for radical measures, such as those which he had demanded in the election campaign (which had led him a good deal farther to the left than before), did not diminish, for despite a sharp upturn in the economy in 1936 there was renewed recession in late 1937. Some achievements, such as the establishment of the U.S. Housing Administration for slum clearance and of the U.S. Maritime Commission to encourage a merchant fleet worthy of the nation, were developments of the New Deal, but most attention had to be concentrated on the second slump. It is possible that it was precipitated by the over-anxiety of the Administration to revert, in the optimism of recovery in 1936, to ideas of economy and orthodox finance, and its readiness to fear a premature boom, but unemployment which had briefly sunk to its lowest point since the 1920s in July 1937 – below 5 million – rose to 11 million by January 1938. This had a very adverse effect on national morale, particularly in view of the Administration's claims to government planning in the economy, and the conservatives cried loudly that the New Deal had failed. By the spring the President, under very heavy pressure from the left (including elements as desperate as Huey Long of Louisiana and as fantastic as the Social Credit Party in the Far West), was convinced that the natural forces of recovery were again proving inadequate and launched the so-called Second New Deal. Its deficit spending was not, even now, the result of the adoption of the theories of Keynes, or anyone else, but simply, once again, a response to the facts: F.D.R. would rather increase public works and unbalance the budget than not help the unemployed.

In fact, the new measures did not cure the recession. Unemployment was still to stand at about 10 million in 1939, and to all appearances (as in 1914) it was the war which at last effectively reflated the American economy. One trouble was that the renewal of the depression caught the Social Security system set up by the Act of 1935 – perhaps in the long term the most important permanent reform of the New Deal – off balance, before it had had time to establish itself and consolidate its funds; it has been argued, indeed, that the sums collected by the government in social security taxes were a factor in causing the renewal of the depression. But it was nevertheless a vital symbol of the revolution in the American mind on the subject of Federal intervention in the social and economic life of the nation, for it took the unprecedented step of co-ordinating Federal and State action on old-age and unemployment insurance. In any case, however, the sums involved were still too small to have a decisive effect in re-stimulating the economy. Nor was the steady progress made by Secretary of State Hull in his policy of reducing international trade barriers by trade treaties (mostly bilateral) sufficiently rapid or extensive to have a crucial effect.

But one development of the President's terms of office was of the utmost importance, even though it was scarcely the result of direct government action at all – the exceedingly rapid growth in the power of labour. This revolution, with its resultant raising of wages (which was in the long run probably the most significant single reflationary factor in national economic life), was perhaps the most important long-term result of the New Deal. At first the President had been only a lagging supporter of labour, but by his second term he had, despite the vicissitudes of his relationship with a number of their leaders, become increasingly warm towards them and increasingly dependent on their political support. The National Industrial Recovery Act had given the right of collective bargaining to labour and set up the Labor Advisory Board. This signalised a fundamental change in the attitude of government, in some cases at the State as well as the Federal level. The extraordinary growth of the AFL is best illustrated by that of its greatest union, the United Mine Workers, from 80,000 to 400,000 members in a single year after the passage of NIRA.

The Wagner-Connery Act of 1935 was very favourable to labour and set up a permanent National Labour Relations Board (NLRB). This was followed by the formation of the Congress of Industrial Organizations (CIO), the first large industrial – as opposed to craft – federation of unions, under the leadership of John L. Lewis, the Mine Workers' leader, in 1936. This body, founded by the Mine Workers, who seceded from the AFL, organised the great and reluctant, indeed reactionary, steel and automobile industries with extraordinary speed, partly through the invention, or use, of the radical and remarkably successful 'sit-down' strike. (As Denis Brogan has put it, 'there were as many claimants for the honour of this invention as there were for the birthplace of Hoover or of the Republican party'). By the beginning of the Second World War labour had become powerfully entrenched in the life of the United States, although at the cost of a split between the AFL and the CIO which was to endure for many years. This marked a lasting alteration in the balance of American society: in a sense it could be considered as the rectification of an imbalance which had persisted since the triumph of industrial capitalism in the late nineteenth century.

As for the economic affairs of the Union, save for the War the New Deal would have gone out with a whimper rather than a bang. New investment which had totalled $9·5 billion between 1925–9 and $1 billion from 1933–5 did not exceed $2 billion in the period 1935–9; other free economies in the Western world fared somewhat better in this respect than the United States. But the New Deal must not be underestimated; the problems of the Economic Blizzard were very grave and very difficult to understand, let alone to remedy. The New Deal gave power, or the promise of power, to the Federal government: more than that, it gave hope to the American people. F.D.R.'s contribution was a determination to go on experimenting until poverty was alleviated, and he broke down in political practice the shibboleths which Keynes was attacking in economic theory. He restored America's belief in its own democracy, and this was of inestimable value when the war came.

Chapter 19

Withdrawal and Return, 1921–41

T HOUGH THE presidential election of 1920 was not, as was
claimed, a 'solemn referendum' on the League of Nations,
because it was also much concerned with other issues, and
though American isolationism in the next two decades was by no
means as complete as historical tradition has had it, the revulsion
of American opinion, in habitual fashion, against involvement in the
affairs of the old world between the two wars was very marked. The
truth is that isolationism as a state of mind was a reality, but that
isolation, in the technological circumstances of the twentieth
century, was impossible. Just as in the case of the British policy of
appeasement of the dictators under Neville Chamberlain in the
1930s, the predominant feature of the American attitude often
seemed to be a failure to face the harsh facts of international life
which, in the words of one American historian, R. W. Van Alstyne,
'held the American public spellbound . . . Pathological in its
devotion to the empty slogan of "Keep out of war!" the public was
fascinated and frightened by the growing spectacle of violence and
lawlessness in Europe. Its education in the strategy of the western
Pacific was yet to come. Pearl Harbor proved to be the best
teacher.'

The question which linked together in 1921 the main international
problems both of Europe and the Far East – largely because of the
ubiquitous nature of sea power – was that of naval rivalry between
Britain and the United States. Even during the Wilsonian period it
had been a recurrent if recessive theme in Anglo-American relations,
and now it squarely faced the Republican administration and its
Secretary of State, Charles Evans Hughes, one-time Presidential
candidate and future Chief Justice of the Supreme Court. The heart
of the question was the hard necessity for Britannia, who had so long
ruled the waves, to reconcile herself to this overt naval equal and
potential naval superior. But within this heart there also lay the fact
that the United States, although unwilling to accept the implications of the situation, now in truth held the balance of power not
only in Europe (as Britain had in many respects long done) but also

in the world as a whole. In Europe the strength of her position was exaggerated by the weakness of Germany and Russia as well as by the exhaustion of Britain and France, but in the Far East it was complicated, as had become clear during the Versailles negotiations, by the existence of the Anglo-Japanese Alliance and the growing American mistrust of and rivalry with Japan.

There were now, however, potent elements in Anglo-American relations making for the friendly settlement of any grave problem between the two peoples; the first signs of compromise were informal British suggestions for naval parity, and the recognition by the British government, in large part as a result of the forceful representations of the Canadian Prime Minister, Arthur Meighen, that in effect the Japanese Alliance must, if necessary, be sacrificed for the sake of understanding with the United States. After the signing of an Anglo-Irish truce on 8 July 1921 (an event of some significance in Anglo-American history), the British government accepted an American invitation to the Washington Naval Conference which assembled later in the year. There, in a dramatic opening speech, Secretary of State Hughes called for a radical programme of naval disarmament, so that, as Mark Sullivan told the tale, the First Sea Lord, Earl Beatty, was seen to come forward in his chair, a 'slightly staggered and deeply disturbed expression' on his face, reminding one of a 'bulldog, sleeping on a sunny doorstep, who has been poked in the stomach by the impudent foot of an itinerant soap-canvasser seriously lacking in any sense of the most ordinary proprieties.' As a British correspondent described it, the urbane Balfour alone of the British delegation appeared unmoved at the continuation of these proposals, which sank more British battleships 'than all the admirals of the world had destroyed in a cycle of centuries'.

After hard bargaining, the United States, Britain, Japan, France and Italy, in one of the few successful disarmament treaties in history, accepted a ratio of roughly 5–5–3–1.7–1.7 in capital ships and aircraft carriers. Fundamentally this agreement was made possible, in this post-war era, by the financial circumstances and the pacific inclinations of the peoples concerned; in the United States the sentiment was mobilised by the formidable isolation leader, Senator Borah. But a price had to be paid for Japan's acceptance of this position of naval inferiority, and this was acceptance in her turn by the United States of an agreement to maintain the *status quo* in the fortification of the insular possessions of the powers in the Pacific, which considerably increased the Japanese ascendancy in the area. Along with these military provisions went political arrangements (embodied in the so-called Four and Nine Power treaties) which were more difficult for the United States to accept, strictly limited though their actual commitments were. In essence they provided as graceful a British escape as possible from the Japanese alliance by merging it in a broader association. The Four Power treaty specifically terminated the alliance, but pledged that the signatories would 'communicate with one another fully and frankly in order to arrive at an understanding as to the most efficient measures to be taken, jointly or separately, to meet the exigencies of the particular situation.' But, weak as this American engagement was, the Senate still added a reservation to the effect that there was 'no commitment to armed force, no alliance, no obligation to join in any defence.' The Nine Power pact reaffirmed the Open Door policy in China, but was accepted by Japan, probably because it constituted only the flimsiest paper obstacle to any designs she might have on the Asian mainland.

The United States thus got her way, by obtaining essential naval equality with Britain and bringing about the end of the exclusive Anglo-Japanese alliance, but the Washington Treaty left Japan in effective control of the North West Pacific, while Britain's influence was still seen as paramount in the Narrow Seas and Mediterranean and along the route from Europe to Australia. The United States, however, dominated all the approaches to the Western Hemisphere and had clearly demonstrated that the crucial fact for the future of sea power was her capacity to outbuild any other maritime nation. Churchill has been critical of this 'annulment' at American behest of the British bond with Japan, which 'caused a profound impression' in that country 'and was viewed as the spurning of an Asiatic Power by the Western World. Many links were sundered which might afterwards have proved of decisive value to peace.' But Japan's recent history had not been of the kind to give much hope that she would be restrained in her urgent international ambitions by such a tie as this. The most that can be said with assurance is that it probably strengthened the hands of the militant and military elements in Japanese life.

The treaty did not, of course, settle the naval question for good, and it only applied to the largest categories of vessel. A Conference at Geneva in 1927, which was left too much in the hands of the naval experts, failed to agree on the restriction of lesser categories, but at London in 1930 an earlier meeting of minds between the pacifist Labour Prime Minister, Ramsay MacDonald, and the Quaker President Hoover was finally consummated and resulted in effective overall Anglo-American parity, if not exact equality. France and Italy did not ratify this treaty, and Japan gave notice that she would not accept the overall fleet ratio, of 100 (U.S.) – 102·4 (G.B.) – 63·6 (Japan), beyond the next naval Conference, when she would demand equality. She in fact renounced the London treaty in 1934, but even more ominous had been the earlier assassination of the Minister who negotiated it on his return to Japan from London. When the 1935 naval conference met, circumstances had been so changed by the aggressive policies of the 'Axis' powers that it in effect abolished all Anglo-American naval limitations and ended serious Anglo-American naval rivalry. Britain was very soon to welcome as large and dominant an American navy as possible, though even after the Second World War some vestigial British jealousy of American naval power could show itself.

Meanwhile, though ostentatiously refusing at first any contact with the League of Nations and persistently rejecting the recommendations of successive Presidents to join the quite autonomous World Court, America gradually began to edge nearer to League affairs by taking part in some of its non-political activities. The Administration commenced, for instance, by sending 'observers' to the Opium Conference of 1924 – what Clemenceau characteristically described as being represented by an ear but not a mouth. But the United States, as we have seen already, could not in fact opt out of the world economy, and her massive overseas investments had profound political, as well as economic, implications. One international problem with which she was intimately associated was that of war debts and reparations. Efforts to solve this had necessarily to include, even to be led by, the American government, since she was the world's largest creditor.

Complex in its details, the situation was simple in its essence, for Britain was a net creditor, being owed more than she owed, whereas France and other associated states were debtors, although owed reparations by Germany. From the beginning the European powers wanted to link their payment of their debts to Germany's payment of reparations, but the United States refused to accept this, partly because she saw the impossibility of the Germans actually paying too much. Britain early proposed an all-round cancellation of debts (analogous to that which she had effected after the Napoleonic wars) for the benefit of world trade, but this the United States refused, rather in the spirit of Coolidge's reported remark, 'They hired the money, didn't they?' Britain therefore announced that she would collect from her European debtors only such sums as were needed to pay her American debt, about the settlement of which an Anglo-American agreement was signed in 1923. But increasing difficulties arose over the payment of vast sums so disruptive of international patterns of trade and exchange, especially in view of the height of the American tariff; and with the Great Depression came nemesis. Starting with Germany, all the powers except Finland (which alone had a favourable trade balance with America) rapidly defaulted on their war debts to the United States. An irritated Congress in 1934 passed the Johnson Act which forbade any person under American jurisdiction to lend money to any government in default on its debts to the United States. Yet, although the debts never have been paid, within seven years the United States was supplying Britain and her Allies on a scale far exceeding that of the First World War. But 'Lend-Lease' was to do this in a fashion which left no legacy of trouble and ill-will remotely comparable to that of the war debts problem in these years.

Very shortly, however, such clouds as these were overshadowed by the far more ominous gathering of the storm of World War II. Though it was to burst out in Europe first, its earliest premonitory symptoms were in Asia and were not checked by one American-promoted agreement, the Kellogg Pact of 1928, under which, in a sanguine flush of Jeffersonian idealism, its signatories renounced war as an instrument of international policy. But it was as a signatory of this pact that America, in the person of Secretary of State Henry L. Stimson, urged an international appeal for the ending of the undeclared hostilities which had broken out between Nationalist China and Soviet Russia in 1929. This was ineffective, but it fore-shadowed the most active American policy in the Far East since Theodore Roosevelt, which began when Japan launched the care-fully prepared Manchuria 'incident' on 18 September 1931. Stimson (whose personal policy it was) certainly was far from being an isolationist, at least in the Far East, and was prepared when he intervened to go up to, and even beyond, the limits of what was politically possible in the face of public opinion within the United States. He lacked, of course, the authority of the Republican Roosevelt, especially because his President, Hoover, was far more pacific, indeed pacifist, than his strong and active Secretary of State, who thus presented the unusual spectacle of the American State Department urging a reluctant, European-oriented, League of Nations to more vigorous action against Japan.

Stimson thought that the League must take the lead, but in-structed the American Minister at Berne to be present at meetings of the Council in Geneva; when requested by the League to do so he appointed a representative to attend such of its meetings as affected the enforcement of the Kellogg Pact; on 23 September he agreed

with the League to send identical notes calling for the withdrawal
of troops; and on 5 October he promised that the American
government would 'endeavor to reinforce what the League does'
and even talked later of 'some form of collective economic sanctions
against Japan'. But, despite all this, the League would do no more
than invoke the Kellogg Pact, through the motions of which the
United States also went. When the League appointed the Lytton
investigating commission, the United States went much further and
delivered a serious warning to the Japanese Ambassador in
Washington. There could be no clearer illustration than this
of the dire results of America's failure to enter the League of
Nations, for without her it was spineless, partly because of its
lack of real and ready muscle, particularly in the Far East.

Other powers, and especially Britain, must also bear a large,
indeed greater, share of the blame. Stimson informed the Foreign
Office in London beforehand that he proposed to reaffirm the Open
Door policy and the territorial integrity of China, but Sir John
Simon, the Foreign Secretary, in typical fashion evaded the issue
by hiding behind the League, and London sent a studiedly casual
reply to Washington. But perhaps Simon had some excuse; not
only was British public opinion very reluctant to undertake any
forceful action, but he might also be pardoned for (in fact was
almost certainly correct in) believing that Stimson had far outrun
his own public and even his own President, for the latter wrote at
the time, we 'will not go along on war or any of the sanctions either
military or economic, for these are the roads to war.' But on
7 January 1932 the Secretary of State acted alone and enunciated
what came to be called the 'Hoover-Stimson doctrine', that the
United States would not recognise agreements effected by means
contrary to the Kellogg Pact. This was a precedent of great importance, although it was in the direct Wilsonian tradition of
moralism in international affairs, particularly *vis à vis* Latin America
and also Soviet Russia, which the United States had steadfastly
refused to recognise since the Bolshevik Revolution. Though it
embodied a typical Jeffersonian overemphasis on the effectiveness
of economic and psychological pressure in international affairs, its
critics must admit that moral factors cannot readily be excluded
permanently from foreign policy; in any case the American readiness
to condemn the use of force and to refuse to recognise the international fruits of it was to have important repercussions in the era
of Red China after the Second World War.

But it certainly did little, if anything, to halt Japanese aggression.
When Japan attacked Shanghai in January 1932 the United States

led Britain in the sending of reinforcements, but Simon still refused the repeated and urgent requests of Stimson to join him in the formal invocation of the Nine Power Treaty. Britain did get a non-recognition motion through the League, but Japan established a puppet state in Manchuria in September 1932, and in 1933 left the League. In 1937 she attacked the Chinese heartland, and by the time of the Munich crisis in September 1938 had Hankow and Canton in her clutches. Though most of the citizens of the Western democracies did not realise it, the Second World War had begun in all but name.

At first, it could be said, F.D.R. was less concerned about international affairs than Stimson and even Hoover. He had been Vice-Presidential candidate in 1920 on a League ticket, but in 1933 had declared, 'we are not members, and we do not contemplate membership.' Not only was he deeply involved in domestic problems and in seeking essentially domestic solutions to them, but many New Dealers, such as Harry Hopkins, were isolationist in these early years. There was, however, an antithetical, anti-isolationist strain in the Administration, personified by such men as Henry Morgenthau and above all Secretary of State Cordell Hull, who was a Wilsonian low-tariff Democrat from Tennessee and who steadily carried through a programme of bilateral trade treaties (including one with Britain in 1938) during his long tenure of office. But in Congress, and especially perhaps the Foreign Relations Committee of the Senate, which was dominated by Borah, isolationist sentiment was deeper than ever; the isolationist ranks included a number of radical Democrats like Burton K. Wheeler of Montana. As the threat to peace and democracy increased with the growing ascendancy of Hitler and Mussolini in Europe, the tide of isolationism rose ever higher in the United States, but these dangers, combined with this classic display of the ostrich stance, produced a steadily intensifying reaction in the President, who was, after all, not only a Wilsonian but a Roosevelt and a disciple of Mahan, as well as a statesman who had been Assistant Secretary of the Navy during the First World War. So he began a long and in the end – with the aid of Japan – successful struggle to make the reluctant American people face the harsh and unpleasant realities of international life.

This struggle did not begin well. In 1934 the Nye Committee of the Senate commenced a prolonged investigation of the munitions industry, in an effort to indict arms manufacturers for causing wars, and especially for causing America to enter the First World War – an indictment which in a broad sense can only properly lie against mankind as a whole. In 1935, in this state of mind and as a hurried response to Mussolini's invasion of Abyssinia, the first of the famous Neutrality Acts was passed by Congress, making illegal the export for a belligerent of 'arms, ammunition, or implements of war', and giving the President power to forbid belligerent submarines to enter American ports and American citizens to travel on belligerent ships. Hull and the President vainly asked for discretion in the banning of exports, in order that they might distinguish between aggressors and their victims, but reluctantly accepted the bill in any case. In fact the legislation worked in practice against Italy, the aggressor, and this effect was reinforced somewhat by a moral embargo on exports to her which was called for by the Administration. In 1936 a further Neutrality Act strengthened the first; by forbidding, for example, loans to belligerents. In 1937 after the outbreak of the Spanish Civil War, in an attempt to satisfy this consuming and understandable American desire not to become involved in hostilities (which was shared by the European democracies with their policy of Non-Intervention in Spain), an embargo on exports to both sides was specifically enacted, as if in an international conflict. From this Franco and his insurgent forces profited greatly, for their allies, Germany and Italy, were restrained by no fears or scruples from sending large-scale aid.

In the same year a third, and 'permanent', Neutrality Act was passed. To the existing provisions, it added others even more stringent. The President could forbid certain raw materials as well as arms to be carried in American ships; such of these raw materials as were exported to belligerents must also be paid for in cash before leaving the United States; these constituted what came to be known as the 'Cash and Carry' provisions. The prohibition against Americans travelling in belligerent vessels was made absolute, and the arming of American merchant vessels was forbidden. This Act of 1937 was the high-water mark of isolationism. It signalised the complete reversal of Wilson's belief that the United States could tolerate no abrogation of her full rights as a neutral in international law. It was in fact a virtually total, voluntary, renunciation of her rights as a great power to move and trade upon the high seas without let or hindrance, and it was made in the delusory hope that she would thus avoid becoming involved in the armed struggles of the 'outside' world. She was to learn the hard way that she was no longer safe on the inside looking out.

Ever since the enuciation of the Monroe Doctrine, however, Americans had regarded the Western Hemisphere as peculiarly their sphere of interest and influence in the world, and even at the height of isolationist sentiment they remained aware of the need to consolidate the security of this base. Taking up a phrase of his predecessor's, first used during a visit to Latin America, F.D.R. called in his First Inaugural for 'the policy of the good neighbour' in 'the field of world policy'; and the term Good Neighbour came particularly to be applied to the states of the American hemisphere. He went on to talk of 'the neighbour who resolutely respects himself and, because he does so, respects the rights of others', thus by implication announcing the end of the Roosevelt Corollary to the Monroe Doctrine and of the American policy of persistent interference in Latin-American affairs. This new cordiality and increased comprehension of Latin-American feelings on the part of the United States was shortly given full expression in such measures as the repeal of the Platt Amendment (which had given America the right of intervention in Cuba) and the withdrawal of American marines from Haiti. The attitude, despite difficulties over Argentina, was to form in general a satisfactory basis for American policy in the Western Hemisphere during the Second World War, although it was to prove inadequate in the post-war years in face of the pressure from Communism and the desperate poverty of most Latin-Americans.

Meanwhile in Europe things went from bad to worse, and the President issued increasingly urgent warnings to his people that neutrality was not enough, but he never felt – without doubt correctly – that he could afford to move too far ahead of American public opinion, for he was always acutely aware of the disaster which had overtaken Wilson and his policies just because he lost touch with the people. In 1937, for instance, in a famous speech at Chicago, he called for a 'quarantine' of aggressors, but in the full blast of isolationism this backfired, and slowed down the President's policy of educating the public in international realities. Nor were Britain and France in any better case, for their policy of appeasement was now in unrestrained operation, and in 1938 Chamberlain felt unable to take up enthusiastically Roosevelt's secret offer of a Washington economic conference, which earned the verdict from Churchill (in his memoirs, but speaking nevertheless more as statesman than historian), 'That Mr. Chamberlain, with his limited outlook and inexperience of the European scene, should have possessed the self-sufficiency to wave away the proffered hand stretched out across the Atlantic leaves one, even at this date, breathless with amazement.' American rearmament did begin to gather momentum, but even this concrete American power counted for singularly little on the international scene because the world believed that the American people, if not the American President, would refuse to use it except in the sheerest self-defence.

Thus the slide to war in Europe accelerated, unchecked by any of the efforts of Roosevelt to do what little he could by mobilising world, as well as American, opinion against the dictators; and on 1 September 1939 (heralded by the unexpected Nazi-Soviet pact) the war finally came. The President's attempts earlier in the year, after the rape of Czechoslovakia, to obtain alterations in the Neutrality law giving him discretionary power to aid the victims of aggression had proved unavailing, but the limited Cash and Carry provisions of the 1937 Act had expired on 1 May. The main fact, however, was that when the war began the export of munitions of war directly or indirectly to belligerents from the United States was absolutely forbidden. In this respect the position of the Allies *vis à vis* Germany was much less favourable for obtaining essential assistance from America than it had been in 1914. On the other hand, American opinion, while still overwhelmingly isolationist, was much more hostile to Germany than it had been twenty-five years before; Roosevelt's Neutrality Proclamation of 5 September differed markedly from that of Wilson, for the President commented, 'This nation will remain a neutral nation, but I cannot ask that every American will remain neutral in thought as well.' So deep was American mistrust of tyranny and dislike of such things as the German persecution of the Jews that in October 1939 a public opinion poll showed that, although 99 per cent of the American people favoured neutrality, only 2 per cent were pro-German as compared with 84 per cent who favoured the Allies.

The President accordingly called Congress into Special Session on 21 September to amend the neutrality legislation by 'a return to international law'. After a bitter struggle a compromise with the forces of isolationism was reached; the arms embargo was repealed, but Cash and Carry was enforced for all war materials, which must thus become non-American before export and be carried in non-American ships. Travel on belligerent vessels and loans to belligerents were still forbidden, and a new provision excluded American ships altogether from 'combat zones', which were to be defined by Presidential proclamation. But despite these restrictions, the amended legislation was a victory for the Allies, who gained the vital point, the right to purchase American arms and munitions. Its importance is demonstrated by the fact that in the first year of the war 44 per cent of all United States exports went to the British Empire. In fact America was already becoming (and prosperity returned in the process) what F.D.R. was later to call her, the 'great arsenal of democracy', although the necessity of paying in cash soon became a severe strain on allied dollar resources. The neutrality legislation did without doubt, however, reduce the friction over neutral rights both with Germany and Britain.

Thus the situation remained during the first six inactive months of the so-called 'phoney war', but beginning in April 1940 a new phase of the struggle revealed itself with alarming rapidity, following on the total collapse before the triumphant German forces of Denmark, Norway, Holland, Belgium and France. Within a mere two months an underlying reality which had never been made clear in 1917 was brutally exposed – that the very existence of a free United States might be threatened by a German victory. By now the President was far ahead of American opinion in his desire actively to aid Great Britain which, under Winston Churchill, was standing virtually alone against Germany; the latter was now joined by Italy, in an action described by Roosevelt in famous words, 'the hand that held the dagger has struck it into the back of its neighbor'. Arms began to reach the beleaguered island, the vital ones being fifty over-age destroyers which were in effect exchanged for 99-year American leases on six bases in British territory within the Western Hemisphere, a very significant reinforcement of the security of the United States. On 27 September the German-Italian-Japanese alliance was announced, and in November Roosevelt, contrary to long-standing tradition, stood for a third term, decisively defeating his dynamic internationalist opponent, Wendell Willkie. By the end of the year the acute crisis had passed for Britain.

But the chronic condition, one of great gravity, persisted, for, even setting aside the slenderness of her ultimate chance of triumphing unaided over a Germany bestriding the European continent like a Colossus, she was faced with early strangulation not only by the German U-boats but also by her increasingly crippling lack of dollars to purchase indispensable arms and supplies from the United States. In one of his greatest and most imaginative acts of statesmanship the President evolved the concept of Lend-Lease, by which America's full material might could be placed at the disposal of her Allies without leaving an acrid legacy of war debts when hostilities ceased. After a stiff struggle in Congress, during which Senator Wheeler (in what F.D.R. called 'the most untruthful, the most dastardly, unpatriotic thing that has been said in public life in my generation') called it the 'New Deal's triple A foreign policy' of 'ploughing under every fourth American boy', the bill was passed in March 1941 by substantial majorities. It was very broadly drawn and gave the President power, among other things, to lend or lease any defence article to any foreign country deemed vital to the defence of the United States, and even to communicate any American defence information to any such country.

It forbade the convoying of belligerent vessels by American ships, but this provision was shortly evaded by the establishment of naval patrols 'as far on the waters of the seven seas as may be necessary to the defence of the American hemisphere'. Meanwhile, co-operation with Britain became ever closer, extending not only to staff talks but in August to the Newfoundland meeting of Roosevelt and Churchill which formulated the Atlantic Charter, which was in fact an astounding statement of joint war aims by a belligerent Britain and a non-belligerent United States. In July American troops had taken over from those of Britain in Iceland, and during this period the American navy escorted a British division to Singapore. The first American vessel had been sunk by a U-boat in the spring and on 31 October an American warship was sunk with the loss of 100 hands. Despite the German invasion of Russia on 22 June 1941 and the extension of Lend-Lease aid to the Soviet government (which, at last, the Roosevelt Administration had recognised in 1933), the United States did not make the plunge into full-scale war in Europe. Voluntarily to enter a great modern war is a step which any democracy finds it difficult to take, and in America in 1941 not only was love of peace peculiarly strong but so also were the still highly influential forces of isolationism. No one can say whether America would in time have become totally involved in the German war, but it may well be that Roosevelt's instinct against going off at half cock was profoundly right, because of the risk that the American people might have been bitterly divided on the issue.

In the event, the decision was taken in Tokyo. Before the outbreak of the European war the Japanese Foreign Office had proclaimed a 'new order' in Asia, 'The Greater East-Asia Co-Prosperity Sphere', and had paid no heed to the warnings of Ambassador Grew that Japan's actions, such as the annexation of Hainan and the Spratley Islands, were alienating the American public in the autumn of 1939. In July 1940 the United States began to impose what amounted to piecemeal economic sanctions against the Japanese Empire, and these measures, especially in the case of the embargo on petroleum and certain metals, had a seriously weakening effect upon Japan, in this respect the most vulnerable of great powers. America gave no outright guarantee to Britain and Holland for their Far Eastern possessions, but the Administration (with no buffer, as in Europe, between it and the enemy except distance) was taking a pretty strong line. In September 1940, however, the Japanese forced the Vichy government of France to admit them to Indo-China.

There were protracted efforts at negotiation between Tokyo and Washington in 1941, in which both sides had serious intentions, but the United States was not willing to give Japan the degree of freedom of action which she demanded. In October, liberated from her fear of Russia by Hitler's invasion, Japan decided on war unless the United States had accepted her terms by 25 November. Accordingly, adopting her customary method of dissimulation and treacherous undeclared hostilities, she pretended to continue negotiations while secretly preparing her attack. Despite the fact that the United States had broken the Japanese code, and that Hull had on 27 November written to Stimson (recently, in a remarkable bi-partisan decision of the President, appointed Secretary of War, along with another Republican, Frank Knox, as Secretary of the Navy), 'I have washed my hands of the Japanese situation and it is now in the hands of you and Knox, the Army and Navy', sufficiently urgent warnings of the imminent possibility of war were not sent out by Washington. On Sunday afternoon, 7 December, 'a date that will live in infamy' as the President declared, Pearl Harbor was attacked with the loss to the United States of 8 battleships, 7 other vessels and 188 aircraft. The next day Congress declared war on Japan by 82 votes to 0 in the Senate and 388 votes to 1 in the House, a unanimity which fairly reflected the now suddenly united and unshakeable resolve of the American people whom they represented. In a deliberate act of extraordinary and wanton folly Japan had taken the first step on the direct road to Hiroshima.

Chapter 20

The Second World War, 1941–45

O<small>N</small> 8 <small>DECEMBER</small> the United States was at war against Japan and half at war – 'co-belligerent' (as Mussolini had called it) with Britain – against Germany and Italy. As early as 1940 a firm planning decision had been taken to concentrate, if the United States became involved in a general war, on winning the European struggle first, and it seems unlikely, so profound was the revolution effected in the American mind by the traumatic shock of Pearl Harbor, that she would not soon have entered into open war against Germany. But she was saved from the need to make a decision, for on 11 December, loyal to the Rome-Berlin-Tokyo Axis and matching the Japanese in folly, Germany and Italy declared war on the United States. On the same day Congress reciprocated without even the single dissenting vote which had been cast in the House against war with Japan. During the more than three years of war which followed, despite considerable – chiefly Republican – restiveness from time to time, the United States government adhered unwaveringly to its decision to defeat Germany first. This was in large measure because of the inflexible purpose of General George C. Marshall, who remained Chief of Staff of the Army and the dominating figure in the Joints Chiefs of Staff Committee throughout the conflict, for the Navy, headed by Admiral Ernest J. King, was deeply absorbed in the Pacific war. The President's consistent support of Marshall was crucial in maintaining this vital policy.

But the Far Eastern war would not just wait; within little more than three months of Pearl Harbor Japan had not only taken the whole of the Malay Peninsula and the Philippines but had swept as far south as Java and Port Moresby in New Guinea and as far east as Wake Island and the Gilberts. The main burden of this struggle against Japan fell on the United States alone, and it is a measure of the power that she generated in the war that she by no means rested content with a strategy of containment in the Pacific, but had made giant strides towards the Japanese homeland by the time victory came in Europe. In this latter theatre she had two potent

Allies, Britain and Russia. With the Soviet Union, though there was much goodwill towards her in America, especially on the left, relations were never very close, partly owing to geography, partly to political differences, and partly to the deep-rooted suspiciousness of the Kremlin. With Britain on the other hand there was, despite the real and sharp differences of opinion at all levels, an intimacy of co-operation perhaps unmatched in history between two sovereign nations. This was not only true, in general, at the summit, with the frequent meetings of Roosevelt and Churchill, but was reflected in the establishment of the Combined Chiefs of Staff Committee in Washington, the effective central military directing agency of the war, on which Britain was represented by Sir John Dill, who developed a close friendship with General Marshall. The principle of unity of command over Anglo-American forces, as well as the most cordial Anglo-American co-operation, was epitomised in the career of General Dwight D. Eisenhower in North Africa and Europe.

Yet from the time of her entry into the war, which had been going on for more than two years, the United States immediately became the dominant force in the coalition. Without the Red Army, which was assisted to only a limited degree by American Lend-Lease material (sent in as abundant quantities as the exceedingly restricted transportation routes permitted), the struggle would have been vastly tougher, but it yet remained the case that, taking the global war as a whole, the predominant fact was the power, and especially the industrial power, of the United States. This would still have been true even if it had not been demonstrated beyond doubt in the last stages of the conflict by the production of the atomic bomb, which (though it owed a great deal to British science) could only have been made in the time available by American technological capacity. As Churchill wrote of 1941, albeit after the event, 'Silly people, and there were many, not only in enemy countries, might discount the force of the United States. Some said . . . now we should see the weakness of this numerous but remote, wealthy and talkative people. But . . . American blood flowed in my veins. I thought of a remark which Edward Grey had made to me more than thirty years before – that the United States is like a gigantic boiler. Once the fire is lighted under it there is no limit to the power it can generate.'

This is a highly significant if naturally somewhat Edwardian simile, for as one British military historian, Marcus Cunliffe, has written, the American military mind (particularly in the Second World War, for example, in contrast with the Russian) tended to think it possible 'to win . . . wars by substituting machines for man-power'. (The Russia of the Sputnik era is plainly a very different kettle of fish.) This was in part the result of the Northern victory through material superiority in the Civil War and the subsequent industrial supremacy of the United States, but the North also enjoyed superior numbers and the United States is a relatively populous nation, so that she was also prepared to be more prodigal of men than the United Kingdom, with its much smaller popula-tion. (Thus the Americans always pressed for a direct frontal assault on Hitler's European fortress and mistrusted Churchill's penchant for the indirect attack through the 'soft underbelly' of the Mediterranean area). Even in this greatest of her wars, the total mobilisation of the resources of the United States was never achieved, compared for example with Britain; the war was not for her really 'total', for it had comparatively little physical impact on the American homeland, with no bombs or missiles falling on her soil, and there was, for instance, no conscription of women, although 36 per cent of the civilian labour force was female in 1945. Yet the production curve of the United States reached its peak in October 1943, eighteen months before the end of the war, and it is striking that the first war-time surplus was in aluminium, which had been one of the first serious shortages. America did in a very real sense become the arsenal of democracy.

In effect, American industrialists said to the military, 'Tell us what you want and we will produce it'. But the armed forces often did not really know exactly what they did want, although to some extent they took advantage of British battle experience, which they lacked. (They did so, for example, over tanks, but not over fighter aircraft.) Only General MacArthur among leading American com-manders had fought even a division in battle; General Eisenhower had no battle experience. Furthermore, in the nature of things, the forces lacked the modern technological knowledge to design the best weapons, and so technical faults and production snags occurred quickly; but were ironed out by normal civilian research methods. The military ended by telling industry not what they wanted but what they wanted to do and the civilians devised the best tools for the job. Yet even the industrialists, emerging from the long years of under-production during the depression, did not really understand the capacity of the American productive machine; Donald M. Nelson himself, Roosevelt's first attempt at a 'production Czar', was 'startled' and 'alarmed' when his chief set 45,000 tanks and 60,000 planes as the American target for 1942. In fact these numbers were exceeded. At the beginning of 1942 munitions accounted for only

15 per cent of national production: at the end of the year for something nearer 50 per cent. Expenditure on them was $30 billion in 1942, $60 billion in 1943, and well over $60 billion in 1944. In a short time the vast mass of 10 million unemployed were absorbed into industry and the most acute shortage became that of manpower. Agriculture, on the other hand, achieved great increases in production with 5 per cent fewer workers than at the beginning of the war. Perhaps the most extraordinary evidence of American strength is the fact that in 1944 the overall standard of living of the people of the United States was higher than it had ever been before.

How was this economic miracle achieved? Not, certainly, through meticulous planning and central direction by the Federal government. The President provided inspiration, but a minimum of control: he set targets but left it to industry to produce the goods. And intelligent co-operation at the lower levels often succeeded where co-ordination from the top frequently failed. One manufacturer, for instance, required over $5 million of expansion in his plant to fulfil an artillery contract: local inquiries revealed that 118 of the 121 parts involved could be made in his area in factories not yet absorbed into defence work. To take another example, some thirty-odd units in the washing machine business formed a pool, with three as contractors and the remainder as sub-contractors, and produced $12 million of machine guns. Official advice did begin to play an important part by the end of the war, but much, perhaps most, of the original initiative came from the bottom. In a very real sense, in other words, this greatest American victory, on the home front, was won without proper planning from above. This was very much in the American democratic tradition; one is indeed tempted to say that it is an essential part of the American genius, by which the Federal system limits the effectiveness of central organisation but compensates for it by giving free play to the abundant and vital forces which well up spontaneously from the depths of America's manifold being, from the popular springs of the American democracy. Certainly the political and economic system of the United States before the Second World War was, despite the New Deal, ill adapted to the precise planning of the war effort. As Montagu Norman, the Governor of the Bank of England, is reputed to have said to American Ambassador Joseph P. Kennedy in 1939, 'I see that you people ["folks" is the unquestionably inaccurate word used in the American version] in the United States are contemplating industrial mobilisation. Who's going to run it? God Almighty?'

But this is not to say that the President was unaware of what the was doing. Far from it, for in 1939 he had deliberately suppressed an elaborate blueprint for industrial mobilisation drawn up by Bernard M. Baruch, who had attempted a similar task for Wilson in the First World War. This was not merely because the United States was not in the war and so could not, for political reasons, really start to mobilise for it; it was also a result of F.D.R.'s profound belief, as one historian of the war, Eliot Janeway, expresses it, that 'democracy' is 'more efficient than efficiency . . . It was his judgement that, given only time, America's home front would win the war . . . On the administrative level . . . his realism assumed that, if the country had to depend on Government for leadership, it would lose the war.' There were, however, limits to this, especially after Pearl Harbor brought a united American people fully into the struggle, and when, in October 1942, James F. Byrnes was installed in the White House as a sort of assistant President and began to give forceful economic leadership, there was a vast improvement in the administration of the home front. During 1943 the President took and enforced effective decisions on priorities and on the control of wages and prices, which only rose by 1 per cent after May of that year. But the leopard cannot change his spots, and the President remained in the war much the same pragmatic, eclectic political practitioner of dividing and ruling the members of his administration as he had been in New Deal days. Even this, however, liberated the energies of a number of very energetic subordinates, thoroughly willing, albeit at the price of some administrative rivalries and consequent wastage, to cut through the red tape; as Stimson characteristically declared, when told that the highly efficient Aluminum Company of America was a monopolistic trust, 'I'd rather have some sinful aluminum now than a lot of virtuous aluminum a year from now.'

Sometimes the feuds which resulted were harmful, as that between the Secretary of War, Harry Woodring, and his assistant, Louis Johnson, had been back in 1940, but in the field of co-ordination —as on the Advisory Commission to the Council of National Defence (set up in May of that year) where there was admirable co-operation between two great protagonists of industry and labour, William Knudsen and Sidney Hillman—there was all too often too little power for much to be accomplished. It was therefore not surprising that it was in the realm of shortages (and later, much less seriously, of surpluses) that the gravest difficulties arose, for this was principally a matter of establishing priorities. The need for administrative regulation made itself felt primarily in shortages of steel, aluminium and copper, though there were also serious difficulties over rubber, petroleum, and electric power. The multiplication of agencies by the government, such as the Priorities Board, the Office of Production Management and the Office of Price Administration (to name but a few of the most important ones in this field), did not achieve order, but out of the disorder, as business assumed control, order (or at least products) began to appear. For example, Colt's arsenal at Hartford, Connecticut, was the 'shrine of the military gun-makers', but at the beginning of the European war its output was so limited that only a small portion of the plant was equipped for line production. In June 1940 the Saginaw Steering Gear Division of General Motors, whose private automobile production was still booming, undertook to produce 25,000 machine guns. Without interfering with auto production they had produced blueprints by September, had chosen a site by November, and were in production by April. The contract called for the production of the first gun in 18 months, it was delivered in 11; it called for 160 guns in the 21st month at a cost of $667 per gun, in that month Saginaw delivered 28,728 Brownings at a cost of $141 each. It was by analogous processes of adapting mass production techniques that the United States Navy, which began the war with some 300 combatant ships, ended it (contrary to all the precedents of naval warfare) with over 1,100, and that the American merchant marine, despite all the sinkings, exceeded 36 million tons when peace came.

Out of the apparent political and economic confusion came the greatest feat of military, or any other kind of, production in history. It was a signal triumph of democratic politics, and at bottom it depended, as in the last resort everything must in a democracy, on public opinion. It was because he realised this and because he remained pre-eminently the master of it, that the President retained effective personal control of the government. So great was his ascendancy over the people at large that he was elected to an unheard-of, scarcely imagined, fourth term in 1944, by a majority of electoral votes which, if a little smaller than in 1940, was still very substantial – 432 to 99. Yet up to the very end, in matters of production, it was the industrial judgement, the industrial instinct, which was right, and the political and military opinion which was wrong. By the beginning of 1944 production was so huge that Stimson ordered military procurement programmes to be cut back by more than $12 million, and the President declared, 'Demobilisation begins long before hostilities end'. In fact, this was premature, and the cuts had to be restored, but nothing perhaps illustrates more vividly the paramount importance to the Allied victory of American industrial might.

But weapons do not yet (no one can say what the future holds) win wars by themselves; victory is gained by fighting men using weapons, by 'blood, toil, tears and sweat', or, in the American version of General Patton, 'blood and guts'. (As it was put to me at the time by one G.I., healthily and democratically sceptical of brass hats, 'Yeah! My blood and his guts'.) Civilians at home were not harmed and military casualties were far lighter than they had been in the Civil War relative to population, largely owing to advances in medicine, but, though only 322,000 Americans were killed or missing between 1941 and 1945, compared with more than 600,000 between 1861 and 1865, the United States armed forces suffered more than 1,100,000 casualties in the Second World War. More of these were incurred against Japan than against the European powers, and the two theatres of war were in fact notably separate and distinct from one another, being joined only by the threatened and contracting sea lanes of the British Empire (effective use of the Mediterranean was denied to the Allies for long periods) and by the great maritime routes of the Atlantic and Pacific oceans, which were unified by the continental United States with her control of the Panama Canal. In this, the first truly global war, the dominating strategic position of America in the world became fully apparent; the earth, indeed, became Americocentric for the first time, and was to remain so for some years to come. As Churchill put it in a famous tribute to Roosevelt, in his 'life and by his actions he changed, he altered decisively and permanently, the social axis, the moral axis, of mankind by involving the New World inexorably and irrevocably in the fortunes of the Old'.

Not least among his contributions to victory was his understanding of the fundamental, absolute, importance for the Allies of command of the seas; in this, by temperament and experience, he was at one with Churchill, who long corresponded with the President under the sobriquet, 'Former Naval Person'. Sea power above all else gave real unity to the war and necessitated unified command, and the supreme menace to this freedom of the seas, on the defeat of which all else depended, was the long-standing U-boat threat to the very existence of Britain, the indispensable European base, the unsinkable aircraft carrier, of the Allies. In 1942, 1,161 Allied merchant vessels were destroyed by enemy submarines, but by the beginning of 1943 American production of merchantmen and anti-submarine craft was getting into its stride, and the courage and skill of Allied naval and merchant sailors was having its effect. In September 1943 it was announced that 90 German submarines had been sunk in as many days and by March 1944 Admiral King could state that the U-boats had changed from a menace to a problem. In 1942 65 submarines had been sunk for the loss of 8 million tons of Allied shipping; in 1943 237 submarines for 3½ million tons; and in 1944 241 for 1½ million. The basis for victory had been established.

The conquest of the U-boat, however, was really a defensive achievement. In the Far East an unprecedented naval offensive was necessary to defeat Japan, which was far more formidable as a naval power than Germany, especially in surface ships. Not only was it essential to the liberation of the numerous territories captured by the Japanese, but to the direct assault on Japan itself which was universally believed to be necessary to victory. This new – and, happily, in the event short-lived – imperial domain of Japan was itself as dependent on command of the seas within the huge area over which it spread as were the Allies. Japanese sea power was steadily weakened by a growing American submarine offensive, which in 1944 sank more shipping than the U-boats and developed into an effective full scale blockade of the vulnerable Japanese home islands. In May 1942, when scarcely recovered from the seemingly crippling blow to the surface forces of the United States Navy at Pearl Harbor (naval ship building is traditionally what seems in war a desperately slow process), America defeated a Japanese force in the vital Battle of the Coral Sea off New Guinea, which decisively checked the advance of Japan towards Australasia and in fact began the long ebb of their tide of conquest. In June this was made quite clear by the victory of Midway, which prevented a Japanese invasion of Hawaii. In due course the prodigious expansion of the American navy began to tell; this was a remarkable feat not only of production by the shipyards but also of nautical training, for although (which is often forgotten) the United States is a great maritime nation with all its traditional skills, many of its new officers and ratings had literally never seen the sea before they joined the navy or the marines.

Japan, however, did not, in a strictly military sense, depend exclusively, or even perhaps primarily, on her sea communications to hold her island 'co-prosperity sphere' together, but on aircraft, flying from land base to land base; an attack on a particular island, like the first American offensive in the Pacific, on Guadalcanal in August 1942, was met by reinforcement from the air – the so-called Tokyo Express. Japan developed its air arm, both for attacks on sea and land, to a considerable height of efficiency, though in this it did not compare with Germany. The United States, utilising much British experience, reacted to, and in the end totally defeated,

this strategy by the most important naval development of the war –
the establishment of the supremacy of the aircraft carrier, which in
due course became the new capital ship of the world's navies.
Though this meant that in the great naval battles of this war surface
vessels scarcely ever saw one another because they were fought at
long distances by the aircraft of the respective fleets, it was in fact a
classical reassertion of the importance of sea power, which restored
to the dominant ocean peoples the unrivalled strategic mobility
which is its greatest advantage. From it flowed the masterly Pacific
strategy of Admiral Nimitz and General MacArthur, of by-passing
strong points (whose garrisons as often as not eventually died of
starvation) and attacking weak ones with overwhelming superiority,
thus hopping from island to island until, despite the prolonged,
bitter, unprecedentedly desperate fighting of the ferocious Japanese
soldiery, the Americans were by early in the summer of 1945 in
command of Okinawa in the Ryukus, at the very threshold of Japan
itself. This policy of 'hit 'em where they ain't' would have made
glad the heart of Mahan.

Air strength was equally an indispensable key to success in
Europe and the Middle East. It was through the revolutionary
combination of mobile and armoured forces with air power that
Hitler's *blitzkrieg* had laid Europe at his feet. Moreover his Air
Force reinforced the blockade of Britain and inaugurated the policy
of mass day and night bombing, aimed not only at military targets
but at civilian morale. Britain and the United States had been
pioneers in aviation and as insular powers took naturally to the
idea of strategic bombing, as well as tactical, 'close support' of sea
and land operations from the air. The British had concentrated on
night bombing and so America made its main drive in daylight
raids. By mid-1943 the Allies were able to launch not only '1,000
bomber raids' on single targets but to inaugurate 'round-the-clock'
bombing; by the end of the war the Royal Air Force had dropped
1¼ million tons of bombs on Germany, the U.S.A.F. 1½ million.
The combined air arms lost 20,000 bombers during the war, but
production became so rapid that they ended up with overwhelming
air superiority in all theatres of operations. Similarly, so powerful
did their fighter squadrons become that they destroyed nearly
60,000 German planes. The effects of mass bombing were on the
whole disappointing, but superiority in the air was none the less
vital to the success of Allied arms.

This, though to contemporaries it often seemed agonisingly slow
in coming, was in fact remarkably swift. On the Eastern front,
beginning with their final repulse of the deep German thrust in

the Caucasus and their counter-offensive at Stalingrad in the summer and early winter of 1942, the Russian armies fought their way remorselessly forward through Eastern Europe and into Germany, battling their way into Berlin in the spring of 1945. The Allies, wisely in view of Britain's acute man-power shortage and the time needed to train, equip and deploy America's armies, launched their first offensive in late 1942 in North Africa where sea power and distance limited the forces which could be committed by either side. The British drove the Germans and Italians back westward from the gates of Cairo and an Anglo-American force landed, in the first of their increasingly skilled land and sea, 'combined', operations, in Morocco and Algeria. By May 1943 they had cleared the North African littoral, and in July they landed in Sicily. By the autumn they had entered Naples, Mussolini had been overthrown, and the Italian government had sued for peace, but the Germans tightened their grip on Northern Italy and kept the Allies bogged down in the narrow Italian peninsula until early in 1945. Meanwhile in North-west Europe the great Anglo-American onslaught, long pressed-for by the United States and long (and sceptically) awaited by the Soviet Union, had been prepared to the last detail, and was launched, under the command of General Eisenhower. 6 June 1944 was D Day for this, the greatest of combined operations, which was hailed as such even by Stalin; the critical shortage had been of landing craft, but once again American production had fully met the need, and an armada of no less than 4,000 vessels took part in the landing. In less than seven weeks American forces had broken out of Normandy and within a few days, in an operation of a size and speed unmatched in the war, France was virtually cleared of the enemy. After a winter of slower progress, the Allies moved forward more rapidly again, and on 7 May 1945, Hitler having committed suicide, the Germans surrendered unconditionally. 'V.E. Day' marked the close of the war in Europe.

To the end the Allies had honoured their obligations to the Soviet Union, in particular by refusing insistent German requests to sign a separate peace. Roosevelt indeed had from the beginning determined to pursue a policy of friendship with Stalin; in what, with the advantages of hindsight, appears an excessively sanguine reliance on his own personal persuasiveness and a great underestimate of the ruthless realism of international Communism he had, as it turned out, staked his reputation as an international statesman, especially at the Yalta conference of 1944, on continuing accord between Washington and Moscow. He had sometimes looked, at the Teheran conference with Stalin and Churchill for instance, as if he was deliberately cultivating Russia at the expense of close relations with Britain, and the whole American concept of the United Nations, established towards the end of the war, had, by giving commanding influence to the Security Council and the three Great Powers, been based on the expectation of Russian-American co-operation. But the increasingly arbitrary Stalin, his land devastated by the Nazis and fearful of the whole outside, capitalist, world, not only proved suspicious and intractable but began, especially in Poland, to establish an iron Russian-Communist control over the lands he occupied in Eastern Europe – in Western Europe the analogous operation by the Allies was, in contrast, known as Liberation. By April 1945 the patience and bonhomie even of F.D.R. was wearing thin, and he wrote to Churchill of the Russians, 'We must be firm, however, and our course thus far is correct'.

It was one of the last messages he penned. On 12 April, exhausted by over twelve years – including more than three of gruelling war – in the heaviest job on earth, the President died of a massive cerebral haemorrhage. The light which had so long shone as the focal point of American life was suddenly extinguished, but the gloom seemed almost as dark outside the United States; no Briton who lived through those years could fail to be conscious of it or to echo the verdict of the noblest of contemporary Englishmen, 'the greatest American friend we have ever known, and the greatest champion of freedom who has ever brought help and comfort from the new world to the old'.

His successor, Harry S. Truman, in due time to become one of the most capable of American Presidents, was inexperienced in international affairs, and when, in the last stages of the European war, Churchill urged him to order Eisenhower to meet the Red Army as far to the east as possible, and especially to take Berlin, he accepted the view of his military advisers that the sole aim of America in the war should be to win a total military victory as soon as possible. In the words of General Marshall, 'The single objective should be quick and complete victory'. This rather characteristic American view, that international political problems must be susceptible of total, in war military, solution, was in its way as tinctured with naiveté as Roosevelt's confidence that he could 'handle' Stalin; how wrong it was and is Americans were to learn by painful experience. As General Omar N. Bradley, who was to be Chief of Staff when the lesson was at its most painful – in Korea in 1950 – put it later, 'As soldiers we looked naively on this

British inclination to complicate the war with political foresight and non-military objectives'. But this was not the only motive, apart from an honourable feeling for gallant comrades-in-arms, for continuing to conciliate the Russians: the Japanese war seemed very far from over, despite devastating American air raids on Tokyo. Though at Okinawa more Japanese (7,800) had been taken prisoner than ever before, 110,000 had died in the defence of the island: how many American casualties would the conquest of Japan itself cost? It was not until he was actually at the Potsdam Conference in July 1945 that President Truman received information that the first atomic bomb had been successfully exploded at Alamogordo in the New Mexico desert. Even then no one knew absolutely, for sure, what its military or political effects would be. But at Potsdam the Russians for the first time specifically undertook to enter the war against Japan, which they indeed hastily did in its very last days.

The harnessing of nuclear fission for military purposes (from which its peaceful use was to develop later, as has, alas, so often been the case with human progress) was without question the most important outcome of the Second World War, adding a new dimension to the affairs of men. It was the most decisive demonstration that there could well be that the future of mankind, for ill or good, lay in large measure in the hands of the scientists. It had been an American-British-Canadian scientific achievement, drawing on the accumulated resources of international scientific knowledge and made practicable by American industry. Germany, before Hitler's time a leader in science among the nations, had been on the track of the atomic bomb, but, whether or not she could have made one, had put all her available technical resources into the development of rockets, unmanned aircraft and guided missiles, in which she far outstripped the Allies. These V1s and V2s had come too late to have any decisive effect on Hitler's fortunes, but when combined in the post-war era with the nuclear knowledge of the free world of the West, were rapidly to usher in the awesome era of the Inter-Continental Ballistic Missile with its nuclear warhead.

Meanwhile, understandably and properly conscious of its life-saving potential if it brought the war to an early close, but rejecting out of hand any actual and specific preliminary demonstration to the Japanese of its almost unimaginable power, President Truman, strongly supported by his countrymen and his British allies, called on the Japanese government, in general terms, to capitulate. When they did not do so, an American B 29, on 6 August 1945, dropped an atomic bomb on Hiroshima, where it killed 79,000 persons almost instantly. Three days later another was dropped on Nagasaki, with comparable effect. Next day the Japanese ministers, pressed by the Emperor personally, sued for peace, and Japan surrendered on 14 August, scarcely more than a week after the first bomb. Thus came final and total victory in the Second World War, under the shadow of the mushroom cloud which was henceforth to hang over the affairs of men.

Chapter 21

The American Ascendancy
and the Cold War, 1945–63

WHEN THE war ended, the United States was at an unprecedented peak – perhaps also the ultimate peak – of
her international power. Not only had she been the
principal agent of Allied victory, but when it was gained she
possessed a monopoly of the atomic bomb. She alone among the
great belligerents had suffered no war damage except in operations
overseas, and her industrial and agricultural strength were absolutely
greater when she emerged from the war than when she entered it.
In 1948, it has been estimated, America enjoyed some 40 per cent
of the world's income, and her gross national product was five
times that of the next largest national income at that date, the
British. In 1952 the annual average *per capita* income of the American
people was $1,823, while the next highest, the Canadian, was only
two-thirds of that sum. In these years, it has been claimed, the
United States, with about one-sixteenth of the world's population,
produced one-third of all the world's goods and one-half of the
world's manufactured goods. This was reflected in her military
power, for, in addition to her unique atomic predominance, she
easily led the world in aircraft and soon seemed to have established
a lead in rocketry – now almost by definition nuclear – while her
navy was at least equal in strength to all the other major navies o
the world combined. She was without question the most powerful
nation ever.

This unrivalled power resulted in an unprecedented American
ascendancy in international affairs. Had Franklin D. Roosevelt
survived the war, his personal and official influence would greatly
have exceeded that of Woodrow Wilson in 1918–19, but the question
which worried the world in 1945 was whether the United States
would in fact stay in it, or whether she would once more opt out
as she had done in the days of the League of Nations. In the light
of her pre-war history she answered this question with what might
well seem an extraordinarily unequivocal acceptance of her role,

not of participation only but of leadership, in international events. In fact isolationism was dead, or at least quite moribund. A few Republican voices from the past, like that of Hoover, and from the present, like that of Senator Robert A. Taft of Ohio, might talk of withdrawing into 'fortress America', but they were speaking the language of political opposition and in any case defined the fortress (as Hoover did in 1950) in a distinctly post-1941 fashion – to include Japan, Formosa and the Philippines on the one hand and Great Britain on the other. This collapse of isolationism was perhaps inevitable for an intelligent people in the age of the jet and the missile. Certainly the United States never made any serious move to disengage herself either in the Far East or in Europe: she did not even undertake the 'agonising reappraisal' of her policy of participation with which one of her Secretaries of State in a mood of vexation threatened the 'recalcitrant' Europeans. Indeed, once the United States was clearly committed to international leadership (such, Americans might wryly reflect, is human nature, which is never satisfied), the nations of the world, including even her Allies, tended to go to the other extreme and to become suspicious and even resentful of what they sometimes called the 'inflexibility' and 'belligerence' of American policy throughout the world.

In the detailed course of events, naturally, these general trends were not at once or always apparent. The United Nations, with bipartisan support from the American parties (made effective by Senator Arthur H. Vandenberg of Michigan, a converted isolationist and the most authentic Republican spokesman of these years), had already come into existence at the close of the war. Designed to avoid what was regarded as the excessive idealism of the League of Nations, it concentrated even greater power than its predecessor had done in the Council, known as the Security Council, which was frankly an instrument of the great powers (technically including France and China, but with the effective control in the hands of the 'Big Three' – America, Russia and Britain, which last-named soon began to lose out in influence to her giant companions). Each of these five possessed a veto upon any action of the Council. Thus the whole operation of the United Nations depended essentially upon the co-operation between Russia and the United States for which Roosevelt had hoped. Churchill, though he went along with the idea, had always been less sanguine about the Soviet Union; as he wrote later, 'We can now see the deadly hiatus which existed between the fading of President Roosevelt's strength and the growth of President Truman's grip of the vast world problem . . . The indispensable political direction was lacking at the moment when it was most needed. The United States stood on the scene of victory, master of world fortunes, but without a true and coherent design . . . Thus this climax of apparently measureless success was to me a most unhappy time. I moved amid cheering crowds . . . with an aching heart and a mind oppressed with forebodings.'

At first President Truman persevered in the effort to work with Stalin, but he began to see clearly how impossible this might be at the Potsdam Conference, when the Russians remained absolutely obdurate against free elections in the states of Eastern Europe. Nevertheless, when the war ended, immediate and rapid American demobilization was begun and Lend-Lease was terminated abruptly, so that it was not until the summer of 1946 that a marked change in American opinion began to appear. This owed much to the famous warning of Churchill himself, given on American soil in the presence of President Truman at Fulton, Missouri, in March 1946, which called attention to the fact that was to dominate the affairs of mankind for more than a decade to come, especially until the death of the tyrannical Stalin: 'From Stettin in the Baltic to Trieste in the Adriatic, an iron curtain has descended across the Continent . . . I do not believe that Soviet Russia desires war. What they desire is the fruits of war and the indefinite expansion of their power and doctrines . . . I am convinced that there is nothing they admire so much as strength, and there is nothing for which they have less respect than weakness, especially military weakness.'

At first the speech was badly received in the United States, but from Moscow the missives of George F. Kennan of the American Embassy cogently emphasised the need for a policy of 'containment' of Soviet expansion; and realistic recognition of the situation, to which Bernard Baruch in April 1947 gave the name 'the cold war', soon became widespread in the United States. The Americans had learned fast, or, as one of them wrote, 'Our long-preserved virginity of mind has at last been deflowered by the facts'. The world, and particularly the United States, had to live with this problem of the great divide – part great-power rivalry, part economic competition, part fundamental ideological antipathy – up to the present day and beyond, for when at last in the 1960s some signs of a thaw in American-Russian relations became apparent, Communist China had already stepped into the Soviet shoes as the belligerent, adamantine, self-designated *ex cathedra* voice of the true Marxist gospel of the inevitability of violent conflict with the capitalist world, which America led and dominated.

The government of the United States had formally taken up the challenge when in March 1947 the Truman Doctrine brought aid to disordered Greece and vulnerable Turkey, and promised it to other nations whose freedom was threatened either from within or from without by Communism. But America did not remain content with such negative measures of piecemeal defence, and three months later Secretary of State George C. Marshall, as great a figure in peace as in war, launched the splendid plan of American financial aid, to combat 'hunger, poverty, desperation and chaos' in Europe (and later elsewhere), which bore his name. This policy of unprecedented international generosity appealed to the deeply humanitarian and charitable instincts of the American people, but it also gained massive support, despite President Truman's declaration that 'This is in no way a threat', from the belief, probably well founded, that it was necessary to halt the flood of Communist subversion and military domination in Europe. It was offered to the Soviet-controlled countries of Europe as well as to those in the West, but only Czechoslovakia made any overt attempt to accept it, and it was characteristic that this abortive Czech desire to co-operate with the West was followed in February 1948 by a Communist coup in Prague which established completely effective Soviet dominion. So the lines of the cold war were drawn, and froze and hardened.

A Russian attempt to seize control of West Berlin by blockade began in June 1948, and was, after a period of months, decisively defeated by an Anglo-American airlift of supplies to the beleaguered city; joint East-West control of Germany collapsed and the Allies set up the West German Federal Republic. Long negotiations, prompted by Canada and Britain, ended in March 1949 with the formation of the North Atlantic Treaty Organisation, perhaps the most important single step in post-war American foreign policy. This treaty in effect committed the United States irrevocably to come to the defence (of course on a reciprocal basis) of Britain, France, the Benelux countries, Canada, Italy, Norway, Denmark, Iceland, Portugal, and in later years Germany, Greece and Turkey. It circumscribed Russia and became the backbone of American diplomacy: it brought Soviet expansion in Europe to a halt.

But American policy during the two post-war Democratic administrations did not succeed so well on its second front, in the Far East, especially in the eyes of Republican critics; it was here that bi-partisanship in the foreign policy of the United States, always a seemingly tender plant, first withered. The democratisation of Japan, it is true, proceeded with astonishing speed and, on the surface at least, remarkable success under the pro-consulship of General MacArthur. How firm free institutions there would prove in the long run remained to be seen, but Japan, disarmed and powerfully conscious of the drastic and fearful nature of her defeat, was held until the present time within the American orbit.

On the mainland of Asia, in vast and teeming China, however, the story was very different. The Nationalist government of the Christian Chiang Kai-shek, with his American-educated wife, had become the focus of America's warm hopes for a friendly and democratic China, with the long-suffering people of which, both in the mission field and in a vague political sense, the Americans had long felt a curious but influential bond; this was continually strengthened by the so-called 'China lobby' which sprang up in American politics (especially centring in California). The Nationalists had long been locked in a deadly civil war, with the Chinese Communist forces of Mao Tse-tung, which was in a sense scarcely interrupted by the Japanese conflict. American efforts (in the optimistic period when the United States hoped to work with Communism) to reconcile Chiang and Mao failed totally, as did her efforts, by lavish aid, to bolster up the Nationalist cause. The truth was that the Kuomintang was undemocratic, corrupt and incompetent, and its armies seemed to melt swiftly away before the advance of the ruthlessly efficient forces of the Red authorities, who, perhaps for the first time in modern Chinese history, made a really effective appeal to Chinese nationalist sentiment, and who were certainly to weld this great land for the first time into a modern state. By 1949 the mainland of China was entirely in Communist hands, and Chiang had fled to Formosa.

This catastrophic upheaval in the balance of power of the cold war, signalised in the treaty of 15 February 1950 between Mao and Stalin (who had not aided the Red Chinese during most of their long struggle towards victory), had a profound effect upon American public opinion. Fundamentally perhaps this effect was the result of two painful facts which Americans were suddenly forced to grasp fully for the first time. One was the real extent of Communist power, encompassing in Europe and Asia, as one Russian was to claim in 1956, '25 per cent of the world's territory, . . . upwards of 35 per cent of its total population, . . . and roughly 30 per cent of its industrial production': the cold war suddenly became veritably a war on two fronts. The other fact, and it was in some ways more traumatic in its effect, was that there are real, if not quite inflexible, limits to the power of the United States. It was not merely that she had in her history won outright every war in which she had engaged (except that of 1812), and had come to believe not only in the possibility but even the indispensability of total victory: it was that her fabulous success story in filling a virtually empty sub-continent in an astonishingly brief span of history, in dominating a hemisphere of weak and ineffective neighbours, and in leading world coalitions to victory on two occasions against Germany and her Allies, had bred in her bone the belief that there was no problem that she could not 'lick'. (It was not for nothing that contemporaries of General Ulysses S. Grant had noted in the Civil War that his initials stood both for 'United States' and 'Unconditional Surrender'.) And apprehension of these facts was made more excruciating for the Americans by their psychology of haste and hustle: American problems in the American mind ought not only to be solved for ever and a day but to be solved in a hurry. When, therefore, the cold war seemed both to become more menacing and to stretch onwards into the indefinite future, the American people found the situation hard to accept.

One result of this was the sudden outburst in the 1950s of xenophobia and near-hysterical mass intolerance associated with the name of Senator Joseph R. McCarthy of Wisconsin, for so unprecedented a 'defeat' for America *could*, to many Americans, only be the result of treason. Another was the rejection of the Democrats at the polls in 1952, accompanied by the vilification of Secretary of State Dean Acheson, whose name was, inevitably, closely linked with the 'failure' of the China policy of the State Department. (In cold fact, it is virtually certain that nothing but the outright, full-scale, military intervention of the United States in China – unthinkable under any administration – could have saved the Nationalists and prevented the establishment of the Chinese People's Republic). Another was, perhaps, the six-year personal control over American foreign policy of President Eisenhower's Secretary of State, John Foster Dulles, who became the incarnation of Republican resolution in the cold war, especially against China; he believed in the policy of resolute confrontation with the Communist powers, and became responsible for the phrase 'brinkmanship' to describe its risks, which he was, he claimed, prepared to face unflinchingly even in the nuclear age. But before these things came to pass, America was to get rid of some of its frustrations (though for a period they seemed to intensify) in the Korean crisis which resulted from the invasion of South Korea on 25 June 1950 by Communist-dominated North Korea.

To his very great credit President Truman came to the aid of

South Korea and rallied the United Nations to do the same; the Security Council was for once not paralysed by the Russian veto because the Soviet representative was boycotting its meetings in an effort to force the organisation to admit Red China. This absence was in fact an important element in delaying American recognition of Pekin (which was being contemplated by the Administration at this very time, urged on by the British government which had already taken the plunge) for at least the fourteen years to date. Since the attack was a total surprise, the United Nations' forces which were rushed in (the vast bulk of them, apart from the South Koreans, was and continued to be American) were almost driven into the sea, but proved just able to hold the port of Pusan at the southern tip of the Korean peninsula. From this base, within a few weeks, the United Nations commander, General MacArthur, launched a brilliant offensive which drove the Communist North Korean forces not merely back across the 38th parallel (the highly artificial border between South and North Korea drawn after the departure of the Japanese) but almost across the Yalu river into Manchuria, so that the General was soon publicly promising his troops that they would be home by Christmas. Instead, decisive intervention by the armies of Red China drove them back 200 miles into South Korea by the end of the year.

At this juncture MacArthur, supported by many Republicans at home, and his pride injured by this humiliation not only of himself but of the strongest power on earth, began to demand all-out war against China; his cry that there is no substitute for total victory struck a deeply responsive chord in American instincts and emotions, but General Bradley, American Chief of Staff in Washington, kept his head, declaring that a war with China when Russia was the heart of aggressive Communism would be the 'wrong war at the wrong place at the wrong time and with the wrong enemy'. When MacArthur deliberately began to appeal over the heads of his government to American public opinion on the issue, President Truman, in a typically courageous action, abruptly dismissed him. After the first shock, responsible American opinion came round to the President's point of view about the need for the civil power to assert its control over this great American military hero, perhaps the most brilliant general in her history. This was not only because of his air of self-righteous flamboyance, which had always irritated many good American democrats, but because suspicion of military authority runs deep in the United States, despite the American penchant for generals as presidents. (It is to be noted that this feeling does not extend to approval of the military as such, and that America's president-generals have been on the whole the least regimental, if not military, of soldiers. The fact arises from the political value of the publicity which war-time generals inevitably get). In part this mistrust of the military reflects a healthy libertarian scepticism about armies, in part perhaps a hatred of the 'red-coats', and in part possibly stems from the anti-Cromwellian tradition inherited from their British forebears.

The dismissal of General MacArthur was followed by a long and frequently bloody stalemate in Korea, which frayed the nerves of the American people, who were unused to such protracted, inconclusive and maddening (though very limited and far-off) blood letting in strange, foreign fields. The war was not ended until 1953, early in the presidency of General Eisenhower, who alone perhaps had the prestige (including military prestige) to bring it to an end by compromise. The Korean War proved probably the most painful stage in the process by which the people of the United States learned the limits of their international power, but it hardened their determination to support Chiang in Formosa and, in the Wilsonian tradition, not to give even the limited moral approval to an aggressive Red China – trying to 'shoot her way into the United Nations' – which diplomatic recognition of the Pekin government would have involved. Washington was also to show more tangible evidence of its displeasure by continuing to maintain to the present time – and with varying successs trying to persuade her allies to maintain – an embargo on the export of 'strategic materials' to Communist countries. But the nations of Western Europe (and elsewhere), more accustomed, many of them, to the chronic drain of distant and minor wars, breathed much easier when the controversial General – who they feared might precipitate a third world war, with all its horrors – had disappeared from the international scene.

For those horrors might now well prove to be nuclear, since, to the dismay of the Western world, three years before even the most pessimistic prophets had believed it possible, in September 1949, the Soviet Union had exploded its first atomic bomb. Even more alarming was to be the detonation of her first hydrogen bomb in 1953, not so very long after that of the first American hydrogen 'device' and perhaps before the testing of what was possibly the first actual United States hydrogen 'bomb' in 1954. The rapidity with which the Russians began to follow in America's footsteps was certainly not slowed down by the American termination, soon after the war, of the atomic partnership with Britain and Canada, as a result of which Britain felt impelled to divert to the production of her own independent atomic weapons (the first of which was exploded in 1952) the very considerable resources which might have kept a continuing joint Anglo-American programme much further ahead of their Communist pursuers. But this decisive and even debilitating Western split, widened by British security leaks (such as that of Klaus Fuchs, revealed in 1950) and by the rising frenzy of McCarthyism (which was exacerbated by the two trials of Alger Hiss culminating in 1950), endured till common sense returned after the disgrace of McCarthy and in face of the evidence provided by the launching of the Soviet Sputnik I in 1957 of the truly formidable nature of the Russian technical challenge. In 1958 the exchange of military atomic information with Britain was recommenced. This renewed Anglo-American co-operation was all the more remarkable because it was to follow only two years after the Suez crisis, the worst Anglo-American dispute of the twentieth century. This was to come, ironically, during the height of the election campaign for his second term of that great Anglo-American figure, President Eisenhower.

The firmness of Secretary of State Dulles in the Far East, especially over the off-shore islands of Formosa (where a state of war, with sporadic raids and shelling, between Chiang and Mao still continued), sent occasional frissons down European backs, but Britain firmly supported the formation of the South East Asia Treaty Organisation (SEATO) – a counterpart, though necessarily a much weaker one, of NATO – in 1954. Not so happy in some of its incidental results was the diplomatic initiative taken by Britain's Anthony Eden in presiding, with French Premier Pierre Mendès-France, over the liquidation of France's empire in Indo-China, for Dulles did not forgive the way in which he was eased aside, in this act of what he probably regarded in his heart of hearts as appeasement of Communism. Nor was Dulles at his best in the short-lived atmosphere of rapprochement with Russia which followed the death of Stalin in 1953 and culminated in the abortive 'summit' conference at Geneva in 1955; it was, after all, only three years since the Republicans had come to office on a wave of election cries that the United States must 'roll back' the Iron Curtain in Eastern Europe. When in fact in 1956 the gallant Hungarian rebellion against the galling Communist yoke took place, the United States was intensely concerned about its relations with its principal ally, Britain, over Suez and had to stand helplessly by while the tanks of its principal enemy ruthlessly re-established Soviet control in Budapest. But even without the Anglo-American crisis, the Secretary of State would have been powerless, for no sane man (and his President was pre-eminently that) could really ever risk a nuclear war where Russia considered that her absolutely vital interests were at stake, even for a cause as noble as that of the Hungarian rebel-patriots. It was the second stage in the lesson of the limits of American power in the atomic age.

Anglo-American co-operation in the Middle East had never been close, partly owing to America's relative lack of interest in this, to her, remote area, partly owing to commercial (especially oil) rivalries, and partly owing to the American feeling that Britain's participation in the affairs of the region was in large degree the unhappy result of British imperialism. This general anti-colonialist atmosphere in which American policy moved was an understandable result of her history, as well as of her determination to try and wean the emergent nations away from the temptations of Communism; it necessarily remained at least a latent cause of friction with the colonial powers who were her chief allies, however quickly (the pace being forced by Britain) they set about disbanding their Empires. Britons on the other hand did not easily accustom themselves to the rapid dwindling of their power, and were deeply shocked when President Nasser of Egypt in July 1956 – largely in pique at America's sudden withdrawal (in view of Egypt's Communist contacts) of its promise to aid in financing the construction of his cherished Aswan High Dam – nationalised the Suez Canal, which had until recently been controlled by Britain, whose people had been bred in the idea that it formed the vital life-line of their Empire.

Prime Minister Eden, believing not only that this was true, but also that Nasser (against whom he was personally resentful) was a kind of new Hitler whom it would be fatal to appease, determined to take firm action in co-operation with France to keep the Canal under international control. For three months Secretary Dulles employed every device which his fertile legal mind could invent to reach a settlement, or postpone a show-down, for neither he nor President Eisenhower was prepared to tolerate the use of force by their allies. On 29 October a much-provoked Israel attacked Egypt, and on 31 October (eight days after the outbreak of the Hungarian revolution) Anglo-French forces, having sent an ultimatum, attacked Egypt and began to land forces to take the Suez Canal Zone, in order 'to separate the belligerents'. A rising outcry in Britain made it clear that the country was passionately divided on this military action, and in the United Nations General Assembly on 2 November the United States in effect led in the condemnation of the Anglo-French action by 64 votes to 5, with Canada abstaining. The military operation was shockingly mishandled and this, combined perhaps with Russian threats on 5 November (the day after their tanks entered Budapest) of the dangers to Britain from rocket attack, led to Anglo-French acceptance of a cease-fire on 6 November, and the ultimate arrival of a UN token force to keep guard around the borders of Israel.

The Administration in Washington had been deeply affronted by the secrecy with which the operation had been planned by the French and British, but when the Russians, in the midst of their gruesome police action in Hungary, began to threaten Britain and France, President Eisenhower at once and publicly declared the solidarity of the United States with its two allies against the Soviet bloc, despite his stated belief that those allies had acted 'in error' in the Middle East. This return towards the normality of the cold war was aided by the increasing number of American voices now raised to deplore the Administration's abandonment of, indeed hostility towards, the actions of its most reliable ally – however misguided – in defence of what her government at least believed to be one of her most vital interests. That the closure of the canal for many weeks with relatively few effects on Britain showed that it was nothing of the sort did not count for as much in the American mind as the growing evidence that the chief result of Western disagreement was Communist penetration of the Middle East. This conviction found remarkable expression when in 1958, under the so-called Eisenhower Doctrine, the United States sent troops to the Lebanon at the request of its government while Britain simultaneously sent them to Jordan at the request of King Hussein.

The doctrine stated that the Congress was prepared for the President 'to employ the Armed Forces of the United States as he deems necessary to secure and protect the territorial integrity and political independence of any ... [Middle Eastern] nation ... requesting such aid against overt aggression from any nation controlled by international communism'; it followed in this a precedent established a few years before over the off-shore islands of Formosa. It was a significant constitutional innovation, for it meant that the Congress had, in specific areas, virtually surrendered its jealously guarded power of declaring war to the President and Commander-in-Chief, an action which was in accord with the realities of the rocket age. Not only had the United States now stretched her protecting arm over the Middle East, as well as Europe and the Far East, but Anglo-American amity had been remarkably restored, largely through the determination of Britain's new Prime Minister,

Harold Macmillan, whose doctrine of Anglo-American 'interdependence' was reciprocated by his old war-time friend, the President.

Dulles, more perhaps than any other American Secretary of State, was oriented rather towards France and Germany than towards Britain, and it was with Germany, in the person of Chancellor Adenauer, that he established the closest relationship. It was in no small measure due to Dulles that, after many disappointments and frustrations, the American ideal of a united Europe, fostered ever since the Second World War, began to realise itself, with the formation of the European Economic Community by France, Germany, Italy and the three Benelux countries in 1957. At first, Britain's Conservative government stood aloof, as its Labour predecessor had done from the forerunner of the Common Market, the European Coal and Steel Community. But with the entry of President Kennedy, who had a deep knowledge of Britain, into the White House in the spring of 1961 Prime Minister Macmillan decided to try and make full European unity a reality by applying in July of that year for Britain to join the Six. The new President indeed, echoing Macmillan's own phrase, set his sights on the broad goal of unity for the whole North Atlantic area, calling in a Fourth of July speech at Independence Hall in Philadelphia in 1962 for a new 'Declaration of Interdependence', for a true 'Atlantic partnership'. But after protracted negotiations General De Gaulle vetoed the admission of Britain into the Common Market early in 1963. The European Economic Community remained united, but it showed a tendency to be inward-looking and did not appear likely, even without the United Kingdom, to take very rapid steps towards political unity, or greater solidarity with the United States, as long as President De Gaulle presided over its destinies. Not that he has so far proved in the crunch to be a bad ally to the United States, but he was determined to follow an independent 'European', or at least French, line, which he carried farthest in a field remote from the affairs of Europe – his recognition of the Red Chinese government in January 1964.

And the foreign policy of the United States continued to be dominated by the Cold War, though its character underwent deep, if sometimes not very clear-cut, changes in the second administration of President Eisenhower. The first factor making for change was that the Communist threat became much more formidable with the growth of Russian technical competence and power. The second was that China began unmistakably to emerge as the more militant and also anti-American of the two Communist powers.

Yet despite the increasing talk by Premier Khruschev, as he became firmly seated in the saddle at the Kremlin, of 'peaceful', if 'competitive' 'co-existence', President Eisenhower's undoubtedly sincere desire for peace did not produce a marked amelioration of America's relations with Russia, even after the resignation and death of Dulles in the spring of 1959. The visit of Khruschev to the United States in September 1959 led, it is true, to the summoning of a summit conference at Paris in May 1960. This ill-fated meeting never took place, although all the principals were actually assembled in the French capital, because of the refusal of President Eisenhower in effect to apologise for the deep reconnaissance flights of American stratospheric planes over the Soviet Union, of which Russia had obtained irrefutable evidence when it shot down one of these aircraft early in the month. The summit leaders departed in disarray and the President's term of office ended with American-Russian relations at a low ebb.

His successor's all-too-short tenure of the Presidency brought the struggle with the Communist bloc to a new height of tension. Though there was a sharp crisis over Berlin in 1961, the intensification of the cold war was principally due to the growth of the Communist threat to Latin-America, which is, because of its desperate poverty and its political disunity and chaos, the Achilles heel of the United States. Thus the revolutionary régime of Fidel Castro in Cuba had by 1961 plainly become a Communist dictatorship in the closest connection with the Soviet Union: this was not the cold war comfortably remote in Berlin or Laos but ninety miles from the shores of Florida, in an island which had for many years had the closest bonds with the United States, even amounting, from the end of the Spanish-American war until the Presidency of Franklin D. Roosevelt, to the right of armed American intervention for a wide range of reasons. The young President in Washington, inheriting an incomplete plan from the outgoing Republican administration, allowed on 17 April 1961 a totally abortive invasion of Cuba by Cuban exiles trained and armed through the good offices of the Central Intelligence Agency of the United States. (It was not the first time since its inception after the Second World War that this agency, under the direction of Alan W. Dulles, a brother of the late Secretary of State, had aroused criticism and alarm by the apparent extent of its power, by its not infrequent clumsiness, and by the degree to which, for security reasons, it appeared to be beyond the control of the Executive, let alone the Legislature.) Certainly those who predicted the rapid collapse of Castro were hopelessly wrong, and for American intelligence the

CIA bore the chief responsibility. Mr. Dulles has denied that it misled the Administration over the Bay of Pigs fiasco, but he has not allayed the doubts, similar to those which have arisen on other occasions in American history, as to the quality of work of American intelligence, which has seemed sometimes much too ready to believe what it wants to believe. This disaster achieved the worst of two worlds: the United States incurred the odium of invading Cuba, but did not have the compensation of success, which could only have been achieved by the decisive use of her own military forces.

The experience, however, was not lost on the brilliant political mind in the White House. President Kennedy developed in the fire of this crisis a tempered circumspection, a balance and a resolution which placed him soon on the highest level of international statesmanship. Whether Khruschev was unduly impressed by the incredible incompetence of the Bay of Pigs decision, whether he was not unduly impressed by the youthful President when they met in Vienna in the summer of 1962, or whether he was misled by some internal Soviet situation or Communist tactical calculation, he suddenly and secretly in the autumn of 1962 began to prepare for the dispatch of Soviet nuclear missiles to Cuba, a step which might, if it had come off, have altered the entire balance of nuclear power between East and West by bringing the heartland of the United States under potential fire from medium-range rockets. It was on the face of it a reckless gambler's throw on the part of Russia, one which carried fearful risks.

This time American intelligence did not err. On 22 October 1962 the President broadcast the facts and published the evidence, forthwith imposing an air and naval quarantine on Cuba. This was tantamount to an act of war, and for six days of extreme tension the world stood breathless on the real brink of a nuclear holocaust. On the whole America's allies stood very firmly by her, but never had they so clearly seen how powerless they were to influence the issue: now they fully grasped for the first time how absolutely the destiny of mankind lay in the hands of the United States in its relations with Russia. On 28 October Premier Khruschev flatly announced that the Soviet Union would withdraw its offensive missiles from Cuba, and in due course it did so. This was an unmitigated public defeat for Russia, but nothing became President Kennedy better than his moderation in victory. Not only did he refrain from any action which might damage Russian susceptibilities further, but he showed during the following year (when urged on by Prime Minister Macmillan) a readiness to persevere once again and even with greater vigour in seeking a Russian-American *détente*, especially over nuclear disarmament. It was as if this second Cuban crisis – from which, unlike the earlier one, the President emerged successfully – had still further deepened his humanity and his sense of the enormous responsibilities of the most powerful office in the world, that office which he had sought in an almost carefree fashion but two years since.

After negotiations which had continued on and off and in varied forms since the end of the Second World War the United States, Russia and Britain (but not France) signed, on 5 August 1963 in Moscow, a treaty providing that they would ban all nuclear tests above ground. It might seem a mouse to have produced from such a mountain of labour and it might yet prove an abortive birth, but to the human race – whose pollution of the air they breathed by their predominantly military nuclear explosions might, on not too distant a day, have reached the point of deadly peril – it offered at worst a respite from, and at best possibly even the beginning of the end of, at least one phase of the cold war. (It was perhaps not without some significance that it was followed on 16 August by an American-Russian agreement on a modest joint programme of experiments in space with weather and communications satellites.) Whether or not it was to lead in the end to a real Russo-American rapprochement, the test-ban treaty was peculiarly associated with the Presidency of John F. Kennedy. There seemed little doubt to many acute observers that it was the direct result of the Cuban confrontation, where American firmness had brought home to the Soviet Union (and to Kennedy and Khruschev personally) the degree and imminence of the danger to humanity; and the confrontation itself from which the President emerged with such enhanced stature had in some degree been precipitated by his own earlier and, as it seems, youthful folly at the Bay of Pigs. Perhaps as remarkable as the achievement in signing the treaty was that of getting it through the Senate, with relative rapidity, by a comfortable margin, and without too great a fanfare of opposition oratory to mar its effect.

The world, even if it was wrong to do so, began to cherish once more the glimmerings of hope for an end to the threat of nuclear war, as President Kennedy, though with his now characteristic coolness and caution, pressed on with proposals for further disarmament; he even suggested to the United Nations on 20 September a joint American and Russian expedition to the moon. There seemed every expectation that, in the fullness of his youth and vigour, he would be re-elected in 1964: instead he was shot by an assassin during a visit to Dallas, Texas, on Friday 22 November 1963. The extent to which the world had in a short space come to place reliance on his leadership was demonstrated by the unprecedented, spontaneous and extraordinary outburst of grief around the globe. No death in history had so immediately affected so many of mankind.

His successor, Lyndon Baines Johnson of Texas, who had been Senate majority leader for some years during the Eisenhower period and an active contestant for the Democratic nomination for the Presidency in 1960, was a much better-known figure than Vice-President Truman had been when he succeeded Roosevelt, but his skills and experience had been very largely confined to domestic affairs. He pledged himself to continue the foreign, as well as domestic, policies of his predecessor, but the world had to wait for him to prove himself in international affairs, and perhaps would have to do so until – and if – he should be elected to a second term. Problems there were in plenty in his first year of office – in the Middle East, in Vietnam, and especially in Latin-America, where unrest in Panama over the American Canal and its American-ruled zone, burst into flame with severe rioting in January 1964. This was not only politically – and even, for a nation with such deep anti-colonialist sentiments, morally – embarrassing in itself (the enormous power of the American giant among its neighbours in the Western Hemisphere ensured that it was *in itself* no more than that) but conjured up in the American mind alarming visions of Central and South America following Cuba into the Communist camp. It was indeed this fear which now gave such an air of urgency to the reactions of the United States to affairs in Latin-America.

Here, in a hemisphere long regarded as sacrosanct from outside interference under the Monroe Doctrine, the cold war struck closest home. The world struggle had, it is true, changed its character markedly during President Kennedy's administration. This was no doubt due to a great complex of causes, including a number of antithetical ones. Such were the Kremlin's increased sense both of America's firmness and of her readiness to negotiate; the rising standard of Soviet living (combined with demands from the peoples of the U.S.S.R. themselves for the continuation of the process) and the failure of Soviet agriculture; and the dramatic growth of Russian missile, and above all nuclear, power and the Soviet government's full realisation of the impossibility of nuclear war. The change in the Communist camp, however, unquestionably seemed to owe

most to the growing antipathy – indeed outright hostility – between
Russia and China. No one in the West could say that this breach
would not be repaired, and the Soviet Union had certainly not
ceased to desire the world-wide victory of Communism (even if she
wished it to be her own variety and even if she had become more
cautious in her use of weapons in the struggle with the West), but
there was at least a distinct probability that now the main factor
moving Russia towards a *détente* with the United States was her
fear of her great Communist ally. China is (as General De Gaulle,
with his characteristic kind of realism, had declared as long ago as
1959), with her 'numberless and impoverished, indestructible and
ambitious' masses, 'building through trial and hardship a power
which cannot be measured and casting her eyes about her on the
open spaces [of Russia] over which she must one day spread'. In
the opinion of many experts this China might perhaps at any time
explode her first nuclear weapon.

Thus the nature of the cold war had changed, and the world
might hope for the continued amelioration of Russian-American,
if not for some time of Chinese-American, relations. None the less
the West could not count upon it. And how, should the Communist
bloc re-unite Moscow and Peking, did the balance of power rest in
the cold war in 1964? The strength of China was as yet emergent
only, however formidable it seemed to be, but that of the Soviet
Union had increased at a rate which few indeed would have ven-
tured to predict fifteen years before. In the long perspective of
history, it might be argued, the United States had been the supreme
and unchallenged international power (in the words of *1066 and
All That* 'top nation') which she was in 1945, for a much shorter
period than most of her predecessors, for within 5 years her
supremacy was being challenged, and within little more than 10
years very seriously challenged, by Communist Russia, while a less
bitter but real rivalry may yet develop with a resurgent and united
Europe. (In the late 1940s, for example, the days of the 'dollar gap',
the dollar dominated the economic life of the world even more than
the pound sterling of Britain had done in the nineteenth century,
but by the 1960s there had been two serious 'runs' on the once-
scarce dollar, which would have seemed inconceivable a decade
earlier). How strong the Soviet Union is and above all how far she
may have caught up the United States is perhaps the most important, yet most vexed and difficult, question in international affairs
today.

Though America's population had increased by 47 millions
between 1940 and 1960 and that of Russia over a similar period

by only 18 million, owing largely to the war, the totals in their last censuses were 183 million and 208 million respectively; their respective birth rates are at present estimated at 22·4 and 25 per 1,000, and their death rates at 9·5 and 7·5 per 1,000, which seems to give Russia a population advantage. (The low Russian death rate is no doubt in part due to the more youthful age structure of the Soviet Union.) The basic resources and geographical situation of the United States appear much greater and more favourable, but those of the Soviet Union are, so far, less well explored and less fully exploited. The economists disagree widely on another question, but it appears likely that the total national income of the U.S.S.R. is only some 60 per cent of that of the United States; Soviet industry is producing considerably less and Soviet agriculture very much less than American. Even more contentious, and also important, is their relative rate of economic growth, and estimates have fluctuated wildly of late, from one that Soviet growth is five times as fast as that of the United States (made in 1962) to one that the Russian is only half that of the American (made in 1964). It appears likely that the Soviet rate of growth, if – as seems very probable – it has substantially exceeded that of the United States in recent years, has not done so by the very large margins sometimes claimed. In the past, it is true, the curves of national rates of economic growth have tended to flatten out in due course – so that the Russians might be expected perhaps to go on for some years narrowing the gap between them and the Americans – but it is far from certain that this will always be so, especially in this cybernetic age.

In military strength, however, and in the technology on which it now so greatly depends, the Russian challenge to the United States is without doubt real and formidable. Her navy (in view especially of America's *Polaris*), as well as her air force, are no doubt inferior, but her army is much stronger. The crucial problem, however, is to assess her nuclear missile power, which is peculiarly difficult not only because of the secrecy with which it is surrounded but also because of the capacity of the Soviet system to concentrate an extraordinary proportion of its national effort in particularly valued fields, of which this is one. If her military strength in this unique and vital area is commensurate with her performance in the space race since her launching of the world's first satellite in 1957 (in which race the United States seems to be beginning to catch up only in 1964), the two super-powers have indeed reached by 1964 a stalemate of nuclear power, a balance of nuclear terror. And in this absolute sphere, enough – to the common eye – is unquestionably enough. The solitary ascendancy that the United States enjoyed in 1945 has disappeared, enormous though her power still is: now the American people must live with Russia, unless they or the Soviet government decide that they must die together, along perhaps with the whole human species.

Chapter 22

Post-War America

T HE UNITED STATES emerged from the Second World War not only the strongest power on earth but the richest nation in history, and the years which immediately followed increased both that financial ascendancy and that wealth. Yet the world watched the economic fortunes of the titan with much the same anxiety that it asked itself whether in international affairs the American people might not withdraw into their accustomed shell and leave it in the lurch, for interested observers were beginning to appreciate the degree to which the Great Depression of the 30s had spread outward from the United States. Chronically reminded by the ever-present dollar gap – the result fundamentally of the world's post-war poverty and America's abundance – of their dependence on the American economy, the governments, and especially those of Western Europe, came with some justification to accept the current saying that in economic matters, 'when America sneezes, Europe catches a cold'. So they watched the American economic barometer with almost as much slightly apprehensive interest as the people of the United States themselves. The question uppermost in those interested minds (Keynesian almost to a man) was, 'Will the Economic Blizzard return?'

In the nearly twenty years which have elapsed, the American answer has been almost as clear a negative as that given about a return of isolationism. In fact, as so often happens in human affairs, the problems of yesterday, which filled the minds of the world's economists in 1945, no longer proved to be the problems of today, and the dominant difficulty turned out to be, not deflation, but inflation: Whirl was king, having deposed Zeus. War, the great consumer, had once more created a huge back-log of unfulfilled demand, and the predominant problem of peace, in America as well as elsewhere, was to supply it – the very opposite of the pre-war problem of creating demand to meet the over-supply. In due time, when this deflationary situation showed signs of re-emerging in the recessions of 1953/4, 1957/8 and 1960/1 natural trends – national as well as international – in the economy, fortified where necessary by appropriate government measures of a Keynesian character, prevented the return of anything like a great slump. One factor of importance in maintaining the economy's momentum, especially in the period of the Korean War, was the consistently high, indeed enormous, expenditure of the Federal government on national defence, and later on space development. Another – related as well as possibly more important – was the amount of this and other expenditure which took place overseas, both under programmes of military aid and under the Marshall Plan, which, by the bizarre economic process of virtually free gift, went far to solve the acute problem of America's excessively favourable balance of payments – the obverse of the dollar gap. A less paradoxical way of aiding Europe and the world to trade with America was by continual and not totally unsuccessful Administration efforts to lower the American tariff – most effectively perhaps by bilateral and other executive trade agreements. But the immediate post-war period remained one of acute shortages at home, and desperate shortages abroad.

Yet though the struggle which faced the Fair Deal, as President Truman called his domestic programme, was to try and control rising prices rather than to try and prevent their fall as the New Deal (of which it was a continuation) had done, this Democratic régime was almost as willing as its predecessor to use the full force of the Federal government's authority and influence for economic purposes. This made certain that there was to be no return to extreme pre-war concepts of a ruggedly individualistic economy, and even when President Eisenhower led the Republicans into power once again in 1953, although big business reasserted its influence, the clock was not put back; more conservative financial policies might prevail, but the President's moderation meant that Washington did not contemplate any real abdication of its domestic authority, much as the small if vocal and influential 'Neanderthal' wing of the party might desire it.

President Truman, although he was – once he found his feet, especially after his unexpected victory in the presidential election of 1948 – far from pulling his punches with his political opponents, never became so bitterly hated by business-men as F.D.R., that 'traitor to his class', had been, nor was he himself perhaps so hostile to them. Indeed, in his early years in the White House he relied a good deal on an old friend, John Snyder, who was a St. Louis banker, while his most immediate contretemps were with labour, which was jockeying for position in the post-war uncertainty. There were major strikes in the automobile industry and the coal mines, and only vigorous Presidential action in taking over the railroads prevented an unprecedented national rail strike in May 1946. While a political battle over the continuation, and even strengthen, ing, of Federal price controls went on, prices continued to mount-until by December 1946 they were 33 per cent above the level of December 1941. In the confusion there were even patches of un-employment amidst the overall shortages, which prevailed parti-cularly, for example, in new cars and housing. There was a considerable post-war restlessness, which showed itself in such things as two serious Northern race riots, as well as a number of Southern lynchings. The Congress which was elected in the fall of 1946 on the slogan 'Had enough?' was Republican for the first time since Hoover.

The worst, however, was over. In 1947 the shortages began to disappear as civilian production really got into its stride, and the price-rise slowed down. The American standard of living, especially of labour which now began more and more to think of itself as middle class, was far higher than ever before. The federal govern-ment's wide programme of educational aid to ex-service men (in American official terminology called the 'G.I. Bill of Rights for Veterans') was typical, and it benefited 4 million youths in 1947. But this Congress, the 80th, under the leadership of 'Mr. Republican' Taft, asserted itself chiefly by refusing to accept the President's many recommendations for social and economic legislation. Its single really significant piece of law-making was the Taft-Hartley Act, passed over one of Truman's 62 Presidential vetoes. This measure severely regulated the functions of trade unions, as for example by making them liable to be sued for breach of contract and damages; by ordering publication of unions' accounts (impor-tant in view of the considerable corruption in certain American labour organisations, which had in fact even been infiltrated to a limited extent by ex-gangsters after the repeal of Prohibition); by enjoining a compulsory 80-day cooling-off period before strikes; by denying National Labor Relations Board facilities to unions whose officers failed to sign affidavits that they were not Communists; and by prohibiting the 'union shop', which in the United States means that a worker must join a union after he has been hired. (This provision was repealed in 1951 and the only restriction left was the prohibition of the more extreme 'closed-shop', the system which forbids even the hiring of the non-union man.) Unpopular as the Act has always been with labour, it has remained substan-tially the basis of labour-management relations in the United States, and has been perhaps a not unsuccessful one. The President's answer to what he castigated as the 'do-nothing' Republican Congress was to move decidedly to the left in his 1948 campaign platform.

His prospects in the election appeared gloomy indeed, for he was opposed not merely by a highly competent and exceedingly confident Republican, Governor Thomas E. Dewey of New York, but by no less than two splinter Democratic candidates; on the left, Henry A. Wallace, Truman's predecessor as Vice-President, running on an anti-cold-war Progressive ticket, and on the right, Governor J. Strom Thurmond of South Carolina, the 'Dixiecrat' candidate put up by the Deep South in resentment against the increasingly liberal racial policy of the Administration, which had demanded from the 80th Congress legislation against lynching and the poll tax, and a permanent Fair Employment Practices Commission. After a vigorous 'whistle-stop' campaign which was very much in character, 'Give 'em Hell Harry' was still judged to have no chance by either the Republicans or the newly professionalised pollsters; but he won by a plurality of 24 to 22 million votes. Taft was as aghast as George Gallup, who was the high priest of the now-dominant cult of consumer-research in this political incarnation; to the latter's lament, 'I just don't know what happened', the former (President's son that he was) piped sombrely, 'I don't care how the thing is explained. It defies all common sense for the country to send that roughneck ward politician back to the White House'. The President said, 'I just hope – I hope so much I am worthy of the honor'.

Though the right (as well as the left) of the Democratic party, which once more controlled the Congress, had been shown the limitations of its power in a presidential election, the Bourbons of the South could still prove their strength on Capitol Hill in their accustomed conservative alliance on domestic measures with the Republican minority. Despite this opposition, however, a few Fair Deal measures, such as a Federal housing programme, increased public power and rural electrification, and stronger price supports for agriculture were passed in 1949, and did much to check the first of the post-war down-turns in demand at the end of the year. (In one field, where Executive action alone was necessary, real progress was made during the long Korean War, that of abolishing racial segregation in the armed forces.) But in 1950 inflation once more increased with the now incipient boom in the economy which the war was to do much to maintain, and before long the dollar was worth only 59 cents compared with 1939, the cost of food being particularly high. But with this rich ripeness of American life came some rottenness; there were accusations of political corruption in high places (where, of course, Democrats had been for nigh-on twenty years); one million of the nation's children were in trouble with the police in 1951; and under the probing of the Kefauver Committee of the Congress and the glaring lights of TV the American people saw with their own eyes the criminals who made big business out of illegal gambling in the United States. These things added to the mood of frustration over the Korean stalemate as Truman's second term ran out, but perhaps the most important issue, emotionally speaking, of the presidential election of 1952 was the accusation that the Administration was 'soft on Communism'.

Fanned by aspiring politicians like the Republican Richard M. Nixon of California, the fires of popular intolerance burned high for some years in one of those bursts of near-hysterical pressure to conformity to which American public opinion is on occasion prone; indeed, as Tocqueville long ago foresaw, the tyranny of the majority was to be one of the great problems of democracy and in particular – because it was the first great democracy – of the United States. Striking contrasts can arise (with anti-immigrant and anti-foreign, anti-German and anti-Russian, anti-'atheist' and anti-Communist passions) between the deep and real devotion of the American system to the idea of liberty and the alarming practical power of the mass of the people – or those who claim to speak for them – to impose a 'patriotic', near-uniform set of views on those who would exercise their freedom to disagree. Genuine individualism, with its almost indispensable flavour of eccentricity, is often perhaps more difficult to maintain in America than in Britain, despite American lip-service to the ideal of the individual and the sweeping and specific protections of individual rights embedded in the constitution. In view of the force of the American pack-instinct when in full cry, it is well indeed that the Founding Fathers, at the insistence of those who feared that their work had erred on the side of authority, accepted the first ten amendments – the Bill of Rights – as an integral part of the constitution. In particular, the First Amendment protects the people's liberties against Congress; and the Fifth Amendment, enjoining that 'no person . . . shall be compelled in any criminal case to be a witness against himself, nor be deprived of life, liberty, or property, without due process of law' (especially when reinforced later by the Fourteenth Amendment laying a similar prohibition explicitly on the States), has been an important barrier against encroachments on individual freedom.

But even over such perhaps necessarily and fortunately rigid bulwarks as these, public opinion can wreak considerable havoc with individual lives, especially when led by able and often unscrupulous demagogues. Just such a one was Senator Joseph McCarthy (from, of all states, with its noble Progressive record, Wisconsin) who began in February 1950 a campaign of wild, and in almost every case totally unjustified, accusations of 'communism' against the Administration and a number of figures prominent on the national scene. Under-estimating the degree to which many of the American people, unaccustomed to the grim and novel, sudden and seemingly towering spectre of Soviet Communism, were prepared, in their search for scapegoats for the unfortunate facts of international life, to swallow the theory of a Great Conspiracy against the American nation, the Administration played down the issue, which President Truman described as a 'red herring'. Secretary of State Acheson with true Christian charity but perhaps some political rashness had declared that he would not 'turn his back on Alger Hiss', one of the relatively few actual if erstwhile communists in public life, who was convicted of perjury in 1950. But Hiss was a symbolic figure, who had been present in a minor role at the Yalta conference, when Roosevelt had most fully implemented that Democratic policy towards the Soviet Union which even a man of such integrity as Taft declared at this time had 'surrendered to every demand of Russia . . . and promoted at every opportunity the Communist cause in China'. In a sense, as Alistair Cooke pointed out, it was the whole New Deal generation which Republicans now tried to put on trial, for in the deep uncertainties of the Great Depression and its entirely different climate of opinion some radicals had not surprisingly toyed with the potent and explosive ideas of Marx.

The trial of 'left-wing' America, however, was far indeed from a fair or dispassionate one. Personally affable and with a sort of genius for rambunctious publicity 'Joe' McCarthy rode the wave of popular fear with ever more exaggerated and fraudulent accusations. His original constitutional base was the Chairmanship of the Committee on Government Operations of the United States Senate, and he was able to use it very effectively because of the powers, most of them proper and necessary, of Congressional Committees for inquiry and investigation. Acting like a sort of cross between Parliamentary committees and Royal Commissions in Britain, the committees, and sub-committees, of the Congress have always, and perhaps increasingly in recent years, played a most important part in American political life; they have powers of subpoena and interrogation, but they are not subject to the strict rules of evidence or codes of procedure of courts of law. This can have advantages in ruthless and effective 'probes', but, even though so many American politicians are lawyers, a committee can, in malign or careless hands, do devastating and often unjustified damage to the reputations of individuals. This was pre-eminently so in the case of McCarthy, whose influence was for a period so great that it was certainly a factor in the Democratic defeat in the election of 1952, during which even General Eisenhower did not repudiate this unwelcome ally and after which Secretary Dulles carried out a 'purge' of the State Department which proved very damaging to its morale. But as all wise observers of the United States had known it would, the fire soon burned itself out: McCarthy went too far, especially in his attacks on the Army, and in 1954, in a procedure only used three times before in 167 years, he was formally censured by the Senate. This condemnation by his fellow members of what has been called the most exclusive club in the world curiously but clearly ended his political power, and he died in obscurity soon afterwards.

General Eisenhower, who had defeated Taft on the first ballot at the Republican Presidential Convention in 1952, was very much the nominee of the liberal wing of the party, but his overwhelming victory, by 442 electoral votes to 89 for Democrat Adlai Stevenson (a lead which the President even bettered a little in 1956), at first increased in this politic soldier but non-political statesman an inherent tendency to think of himself as in some sense above party. The Presidency does indeed always have this dual function – headship of the state and leadership of the President's party – and Eisenhower in some degree saw himself initially (more perhaps than any of his predecessors except Washington) as a sort of temporary and elected constitutional monarch, presiding over the destinies of all the people. But it is also true that, since Jefferson and Jackson, the American political system has seldom worked well unless the President has given decisive leadership through the only effective instrument he has, his party; and even though after 1954 he had to work with Democratic Congresses – in which the skilful and moderate Senate leadership of Lyndon B. Johnson greatly aided him – he gradually began to take a firmer 'party' line. (Even after his attitude became markedly more conservative he could still count upon a good deal of Bourbon-Democratic support.)

Yet from the beginning his policies in some degree justified the description 'dynamic conservatism', which, in an era when many young people no longer remembered the Depression, had a wide appeal. (In 1956, be it noted, the majority voted for Eisenhower but against the Republicans.) Fiscally orthodox under the early influence of his first Secretary of the Treasury, George Humphrey, he was greatly concerned to disprove the accusation that his was a 'Business Administration' of 'nine millionaires and a plumber' (his Secretary of Labor), and would probably have consented to heavy deficit spending if the two recessions of his presidency had not quickly straightened out. Despite early economies even in military spending (easier for him than for non-military leaders to effect) Federal spending continued to rise, from $74 billion in 1953 to $80 billion in 1959. In part this was due to public alarm, at the state of American defence and technical and scientific education, which Russia's Sputnik provoked in 1957 (the first important Federal Education Act appropriated what many regarded as the inadequate sum of $1 billion in 1958 to be spent over seven years), but it was also due to the President's willingness to continue and even cautiously to expand the social welfare programmes of his predecessors in Washington. Social security was extended, the minimum wage was raised to $1, private housing was encouraged by Federal loans, and the new Department of Health, Education and Welfare was founded. Despite some deliberate efforts to strengthen the arm of private enterprise, as over electric utilities in the South and over the renunciation of Federal claims to the tidewater oil resources of the United States, it was clear both that the President was often to the left of many right-wing Democrats and that neither the Federal government as a whole nor the Executive branch in particular was going to reverse the trend towards increased power in Washington which had prevailed throughout the century.

Even Secretary of Agriculture Ezra Taft Benson, a Mormon strictly dedicated (perhaps as a first step towards the restoration of a free market in farm produce) to the replacement of rigid price supports by flexible ones as a means of getting rid of the huge agricultural surpluses which built up every year under Congressional protection, was only able to restrict Federal intervention to a very limited extent. National agricultural income during this period dropped 20 per cent on 1951 (though individual farm incomes only did so by 6 per cent), but none of the measures adopted 'cured' the farm problem, which is indeed universal in the Western world in different forms. The surpluses arising from the skill and sweat of American farmers and the subsidies of Washington continued to mount. The Eisenhower years were dubbed with some justice the age of 'affluence', and in familiar fashion riches were still accompanied by corruption; as Burke had put it many years ago in a similar context, the greatly increased wealth of America 'overflowed with a rich redundance ... upon some places where it was ... improper'. Labour prospered as never before, and, in such cases as that of the Teamsters' Union, there was mounting public indignation not only at the corruption but at what seemed to many the over-weaning power of this new estate of the realm; the Landrum-Griffin Act of 1959 accordingly went beyond Taft-Hartley in tightening the nation's regulation of the affairs of the unions. Even the Administration itself seemed to bear some of the taint of decay when the President's powerful chief-of-staff, Sherman Adams, was forced to resign in 1958 over his ingenuous receipt of gifts from a well-wisher. In measured terms in the same year one of America's leading economists, J. K. Galbraith, who had – in all probability correctly – opined in 1955, in his study of *The Great Crash*, that nothing quite like the Economic Blizzard could happen again, took *The Affluent Society* (as he called this book) to task for spending too much on private enjoyment and too little on social improvement.

But in one sphere mounting public concern, and tension, over just such a social issue became apparent during these years, even though improvement was very slow: this was the Negro question. The Administration lived up to its promises to continue the Truman policy of desegregation in the armed forces, but the real govern-mental initiative in the race problem – perhaps the most serious of all the domestic issues which face the American people in mid-twentieth century – came from an unexpected, but by no means unprecedented, quarter, the Supreme Court. In different ways, in the eras of Chief Justice Marshall, of the Dred Scott decision, and of Mr. Justice Field, the Court had been a moving force in politics, but it had never perhaps shown the same degree of political initiative as it did under Chief Justice Earl Warren (who fully exemplified, as the long-time Governor of California and a recent Vice-Presidential candidate, the overt and active connection between American political life and the American judiciary, which is also apparent in the widespread practice of election of judges in many of the States). In 1954 the Supreme Court in a unanimous judgement – which is rare enough in the Supreme Court's history in such cases as this to lend verisimilitude to the view that it was the result of a political conviction that the United States could not properly lead the free and multi-racial world until she had tried to put her own house in order on this issue – flatly reversed *Plessy* v. *Ferguson* (1896), declaring that 'separate educational facilities are inherently unequal' and laying down that desegregation must be carried out in the educational institutions of the nation with 'all deliberate speed'.

The states of the South, especially the Deep South, used (and in many cases are still using) all possible means of delaying the implementation of this decision, including elaborate plans in some states for the virtual abolition in the last resort of public state educational systems. In some upper Southern or border states, such as North Carolina, 'token' integration took place; in others, such as Missouri, greater progress was made; but in the hard-core states, especially South Carolina, Alabama, and Mississippi, virtually no advance has yet occurred. In a number of areas, such as New Orleans, even efforts to effect token desegregation provoked violence, while at Little Rock, Arkansas, in 1959, the eyes of the whole world seemed as never before to be focused on this grave 'American dilemma'. Local disorder and the obduracy of Governor Orville Faubus forced the President, for the first time since Reconstruction more than three-quarters of a century before, to send in Federal troops, the 101 Airborne Division. They replaced the local state militia, which the Governor had called out to keep order by preventing Negro children from entering Little Rock High School as ordered by the Federal Courts: the paratroops kept order by admitting the children. But, such is the complexity of the Federal situation that in due course the President as Commander-in-Chief called the state militia, as he is empowered to do by the Constitution, into the 'actual Service of the United States' (that is to say into the 'regular' forces) and, to the mystification of foreign observers, used them to replace the paratroops and to let into school the Negro children the Governor had previously used them to keep out. Analogous legal complexities have made possible the prolonged Southern rearguard action in all areas of the Civil Rights problem.

For the pressure of the race question intensified over other issues besides education. Further progress was made, for instance, over Jim Crow, or segregation, in inter-state transportation (which had already been declared illegal), and after a vitally important spontaneous Negro bus boycott in Montgomery, Alabama (in which the Reverend Martin Luther King emerged as a potential national Negro leader), desegregation even began to make headway also within certain Southern States. There was some progress in the number of Negroes voting in parts of the South, and the Negro vote in the North, particularly in the great urban areas, became an increasingly important factor in politics; in certain districts Negroes were able to make the racial issue the most important plank in election platforms. Yet nothing illustrates more forcibly to the foreigner than this the unique character of American parties, for the Northern Negro vote was for the most part captured not by the old Republican allies of the coloured people but by the radical wing of the Democratic party, that party whose deeply conservative Southern members were directly responsible for maintaining one-party White Democratic rule in the Solid South. On this, as on a number of other, principally financial, issues, these Bourbons in the Congress voted with their right-wing Republican colleagues. A few radical Republicans did the reverse, but they were not sufficiently numerous to prevent prolonged delay over Civil Rights. This was especially so because under the 'seniority rule' – that committee chairmanships, on which the swift passage of legislation so greatly depends, go to the longest-standing members of the majority party with unbroken service on that committee – Southern Democratic Senators particularly, based on their almost impregnable one-party constituencies, had a unique hold over Congressional affairs. Even in the South itself, however, the growing racial tension began to produce unexpected results; one was the great increase in cross-voting (diametrically opposite to 'voting the straight party ticket') by which the Southern electorates tended to support Republican candidates in presidential elections but to continue to return Democrats in the states, because Democratic presidential candidates were, and had to be if they were to win in the North, distinctly liberal.

This was not, however, the only reason that progress seemed to the Negro, painfully, even agonisingly, slow, for the great ally of Southern obstinacy was Northern apathy. It was the turning-away of the Northern majority after Reconstruction, the willingness (understandable in the climate of opinion of the era) to leave the South – that is the White South – to settle its own affairs, which had produced and then perpetuated a situation in which by mid-twentieth century probably far less Negroes in the South were voting and playing an active part in politics than seventy-five years before. And though in the North Negroes exercised, or could exercise, their full political rights, they unquestionably lacked their full social rights; though in much less degree than in the South where over-whelming segregation was the rule, they were still second-class Northern citizens. Widespread, almost universal discrimination existed, for example, in housing, and in the choice of career or job the cards were heavily stacked against the coloured man, despite the rapid growth of pro-Negro white groups, especially, for instance, among students, who were even active in the South itself as 'freedom riders' and participants in lunch-counter 'sit-ins'. Yet one of the most significant, and in the long run hopeful, of all current developments was the continued and probably accelerating migration of the Negro from the South; this had beeen going on ever since the Civil War, but by the early 1960s for the first time more than half the Negro population of the United States lived outside the South. Only one thing perhaps was more important (and this was a much more recent development), the seizing of the initiative by the Negroes themselves: for the first time they began to use their own great weight – they number approximately 20 million, which is better than 10 per cent of the American people – to demand their rights, even in the South.

This process was stimulated by the slowness of official action. President Kennedy, for all his liberalism, which, cool-headed though it might be, was unquestionably real, was incapacitated by the indigestible Southern lump in his own party and was able to effect little, if anything, more than President Eisenhower. He had, however, the appearance of being forced into more vigorous Executive leadership by such developments as the outburst of violence at Birmingham, Alabama, in May 1963. Negro pressure continued to intensify under the inspiration of Negro leaders, albeit reluctant ones in some cases like the author James Baldwin; indeed, traditional organisations of Negro protest, of which the National Association for the Advancement of Colored People (NAACP) was much the largest, began to feel the rivalry of more belligerent and as yet less powerful bodies like the Student Non-Violent Co-ordinating Committee and above all the Southern Christian Leadership Conference of Martin Luther King, which was also pledged to employ only peaceful Gandhian methods of direct action. One sinister development was the rapid rise to prominence – although its exact extent was much disputed – of the Black Muslims, a Negro separatist movement which appeared likely to be willing, if it ever proved practicable, to use violence to attain its goal of total separation between the races – of apartheid in reverse. The fantastic nature of its plan for an independent Negro state within the confines of the United States was, however, a measure of the frustration of some Negroes, and its contempt for the decadence of the white race in America threatened to make dominant in Negro protest a long-standing but hitherto recessive strain of ruthlessness, such as had shown itself in the 1920s in Marcus Garvey's Universal Negro Improvement Association, with its assertion of black supremacy.

The resulting fears that this great minority of Americans might as a whole turn to extremism certainly had as yet no basis in actual facts. American Negroes in overwhelming numbers wanted to be

nothing but '100 per cent Americans', and their restraint and
moderation were in truth remarkable, indeed a wonder to the
world, under whose eyes (through all the media of modern mass
communication) the scenes of basically white-provoked violence in
Alabama and elsewhere took place. The police dogs of Birmingham
came threateningly close to being a derided symbol of American
democracy. Washington, D.C., the nation's capital (governed by
the Congress, and until recently with its citizens unable to vote
even in Presidential elections) has the largest proportion of Negroes
of any great American city (54 per cent of its population) and a
very high rate of crimes of violence, but the huge and well-behaved
national demonstration in the Negro cause which was held there,
by both white and black, on 28 August 1963 was an exemplary
instance of Negro orderliness and even characteristic good humour.

Its announced object had been to pressure Congress to produce
an adequate Civil Rights Bill; measures had been passed with great
difficulty in 1957 and 1960 but both had been greatly watered down
by the threat and use of the filibuster by Southerners in the Senate.
This sacrosanct procedural protection of free speech for the representatives of the states in that august body, which is limited solely
by their own physical endurance in holding the floor, can only be
suspended or altered by a two-thirds majority, which is very difficult
to obtain. By means of the filibuster, in the 1957 Act the authority
granted to the Federal Attorney General to seek court orders to
prevent interference with the right to vote was in practice seriously
undermined in the South by the amendment that convictions for
criminal contempt must be tried by jury: in such cases Southern
juries, which are almost always white, will not convict. Even the
ratification in 1964 of the 24th Amendment, prohibiting the poll
tax which has been so widely used to deprive the Negro of his vote,
might make little difference if it was as widely defied as the 14th
and 15th have so long been.

In June 1964, however, a filibuster against a quite strong Civil
Rights Bill, which had been sent by the House of Representatives to
the Senate, was broken by a two-thirds vote, and the Bill was
passed by the Senate shortly thereafter. This was an important
step forward, and President Johnson, himself a Southerner (for
Texas is, for all its industry and western character, still a Southern
state), is pledged to and has actively pursued Negro rights, but the
whole Negro question as the election of 1964 approached was still
one of the utmost gravity and also uncertainty.

There were problems also in other aspects of domestic affairs
after President Johnson's first months in office. In social and

economic affairs he was even more clearly dedicated to the liberal and progressive policies of his predecessor, and there were some signs, such as the new reforming tax bill long demanded and now obtained by the Administration, that he might yet have somewhat more success in implementing them, partly through the shock of President Kennedy's assassination and partly through his personal standing in the Congress, though such auguries of good will between the White House and Capitol Hill seldom last long in the face of the traditional rivalry between the Executive and Legislative arms. This his predecessor, himself a member of the Senate (now perhaps becoming a more popular and favourite breeding ground for the Presidency than the Governorship of states as in the nineteenth century), had soon discovered. President Kennedy's campaign in 1960 had been essentially a loud cry for a 'new frontier' spirit, a call to 'get the United States moving again' after two terms of Republican 'stagnation'. Despite the appeal of such a platform at a time when something like 7 per cent of the American labour force was unemployed (though in the United States, partly through its traditions of free enterprise and mobility, the 'acceptable' figure of unemployment is much higher than the British $1\frac{1}{2}$ per cent), his victory over Vice-President Nixon was one of the narrowest in the history of American presidential elections.

As might have been expected, perhaps, in so evenly divided a country where there are other representatives of the people besides the President, Mr Kennedy was able to make singularly little headway with his efforts to persuade the Congress to pass measures to improve the economic situation of the United States. This, though it did not become worse, did not improve dramatically; there was a residue of poverty and unemployment in the richest nation on earth – the one having the highest overall standard of living of any people in history – which appeared considerably more blatant than the worst Britain had to show. This economic uncertainty of the United States in the Kennedy period, contrasting so strongly with the pre-eminent strength of the American economy since the Second World War, showed itself in a continuing relative weakness of the dollar in international exchange. The United States really needed the so-called 'Kennedy round' of international tariff negotiations – especially with the Common Market countries – which the President had arranged for 1964, for the rate of America's economic growth had proved relatively slow (as compared for example with some European and other countries) in recent years. This uncertainty continued to prevail at the time of the President's assassination.

Yet this fourth public murder of an American President, with all the grievous shock it entailed at home and abroad, was taken rather remarkably in its stride by the United States. The American vice-presidential system had long been criticised as clumsy and in-efficient, but vigorous steps had been taken to improve this situation since the death of Roosevelt, and Vice-President Johnson was able to assume the responsibilities of office with extraordinary little dislocation. The immediate attention that now focused on the question of the line of succession after the accession of a Vice-President, which has been altered more than once by Congressional legislation, was in itself a healthy sign, and Americans could reflect that their elective monarchy, as it has so often been called, had been able to act in the full spirit of the old world aphorism, 'Le Roi est mort, Vive le Roi'. It was perhaps, for all the horror of its occasion, a not unhappy augury for the future.

Chapter 23

The Government of the United States

THE Declaration of Independence in 1776 set a seemingly indelible stamp of democracy upon the theory of American government, and soon thereafter the United States began to prove itself in practice also the world's first great democratic nation. This belief in objectives which the French were later to describe – in their less successful effort to attain them – as 'liberty, equality and fraternity' pervaded almost all areas of American political life; as the Virginia Bill of Rights (which preceded the Declaration of Independence by three weeks) affirmed, so most Americans believe: 'That all men are by nature equally free and independent, and have certain inherent rights, . . . namely, the enjoyment of life and liberty, with the means of acquiring and possessing property, and pursuing and obtaining happiness and safety . . . That all power is vested in, and consequently derived from, the people; that magistrates are their trustees and servants, and at all times amenable to them. That government is, or ought to be instituted for the common benefit, protection and security of the people . . .' However much the system might from time to time fall short of the ideal – in early oligarchic practices, in intermittent intolerance, in corruption (especially in the great new urban conglomerations), and above all in slavery and racial inequality – the United States remained dedicated to the aim of democracy, not only for itself but for 'all men' everywhere. When they made a deliberate decision – the first nation to do so in quite this fashion – that they would 'assume among the Powers of the earth, the separate and equal station to which the Laws of Nature and of Nature's God entitle them', they felt that 'a decent respect to the opinions of mankind requires that they should declare the causes which impel them to the separation'. As the Russian state, the 'third Rome', has, in the view of many, held before itself a special universal role, so America has, from the beginning, in some sense assumed for herself an exceptional oecumenical destiny – to bring democracy to the whole human race.

And to a considerable extent compared with many other, even European, countries, they practice what they preach; in contrast

with the centralised, monarchical and aristocratic traditional practices of Britain, for instance, initiative in American public life (in
which titles of nobility are unconstitutional) can come to a remarkable degree from below. Democracy is a real thing in the United
States, as no one can doubt who has seen, for example, in the
frequent fashion of the country, a small local community voting to
authorise, and then floating, its own bond issue to finance its own
new school. Not only do representative institutions exist at all levels
of American political life – township, county, city, state and nation –
but there is frequently great vigour and activity in their politics.
Partly because of the extra tier of government in this Federal system
and partly because of the frequency and fixed regularity of elections
under the Constitution, the burden on the citizen is relatively heavy.
In a presidential year he may need to vote in a party primary as
well as a final election, and the ballot paper for the latter may be a
very long and often complex document. He may, as we have
observed, be called upon to vote both for a Presidential and Vice-
Presidential candidate (or rather, in almost all cases, for the electors
who nominally select them), as well as for a Senator and Congressman; he may also have to choose a number of state officers, including
a Governor, Lieutenant Governor, and members of the upper and
lower houses of the State legislature (the former usually known as
State Senator); he may in addition have to pick out from a considerable list of candidates many other officials, ranging from judges
on the State Supreme Court through the sheriff of the county down
to the proverbial dog-catcher of his township; and on top of this
he may have to pronounce upon amendments to the State's constitution and such matters as authorising the public borrowing of
money. It is small wonder that in the United States, as in all
political societies, there are extensive patches of inertia and serious
lapses from probity, and that a popular vote of more than half the
electorate even in a Presidential election is regarded as creditable,
compared with anything over three-quarters in a British General
Election.

   This climate of free activity is jealously guarded by the Constitution. The First Amendment itself laid down that 'Congress shall
make no law respecting an establishment of religion, or prohibiting
the free exercise thereof; or abridging the freedom of speech, or of
the press; or the right of the people peaceably to assemble, and to
petition the government for a redress of grievances.' One present
Justice of the Supreme Court has gone so far as to doubt whether
even laws of slander and libel are constitutional. The journal and
the newspaper, especially the popular press (later developing its

yellow and tabloid forms) soon reached a very wide public in America; this was indeed her most rapid field of cultural growth, and one in which she led the world. Today the power of the American Press is enormous, particularly because of the looseness of such American laws of libel and slander as do exist and the reluctance of judges to hold newspapers in contempt of court even for comment on matters still *sub judice*. Criticism of the overweening assertion by the nation's journalists of their right to be everywhere and know everything in the sacred name of Freedom of the Press has remained even more muted in the United States than in Britain. But it is notable that Walter Lippmann has recently questioned the wisdom of the further growth in influence of the Presidential Press Conference, which has long been so important in the political process that it is often compared to Question Time in the House of Commons.

Similarly, the separation of Church and State is carefully protected, and in modern times there has been constant and important litigation about the extent to which any form of religious instruction whatever is legal in the public – state – schools; hence the great scale and significance of private, denominational education, especially in Roman Catholic 'parochial' schools. Even in the once exclusively Mormon State of Utah this separation exists in considerable degree in fact as well as name. (One vital *de facto* protection of religious liberty in America is simply the existence of so many religions). Perhaps in this we may detect an echo of the English seventeenth-century aphorism, 'No Bishop, No King'. The Second and Third Amendments show clearly the American fear of the military, though the former, which guarantees 'the right of the people to keep and bear Arms', has had unhappy side-effects in making the control of fire-arms, especially in such a state as Texas, more difficult than it already is in a modern industrial society. The zeal for liberty which prompted the Ninth Amendment (although this is so vague that it has never really been used in the Courts) – 'The enumeration in the Constitution, of certain rights, shall not be construed to deny or disparage others retained by the people' – also remains very much alive, as in such active modern bodies as the American Civil Liberties Union. But the fundamental protection of the rights and freedom of the individual is the Anglo-American legal system, which holds men innocent till proven guilty, which generally confines judges to jurisdiction in matters of law rather than fact, which demands for every man a fair trial, and which above all essentially guarantees that that trial shall be by a jury of his peers. These things are enforced by Amendments 6, 7 and 8 of the Constitution: they are basic to American justice and the legal system of the Federal government and the states.

The Constitution, however, is at almost as great pains to protect the institution of property, the economic as distinct from the political rights of the individual, as it is the maintenance of liberty; half of the clauses enumerating the powers of Congress, for instance, are concerned with such matters, and the basic material of American day to day politics has always been economic. Until the present century this has been made more possible than in many other states by the degree of America's isolation, by her insulation from grave perils in foreign policy, but it does produce from time to time a mild appearance of schizophrenia in the divorce of financial, agricultural and commercial realities from the high-flown oratory of political rights. This gap between the theory and practice of American democracy can be seen pre-eminently in the great urban, and also rural, political machines which still exist in many places, and in the residual elements of the old spoils system by which the incoming party still feels remarkably free by European standards to appoint new office-holders from among its members to a number of posts at all levels of government.

The actual bulk of Congressional legislation (as distinct from the time spent on it) has always consisted (and to a considerable extent still does) of the mass of what would be called in Britain private members' bills (though all American legislation technically takes this form). Many of these rush through, like a broken log jam, in the final days and hours of the session; the process of politico-economic bargaining, which produces this spate and is in fact often called log-rolling, is both the perquisite and the duty of the Congressman. Totally reliant for his seat as he is upon the support of his Congressional district rather than his national party, he has always been judged 'back home' in great degree by the quantity of meat from the 'pork barrel' which he gets for his constituents. In earlier days (as we have noted) for rapid economic development, and nowadays for the relief of economic hardship or the stimulation of further prosperity, Federal funds have been sought and received for the building of post offices, fortresses, arsenals, and dockyards, for the construction of post-roads (and in recent times many other forms of highway), for the support at one time of railroad construction and now for the subsidising of airline facilities, for defence plants and vast military contracts, for space agencies with all their huge expenditures, and for many analogous purposes. These funds, appropriated in such Acts, have been little less than a vital ingredient in the daily economic diet of the people.

Nor do the Americans find it as necessary as the British to clothe such economic facts of life in a garb of political or even moral principle when they emerge on the public stage. The 'pressure group' in the politics of the United States, which frequently assumes a sectional or regional character, is not only recognised and accepted, but in effect given an official status, as, for example, by the legislation requiring the registration of the 'lobbyists' of such groups. It is accepted as natural, nay proper, that the agricultural interests of the country, for instance, should band together to form the exceedingly powerful farm bloc, which influences the government in matters large and small; this group has successfully pressed for the maintenance of the Federal subsidies which assist in the production of America's enormous agricultural surpluses. (On a somewhat different plane it long prevented the sale of yellow margarine, which might be mistaken for butter, so that generations of American 'house-guests' participated in the solution of this problem by painfully and incompetently stirring in with a spoon the little packets of yellow powder supplied with each packet of lard-like 'oleomargarine'.) In the same way, manifold industrial pressure groups are always on the alert to effect or prevent changes in the tariff which will favour their products. In recent years, to take two small but significant examples, the American bicycle industry (long in competition with superior British experience) and the watchmaking interests of the United States (always struggling with Swiss expertise) have made their voices clearly heard.

But American libertarian beliefs were none the less deep enough to affect the most basic economic tendencies, as the remaining mistrust of monopolies, of overweaning industrial power, of the 'curse of bigness', still shows. Fundamental facts of great weight – the size of the American market unrestricted by tariff barriers, the richness of American resources, and the scale and sense of efficiency which these encouraged – all tended towards the formation of larger units of industrial organisation, but Administrations have been constantly forced to pay something more than mere lip service to the Jeffersonian ideal of the 'little man', the 'economic backbone of American political democracy', albeit this is an increasingly urban, 'Hamiltonian', civilisation and not the society of farmers that Jefferson envisaged. In fact the United States has, with some justice in mid-twentieth century, been called an oligopoly, dominated by a few vast industrial combinations. But strenuous and not unsuccessful efforts have been made by the government and the people to enforce the continuance of real competition between the giants. And this has been reinforced by emphasis on the idea of 'counter-

vailing power', by which the influence of the great industrial producers is counterbalanced by the strength of the huge distributive
enterprises, by the power of the great trade unions, and in fact by
the pervasive influence of government itself. But even under the
Republican régime of the 1950s the anti-trust activities of the
Attorney General's department remained relatively vigorous. The
importance of this aspect of America's belief in a free society in
which the individual has maximum scope, and the startling contrast
which until very recent times it presented with most of Europe, is
perhaps best illustrated by the fact that it was considered necessary,
in the Webb-Pomerone Act of 1918, specifically to exempt American
firms from anti-trust legislation when engaged in the export trade.

If this paramount concern for individual rights be regarded as a
good, tribute is due to the perspicacity of the Founding Fathers
for embedding bulwarks for their protection deep in the structure
of the Constitution: these remarkably able men were, many of
them, already aware of the danger which Tocqueville had in mind
when he wrote later, 'It is in the examination of the display of
public opinion in the United States that we clearly perceive how
far the power of the majority surpasses all the powers with which
we are acquainted in Europe'. In some cases, these bulwarks proved
ineffective. The so-called Electoral College system for the indirect
election of the President broke down almost at once and was
ruthlessly adapted to produce a highly popular contest, although
not a nation-wide majority vote. The constitutional provision that
States appoint Presidential Electors and the fact that they are
approximately proportionate in number to the population of each
State, combined with the convention that the winning candidate
in each State takes all that State's electoral votes, has continued to
give a disproportionate advantage and influence to the large States.
At least until modern times, when mass publicity has tended to
make it less important, the number of Presidents from great States
like New York and Ohio affords strong evidence of this.

Similarly, the entire omission of, or rather absence of all reference
to, political parties in the Constitution, which reflected the contemporary mistrust of such new-fangled 'factious' organisations, was
quite powerless to prevent the almost immediate growth of the
party system; the Federalists and the Democratic Republicans were
fully fledged and at one another's throats within a decade of the
inauguration of the new government. In due course, with the rise
of Jacksonian Democracy as the heir of the latter, the Whig party
came into existence as a sort of successor of the ill-fated Federalists,

and with the collapse of the Whigs and the successful formation of the new Republican party in the pre-Civil War era, we are on the threshold of the modern, now century-old, political rivalry between the Republicans and the Democrats, soon to be traditionally symbolised by Thomas Nast's cartoon figures, the elephant and the donkey. The two-party structure has indeed become a seemingly unalterable feature of the American political system. 'Third parties' have been frequent, especially though not always in the hands of reformers and zealots – the Greenbackers, the Populists, the Bull Moose Progressives of 1912 and the Progressives of 1948, as well as the conservative, indeed reactionary, Southern Dixiecrats, also in the latter year. These new parties have often served a most valuable purpose, both in giving vent to popular discontent and in stimulating the two great leviathans to action. But none of them has really endured as a continuing third force in the way that the Liberal party has to some extent done in Britain, largely because, where their appeal has not been solely ephemeral, their ideas have been taken over or gradually absorbed by one, or sometimes both, of the major parties.

Time, too, has changed the balance of the Constitution so carefully constructed in 1787. The Supreme Court, it is true, may possibly have asserted its independent sphere of action more decisively in the early years than the Fathers expected, thus strengthening the protection of individual and corporate rights against the power of the Federal legislature and executive, but the essence of the way in which it asserted itself under Chief Justice Marshall was the enormous strengthening of the Union at the expense of the States. With the exception of the period of Southern ascendancy in the 1840s and 1850s and that of the peak influence of Social Darwinism in the 1880s there has been a perceptible tendency towards the increase of Federal power, especially in the twentieth century; since 1933 it has been positively dramatic. And within the Federal government it has been the executive which has acquired most of this new power, for with the exception of a phase of considerable Congressional initiative and influence in the years after the Civil War, the Presidency has gathered more and more of the national leading strings into its own hands. As head of his party and also Head of State the President has become a national leader of immense potency. Though few of the forms of his relationship with Congress have changed, their content has in the long run altered in such a manner as greatly to increase his power. With the growth in the complexity of government, the Civil Service has expanded rapidly in numbers and power, though not yet perhaps equalling those of the great European states in influence; this process the rise of the Bureau of the Budget, as we shall see, vividly illustrates.

With the sudden, huge development in the importance of foreign affairs, the President's clear rights and duties in this field have greatly augmented his strength; and his role as Commander-in-Chief has had exactly the same effect, in peace (or the near-peace of our era) as well as in war. So obvious has this growth in executive influence become that even the hitherto largely neglected, if not ignored, Vice-President has in the years since the Second World War been kept in much closer touch with the executive than heretofore; indeed sometimes he is closer to the President than to the legislature, where his original constitutional duty (presiding over the Senate) lies.

But though in so many ways the tendency towards increasingly centralised governmental power has altered the facts of American politics, if not so frequently the letter of the Constitution, the rigid structure of this basic written instrument has kept very much alive a number of hindrances, in their origin mostly deliberate, to the expansion of the strength of Federal authority. (Washington in the District of Columbia, for example, though it now has the right to choose its quota of Presidential Electors and has become in this century a real national capital, is, with its roughly three-quarters of a million inhabitants, very far from playing the part in the life of its nation that London or Paris do.) The government's own inbuilt system of checks and balances still limits, sometimes strictly so, the range and effectiveness of its activity.

The separation of the Executive, Legislative and Judicial arms makes action in some spheres extremely difficult even now. This is perhaps most obviously the case in legislation, for the fact that no Executive officer may sit in Congress and none except the President address it directly as a body makes it very hard for the Cabinet, which has no collective responsibility – and its members no individual responsibility except to their own head, the President – to get the laws it needs from Capitol Hill. (It is interesting that Hamilton had wished in the very beginning to be allowed to present his report on finance to the House in person but had been refused, and that the Constitution of the Southern Confederacy had actually made it permissible for Congress to 'grant to the principal officer in each of the Executive Departments a seat upon the floor of either House, with the privilege of discussing any measure appertaining to his department'.) Officials can, and do, frequently appear before committees of Congress, but even then they appear only as witnesses and not technically to present their own case, though with the loose rules of procedure in the committees this is not in practice a very clear distinction.

The whole problem is most vividly exemplified in that traditionally central function of the legislature in a Western-type (and particularly Anglo-American) democracy – taxation and finance. With the ramifying complications of modern industrial society and the expanding business of the Federal government the management of financial legislation by the Appropriations Committees of the House and Senate, in consultation with the numerous other committees and sub-committees concerned (the sub-committees, for example, on Public Works, and on Foreign Operations) has become an exceedingly involved and tangled process. This is only alleviated by the fact that Congressional committees have much greater facilities and funds for research and operation than their weaker Parliamentary counterparts in Britain. In 1921 the Bureau of the Budget was formed to advise the President, and through him the Congress, and its power has grown rapidly, so that each year it costs some $30 million and produces a formidable tome of fact, analysis, and recommendation, which sometimes weighs as much as seven pounds! Yet because of the separation of powers the President often has the greatest difficulty in getting the bulk of what he wants, let alone in exactly the form and at the time he wants it. The Budget is never considered as a whole by either House (indeed does not really exist as such) and during a single Congressional session as many as twenty separate, frequently very piecemeal, appropriation bills go through the complicated process of enactment, running the gauntlet of committees of both Houses, then of the two Houses themselves, and finally in many cases of a Conference Committee of the Senate and the House to resolve the differences between their versions of the bill.

But financial legislation simply has to be passed sooner or later, and the President's difficulties in getting other legislation through, as, for example, in recent years on Civil Rights, can be even greater. The committees are on the whole much better at their valuable function of educating the public (and sometimes of influencing them in a less wholesome way) on political issues than at expediting the passage of laws. Indeed Congress, which has its own independent legislative responsibility, is still not only wary of accepting specific measures put forward by the Executive but even seems sometimes chary of overtly recognising that the President has the right to do much more than is specified in the Constitution: 'He shall from time to time give to the Congress Information of the State of the

Union, and recommend to their Consideration such Measures as he shall judge necessary and expedient.' Certainly, though the President's veto is in frequent use today – especially when his party has not got majorities in Congress – the proposal to increase his control over the legislative process by giving him the power to veto parts, rather than merely the whole, of Bills (the so-called 'item veto', which again was embodied in the Confederate Constitution, for appropriation bills) has never been accepted. And Congress, with a House of 435 members and a Senate of 100, is obviously not ideally constituted, despite the Committee system, to initiate and then to accept without undue delay even its own legislative measures. In the view of some critics there has been a grave legislative failure by Congress in the face of pressing domestic problems in the years since the Second World War.

These difficulties, arising from the calculated division of governmental power, are not solved, except in a limited degree, by the party system, which is of course in Britain a crucial element in the effective leadership of, indeed control over, the House of Commons by the government, which is invariably drawn from its majority party.

The American two-party system has been, and still is, an indispensable part of the democratic system of the United States, but the national parties are at bottom coalitions of local parties with deep and literally vital roots in their states. Only during Presidential elections, if then, are these alliances really united throughout the nation, and at those times their traditional cement has been the desire for victory and the perquisites and patronage which it brings, rather than political principle, although the importance of differing Democratic and Republican policies has greatly increased in this century. Yet the Democratic party, especially, still contains totally antithetical reactionary and liberal figures like Senator Eastland of Mississippi and Senator Humphrey of Minnesota. Almost the only occasions when the House and the Senate regularly vote on strictly party lines are in the critical divisions at the beginning of each Congress when the members – all of the Representatives and a third of the Senators being newly-elected – cast their first votes, on such matters as the choice of a Speaker of the House and the organisation of the highly important committees which dominate the procedures of debate, investigation and legislation. But between national elections the parties, especially if they do not control the national government, draw their nourishment from the localities where their basic organisation lies; these grass roots of the parties, which are as important in the great cities as in the old rural areas whence the metaphor arose, are a seemingly inevitable feature of American politics.

If, as not infrequently happens (for instance, for Southern Democrats over the race question), there is a conflict between the policies of a President of one's party and the wishes of one's constituents, the latter must prevail. The support of his party is of nothing like the importance to an American member of Congress that it is to a Member of Parliament, especially because the former must by the Constitution 'be an Inhabitant of that State in which he shall be chosen', and by custom reside in his Congressional district, so that a new constituency can really never 'be found' for a defeated member, although another post or office may be, and often is. Persistent defiance of the Whips in the House of Commons can mean virtual disfranchisement because Independent Members can scarcely exist today: almost all American members tend to independence and frequently ignore the Whips, who are much less powerful figures than their British counterparts. Their superiors in the American system, the Majority and Minority Floor Leaders of the House and the Senate, whose essential task it is to try and control or guide their unruly party cohorts, have an arduous and harassed life, and their success in navigating the legislation of their party through Congress is strictly limited. The fact that the immensely powerful Speaker of the House is very much a party man, elected by the majority party, only alleviates this chronic ailment which arises from the separation of powers. Yet, ironically, even where the Founding Fathers deliberately overrode the principle of separation, as in the requirement that treaties made by the President must be ratified by a two-thirds majority of the Senate, the result was often to make effective action by the government more rather than less difficult.

The rigidity of the Constitution has made this difficulty harder to overcome. Thus, for example, the fixity of election dates (elections are held every 2 years for the House and one-third of the Senate, every 4 years for the President) does not leave to the President as leader of his party as well as of the government that discretion in calling elections which so greatly strengthens the hold over his following of a Prime Minister in Britain, or, for instance, in federal Australia. *Per contra*, a President is greatly weakened in his second term by the fact that – for long by custom and now by law – he cannot run again, and so has much less hold over his party. This inflexibility, too, shows itself – and perhaps to its greatest disadvantage – in the extreme difficulty which has been experienced in amending the Constitution; thus only 24 amendments to the document have been made in the 175 years of its existence, and 10 of these were adopted together in 1791, almost as part of the original instrument. In fact, it has probably been amended much less than was envisaged in 1787, for the more radical of the alternative methods authorised, that of calling another national Convention like that at Philadelphia, has never been employed. (It might well be necessary to do so if the United States should ever enter a supra-national union similar to the European Economic Community.)

This rigidity has certainly not been without its uses. In a country where innovation is so persistently, uniquely, welcomed and whose very population was for three centuries constantly and drastically changing in numbers and composition (on a scale never approached elsewhere and at a rate unsurpassed anywhere until recent years), a constitution too easily amended (let alone an unwritten one like that of Britain, so dependent on custom and tradition) might have altered beyond recognition and possibly very much for the worse. Its inflexibility has helped to preserve the Constitution, with all its very real and very great advantages, and – setting aside the first twelve amendments passed in the first fifteen years – its relatively increasing frequency of amendment (three of the remaining twelve amendments having been passed in the last thirteen years – 25 per cent of the changes in 8 per cent of the time) might suggest that, with the growing homogeneity of American society, greater flexibility may become possible.

Nor must we exaggerate the rigidity. We have seen something of the extent to which Federal authority has expanded, and in fact the range of its activity in economic matters today would have profoundly shocked the majority of the Founding Fathers and might even have surprised Hamilton. Economic organisation in 1787 was still for the most part very localised, but modern industrialism meant that many, if not most, of the important economic units in national life became truly national in scope. Not only is the income of one or two giant corporations today larger than the entire national income of the United States in 1789, but it is vastly greater than the present revenue of many States. This meant that industry outgrew the control of the individual states, making Federal regulation the only alternative to no control at all; and during the twentieth century the American public has gradually made it clear that, addicted though it is to individual economic self-determination, it will not accept the anarchy which threatened during the heyday of *laissez-faire* in the late nineteenth century. Thus the regulatory functions of the Federal government have been enormously expanded, principally through the specific constitutional right of Congress to legislate for inter-state commerce and through the increased use of permanent Federal control bodies like the Interstate Commerce Commission.

Further, the apparently irresistible tendency in all great political federations of the modern world for fiscal strength and hence revenue to fall into the hands of the central government at the expense of the local authorities has enabled Washington, often by the process of offering States 'matching' grants for specific purposes, to extend its influence into many spheres originally quite exclusively the concern of the States. Perhaps the most striking example of this growth of Federal power was the increasingly elaborate system of Federal social security which was begun by the Act of 1935. This provided funds for pensions to the needy aged, for old-age insurance, for unemployment insurance, for benefit payments to the blind, dependent mothers and families, and crippled children, and for extensive public health work. The unemployment insurance plan levied a Federal payroll tax on all employers, but encouraged state action by refunding 90 per cent of these payments if the states set up their own systems. Old age insurance, on the other hand, was entirely national, and employers and employees contributed to the Federal fund out of which pensions were paid. The matching principle was, however, widely applied in the case of public assistance to those already over 65; assistance of up to $15 a month, after a means test, was extended to such aged persons as were indigent, if co-operating states would contribute a like amount. These arrangements have since been added to and altered, though the fundamental overhaul which many have demanded has not been undertaken, and though there has been a tendency for the actual operations, except of old age pensions, to remain predominantly in the hands of the separate states, which may in addition have their own old age pension schemes if they so desire. Nevertheless the whole structure depends on the Federal government, and is an extension of its power beyond the wildest dreams of the late eighteenth century. To such a degree has the American talent for politics enabled its practitioners to adapt, indeed transform, the rigid constitutional arrangements which they inherited from their forebears.

Yet these 'encroachments' of the Federal authority have been strenuously resisted. Sometimes this is the work chiefly of a special sectional interest; thus, the efforts of Administrations in recent years to subsidise education more heavily (this being a State matter) have been to a considerable degree frustrated by Southern fears that it would strengthen the hands of Northern integrationists in the sensitive area (as well perhaps, *per contra*, as by traditional fears aroused in the public at large by Roman Catholic demands that parochial schools be subsidised). Sometimes the special interests have been of a different kind, as in the bitter opposition of the American Medical Association to anything ever so remotely smacking of 'socialised medicine', even for the elderly. But it is not to be denied that such vested interests are far from being a sufficient explanation of the resistance. American political life is still capable of throwing up a deep conservative like Barry Goldwater; or of 'throwing back' with such an atavistic phenomenon as the Birch society (the headquarters of which are in California), or the Minutemen of the West, dedicated to guerilla warfare from the day that Communism comes. These are some of the extreme manifestations which can result from the inbred American conviction, which has been weakened but has never wholly disappeared, that that government is best which governs least, and that the more remote and powerful the government is the less responsive it will be to the will of the people and the more dangerous to their liberties.

Though times have changed, most Americans instinctively expect, and prefer, things which have to be done to be done where possible by the authority which is nearest to them, and closest to the ground – that is in practice by the States. In actual fact it is probable that the division of powers between the Federal government and the states has been the most effective of all the arrangements in the Constitution for the preservation of individual freedom, and this was not really the invention of the Fathers but an unalterable fact of political life which they inherited from *their* forebears. It was part and parcel of the relationship of the colonies to Westminster and to one another, and it remained equally necessary in a federation as large as the United States in 1783 and even more so as she became a vast sub-continental nation.

As Edmund Burke had declared before the American Revolution, 'In large bodies, the circulation of power must be less vigorous at the extremities. Nature has said it. The Turk cannot govern Egypt, and Arabia, and Curdistan, as he governs Thrace . . . He governs with a loose rein, that he may govern at all.' The United States was the first nation, constructed on the enormous scale which has come into its own in the mid-twentieth century, effectively to reconcile size with liberty, and she did it by federation, by selecting for the central government only the essential powers of a modern nation and leaving the rest to the States. Thus she was able to accommodate herself to the wide variety of the sub-continent; to regions as diverse as sub-tropical Florida, prairie North Dakota, industrialised New Jersey and mountainous Washington. More than that, by dividing power she protected liberty. In Russia in the past control from the centre, which ensures unity, has been maintained precisely at the price of liberty: in traditional China provincial freedom tended to be preserved at the cost of unity, but in Communist China it seems likely that the process has been exactly reversed in the Russian fashion. When we become unduly impatient with the cumbersome and creaking antiquity of the American political mechanism, with its inability sometimes to 'get things done' in a hurry (if at all), we may think on these things. Then perhaps, as did that of Burke, our rigour may relent: we may pardon something to the spirit of liberty.

The operation of the Federal system is far from simple. The distinctive feature of it, that the individual citizen owes a simultaneous, dual obligation to both his country and his state, calls for a high degree of political sophistication in many instances, and the conflicts of loyalty which result are never easy to solve and at times of crisis, as on the eve of the Civil War or even over the race issue at the present time, may be intensely difficult. One result of it is the great importance of the Law in the United States and the ubiquity and influence of the legal profession. The inevitable conflicts of jurisdiction, for example, between Federal and State governments not only mean constant reference back to the Constitution by the Courts, which thus exercise great political power, but also entail endless litigation. When we reflect that there is no Federal Common Law as such, only Federal statute and constitutional law, but that there are in essence fifty codes of common law, a differing one in every State, the extreme complexity of the legal system becomes obvious, as well as the reason for the proliferation of American lawyers. It is true that all the States except possibly Louisiana, whose law is derived from the *Code Napoléon*, have some elements of Anglo-American jurisprudence in common, but the diversity is made instantly apparent when we recollect that the punishment for (and of course the mere definition of) murder is very variable, ranging from imprisonment to hanging, the electric chair, or the gas chamber. Similarly, divorce is almost a formality in Nevada but is much more difficult in some other States. These complexities affect legislation and administration as well as the courts, and movement from the law to politics and also back again is an even commoner feature of American, than it used to be (and to a lesser extent still is) of British, life.

In Britain we tend to think of two governmental levels, national and local, with the latter, in these days of the supremacy of statute law, deriving their powers from and subservient to the former. In the American Federal system there is another tier, that of the states, but they are not subordinate to, though they are weaker than, the national government; they have certain powers derived directly from the Constitution or reserved to them by it, which, within their proper sphere, have an equal authority and are equally protected in the courts, both their own and those of the Federal government. Every State has certain powers, which are still very extensive indeed, and each State exercises them in its own way, subject only to the Constitution.

It is true that the fifty patterns of State government have many features in common; the Constitution, for example, lays down that they must be 'republican', and this term in the United States bears as its principal meaning what we might in these days broadly term 'democratic'. Each State has a written Constitution, sometimes not dissimilar from the national Constitution; generally they were first made by constitutional conventions specially summoned for the purpose, and from time to time still are totally overhauled, or created anew, by the same process. Usually they are ratified by a popular vote in the state, and can be (and frequently are) amended by voting on specific amendments at election time. In theory they should be, and originally in practice often were, simple documents embodying basic principles of fundamental law, but increasingly in modern times this distinction between constitution and law has tended to break down. State constitutions have become longer and longer and have in fact included more and more of what is in reality specific legislation.

The governments which are brought into being under these constitutions also run on the whole very true to the same form. There are the traditional arms of government, Executive, Legislature and Judiciary, usually with pretty clearly separated powers. The norm of the Executive is a Governor and Lieutenant-Governor; of the Legislature two elected chambers (one elected in proportion to population, the other representing counties or similar units); and of the Judiciary a supreme and inferior courts. There are numerous and not very important differences in nomenclature. Thus the legislature of Massachusetts is called 'The General Court' and consists of a Senate and a House of Representatives; the lower house of the Virginia legislature, on the other hand, is known as the House of Delegates. There are some not unimportant differences in procedure: thus the legislature of Nebraska notes and displays its votes in a 'division' on an electric tally board on which each member records his individual vote from his seat; and the State of New York has a Court of Appeals superior to its Supreme Court, which is in fact its court of original jurisdiction for crime. There are a few really significant differences in structure; thus Nebraska again, alone among the states, has a unicameral legislature. The attitudes of states on certain questions do of course differ widely. Some states have much looser control of great business corporations than do others; some, especially in the West, employ the initiative, the referendum or the recall, and others do not; some states popularly elect a far wider range of officials, including judges, than do others.

Nothing perhaps so sharply crystallises the different attitudes of the British and American peoples to democratic government than does the surprised, even shocked, British scepticism about the election of judicial officers in many American states, unless it be the election of police officials, such as sheriffs. Our long tradition of centralised monarchical government in which judicial power spread out through the years from its fount and origin, the kingship, and in which, even in the days of aristocratic control of the constitution, power always seemed to, and mostly did, descend from above, predisposes us to think of appointment as almost the only conceivable, let alone efficient and upright, way of choosing judges. In our courts, after all, cases are *Regina* v. *Jo Snook*: in the courts of some states in the United States, on the other hand, they are *The People* v. *John Doe*. This is more than a difference of terminology, for it reflects the fundamental and pervasive American belief that the people are in very truth, in practice as well as in theory, the source of all political power, judicial as well as legislative and executive. This being so, the election of judges seems to many Americans the most logical and natural thing in the world.

This thorough-going democracy does have effects at the lower levels of government, which operate under the jurisdiction of the State – county, city and township. These inferior organs of government, for instance, are quite likely, if the State does not choose to act, to do so themselves on local issues, on their own initiative, in a way without real parallel in Britain. An obviously bizarre example is a recent prohibition of smoking in a local Texas community, but an illuminating one at all levels was brought forcibly home to one foreigner who was in the act of travelling across the United States in 1946 on the day that Congress officially 'declared peace'. During the war uniform national daylight-saving, which was of great economic importance, could not be legislated by Congress because it had not the authority under the Constitution, but it was enforced by Presidential Proclamation under the war power. When the war ended, so did the legal effect of the Proclamation, and the United States, to the considerable perplexity of the migrant stranger (already sufficiently confused by the existence of the five different time zones of North America), reverted in the matter of time to her normal, somewhat permissive, pattern of self-government. The Federal government could take no action in the continental United States except in the District of Columbia; if any State chose to take action it could do so, either by enforcing or forbidding daylight-saving; but if a State did not choose to take any action, virtually any local community, down as low as a township, could do so. Thus the United States became a veritable patchwork of light and shade, and one moved across its broad expanses, never quite sure at exactly what hour one's watch should stand.

In a manner more familiar in this country, local authorities have a vital role (often more vital indeed than in Britain) to play in many spheres. The effective control of education, for example, may be very much more localised. Police, in our fashion, is essentially a local matter; there are State police forces, but they tend to operate to a large extent on the State's highways. The Federal Bureau of Investigation (FBI), under its long-standing head, J. Edgar Hoover, has steadily augmented its power in recent times, but it is still not a full police force in our sense of the term. Even the increased use of Federal Marshals – technically officers of the Federal courts – and their use in greater numbers, almost like bodies of police, in the last few years, especially in race disputes, begins to look as if it may one day come to fill this gap in Federal law enforcement, but there still is at present a lack of actual Federal power, short of the use of the armed forces, and this may in itself very often be undesirable.

But even at this fundamental level, there is at some times and in some places a dichotomy between theory and practice in American politics such as we have seen in earlier days. The actual human beings on whom the whole government at bottom depends are not always as active as the system wants them, needs them, to be. The really fundamental political figure, the ward heeler, who tends the basic unit of American political life, the ward, and whose primal function is to 'get out the vote', can still exercise a remarkable degree of local influence. And on these foundations political machines of the traditional type can still be raised in both city and country, albeit the new political boss is usually a much more sophisticated operator than the old one. None the less, professional politicians are still a very live reality, and politics is a profession which is paid – and can pay very well indeed even yet. But now the politician cannot command his unquestioning legions as his pre-decessor did; he must persuade them, or capitalise more subtly than heretofore upon their sloth, upon their natural human dis-inclination to 'put themselves out' for politics.

The future of American politics, indeed, will depend, as Americans believe it must and should, upon the people themselves, upon their activity, their rectitude and their wisdom.

Chapter 24

The American Way

I F THE FUTURE of the United States depends fundamentally upon
the individual American, taken in the mass, so, in remarkable
degree, does the future of mankind, for few indeed are the nooks
and crannies of the world to which America's influences does not
now in some measure percolate.

Though her anti-imperialist habits and cast of mind have reasserted themselves since the time when she acquired her own real,
if relatively limited and short-lived, colonial empire at the turn of
the century, her Marxist enemies certainly regard hers as overwhelmingly the most powerful and widespread manifestation of
'capitalist imperialism'. And, though she some time ago granted the
Philippines their independence, she does in truth retain sovereignty
or quasi-sovereignty in a few places which serve as fairly distant
outposts for the defence of the United States and what we have
called the free world, such as the Panama Canal Zone, Okinawa,
Guam, American Samoa and a number of other Pacific island
territories. Hawaii, which is in mid-Pacific nearly 2,500 miles from
the American mainland, and Alaska, which is only 50 miles from
Russia (the Diomede Islands in the Bering Strait are actually
shared between the United States and the Soviet Union), have now
been made part of America proper as the 50th and 49th states,
and Puerto Rico in the Caribbean is called a 'commonwealth' but
remains in essence a Territory of the United States. Much more
widespread (and in the early rocket-age they were probably much
more important) are the American bases maintained by treaty
throughout the world. They range from the *Polaris* nuclear missile
submarine base at Holy Loch in Britain, through manifold European,
Mediterranean and Middle Eastern bases, to those in the Orient,
in such places as Japan and Formosa. Not unnaturally, seeking as
they do the world-wide containment of international Communism,
the vast ramifications of this military system are described by the
Communist bloc as (and to a great degree no doubt are genuinely
believed to be) 'imperialist' and thus potentially – indeed by
Marxist dogma inevitably – aggressive.

This American system is a remarkable military effort to hem in the Communist powers and to prevent them from spreading their dominion over the whole of Eurasia, and *a fortiori* beyond it into Africa and across the seas. Eurasia is 'the world-island', as Mackinder called it, which, with the exception of Western Europe, already runs some real risk of falling into the Communist sphere of influence. But the success of the containment policy has been remarkable, despite current weak spots such as South East Asia, and the fundamental strategic position of the free world is not without great advantages against what some have claimed to be this geostrategically decisive Eurasian world-island. The American, and Atlantic, base is very strong, for the United States – herself enjoying an insular position – has in fact taken over the British tradition of highly mobile sea-power (augmented today by air power), even if it has been transformed almost beyond recognition by the technological revolution of the past century. Essentially, however, America, by controlling the sea and air lanes of the globe, is trying to maintain the independence – and opportunity for development in freedom – of the peoples on the periphery of the Eurasian land-mass, as well as those in more distant lands, rather as Britain, in the earlier age of European ascendancy, tried to prevent the conquest of Europe by a single authoritarian power.

But this world conflict is not by any means solely, even predominantly, the result of an old-fashioned great-power rivalry between the United States on the one hand and the Soviet Union and the Chinese People's Republic on the other: it is the outcome of a deep ideological division, in some ways more akin to the even more old-fashioned religious struggles of the sixteenth and seventeenth centuries, but with the profound difference that then it was only a hypothetical kingdom of heaven which was believed to be at issue, but that now it is the actual destiny of humanity which we know to be at stake. The so-called free world, and especially 'the West' (Europe and its direct lineal descendants overseas, most notably in North America and Australasia), shares today in some degree a number of real, if variable and intangible, values, such as those 'rights and freedoms' adumbrated in the United Nations 'Universal Declaration of Human Rights' of 1948; and in such a 'free society', in its many and differing forms of 'democracy', the individual citizen must play a vital part. Because of the crucial position of international leadership which the power of the United States has thrust upon her, much of the fate of the human race in practice rests with the American people. How well are they fitted for this role? And in particular how suitable is their form of government to this unique international leadership?

At first sight, and certainly in the minds of many critics, the Constitution of the United States, and especially its separation and limitation of the powers of the national government, is ill adapted to the conduct of a world-wide foreign policy in mid-twentieth century. Among the most notable criticisms which have been voiced are those of the requirement of a two-thirds majority in the Senate for the ratification of treaties (fatal, for example, to America's entry into the League of Nations which her President had pressed upon the signatories of the repudiated Versailles Treaty); of the need of Congressional appropriations to make good international commitments undertaken by the Executive branch of the government (resulting, for instance, in the periodic struggle in the Congress, and especially the House, over the sums to be voted for foreign aid); and of the constitutional provision that 'The Congress shall have Power . . . To declare War' (obviously liable to be anomalous, indeed superfluous, when her heartland is vulnerable within literally a few minutes to her major potential enemy's 'first strike'). These criticisms are not without substance; one case in point could be the recent prohibition, on Congressional initiative, of American aid to countries which do not take 'appropriate steps' to prevent their ships or aircraft from calling at Cuba, a prohibition which probably went well beyond the desires of the State Department.

In fact, however, though the process of discussion and decision between Executive and Congress may be slow and sometimes clumsy and though Executive formulation of policies may be inhibited by it, the number of occasions in post-war years when it has sharply or severely set back American foreign policy have been few and far between. There has been no recent rebuff to the President by the legislature remotely comparable, for example, to the rejection of the European Defence Community, which was sponsored by the French government, in the French National Assembly on 30 August 1954. Furthermore, the amendment to the Constitution proposed in the 1950s by Senator John W. Bricker of Ohio, which would greatly have curtailed the 'prerogative' of the President in making 'executive agreements' (as opposed to 'treaties' which need Senatorial assent), has not been passed. Indeed, the President's already dominating powers in the sphere of foreign policy on the whole grew steadily and substantially under President Johnson's four predecessors. His power as Commander-in-Chief, in particular, as befits the existence of the cold war (a twilight condition, neither peace nor war), has greatly expanded to suit conditions in which instant decisions of the utmost gravity need to be made and in which the armed forces of the United States regularly number more than 2¾ million men. (In addition, the power of the military, of the Pentagon, has enormously – in view of some dangerously – increased in recent years. The influence of Secretary of Defense Robert McNamara, for example, is very great, though he has used it in considerable degree to keep the military in order.) President Truman alone, from his desk in the White House, in fact committed the United States to war in Korea in 1950, and in 1964 the special telephone, the 'hot line' direct to the Kremlin, which stands at the elbow of President Johnson, is a startling symbol of that power. Certainly under its present machinery for the conduct of foreign policy the United States has irrevocably committed itself, in a manner scarcely conceivable 30 years ago, to a number of international organisations such as the United Nations and to a positive network of 'permanent' and 'entangling' alliances.

Yet the success of America's leadership must depend in great measure upon the impact made by the American people upon the minds and hearts of the other peoples of the earth. Because the United States is a deeply democratic society, no constitutional machinery could work effectively in America which allowed government policy to go beyond what the electorate will in the long run support: it is certainly right that the political institutions of the country should be responsive to the wishes of the people in foreign as well as domestic affairs, for such is the only stable, or even possible, basis of policy in a democracy. This is indeed a fundamental fact in the free world at large, for it will be the more truly the free world the more the policies of its governments are in accordance with the wishes of their respective peoples. It is perhaps the main problem of all international diplomacy in this egalitarian age that, as Mahan foresaw long ago, it is necessary to bring not merely governments but peoples to accord. This imposes significant limitations on American leadership, which cannot use the full and terrible might of the American military machine, not only because nuclear war is in literal truth a last, a desperate, resort – President Johnson has flatly declared it to be impossible – but also because, deep down, Americans know that their allies must be persuaded and cannot be commanded.

This is not as great a disadvantage as it sometimes seems to be *vis à vis* the ostensibly limber ability of the autocratic Communist monoliths to manipulate their puppets' strings. Russia, China and the East European states themselves are all in some measure dependent upon the support of their peoples, and no fact of the cold war – one frequently forgotten by the free nations even after the Berlin wall provided a permanent and astounding dramatisation of it – has been more consistent and remarkable than the steady flow of refugees, day after day, hour after hour, in their thousands and tens of thousands, through the Iron Curtain. Indeed, the great, the persistent, hope of America and the West must be that the pressure of the Russian people for a higher standard of living, long silent but perhaps ultimately irresistible, may in the end of itself produce the decay, if not the collapse, of the aggressive and tyrannical policies of Soviet Communism. For the good things of life can only be produced on this scale by massive scientific and technological education at the highest level: is it possible that the indispensable freedom of scientific inquiry which this entails can long subsist with a rigid control of social and political thought? Can the Russian mind endure permanently half slave and half free? It seems most unlikely that the Soviet government can match the performance of the United States in the competition of co-existence without allowing more and more freedom to the Russian people.

In a sense this orientation towards America has long been implicit even in the Russian ethos itself. In 1937 J. B. Priestley wrote, at the height of the Great Depression, 'America is definitely in front . . . Russia can turn the old economic and political system upside down, but no sooner has she done so than she takes a long look at America.' In the post-war years, at the height of the American-Russian rivalry, few things have been more significant than the way in which Soviet economic objectives, even the sacred Five Year Plans, have tended to be conceived in relation to American achievements; and recently Mr Khruschev has not contented himself with promising to overtake American production in x years, but has also directed the attention of Russian farms to the superior actual agricultural methods of the capitalist American farmer. Thus not only the world outside the Iron Curtain, but even to some extent the bloc within it, look to the American example. This is at bottom a phenomenon which is distinct from the positive international leadership for which the West looks to the United States. Self-conscious, if not introspective, as the American people may be, and concerned as they are about the 'image' they present to the outside world, there is a strict limit to their ability – or that of any people – consciously to project themselves on the minds and television screens of mankind. They are, as it were, as greatly in the grip of their unconscious as of their conscious national identity. What is this American *persona*, this mode of living which thus so deeply concerns humanity?

It has certain obvious features, what may perhaps be thought of as the more superficial aspects of 'coca-colonisation'. Indeed, much that is merely modernity is in fact often called American, but because she has, as the great pioneer democracy, had so distinct an influence, there is a sense in which to be 'with it' does really mean to be with America. Novel architecture, popular music, modern dancing, the hectic search for 'relaxed' living, the jeans of the young, the cocktails of the old, the pungent phrases of the language ('O.K.' must be the first universal phrase of 'one world') – all these things, and many more, have some deep American roots. But does America have anything more than this to offer, anything broader and deeper? Is there a separate, a new, 'American civilisation', as some sociologists would have us believe? Not perhaps this, for in essence the United States has certainly continued the European, and especially the British, tradition in the new world. She has been a part of – indeed the greatest embodiment of – the massive movement of the European peoples into the vast and sparsely inhabited lands of the globe – in North and South America, in Australia, in Africa – during modern times.

But she is a very distinct entity, and there clearly is something which we may call – it is the Americans' own and favourite phrase – an 'American way of life'. We are now perhaps beyond the recent reaction of scholars, especially historians, against the whole idea of national character (provoked largely by dislike of extreme racial theories): we can accept the fact that groups of men acquire identifiable traits, even if through environment rather than heredity. Certainly the 'American character' seems likely to have been very preponderantly the result of the American environment since the genetic composition of the American people, every one of whom is either an immigrant or descended from an immigrant, has been, especially during the last hundred years, of a variety and complexity possibly unprecedented in history. This fact of 'recency of arrival', as Professor D. M. Potter writes, has 'perhaps . . . given to Americans a somewhat compulsive preoccupation with the question of their Americanism . . . If . . . their ethnic, religious, linguistic and political heritage is mixed, . . . nationality can hardly exist at all unless it takes the form of a common adjustment to conditions of a new land, a common commitment to shared values, a common esteem for certain qualities of character, or a common set of adaptive traits and attitudes. It is partly for this reason that Americans, although committed to the principle of freedom of thought, have nevertheless placed such heavy emphasis upon the obligation to accept certain undefined tenets of "Americanism".'

It is obviously logical that the Americans, in the process of creating a nation with a distinctive manner of existence, should have transformed the whole legal conception of citizenship among the nations by persisting until successful in establishing the right of naturalisation in a new country, as opposed to the old European idea of indefeasible allegiance. It is also characteristic that they should have insisted on this, perhaps the most fundamental of individual political rights – the right of the ordinary man to choose his habitation – for the American way of life is essentially one for the masses. The very opening sentence of the *Democracy in America* of Alexis de Tocqueville – most percipient and one of the earliest of all commentators upon the American scene – reads, 'Among the novel objects that attracted my attention during my stay in the United States, nothing struck me more forcibly than the general equality of conditions'. Many, perhaps most, Americans have believed from the beginning not only that self-government in liberty is a natural, a sacred, right of every individual, but that every man is the best judge and guardian of his own interests. This helped to liberate the energies of the people in an almost unprecedented manner and is one of the prime sources of American strength; as Tocqueville noted later, 'Democracy . . . produces . . . an all-pervading and restless activity, a superabundant force, . . . which may, under favourable circumstances, beget the most amazing benefits'.

The rich American sub-continent and the free yet relatively stable Constitution of the United States provided just such favourable circumstances for this American doctrine of self-help, firmly based as it is on the fact of human self-interest. The overwhelming mass of mankind tends to be primarily concerned with earning its living, and each individual's pursuit of his own material interest is the giant furnace which powers the human machine. As Adam Smith – himself concerned even in 1776 to explain the extraordinary prosperity of the American colonies – expressed it in *The Wealth of Nations*: 'It is not from the benevolence of the butcher-the brewer, or the baker that we expect our dinner, but from their regard to their own interest'. The 'principal object of . . . Government' in America has been, as Tocqueville puts it, 'to insure the greatest degree of enjoyment and the least degree of misery to each of the individuals' of the nation. This, combined with the premium placed on resourcefulness by the conditions of a virgin land and the theoretical economic belief in private enterprise uninhibited by government interference, helped to produce not only a national habit of intense and assiduous labour, incessant and purposive animation, but also unusual mechanical ingenuity, high technical skill and sharp commercial acumen. In modern times it has been observed – not without some truth – that America's genius lies rather in technology than in 'pure' science: that its pragmatic character has both given supreme prestige to 'Business' and given most encouragement to those intellectual disciplines which have concrete objectives in view. The Industrial Revolution, which had its first vital manifestation in eighteenth-century Britain, already owed much to the economic effects of the American colonies on the mother country, and, though the Anglo-American commercial connection remained very important in the first half of the nineteenth century, it was to have much its most dynamic demonstration in the prodigious productive achievements of mid-twentieth-century America.

This concentration on worldly goods was, and still is, the subject of much foreign (especially European) as well as American criticism: it was, as Professor Potter points out, Washington Irving – an American Anglophile – who 'coined' the 'classic phrase concerning "the almighty dollar, that great object of universal devotion throughout the land".' Tocqueville wrote, 'I know of no country, indeed, where the love of money has taken stronger hold on the affections of men'. In this sense 'American materialism' is a real force, and it has in one way been strengthened by the lack in the American system of almost any other reward for success except money. The earning of one's daily bread, and some cake too, has a powerful tendency to develop into the pursuit of wealth, not so much for its own sake as for the power it gives and the prestige it brings. Yet it is supercilious hypocrisy of the stupidest kind to pretend that the promise of riches is not one of the supreme attractions of the American way of life to the toiling masses of mankind. Furthermore the fact of economic well-being is indispensable to civilisation, as the philosophers have noted from ancient times. A certain scale of income is not only necessary to life but to any hope for the good life: it is also true that goods or money are not only the cure for poverty but also the most potent of solvents of superstition, ignorance and fear. The much publicised 'quiet American' and 'ugly American' may perhaps arouse mistrust in the 'under-developed' countries: the much more universally recognised rich American is a figure both widely envied and actively emulated.

This belief in the search for wealth, combined with a faith in inherited property, militates against what Tocqueville called the American 'idol' of equality, for he also observed, 'I know of no country . . . where a profounder contempt is expressed for the theory of the permanent equality of property'. Generations of

American analysts of the United States have tended to follow Tocqueville in his emphasis on equality, partly perhaps because they have a natural, native inclination to believe in the existence of American equality. Yet this has led them to define the term in such a special way that some of them are to be found not too far from the Orwellian position that all Americans are equal but some are more equal than others. Thus equality of talents and equality of attainments go out with the bathwater of equality of property, and even equality of rights and opportunity are in practice left somewhat weakened. Equality in Australia, for example, is in many respects much more thorough-going. As Sir Keith Hancock has written, the levelling process in Australia 'is obviously different from that equality which observers from De Tocqueville to M. Siegfried have remarked in the democracy of America. The Australians are not content merely to attack privilege nor to remove the handicaps which birth has imposed upon capacity. Rather they tend to ignore capacities in their preoccupation with needs. Equality of opportunity [as in America] implies free scope for natural talent, which must create new inequalities; whereas what Australian democracy desires is equality of enjoyment.'

Yet many of these American students of America have been reluctant to use the experience of other lands to illuminate their own, and this has resulted sometimes in an excessive introspection, and even parochialism, in their self-analysis. This reluctance to look beyond the American experience has perhaps arisen partly from an almost atavistic fear of being influenced by the corrupt old world whose dust they had shaken from their feet, and partly from the fact that the American achievement has been so astounding and seems so logical that even the most liberal and self-critical American finds it hard to believe that the American way can fail to be acceptable to others once they have been 'exposed' to it. The assumptions on which it is based are simple, indeed so shatteringly simple that Americans are often mystified when the practice of their own system does not live up to its theory. Profoundly though early Americans were influenced by Calvinism, even they – elect as they believed themselves to be – thought of America as a new Zion, and somewhere along the line in later American history the sense of original sin (except within the relatively narrow confines of revivalistic religion) became lost or submerged, and about the time of Jefferson was replaced as the dominant feature of the American ethos by a sanguine optimism and by belief in the progress, if not perfectability, of man. The American was long sceptical of history and tradition and still tends to revert if he can to first principles, while the reality of American isolation until recent times did in fact insulate him to a considerable degree from the impact of other nations. It is this conflict between what he believes must be right and the harsh extraneous facts of life of the outer world which in some measures explains such recent phenomena as the fourteen-year-old refusal of the United States to recognise the actual government of China.

Somehow, too, these facts explain the curious impression often made by Americans upon the minds of outsiders – an impression of simplicity merging into naiveté, of directness verging upon in-genuousness, and of youthfulness which is sometimes hard to distinguish from what the outsiders conceive of as immaturity. This impression is made deeper by the very sentimental character of many Americans, who have not been dragooned like the British into concealing their often profound emotional feelings by main-taining a stiff upper lip. The skin of American 'toughness' is perhaps thinner than that of English reserve, and passion will keep breaking through. As the years pass and as the American experience becomes more worldly, in some ways more painful, and more like that of others, a change is taking place and scepticism and cynicism are strengthening their hold. But curiously, even now, it is frequently American innocence which makes the strongest impact on the European visitor, as in American myth it ought to be: the freshness, straightforwardness and vigour (as President Kennedy called it – and he had ample subtlety and sophistication to boot) are the real charisma of America.

For it would be the grossest misrepresentation to think of its undoubted, and at bottom undoubtedly salutary, concern for material things as being the only, or even perhaps the dominating feature of the American way of life. To put it at its lowest level, America is not only the richest nation in history, but the most generous – and this is not a simple cause-effect relationship. When Adam Smith talked of the self-interest of the butcher and the baker, he went on to say, 'We address ourselves, not to their humanity but to their self-love . . .': in business this may be true in America, but in social life nothing could be farther from the truth. American individual hospitality and kindness give it the daily lie; it was an American businessman, albeit one living in Britain, George Peabody, who set the fashion for the institutional philanthropy of the wealthy in the modern 'foundation' era when he established the Peabody Endowment in mid-nineteenth century; and the Marshall Plan and current 'Point Four' programmes for economic aid to the underdeveloped areas of the world, even though there is a – fully recognised – element of self-interest in both, have lifted charity on to a new international and governmental plane.

On an altogether different level, the Americans can be vindicated from the charge of mere materialism because they are in some sense a very religious people: no less a person than Walt Whitman wrote, 'I say the real and permanent grandeur of these States must be their religion'. They are a nation of church-goers at any rate, their average rate of attendance on Sundays being more than four times that of Britain. It is true that there is a strong social element in American church membership, for there is no better way in the United States of settling into, or becoming identified with, a community. But the remarkable growth of, and public interest in, monasticism in America in recent years, for instance, cannot be comfortably shrugged off in the same way: men may go to church for social reasons in mid-twentieth century, they certainly do not enter monasteries. Similarly, there is a real American intellectual revival going on in religion, associated with such influential figures as Reinhold Niebuhr. And this is symptomatic of a widely-spread support for religious institutions in the United States despite the extremely rigid separation of church and state.

But there are other religious nations in the world who do not appear to follow primitive Christian principles in politics; one of the most interesting features of America is its application, in a fashion, of moral, almost religious, beliefs to political life, and, *per contra*, the distinctly democratic tendencies evident in religion – even, relatively speaking, in the Roman Catholic Church. In religion, as in politics, no people have ever so fully espoused the priesthood of all believers; as the American historian George Bancroft wrote approvingly of Calvinism, 'It established a religion without a prelate, a government without a king'. And the Declaration of Independence, and sometimes the Constitution, partake of the character of holy writ; as Lincoln said, 'I have never had a feeling, politically, that did not spring from the sentiments embodied in the Declaration of Independence'. Certainly there is a profoundly religious feeling about certain aspects of politics in America. It was characteristic of Jefferson to declare that 'The God who gave us life, gave us liberty at the same time', but it was, equally characteristically, Lincoln who gave fullest expression to the American sense of the deep moral purpose of democracy, in the famous words on the battlefield of Gettysburg:

'Four score and seven years ago our fathers brought forth on this continent, a new nation, conceived in Liberty, and dedicated to the proposition that all men are created equal.

'Now we are engaged in a great civil war, testing whether that nation or any nation so conceived and so dedicated, can long endure. We are met on a great battle-field of that war. We have come to dedicate a portion of that field, as a final resting place for those who here gave their lives that that nation might live. It is altogether fitting and proper that we should do this.

'But, in a larger sense, we can not dedicate – we can not consecrate – we can not hallow – this ground. The brave men, living and dead, who struggled here, have consecrated it, far above our poor power to add or detract. The world will little note, nor long remember what we say here, but it can never forget what they did here. It is for us the living, rather, to be dedicated here to the unfinished work which they who fought here have thus far so nobly advanced. It is rather for us to be here dedicated to the great task remaining before us – that from these honored dead we take increased devotion to that cause for which they gave the last full measure of devotion – that we here highly resolve that these dead shall not have died in vain – that this nation, under God, shall have a new birth of freedom – and that government of the people, by the people, for the people, shall not perish from the earth.'

There is thus a persistent evangelical, missionary, air about American life, and one that rings true whatever its practical failings; this is what Bryce described as 'their peculiar buoyancy, and what one may call their airy hopefulness in discussing even the weak points of their system . . . They have a boundless faith in free inquiry and full discussion'. They are, he observed, 'a moral and well-conducted people', and 'they trust . . . to the generally sound moral tone of the multitude, to a shrewdness which after failures and through experiments learns what is the true interest of the majority, and finds that this interest coincides with the teachings of morality.' Perhaps above all, even after two world wars and the Great Depression, what Bryce wrote earlier is true; 'They are a hopeful people. Whether or no they are right in calling themselves a new people, they certainly seem to feel in their veins the bounding pulse of youth.'

Energy, driving, enthusiastic energy, is certainly one of the most striking features of American life. Bernard Shaw talked of the 'volcanic political instinct' of America, but the sense of massive reserves of power is characteristic of a much wider range of American activity. It is fed by the fact that Americans are not content that their posterity should attain the good things of life; their democracy leads them in theory to demand, and expect, that each American should be able to enjoy them here and now. A French observer noted in 1940, 'While in France we consider it takes three generations to go from shirt-sleeves to wealth, here, in America, where accelerated speed is an important element of success, it takes but one generation to complete the same process.' But this energy, and the mobility which goes with it (both owing something to the frontier tradition), have been an enormous economic asset to America, as well as keeping political inventiveness and social humanitarianism alive and vital.

It is, however, not without its dark side. Vitality can sink easily into violence, liberty – in the old phrase – into licence. The habits of the open frontier (startlingly lacking in law enforcement agencies and in order compared to its Canadian counterpart with its North West Mounted Police); the appalling problems of social discipline posed, especially in the great cities, by immigration; and even the American addiction to freedom itself (Shaw typically told the Americans, 'You put up in New York Harbor a monstrous idol which you called "liberty" ') – these and other factors combined to produce in the United States a rate of violent crime probably unequalled in the western world. Four American Presidents have been assassinated in less than a hundred years; lynch law was for many years endemic in parts of the Union, especially the South; and in 1955, for example, with a population some four times the size of Britain, the United States had a total of 6,850 cases of murder and non-negligent manslaughter compared with 125 cases of murder of persons over 12 months of age in England and Wales. That is a rate of murder well over ten times as high, even on the basis of computation most favourable to the United States. This strain of violence never seems to the foreigner to be far beneath the surface of American life.

Similarly, though less gravely, American drive can (as elsewhere in the democratic world) generate restlessness and discontent and degenerate easily into the sort of lifetime's activity, pursued automatically and without any real attempt by the pursuer to gauge its worth to him and to society, that is so vividly depicted in Arthur Miller's *Death of a Salesman*. Less serious in detail and to the individual, but perhaps more so in its penetration of the whole of national life is the cult of the advertisement and the domination of the public-relations man, typified in 'Madison Avenue'. With the enormous prestige of Business and the increasing need (as the natural forces of American expansion perhaps tended to wane with the closing of the frontier) for the deliberate creation of economic demand, the power of the advertising agency waxed, and the influence of these often 'hidden persuaders' spread out into many branches of American life. Some critics believe that this has seriously sapped the strength of the American character and its capacity to deal with the increasingly complex problems of its affluent urban society.

This is not an exclusively American organism but it is one which appears there in its most virulent form. Americans have always taken particularly easily to advertising, for reasons which seem not unconnected with their penchant for overstatement; partly it appears to be the 'promotional' habit of mind acquired in the development of a wilderness, partly the need to talk loudly to keep up the courage of the people in new and uncertain conditions and the insecurity that they, from time to time, naturally produce, and partly the fact that for so long so much of America's achievement was necessarily presumptive. As Sydney Smith irritatedly put it nearly a century and a half ago: 'Other nations boast of what they are or have been, but the true citizen of the United States exalts his head to the skies in the contemplation of what the grandeur of his country is going to be.' 'Others appeal to history; an American appeals to prophecy and with Malthus in one hand and a map of the back country in the other he boldly defies us to a comparison with America as she is to be and chuckles in delight over the splendours the geometrical ratio is to shed over her story.'

The Mississippi Valley frontiersmen of that era were indeed, as Professor R. A. Billington notes, 'insufferable braggarts'; they would cry, 'I can wade the brown Mississippi, jump the Ohio, step across the Nolachucky, ride a streak of lightning, slip without a scratch down a honey locust tree, whip my weight in wildcats, and strike a blow like a falling tree.' This American is an advertising man by nature. But he is a consumer too, and, as Turner pointed out many years before, his imagination was and still is kindled by dreams of the future, whether by the latest labour-saving device or a broader prospect. 'His vision saw beyond the dank swamp at the edge of the great lake to the lofty buildings and jostling multitudes of a mighty city; . . . behind the harsh life of the loghut and the sod house to the home of his children, where should dwell comfort and the higher things of life . . .' Never was such fertile soil for the salesman.

Nor is advertising, let alone business, to be despised; it is a bacterium with powerful beneficial uses as well as unpleasant mutations. 'Promotion', as well as American energy, skill and resources, has helped to produce the economic miracle of modern

America. For this, indeed, all things seem to have worked together, and in the deeply perceptive view of W. E. Rappard perhaps the most important element in the process has been American democracy. What is unique economically about America is what he diagnoses as the 'social depth' of a very homogeneous consumer demand; it is not rationalised mass production in large units which has been distinctive in the United States and which has made it 'the paradise of the standardised product', but the high degree of predictability and uniformity, as well as the vast size, of popular demand. The *Admass* which Priestley has criticised has in fact had enormous economic advantages. And it has resulted among other things from the American axiom that all men should participate in American life; from the American's need for solidarity, for identification with his fellow Americans, which expresses itself partly in ardently desiring the same things as the Joneses; and from the American belief in progress, and hence constant willingness to accept technical, as well as political and social, change. Though this characteristic has borne its lushest fruits in recent years, and has perhaps gained strength from the increasing homogeneity which has begun to result from the restriction of immigration forty years ago, it was clearly visible as early as the Jacksonian era. It was Tocqueville, once again, who wrote, 'America is a land of wonders, in which everything is in constant motion and every change seems an improvement. The idea of novelty is there indissolubly connected with the idea of amelioration. No natural boundary seems to be set to the efforts of man; and in his eyes what is not yet done is only what he has not yet attempted to do.'

He also observed that in America 'the power of the majority' is 'not only preponderant, but irresistible', and that Americans believe 'that there is more intelligence and more wisdom in a great number of men collected together than in a single individual'. When Jefferson Davis was attacking the whole basis of the American Union he declared that it was not 'a Government of one people . . . formed by a mass', but a compact between its sovereign member states. Whatever in fact the Founding Fathers intended, the United States has derived much of its strength from the fact that it is a government by the mass of the people. Nor has a persistent and vigorous strain of yeasty individualism been lacking to leaven the popular lump; although its effects have sometimes been limited, the better side of the Jeffersonian tradition – that concerned with the rights of the individual – has continued to exist within an increasingly Hamiltonian society. But the essential and most important fact about the United States is that it has, from a remarkably early period, wholeheartedly, and on the whole with extraordinarily few reservations, accepted the dictum to which in Britain Gladstone cautiously attained in 1864 after so much doubt and travail; 'I venture to say that every man who is not presumably incapacitated by some consideration of personal unfitness or of political danger, is morally entitled to come within the pale of the constitution.'

Partly this gave strength to America, as we have seen, on material grounds; economically, as well as politically, it meant numbers. It meant that many Americans had what Burke wanted for only an oligarchy of Englishmen, a stake in the country. As Lincoln put it, in his familiar fashion: 'Friend, the Lord prefers common-looking people. That is the reason he makes so many of them.' But even more it gave strength because of its moral force, which thus has the widest possible base. Tocqueville rightly said that the Americans 'acknowledge the absolute moral authority of the reason of the community, as they acknowledge the political authority of the mass of citizens; and they hold that public opinion is the surest arbiter of what is lawful or forbidden, true or false. The majority of them believe that a man will be led to do what is just and good by following his own interest rightly understood.' It is this which fitted her so well for dominance, in what a not uncharacteristic American, Henry Wallace, rather characteristically called 'the century . . . which can be and must be the century of the common man'. Where the old world has had aristocracies, the rule of the best, America has had, in so far as she ever admits special groups to leadership, to invent the term 'elites', 'chosen' not so much *for* ability as *by* the people.

And what superior method can there be for mankind in the future? As Lincoln once more put it, 'Why should there not be a patient confidence in the ultimate justice of the people? Is there any better or equal hope in the world?' This belief in the dignity and the rights of all men is the very marrow of America's bones, and it is the reason why the Negro question, which is basically concerned with the civil rights of all Americans of whatever colour or creed, is more than a current American dilemma: it is a crisis of the American conscience, and an equitable as well as a successful domestic solution of it is fundamental to the triumph of the American way.

Here, in this perplexing and painful problem, indeed, all that is new and best in America confronts the legacy of one of the oldest and most iniquitous institutions of man – human chattel slavery. Nearly all other Americans save the Negroes came to America more or less of their own free will; they were in an almost literal fashion made free and equal by the bold act of crossing the oceans, and even more by 'making good' in the new society. (How extraordinarily revealing this American usage, 'make good', is! To succeed in the economic and social sense carries also the moral imprimatur of the word 'good' and the implications of individual effort inherent in the word 'make'). Yet, because it was exclusively associated with a single race, American slavery was not only a peculiarly abhorrent form of servitude but a constant and glaring affront to the fundamental article of the American creed. As Lincoln put it during his election struggle in 1858 with the Democratic Senator Stephen A. Douglas in Illinois; 'I adhere to the Declaration of Independence. If Judge Douglas and his friends are not willing to stand by it, let them come up and amend it. Let them make it read that all men are created equal, except negroes.' From this issue resulted the agonising convulsion of the Civil War, the greatest ordeal of the United States.

But it was not a war for the Negro only. Once again Lincoln expressed the essence of the matter when discussing the Know-Nothing, or Nativist, party, which embodied the recurrent anti-immigrant passions of native Americans and which was at its zenith in 1855: 'I am not a Know-Nothing; that is certain. How could I be? How can any one who abhors the oppression of Negroes be in favor of degrading classes of white people? Our progress in degeneracy appears to me to be pretty rapid. As a nation we began by declaring that 'all men are created equal'. We now practically read it "all men are created equal, except Negroes". When the Know-Nothings get control, it will read "all men are created equal, except Negroes and foreigners and Catholics". When it comes to this, I shall prefer emigrating to some country where they make no pretence of loving liberty – to Russia, for instance, where despotism can be taken pure, and without the base alloy of hypocrisy.' America – truly, in P. J. Bailey's words, 'half-brother of the world' – has always, even at the height of her isolation, partaken of what Lincoln called 'the spirit which prized liberty as the heritage of all men, in all lands everywhere'. And no particular dogma, no special panacea, has ever been as important to the bulk of Americans as the right of all citizens to pursue their own lives, their own individual ends, with as great a measure of freedom as possible.

In just such a faith must lie the best hope for twentieth-century man. The whole world itself is now becoming 'the great Melting-Pot', the 'Crucible . . . where all the races . . . are melting and re-forming'. With the mixing of peoples comes the clash of differing creeds with their widely varying roots. And with the increasing scope, scale and solidity of 'man-made', 'practical', knowledge in science and in history, there contrasts the growing confusion resulting from the conflict of diverse supernatural beliefs one with another and from the difficulty of reconciling theological dogma with reality. And when, with the establishment of such ideas as relativity and the growing awareness of the philosophic difficulties of determinism in science itself, there comes even further cause for doubt, scepticism, which is already deep over religion, spreads even further. In this state of flux and of uncertainty, what is left but Man? What aim can humanity sanely set before itself save to follow the genius of the species in freedom?

America, by freeing men to some extent from a number of the confining and cramping restrictions of their past – the burden of poverty, the limitations imposed by popular ignorance, the bigotry of priests, the tyranny of kings, the arrogance of the great – set her face firmly on the right path. If the alternative to following that path is the doctrine which forces unhappy human nature on to the Procrustean bed of Communist theory, can mankind hesitate for a moment? For the American system, despite all its grave faults and defects, and despite all its intractable problems (both unique and common to modern industrial society everywhere), has gone far to liberate human nature, and carries within itself the sovereign remedy of self-reform, as well as the hope of strength to effect it. The outlook in Europe and the world is still in some ways sombre, but the extent to which, and the ways in which, it is not, are in considerable degree a result of the more sanguine influence of America upon mankind, especially in this century.

It remains perhaps as true today as it was three-quarters of a century ago, when Bryce penned the words (which conclude his great work on *The American Commonwealth*), that

'This less sombre type of thought is more common in the United States than in Europe, for the people not only feel in their veins the pulse of youthful strength, but remember the magnitude of the evils they have vanquished, and see that they have already achieved many things which the Old World has longed for in vain. And by so much as the people of the United States are more hopeful, by that much are they more healthy. They do not, like their forefathers, expect to attain their ideals either easily or soon; but they say that they will continue to strive towards them, and they say it with a note of confidence in the voice which rings in the ear of the European visitor, and fills him with something of their own sanguine spirit . . . And that America marks the highest level, not only of material well-being, but of intelligence and happiness, which the race has yet attained, will be the judgment of those who look not at the favoured few for whose benefit the world seems hitherto to have framed its institutions, but at the whole body of the people.'

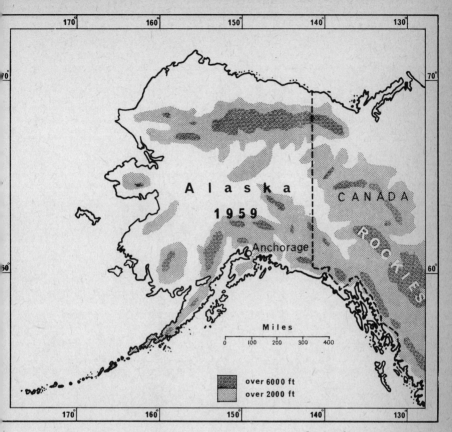

Same scale as main map

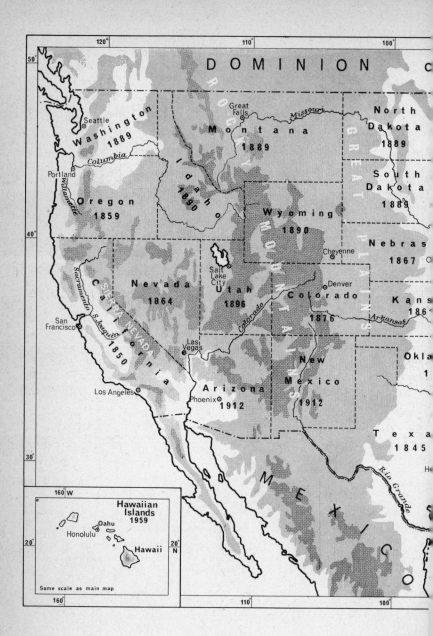

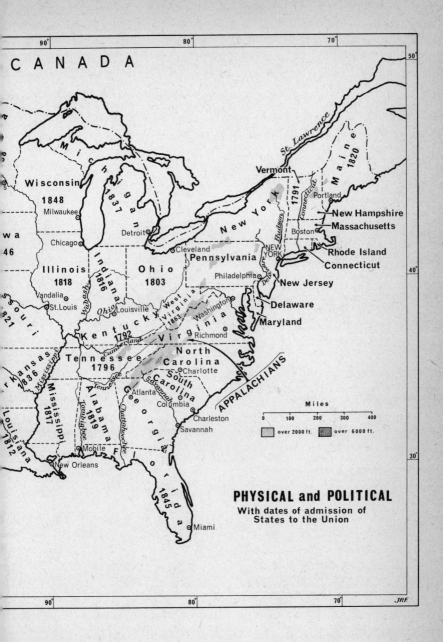

PHYSICAL and POLITICAL
With dates of admission of
States to the Union

The Declaration of Independence and The Constitution of the United States

---

THE DECLARATION OF INDEPENDENCE

WHEN IN THE Course of human Events, it becomes necessary for one People to dissolve the Political Bands which have connected them with another, and to assume among the Powers of the Earth, the separate and equal Station to which the Laws of Nature and of Nature's God entitle them, a decent Respect to the Opinions of Mankind requires that they should declare the causes which impel them to the Separation.

We hold these Truths to be self-evident, that all Men are created equal, that they are endowed by their Creator with certain un-alienable Rights, that among these are Life, Liberty, and the Pursuit of Happiness – That to secure these Rights, Governments are instituted among Men, deriving their just Powers from the Consent of the Governed, that whenever any Form of Government becomes destructive of these Ends, it is the Right of the People to alter or to abolish it, and to institute new Government, laying its Foundation on such Principles, and organizing its Powers in such Form, as to them shall seem most likely to effect their Safety and Happiness. Prudence, indeed, will dictate that Governments long established should not be changed for light and transient Causes; and accordingly all Experience hath shewn that Mankind are more disposed to suffer, while Evils are sufferable, than to right themselves by abolishing the Forms to which they are accustomed. But when a long Train of Abuses and Usurpations, pursuing in-variably the same Object, evinces a Design to reduce them under absolute Despotism, it is their Right, it is their Duty, to throw off such Government, and to provide new Guards for their future Security. Such has been the patient Sufferance of these Colonies; and such is now the Necessity which constrains them to alter their former Systems of Government. The History of the present King of Great Britain is a History of repeated Injuries and Usurpations, all having in direct Object the Establishment of an absolute Tyranny over these States. To prove this, let Facts be submitted to a candid World.

He has refused his Assent to Laws, the most wholesome and necessary for the public Good.

He has forbidden his Governors to pass Laws of immediate and pressing Importance, unless suspended in their Operations till his Assent should be obtained; and when so suspended, he has utterly neglected to attend to them.

He has refused to pass other Laws for the Accommodation of large Districts of People, unless those People would relinquish the Right of Representation in the Legislature, a Right inestimable to them, and formidable to Tyrants only.

He has called together Legislative Bodies at Places unusual, uncomfortable, and distant from the Depository of their public Records, for the sole Purpose of fatiguing them into Compliance with his Measures.

He has dissolved Representative Houses repeatedly, for opposing with manly Firmness his Invasions on the Rights of the People.

He has refused for a long Time, after such Dissolutions, to cause others to be elected; whereby the Legislative Powers, incapable of Annihilation, have returned to the People at large for their exercise; the State remaining in the mean time exposed to all the Dangers of Invasions from without, and convulsions within.

He has endeavoured to prevent the Population of these States; for that Purpose obstructing the Laws for Naturalization of Foreigners; refusing to pass others to encourage their Migrations hither, and raising the Conditions of new Appropriations of Lands.

He has obstructed the Administration of Justice, by refusing his Assent to Laws for establishing Judiciary Powers.

He has made Judges dependent on his Will alone, for the Tenure of their Offices, and the Amount and Payment of their Salaries.

He has erected a Multitude of new Offices, and sent hither Swarms of Officers to harrass our People, and eat out their Substance.

He has kept among us, in Times of Peace, Standing Armies, without the consent of our Legislatures:

He has affected to render the Military independent of and superior to the Civil Power.

He has combined with others to subject us to a Jurisdiction foreign to our Constitution, and unacknowledged by our Laws; giving his Assent to their Acts of pretended Legislation:

For quartering large Bodies of Armed troops among us:

For protecting them, by a mock Trial, from Punishment for any

Murders which they should commit on the Inhabitants of these States:

For cutting off our Trade with all Parts of the World:

For imposing Taxes on us without our Consent:

For depriving us, in many Cases, of the Benefits of Trial by Jury:

For transporting us beyond Seas to be tried for pretended Offences:

For abolishing the free System of English Laws in a neighbouring Province, establishing therein an arbitrary Government, and enlarging its Boundaries, so as to render it at once an Example and fit Instrument for introducing the same absolute Rule into these Colonies:

For taking away our Charters, abolishing our most valuable Laws, and altering fundamentally the Forms of our Governments:

For suspending our own Legislatures, and declaring themselves invested with Power to legislate for us in all Cases whatsoever.

He has abdicated Government here, by declaring us out of his Protection and waging War against us.

He has plundered our Seas, ravaged our Coasts, burnt our Towns, and destroyed the Lives of our People.

He is, at this Time, transporting large Armies of foreign Mercenaries to compleat the Works of Death, Desolation, and Tyranny, already begun with circumstances of Cruelty and Perfidy scarcely paralleled in the most barbarous Ages, and totally unworthy the Head of a civilized Nation.

He has constrained our fellow Citizens taken Captive on the high Seas to bear Arms against their Country, to become the Executioners of their Friends and Brethren, or to fall themselves by their Hands.

He has excited domestic Insurrections amongst us, and has endeavoured to bring on the Inhabitants of our Frontiers, the merciless Indian Savages, whose known Rule of Warfare, is an undistinguished Destruction, of all Ages, Sexes and Conditions.

In every stage of these Oppressions we have Petitioned for Redress in the most humble Terms: Our repeated Petitions have been answered only by repeated Injury. A Prince, whose Character is thus marked by every act which may define a Tyrant, is unfit to be the Ruler of a free People.

Nor have we been wanting in Attentions to our British Brethren. We have warned them from Time to Time of Attempts by their Legislature to extend an unwarrantable Jurisdiction over us. We have reminded them of the Circumstances of our Emigration and Settlement here. We have appealed to their native Justice and Magnanimity, and we have conjured them by the Ties of our common Kindred to disavow these Usurpations, which, would inevitably interrupt our Connections and Correspondence. They too must have been deaf to the Voice of Justice and of Consanguinity. We must, therefore, acquiesce in the Necessity, which denounces our Separation, and hold them, as we hold the rest of Mankind, Enemies in War, in Peace, Friends.

We, therefore, the Representatives of the UNITED STATES OF AMERICA, in General Congress, Assembled, appealing to the Supreme Judge of the World for the Rectitude of our Intentions, do, in the Name, and by Authority of the good People of these Colonies, solemnly Publish and Declare, That these United Colonies are, and of Right ought to be, FREE AND INDEPENDENT STATES; that they are absolved from all Allegiance to the British Crown, and that all political Connection between them and the State of Great Britain, is and ought to be totally dissolved; and that as FREE AND INDEPENDENT STATES, they have full Power to levy War, conclude Peace, contract Alliances, establish Commerce and to do all other Acts and Things which INDEPENDENT STATES may of right do. And for the support of this Declaration, with a firm Reliance on the Protection of Divine Providence, we mutually pledge to each other our Lives, our Fortunes, and our sacred Honor.

CONSTITUTION OF THE
UNITED STATES OF AMERICA

PREAMBLE

WE THE PEOPLE of the United States, in order to form a more perfect Union, establish justice, insure domestic tranquillity, provide for the common defense, promote the general welfare, and secure the blessings of liberty to ourselves and our posterity, do ordain and establish this Constitution for the United States of America.

ARTICLE I

SECTION 1. All legislative powers herein granted shall be vested in a Congress of the United States, which shall consist of a Senate and House of Representatives.

SECTION 2. The House of Representatives shall be composed of members chosen every second year by the people of the several States, and the electors in each State shall have the qualifications requisite for electors of the most numerous branch of the State Legislature.

No person shall be a representative who shall not have attained to the age of twenty-five years, and been seven years a citizen of the United States, and who shall not, when elected, be an inhabitant of that State in which he shall be chosen.

Representatives and direct taxes shall be apportioned among the several States which may be included within this Union, according to their respective numbers which shall be determined by adding to the whole number of free persons, including those bound to service for a term of years, and excluding Indians not taxed, three-fifths of all other persons. The actual enumeration shall be made within three years after the first meeting of the Congress of the United States, and within every subsequent term of ten years, in such manner as they shall by law direct. The number of representatives shall not exceed one for every thirty thousand, but each State shall have at least one representative; and until such enumeration shall be made, the State of New Hampshire shall be entitled to choose three, Massachusetts eight, Rhode Island and Providence Plantations one, Connecticut five, New York six, New Jersey four, Pennsylvania eight, Delaware one, Maryland six, Virginia ten, North Carolina five, South Carolina five, and Georgia three.

When vacancies happen in the representation from any State, the executive authority thereof shall issue writs of election to fill such vacancies.

The House of Representatives shall choose their Speaker and other officers; and shall have the sole power of impeachment.

SECTION 3. The Senate of the United States shall be composed of two senators from each State, chosen by the legislature thereof, for six years and each senator shall have one vote.

Immediately after they shall be assembled in consequence of the first election, they shall be divided as equally as may be into three classes. The seats of the senators of the first class shall be vacated at the expiration of the second year, of the second class at the expiration of the fourth year, and of the third class at the expiration of the sixth year, so that one-third may be chosen every second year; and if vacancies happen by resignation, or otherwise, during the recess of the legislature of any State, the executive thereof may make temporary appointments until the next meeting of the legislature, which shall then fill such vacancies.

No person shall be a senator who shall not have attained to the age of thirty-years, and been nine years a citizen of the United States, and who shall not, when elected, be an inhabitant of that State for which he shall be chosen.

The Vice President of the United States shall be President of the Senate, but shall have no vote, unless they be equally divided.

The Senate shall choose their other officers, and also a President pro tempore, in the absence of the Vice President, or when he shall exercise the office of President of the United States.

The Senate shall have the sole power to try all impeachments. When sitting for that purpose, they shall be on oath or affirmation. When the President of the United States is tried, the Chief Justice shall preside: And no person shall be convicted without the concurrence of two-thirds of the members present.

Judgment in cases of impeachment shall not extend further than to removal from office, and disqualification to hold and enjoy any office of honor, trust or profit under the United States; but the party convicted shall nevertheless be liable and subject to indictment, trial, judgment and punishment, according to law.

Section 4. The times, places and manner of holding elections for senators and representatives, shall be prescribed in each State by the legislature thereof; but the Congress may at any time by law make or alter such regulations, except as to the places of choosing senators.

The Congress shall assemble at least once in every year, and such meeting shall be on the first Monday in December, unless they shall by law appoint a different day.

Section 5. Each House shall be the judge of the elections, returns and qualifications of its own members, and a majority of each shall constitute a quorum to do business; but a smaller number may adjourn from day to day, and may be authorised to compel the attendance of absent members, in such manner, and under such penalties as each House may provide.

Each House may determine the rules of its proceedings, punish its members for disorderly behaviour, and, with the concurrence of two-thirds, expel a member.

Each House shall keep a journal of its proceedings, and from time to time publish the same, excepting such parts as may in their judgment require secrecy; and the yeas and nays of the members of either House on any question shall, at the desire of one-fifth of those present, be entered on the journal.

Neither House, during the session of Congress, shall, without the consent of the other, adjourn for more than three days, nor to any other place than that in which the two Houses shall be sitting.

Section 6. The senators and representatives shall receive a compensation for their services, to be ascertained by law, and paid out of the Treasury of the United States. They shall in all cases, except treason, felony and breach of the peace, be privileged from arrest during their attendance at the session of their respective Houses, and in going to and returning from the same; and for any speech or debate in either House, they shall not be questioned in any other place.

No senator or representative shall, during the time for which he was elected, be appointed to any civil office under the authority of the United States, which shall have been created, or the emoluments whereof shall have been increased during such time; and no person holding any office under the United States shall be a member of either House during his continuance in office.

SECTION 7. All bills for raising revenue shall originate in the House of Representatives; but the Senate may propose or concur with amendments as on other bills.

Every bill which shall have passed the House of Representatives and the Senate, shall, before it becomes a law, be presented to the President of the United States; if he approve he shall sign it; but if not he shall return it, with his objections to that House in which it shall have originated, who shall enter the objections at large on their journal, and proceed to reconsider it. If after such reconsideration two-thirds of that House shall agree to pass the bill, it shall be sent, together with the objections, to the other House, by which it shall likewise be reconsidered, and if approved by two-thirds of that House, it shall become a law. But in all such cases the votes of both Houses shall be determined by yeas and nays, and the names of the persons voting for and against the bill shall be entered on the journal of each House respectively. If any bill shall not be returned by the President within ten days (Sundays excepted) after it shall have been presented to him, the same shall be a law, in like manner as if he had signed it, unless the Congress by their adjournment prevent its return, in which case it shall not be a law.

Every order, resolution, or vote to which the concurrence of the Senate and House of Representatives may be necessary (except on a question of adjournment) shall be presented to the President of the United States; and before the same shall take effect, shall be approved by him, or being disapproved by him, shall be repassed by two-thirds of the Senate and House of Representatives, according to the rules and limitations prescribed in the case of a bill.

SECTION 8. The Congress shall have the power to lay and collect taxes, duties, imposts and excises, to pay the debts and provide for the common defense and general welfare of the United States; but all duties, imposts and excises shall be uniform throughout the United States;

To borrow money on the credit of the United States;

To regulate commerce with foreign nations, and among the several States, and with the Indian tribes;

To establish an uniform rule of naturalization, and uniform laws on the subject of bankruptcies throughout the United States.

To coin money, regulate the value thereof, and of foreign coin, and fix the standard of weights and measures;

To provide for the punishment of counterfeiting the securities and current coin of the United States;

To establish post offices and post roads;

To promote the progress of science and useful arts, by securing for limited times to authors and inventors the exclusive right to their respective writings and discoveries;

To constitute tribunals inferior to the Supreme Court;

To define and punish piracies and felonies committed on the high seas, and offenses against the law of nations;

To declare war, grant letters of marque and reprisal, and make rules concerning captures on land and water;

To raise and support armies, but no appropriation of money to that use shall be for a longer term than two years;

To provide and maintain a Navy;

To make rules for the government and regulation of the land and naval forces;

To provide for calling forth the militia to execute the laws of the Union, suppress insurrections and repel invasions;

To provide for organizing, arming, and disciplining, the militia, and for governing such part of them as may be employed in the service of the United States, reserving to the States respectively, the appointment of the officers, and the authority of training the militia according to the discipline prescribed by Congress;

To exercise exclusive legislation in all cases whatsoever, over such district (not exceeding ten miles square) as may, by cession of particular States, and the acceptance of Congress, become the seat of the Government of the United States, and to exercise like authority over all places purchased by the consent of the legislature of the State in which the same shall be, for the erection of forts, magazines, arsenals, dock-yards, and other needful buildings; – And

To make all laws which shall be necessary and proper for carrying into execution the foregoing powers, and all other powers vested by the Constitution in the Government of the United States, or in any department or officer thereof.

Section 9. The migration or importation of such persons as any of the States now existing shall think proper to admit, shall not be prohibited by the Congress prior to the year one thousand eight hundred and eight, but a tax or duty may be imposed on such importation, not exceeding ten dollars for each person.

The privilege of the writ of habeas corpus shall not be suspended, unless when in cases of rebellion or invasion the public safety may require it.

No bill of attainder or ex post facto law shall be passed.

No capitation, or other direct, tax shall be laid, unless in proportion to the census or enumeration herein before directed to be taken.

No tax or duty shall be laid on articles exported from any State.

No preference shall be given by any regulation of commerce or revenue to the ports of one State over those of another; nor shall vessels bound to, or from, one State, be obliged to enter, clear, or pay duties in another.

No money shall be drawn from the Treasury, but in consequence of appropriations made by law; and a regular statement and account of the receipts and expenditures of all public money shall be published from time to time.

No title of nobility shall be granted by the United States: And no person holding any office of profit or trust under them, shall, without the consent of the Congress, accept of any present, emolument, office, or title, of any kind whatever, from any King, Prince, or foreign State.

SECTION 10. No State shall enter into any treaty, alliance, or confederation; grant letters of marque and reprisal; coin money; emit bills of credit; make any thing but gold and silver coin a tender in payment of debts; pass any bill of attainder, ex post acto law, or law impairing the obligation of contracts, or grant any title of nobility.

No State shall, without the consent of the Congress, lay any imposts or duties on imports or exports, except what may be absolutely necessary for executing its inspection laws: and the net produce of all duties and imposts, laid by any State on imports or exports, shall be for the use of the Treasury of the United States; and all such laws shall be subject to the revision and control of the Congress.

No State shall, without the consent of Congress, lay any duty of tonnage, keep troops, or ships of war in time of peace, enter into any agreement or compact with another State, or with a foreign power, or engage in war, unless actually invaded or in such imminent danger as will not admit of delay.

ARTICLE II

SECTION 1. The executive power shall be vested in a President of the United States of America. He shall hold his office during the term of four years, and, together with the Vice President, chosen for the same term, be elected, as follows:

Each State shall appoint, in such manner as the legislature thereof may direct, a number of electors, equal to the whole number of senators and representatives to which the State may be entitled in the Congress; but no senator or representative, or person holding an office of trust or profit under the United States, shall be appointed an elector.

The electors shall meet in their respective States, and vote by ballot for two persons, of whom one at least shall not be an inhabitant of the same State with themselves. And they shall make a list of all the persons voted for, and of the number of votes for each; which list they shall sign and certify; and transmit sealed to the seat of the Government of the United States, directed to the President of the Senate. The President of the Senate shall, in the presence of the Senate and House of Representatives, open all the certificates, and the votes shall then be counted. The person having the greatest number of votes shall be the President, if such number be a majority of the whole number of electors appointed; and if there be more than one who have such majority, and have an equal number of votes, then the House of Representatives shall immediately choose by ballot one of them for President; and if no person have a majority, then from the five highest on the list the said House shall in like manner choose the President. But in choosing the President, the votes shall be taken by States, the representation from each State having one vote; a quorum for this purpose shall consist of a member or members from two thirds of the States, and a majority of all the States shall be necessary to a choice. In every case, after the choice of the President, the person having the greatest number of votes of the electors shall be the Vice President. But if there should remain two or more who have equal votes, the Senate shall choose from them by ballot the Vice President.

The Congress may determine the time of choosing the electors, and the day on which they shall give their votes; which day shall be the same throughout the United States.

No person except a natural born citizen, or a citizen of the United States, at the time of the adoption of this Constitution, shall be eligible to the office of President; neither shall any person be eligible to that office who shall not have attained to the age of thirty-five years, and been fourteen years a resident within the United States.

In case of the removal of the President from office, or of his death, resignation, or inability to discharge the powers and duties of the said office, the same shall devolve on the Vice President, and the Congress may by law provide for the case of removal, death, resignation, or inability, both of the President and Vice President, declaring what officer shall then act as President, and such officer shall act accordingly, until the disability be removed, or a President shall be elected.

The President shall, at stated times, receive for his services, a compensation, which shall neither be increased nor diminished during the period for which he shall have been elected, and he shall not receive within that period any other emolument from the United States, or any of them.

Before he enter on the execution of his office, he shall take the following oath or affirmation: – 'I do solemnly swear (or affirm) that I will faithfully execute the office of President of the United States, and will to the best of my ability, preserve, protect and defend the Constitution of the United States.'

SECTION 2. The President shall be Commander in Chief of the Army and Navy of the United States, and of the militia of the several States, when called into the actual service of the United States; he may require the opinion, in writing of the principal officer in each of the Executive Departments, upon any subject relating to the duties of their respective offices, and he shall have power to grant reprieves and pardons for offenses against the United States, except in cases of impeachment.

He shall have power, by and with the advice and consent of the Senate, to make treaties, provided two thirds of the Senators present concur; and he shall nominate, and by and with the advice and consent of the Senate, shall appoint ambassadors, other public ministers and consuls, judges of the Supreme Court, and all other officers of the United States, whose appointments are not herein otherwise provided for, and which shall be established by law: but the Congress may by law vest the appointment of such inferior officers, as they think proper, in the President alone, in the courts of law, or in the heads of departments.

The President shall have power to fill up all vacancies that may happen during the recess of the Senate, by granting commissions which shall expire at the end of their next session.

SECTION 3. He shall from time to time give to the Congress information of the state of the Union, and recommend to their consideration such measures as he shall judge necessary and expedient; he may, on extraordinary occasions, convene both Houses, or either of them, and in case of disagreement between them, with respect to the time of adjournment, he may adjourn them to such time as he shall think proper; he shall receive ambassadors and other public ministers; he shall take care that the laws be faithfully executed, and shall commission all the officers of the United States.

SECTION 4. The President, Vice President and all civil officers of the United States, shall be removed from office on impeachment for, and conviction of, treason, bribery, or other high crimes and misdemeanors.

ARTICLE III

SECTION 1. The judicial power of the United States shall be vested in one Supreme Court, and in such inferior courts as the Congress may from time to time ordain and establish. The judges, both of the supreme and inferior courts, shall hold their offices during good behaviour, and shall, at stated times, receive for their services, a compensation, which shall not be diminished during their continuance in office.

SECTION 2. The judicial power shall extend to all cases, in law and equity, arising under this Constitution, the laws of the United States, and treaties made, or which shall be made, under their authority; to all cases affecting ambassadors, other public ministers and consuls; to all cases of admiralty and maritime jurisdiction; to controversies to which the United States shall be a party; to controversies between two or more States; between a State and citizens of another State; between citizens of different States; between citizens of the same State claiming lands under grants of different States, and between a State, or the citizens thereof, and foreign States, citizens, or subjects.

In all cases affecting ambassadors, other public ministers and consuls, and those in which a State shall be party, the Supreme Court shall have original jurisdiction. In all the other cases before mentioned, the Supreme Court shall have appellate jurisdiction, both as to law and to fact, which such exceptions, and under such regulations as the Congress shall make.

The trial of all crimes, except in cases of impeachment, shall be by jury; and such trial shall be held in the State where the said crimes shall have been committed; but when not committed within any State, the trial shall be at such place or places as the Congress may by law have directed.

SECTION 3. Treason against the United States, shall consist only in levying war against them, or in adhering to their enemies, giving them aid and comfort. No person shall be convicted of treason unless on the testimony of two witnesses to the same overt act, or on confession in open court.

The Congress shall have power to declare the punishment of treason, but no attainder of treason shall work corruption of blood, or forfeiture except during the life of the person attainted.

ARTICLE IV

SECTION 1. Full faith and credit shall be given in each State to the public acts, records, and judicial proceedings of every other State. And the Congress may by general laws prescribe the manner in which such acts, records and proceedings shall be proved, and the effect thereof.

SECTION 2. The citizens of each State shall be entitled to all privileges and immunities of citizens in the several States.

A person charged in any State with treason, felony, or other crimes, who shall flee from justice, and be found in another State, shall on demand of the executive authority of the State from which he fled, be delivered up, to be removed to the State having jurisdiction of the crime.

No person held to service or labor in one State, under the laws thereof, escaping into another, shall, in consequence of any law or regulation therein, be discharged from such service or labor but shall be delivered up on claim of the party to whom such service or labor may be due.

SECTION 3. New States may be admitted by the Congress into this Union; but no new State shall be formed or erected within the jurisdiction of any other State; nor any State be formed by the junction of two or more States, or parts of States, without the consent of the legislature of the States concerned as well as of the Congress.

The Congress shall have the power to dispose of and make all needful rules and regulations respecting the Territory or other property belonging to the United States; and nothing in this Constitution shall be so construed as to prejudice any claims of the United States, or of any particular State.

SECTION 4. The United States shall guarantee to every State in this Union a republican form of Government, and shall protect each of them against invasion; and on application of the legislature, or of the executive (when the legislature cannot be convened) against domestic violence.

ARTICLE V

The Congress, whenever two thirds of both Houses shall deem it necessary, shall propose amendments to this Constitution, or, on the application of the legislatures of two thirds of the several States, shall call a convention for proposing amendments, which, in either case, shall be valid to all intents and purposes, as part of this Constitution, when ratified by the legislatures of three fourths of the several States, or by conventions in three fourths thereof, as the one or the other mode of ratification may be proposed by the Congress; provided that no amendment which may be made prior to the year one thousand eight hundred and eight shall in any manner affect the first and fourth clauses in the Ninth Section of the First Article; and that no State, without its consent, shall be deprived of its equal suffrage in the Senate.

ARTICLE VI

All debts contracted and engagements entered into, before the adoption of this Constitution, shall be as valid against the United States under this Constitution, as under the Confederation.

This Constitution, and the laws of the United States which shall be made in pursuance thereof; and all treaties made, or which shall be made, under the authority of the United States, shall be the supreme law of the land; and the judges in every State shall be bound thereby, anything in the Constitution or laws of any State to the contrary notwithstanding.

The senators and representatives before mentioned, and the members of the several State legislatures, and all executive and judicial officers, both of the United States and of the several States, shall be bound by oath or affirmation, to support this Constitution; but no religious test shall ever be required as a qualification to any office or public trust under the United States.

ARTICLE VII

The ratification of the conventions of nine States shall be sufficient for the establishment of this Constitution between the States so ratifying the same.

Done in convention by the unanimous consent of the States present the seventeenth day of September in the year of Our Lord one thousand seven hundred and eighty-seven and of the Independence of the United States of America the twelfth. In witness whereof we have hereunto subscribed our names.

Amendments to the Constitution

ARTICLE I

Congress shall make no law respecting an establishment of

religion, or prohibiting the free exercise thereof; or abridging the freedom of speech, or of the press; or the right of the people peaceably to assemble, and to petition the Government for a redress of grievances.

ARTICLE II

A well regulated militia, being necessary to the security of a free State, the right of the people to keep and bear arms, shall not be infringed.

ARTICLE III

No soldier shall, in time of peace be quartered in any house, without the consent of the owner, nor in time of war, but in a manner to be prescribed by law.

ARTICLE IV

The right of the people to be secure in their persons, houses, papers, and effects, against unreasonable searches and seizures, shall not be violated, and no warrants shall issue, but upon probable cause, supported by oath or affirmation, and particularly describing the place to be searched, and the persons or things to be seized.

ARTICLE V

No person shall be held to answer for a capital, or otherwise infamous crime, unless on a presentment or indictment of a grand jury, except in cases arising in the land or naval forces, or in the militia, when in actual service in time of war or public danger; nor shall any person be subject for the same offense to be twice put in jeopardy of life or limb; nor shall be compelled in any criminal case to be a witness against himself, nor be deprived of life, liberty, or property, without due process of law; nor shall private property be taken for public use, without just compensation.

ARTICLE VI

In all criminal prosecutions, the accused shall enjoy the right to a speedy and public trial, by an impartial jury of the State and district wherein the crime shall have been committed, which district shall have been previously ascertained by law, and to be informed of the nature and cause of the accusation; to be confronted with the witnesses against him; to have compulsory process for obtaining witnesses in his favor, and to have the assistance of counsel for his defense.

ARTICLE VII

In suits at common law, where the value in controversy shall exceed twenty dollars, the right of trial by jury shall be preserved, and no fact tried by a jury, shall be otherwise re-examined in any court of the United States, than according to the rules of the common law.

ARTICLE VIII

Excessive bail shall not be required, nor excessive fines imposed, nor cruel and unusual punishments inflicted.

ARTICLE IX

The enumeration in the Constitution, of certain rights, shall not be construed to deny or disparage others retained by the people.

ARTICLE X

(Articles I to X were adopted in 1791)

The powers not delegated to the United States by the Constitution, nor prohibited by it to the States, are reserved to the States respectively, or to the people.

ARTICLE XI (1798)

The judicial power of the United States shall not be construed to extend to any suit in law or equity, commenced or prosecuted against one of the United States, by citizens of another State or by citizens or subjects of any foreign State.

ARTICLE XII (1804)

The electors shall meet in their respective States, and vote by ballot for President and Vice President, one of whom, at least, shall not be an inhabitant of the same State with themselves; they shall name in their ballots the person voted for as President, and in distinct ballots the person voted for as Vice President, and they shall make distinct lists of all persons voted for as President, and of all persons voted for as Vice President, and of the number of votes for each, which lists they shall sign and certify; and transmit sealed to the seat of the Government of the United States, directed to the President of the Senate. The President of the Senate shall, in the presence of the Senate and House of Representatives, open all the certificates and the votes shall then be counted. The person having the greatest number of votes for President, shall be the President, if such number be a majority of the whole number of electors appointed, and if no person have such majority, then from the persons having the highest numbers not exceeding three on the list of those voted for as President, the House of Representatives shall choose immediately, by ballot, the President. But in choosing, the President, the votes shall be taken by States, the representation from each State having one vote; a quorum for this purpose shall consist of a member or members from two-thirds of the States, and a majority of all the States shall be necessary to a choice. And if the House of Representatives shall not choose a President whenever the right of choice shall devolve upon them, before the fourth day of March next following, then the Vice President shall act as President, as in the case of the death or other constitutional disability of the President. The person having the greatest number of votes as Vice President, shall be the Vice President, if such a number be a majority of the whole number of electors appointed, and if no person have a majority, then from the two highest numbers on the list, the Senate shall choose the Vice President; a quorum for the purpose shall consist of two-thirds of the whole number of Senators, and a majority of the whole number shall be necessary to a choice. But no person constitutionally ineligible to the office of President shall be eligible to that of Vice President of the United States.

ARTICLE XIII (1865)

SECTION 1. Neither slavery nor involuntary servitude, except as a punishment for crime whereof the party shall have been duly convicted, shall exist within the United States, or any place subject to their jurisdiction.

SECTION 2. Congress shall have power to enforce this article by appropriate legislation.

ARTICLE XIV (1868)

SECTION 1. All persons born or naturalized in the United States, and subject to the jurisdiction thereof, are citizens of the United States and of the State wherein they reside. No State shall make or enforce any law which shall abridge the privileges or immunities of citizens of the United States; nor shall any State deprive any person of life, liberty, or property, without due process of law; nor deny to any person within its jurisdiction the equal protection of the laws.

SECTION 2. Representatives shall be apportioned among the several States according to their respective numbers, counting the whole number of persons in each State, excluding Indians not taxed. But when the right to vote at any election for the choice of electors for President and Vice President of the United States, Representatives in Congress, the executive and judicial officers of a State, or the members of the legislature thereof, is denied to any of the male inhabitants of such State, being twenty-one years of age, and citizens of the United States, or in any way abridged, except for participation in rebellion, or other crime, the basis of representation therein shall be reduced in the proportion which the number of such male citizens shall bear to the whole number of male citizens twenty-one years of age in such State.

SECTION 3. No person shall be a Senator or Representative in Congress, or elector of President and Vice President, or hold any office, civil or military, under the United States, or under any State, who, having previously taken an oath, as a member of Congress, or as an officer of the United States, or as a member of any State legislature, or as an executive or judicial officer of any State, to support the Constitution of the United States, shall have engaged in insurrection or rebellion against the same, or given aid or comfort to the enemies thereof. But Congress may by a vote of two-thirds of each House, remove such disability.

SECTION 4. The validity of the public debt of the United States, authorised by law, including debts incurred for payment of pensions and bounties for services in suppressing insurrection or rebellion, shall not be questioned. But neither the United States nor any State shall assume or pay any debt or obligation incurred in aid of insurrection or rebellion against the United States, or any claim for the loss or emancipation of any slave; but all such debts, obligations and claims shall be held illegal and void.

SECTION 5. The Congress shall have power to enforce, by appropriate legislation, the provisions of this article.

ARTICLE XV (1870)

SECTION 1. The right of citizens of the United States to vote shall not be denied or abridged by the United States or by any State on account of race, color, or previous condition of servitude.

SECTION 2. The Congress shall have power to enforce this article by appropriate legislation.

ARTICLE XVI (1913)

The Congress shall have power to lay and collect taxes on incomes, from whatever source derived, without apportionment among the several States, and without regard to any census or enumeration.

ARTICLE XVII (1913)

SECTION 1. The Senate of the United States shall be composed of two senators from each State, elected by the people thereof, for six years; and each senator shall have one vote. The electors in each State shall have the qualifications requisite for electors of the most numerous branch of the State legislatures.

SECTION 2. When vacancies happen in the representation of any

State in the Senate, the executive authority of such State shall issue writs of election to fill such vacancies: Provided, That the legislature of any State may empower the executive thereof to make temporary appointments until the people fill the vacancies by election as the legislature may direct.

SECTION 3. This amendment shall not be so construed as to affect the election or term of any senator chosen before it becomes valid as part of the Constitution.

ARTICLE XVIII (1919)

SECTION 1. After one year from the ratification of this article the manufacture, sale, or transportation of intoxicating liquors within, the importation thereof into, or the exportation thereof from the United States and all territory subject to the jurisdiction thereof for beverage purposes is hereby prohibited.

SECTION 2. The Congress and the several States shall have concurrent power to enforce this article by appropriate legislation.

SECTION 3. This article shall be inoperative unless it shall have been ratified as an amendment to the Constitution by the legislatures of the several States, as provided in the Constitution, within seven years from the date of the submission hereof to the States by the Congress.

ARTICLE XIX (1920)

SECTION 1. The right of citizens of the United States to vote shall not be denied or abridged by the United States or by any State on account of sex.

SECTION 2. Congress shall have power to enforce this article by appropriate legislation.

ARTICLE XX (1933)

SECTION 1. The terms of the President and Vice-President shall end at noon on the 20th day of January, and the terms of Senators and Representatives at noon on the 3rd day of January, of the years in which such terms would have ended if this article had not been ratified; and the terms of their successors shall then begin.

SECTION 2. The Congress shall assemble at least once in every year, and such meeting shall begin at noon on the 3rd day of January, unless they shall by law appoint a different day.

SECTION 3. If, at the time fixed for the beginning of the term of the President, the President elect shall have died, the Vice President elect shall become President. If a President shall not have been chosen before the time fixed for the beginning of his term, or if the President elect shall have failed to qualify, then the Vice President elect shall act as President until a President shall have qualified; and the Congress may by law provide for the case wherein neither a President elect nor a Vice President elect shall have qualified, declaring who shall then act as President, or the manner in which one who is to act shall be selected, and such person shall act accordingly until a President or Vice President shall have qualified.

SECTION 4. The Congress may by law provide for the case of the death of any of the persons from whom the House of Representatives may choose a President whenever the right of choice shall have devolved upon them, and for the case of the death of any of the persons from whom the Senate may choose a Vice President whenever the right of choice shall have devolved upon them.

SECTION 5. Sections 1 and 2 shall take effect on the 15th day of October following the ratification of this article.

SECTION 6. This article shall be inoperative unless it shall have been ratified as an amendment to the Constitution by the legislatures of three-fourths of the several States within seven years from the date of its submission.

ARTICLE XXI (1933)

SECTION 1. The eighteenth article of amendment to the Constitution of the United States is hereby repealed.

SECTION 2. The transportation or importation into any State, Territory, or possession of the United States for delivery or use therein of intoxicating liquors, in violation of the laws thereof, is hereby prohibited.

SECTION 3. This article shall be inoperative unless it shall have been ratified as an amendment to the Constitution by conventions in the several States, as provided in the Constitution, within seven years from the date of the submission hereof to the States by the Congress.

ARTICLE XXII (1951)

No person shall be elected to the Office of the President more than twice, and no person who has held the office of President, or acted as President, for more than two years of a term to which some other person was elected President shall be elected to the office of President more than once. But this Article shall not apply to any person holding the office of President, or acting as President, during the term within which this Article becomes operative from holding the office of President or acting as President during the remainder of such term.

ARTICLE XXIII (1961)

SECTION 1. The District constituting the seat of Government of the United States shall appoint in such manner as the Congress may direct:

A number of electors of President and Vice President equal to the whole number of Senators and Representatives in Congress to which the District would be entitled if it were a State, but in no event more than the least populous State; they shall be in addition to those appointed by the states, but they shall be considered, for the purposes of the election of President and Vice President, to be electors appointed by a State; and they shall meet in the District and perform such duties as provided by the twelfth Article of amendment.

SECTION 2. The Congress shall have power to enforce this Article by appropriate legislation.

ARTICLE XXIV (1964)

The right of citizens of the United States to vote in any primary or other election for President or Vice-President, for electors for President or Vice-President, or for Senator or Representative in Congress, shall not be denied or abridged by the United States or any state for reason of failure to pay any Poll Tax or other tax.

Appendix II

THE ELECTION OF THE PRESIDENT

T HE COMPLEX system by which the President is elected
constitutes the real, as well as symbolic, hard core of
American politics, and a more consecutive account of its
operation than has been possible in the main body of the text is
worth giving.

Presidential elections take place every four years – in fact in each
leap year.

The process falls into two distinct phases. The first is the selection
of the candidates who will run against each other in the final
election; this phase ends with the national party Conventions in
mid-summer, when the candidates are chosen by the parties'
delegates. The second phase is the actual election itself, which in
practice ends on Election Day – 'the Tuesday following the first
Monday in November' – but which formally culminates in the
Inauguration of the successful candidate as President 'at noon on
the 20th day of January' in the following year.

First Phase

In fact Presidential aspirants begin to jockey for political position
even before the year of the election itself, but the first formal stage
of the procedure is the selection by the parties of delegates to their
national conventions, which are held in June, July or August of
election year. These delegates are chosen in three different ways in
the various States. (Morphologically each is in a sense a legacy of
the three main steps in the constitutional development of the
United States – caucus, convention and primary.)

In the first case delegates are chosen by small meetings, or caucuses, of party leaders in the States (4 States in 1964); in the second
they are chosen by State conventions – miniature conventions held
in the States (29 States); in the third by State primary elections
(15 States and the District of Columbia). In Georgia the Republicans employ conventions and the Democrats the caucus; in Alabama,
also, the Republicans use the convention, but the Democrats hold
a primary.

Primary elections are limited to the members and followers of one party and were once purely party affairs, but they are now organised by State officials under State law, in order to ensure that they are fairly conducted; they are in effect party heats to determine who may run as electors on behalf of the party in the final election. The presidential primary thus selects party delegates to the Convention; it may in some cases also express a preference among the possible candidates for the presidential and vice-presidential nominations, in others it may leave the choice to the discretion of the delegates. In some States the voter may 'write in' the name of his favourite candidate on the ballot if it does not appear there officially. The presidential primary may help to show whether a candidate is a good 'vote-getter', but even great primary victories are not necessarily a sure guide to nomination by a Convention, because State delegations are not absolutely bound by primary results and because not all Presidential 'possibles' choose to become candidates in primaries. The primaries are held between March and June.

The two great party Conventions, whose delegates have been chosen in these three ways, meet during the summer, sometimes in the same city one shortly after the other. (Normally only those of the two major parties are of any great importance; in 1960, for instance, the Democratic and Republican candidates got over 99 per cent of the popular vote in the final election.) The Convention system has been used for well over a century and with its colourful rituals of applauding, cheering, marching and so on, it provides much of the drama and fun of American politics. The Conventions have now come to number 1,200 and more delegates from all the States and territories of the United States. Their main function is to choose the Presidential candidate by publicly 'balloting' the delegations, some of which cast their votes unanimously and some of which are divided. Leaders of delegations in succession announce their votes over the public address system of the vast convention hall. There has been an increasing tendency in recent years for delegations to be initially pledged to a candidate and for a decision to be made in the first few ballots. In the past it often took very many ballots to come to a decision, and Conventions sometimes lasted 2 or 3 weeks rather than the usual 3 or 4 days of the present time. With modern national mass media of publicity it is easier for clear 'possibles' to emerge beforehand and more important that the proceedings of the Convention, which are televised to millions of citizens' homes, should be somewhat less wild and considerably shorter than they sometimes used to be.

Candidates become 'possibles' by making a name for themselves in State or national affairs. Of the last six Presidents, two were Vice-Presidents when coming to office (Truman and Johnson), one was Secretary of Commerce (Hoover), one Governor of a powerful State (Roosevelt), one a great military figure (Eisenhower), and one a Senator (Kennedy). The Constitution lays down that the President must be a natural-born citizen of 35 or over who shall have been resident in the United States for fourteen years. A candidate should have strong support in his State and region as well as a national following. There is often an attempt to 'balance the ticket' of the party by having, for instance, a Southern Vice-Presidential candidate with a Presidential candidate from the North, or an easterner with a westerner. The Vice-Presidential candidate is chosen by the Convention after the Presidential candidate, and the latter's wishes as to who he wants as his running mate are very important.

The Convention, as well as choosing Presidential and Vice-Presidential candidates, also draws up and agrees the party's programme, or Platform, for the election. This is done after the Platform Committee has heard the views of various groups, such as farmers, Negroes, labour unions and ex-servicemen (known as Veterans). In 1960, for example, the Republican platform contained 'planks' on foreign policy, defence, government reorganisation, economic growth, farm policy and civil rights. Sometimes, because it is very broadly drawn in order to attract as many supporters as possible, the planks of the Platform may be hard to reconcile with one another.

When their task is done each of the Conventions, which are the great pre-election climax and bring the preliminaries of the contest to a close, is addressed by the successful candidate in an Acceptance speech. This final rallying of the faithful sets the tone for the Campaign, which now begins.

Second Phase

For the period of this election battle each party has a real leader. (The Presidential candidate is always the leader of his party. The opposition party really has no national leader between elections.) Other candidates (e.g. for Congress) may hope to get in on the President's 'coat tails' if his campaign performance is good. And he hopes that his vote will be 'bumped up' in certain places by strong local candidates. Sometimes the Presidential candidate does better in a State than those running for other offices on his ticket: sometimes he does worse. For example, in the 1960 Presidential election:

	Massachusetts	Minnesota
Kennedy (Democrat)	1,487,174	779,933
Senator (Democrat)	1,050,725	884,168

The Democrats carried both States, but the President ran very well ahead of the Senatorial candidate in his home State (Massachusetts), well behind the Senatorial candidate in Minnesota.

The election is a matter of patronage as well as principles. A candidate for State office who is elected will have some State patronage at his disposal; a candidate elected to the U.S. Congress will have Federal patronage channelled through him to his State, if his party also wins the Presidency. This patronage may include jobs, political favours, government contracts, and construction works such as new government buildings, highways, dams and defence plants. Though office-holding changes following Presidential elections have been very greatly restricted in modern times there are still some 'spoils' for the victors. A considerable number of important Federal jobs may be filled with appointees of the incoming President, but over 90 per cent of all Federal employees now have security of tenure. In the course of the campaign the Presidential candidate meets local leaders and arrives at understandings with them, and he will keep a close watch on the degree of loyalty shown by members of his party to him while the campaign is on.

Campaigning for the Presidency is the most strenuous political feat in the world. In the course of it the candidates will travel many thousands of miles and address hundreds upon hundreds of groups and meetings all over the country. In addition to physical stamina the campaign requires huge sums of money.

Various national committees spent about $25 million on the Presidential campaign of 1960. This ignores the spending of State and local groups in support of the national ticket. Total cost for campaigns at all levels in 1960 was probably about $175 million. These funds were used to pay for radio and television time, campaign literature, signs, buttons and the very important private opinion polls. It has been estimated that over 11 per cent of the people contributed to the campaign in 1960, but the major source of funds was from large donors. Forty-one per cent of all reported campaign income came from 5,300 individuals who contributed over $500 apiece.

Most of the direct participation of organised labour and business in financing the campaign in 1960 was in support of voter registration drives. Some of this activity was non-partisan and it is impossible to give any estimate as to the extent of their contribution. Attempts have been made both to limit the total costs of campaigns and to lessen the dependence of the parties on a few large contributors. In 1960 there was a legal limit of $3 million on the expenditure of a national committee. However, there was no limit on the number of *ad hoc* national or local committees which could be organised in support of each candidate.

On polling day all qualified citizens may vote. The right to vote is determined by State law, under the Constitution as interpreted by the Supreme Court. In Georgia and Kentucky all citizens over 18 can vote. In Alaska the voting age is 19 and in Hawaii it is 20, but in all other States the right to vote comes with the 21st birthday. Residence and literacy requirements vary from State to State.

How many citizens actually do vote? In 1960 just over 64 per cent of the civilian population of voting age cast ballots. There are a number of reasons why there is this relatively light turn-out even for Presidential elections. The fact that the voter has to make the effort to get his name on the electoral register deters some; confusion arising from the presence of so many names on the ballot and frequency of elections may stop others; residence requirements temporarily disfranchise the numerous Americans who move frequently. But much the most important factor is discrimination against the Negro in the South.

There is a wide variation in the extent of voting in the various States – from under 26 per cent of the civilian population of voting age in Mississippi to nearly 81 per cent in Idaho and New Hampshire; the eleven States with the lowest percentage of voter participation are all Southern. A major reason for this variation was given by the United States Commission on Civil Rights in its 1961 Report to the President and Congress. 'In some 100 counties in eight Southern States there is reason to believe that Negro citizens are prevented – by outright discrimination or by fear of physical violence or economic reprisal – from exercizing the right to vote.'

When they complete their ballots, the people are theoretically voting for presidential electors in the so-called Electoral College, but in fact for a Presidential candidate, since the electors in each State are pledged to a particular candidate and the candidate who wins in that State traditionally takes *all* the State's electoral votes. Each State has a number of electors equal to its representation in Congress (that is $x+2$); the total number in the Electoral College is 538. This makes contests in States with a large population, and hence large representation in the House of Representatives, of exceptional importance. (In 1964 New York – having 41 Representatives and its 2 Senators – has 43 electoral votes, California 40 and Nevada 3. The District of Columbia has 3.) A candidate to be elected must win a majority, 270 out of 538, of the votes of the Electoral College. It is theoretically possible to elect a 'minority President' (one without a popular majority) but it has only happened once during the last century in a straight two-party fight (in 1888). It can happen somewhat more easily when there are more than two serious parties contesting the election, as in 1948, when Truman had 24,106,000 votes and his three opponents 24,294,000. In 1960 the popular contest was exceedingly close (34,227,000 to 34,109,000) but President Kennedy still won by 303 to 219 electoral votes. Thus in both 1948 and 1960, taking all parties into account, there were less Democratic popular votes than non-Democrat.

In the complex process of adapting this cumbersome system to the democratic needs of a popular election, reform by constitutional amendment has often been considered but not carried through. The system as it exists gives great importance to the vote of the large northern industrial cities since they tend to hold the balance of power in the States with the largest electoral votes. Traditionally it is held that the Democrats must take most of the Southern States and most of the north-eastern industrial States in order to win.

On Election Day in early November the people finally cast their ballots. They may do so by hand or on a voting machine, but in either case voting will be in secret. Tension mounts throughout the day, and because polling stations report separately as soon as they are closed there is great excitement as the returns come in. When the result appears certain the defeated candidate, by custom, 'concedes' victory to his opponent. In mid-December the members of the Electoral College meet in their separate States and formally cast their votes for the candidate who has won. The documents are then dispatched from the State capitals to the President of the United States Senate in Washington; he opens and counts them in the Hall of the House of Representatives on 6 January in the presence of both houses of Congress.

At noon on 20 January the new President 'enters on the execution of his office' in a solemn Inauguration ceremony which includes an address by the President, who also takes (usually before the Chief Justice) the 'Oath or Affirmation' specified in the Constitution:

'I do solemnly swear (or affirm) that I will faithfully execute the Office of President of the United States, and will to the best of my Ability, preserve, protect and defend the Constitution of the United States.'

MAIN STEPS IN THE ELECTION OF A PRESIDENT

Stage 1. March to June	Selection of delegates to National Party Conventions (by caucus, state convention, or primary election in states).
Stage 2. June to August	National Party Conventions select their Presidential and Vice-Presidential candidates.
Stage 3. Thereafter till November	The Election Campaign.
Stage 4. Early November	Election Day.
Stage 5. December	Casting of Electoral Votes, a largely formal process.
Stage 6. 20 January of the succeeding year	The Inauguration of the new President.

Books for further reading

The Harvard Guide to American History, Cambridge, Mass., 1954, is a comprehensive historical bibliography. A more general bibliography is

The Library of Congress, *A Guide to the Study of the United States of America*, Washington, 1960.

H. C. Allen and C. P. Hill, *British Essays in American History*, New York and London, 1957.

H. C. Allen, *The Anglo-American Relationship since 1783*, London, 1959.

Wayne Andrews (Editor), *Concise Dictionary of American History*, New York and London, 1962.

T. A. Bailey, *A Diplomatic History of the American People*. New York, 1955.

S. F. Bemis, *A Diplomatic History of the United States*, New York, 1955.

A. C. Bening and T. C. Cochran, *The Rise of American Economic Life*, New York, 1964.

R. A. Billington, *Westward Expansion: A History of the American Frontier*, New York and London, 1960.

W. E. Binkley and M. C. Mooss. *A Grammar of American Politics*, London, 1950 and New York, 1958.

D. J. Boorstin (Editor), *Chicago History of American Civilization* (multi-volume series), Chicago.

D. W. Biogan, *Introduction to American Politics*, London, 1954. (*Politics in America*, New York, 1955).

F. J. Brown and J. S. Roucek, eds. *One America: The History, Contributions, and Present Problems of Our Racial and National Minorities*, New York, 1952.

W. J. Cash, *The Mind of the South*, New York, 1960.

T. C. Cochran and W. Miller, *The Age of Enterprise; A Social History of Industrial America*, New York, 1942.

M. F. Cunliffe, *George Washington; Man and Monument*, Boston, 1959.

M. E. Curti, *The Growth of American Thought*, New York, 1951.

M. B. Davidson, *Life in America*. Boston, 1951. 2 vols.

H. U. Faulkner, *American Economic History*, New York and London, 1960.

J. H. Franklin, *From Slavery to Freedom; A History of American Negroes*, New York, 1956.

Frank Freidel, *America in the Twentieth Century*, New York, 1960.

J. K. Galbraith, *The Affluent Society*, Boston and London, 1958.

Richard Hofstadter, *The Age of Reform; from Bryan to F.D.R.*, New York, 1955.

Richard Hofstadter, *The American Political Tradition and the Men Who Made It*. New York, 1948.

J. G. E. Hopkins, *Concise Dictionary of American Biography*, New York, 1964.

M. A. Jones, *American Immigration*, Chicago, 1960.

A. H. Kelly and W. A. Harbison, *The American Constitution*, New York, 1955.

V. O. Key, Jr., *Politics, Parties & Pressure Groups*, New York, 1964.

Perry Miller, *The New England Mind* (2 volumes), Cambridge, Mass., and London, 1939 and 1953.

S. E. Morison and H. S. Commager, *The Growth of the American Republic* (2 volumes), New York and London, 1962.

R. B. Morris (Editor), *Encyclopedia of American History*, New York and London, 1961.

A. M. Potter, *American Government and Politics*, London, 1955.

J. G. Randall, *The Civil War and Reconstruction*, Boston, 1937.

D. Riesman and others, *The Lonely Crowd; a Study of the Changing American Character*, New Haven, 1950.

B. P. Thomas, *Abraham Lincoln; a Biography*, New York, 1952.

J. A. Woods, *Roosevelt and Modern America*, New York and London, 1959.

Esmond Wright, *Fabric of Freedom, 1763–1800*, New York, 1961.

Index

Index

371